THE ISLE
OF NOISES

To my
Father on his
42nd Birthday,
13 April 1990

THE ISLE OF
NOISES

Mark J. Prendergast

ST. MARTIN'S PRESS / NEW YORK

Library of Congress Cataloging-in-Publication Data

Prendergast, Mark J.
    The isle of noises / Mark J. Prendergast.
        p.   cm.
    ISBN 0-312-03982-4
    1. Rock music—Ireland—History and criticism.   I. Title.
    ML3534.P74   1990   89-27044
    782.42166′09415—dc20   CIP
                                                                                   MN

First published in Ireland by The O'Brien Press Ltd.

First U.S. Edition
10 9 8 7 6 5 4 3 2 1

DEDICATION

This work is a culmination of experiences —

to Elizabeth Prendergast

Contents

4 Modern Music *page* 143

From progressive rock onwards • Jimi Slevin • pub rock • Bees Make Honey •
The Boomtown Rats • punk realism • The Radiators from Space • punk in the
UK and USA • Northern Ireland — The Undertones, Stiff Little Fingers • the
South — Dark Space, The Blades • essential groups, essential recordings

U2 — a history of the group from Trinity College days to worldwide
superstars in 1980s • analyses of records including Boy, October, War • the
making of The Unforgettable Fire • The Joshua Tree

The avant-garde • The Virgin Prunes • Roger Doyle • Stano • Nigel Rolfe

Postscript — an A-Z of some important performers: Auto da Fé, Big Self,
Blue in Heaven, Cactus World News, Paul Cleary, Chris de Burgh, Johnny
Duhan, Fastway, Na Fíréin, The Fountainhead, Haa Lacka Binttii, Hotwire, In
Tua Nua, Jolyon Jackson, The Mama's Boys, Metropolis, Microdisney, Gary
Moore, Sinéad O'Connor, Michael O'Shea, The Rhythm Kings, Barry Ronan,
Ruefrex, Feargal Sharkey, The Stars of Heaven, That Petrol Emotion, Pierce
Turner, Andy White

Coda   *page* 263

Band Aid • Live Aid • In Remembrance of Philip Lynott • Self Aid • Not the End
but the Beginning

Appendixes

Preface to the American Edition

Being black and Irish many people would expect me to have a deeply schizophrenic character, a sort of rootlessness. On the contrary growing up in an Irish Rock culture I felt akin to a variety of musics, especially those born out of America. Bono of U2 has talked about the spiritual connections between Ireland and the United States, specifically between the heart and soul of the Gaelic spirit and that of American gospel, blues, and country. For my part I've always felt something special for the music of Jimi Hendrix, The Byrds, Arthur Lee, Bob Dylan, The Doors, The Grateful Dead, Simon & Garfunkel, John Coltrane, Miles Davis, Tim Buckley, Big Star, Keith Jarrett and so forth. Surveying Irish Rock over three decades the American influences are obvious.

The aim of this book was to lay bare Irish Rock culture for all and sundry to see. It was never aimed at any market nor written specifically for the Irish, wherever they may find it. Anybody, anywhere with even a morsel of interest in rock music history will readily relate to the stories of inspiration, heartbreak, love, and commitment that make up the panoply of Irish rock history. For Americans, whose folk sources lie dotted around Europe the impact of their liberated music of the '60s was to have a profound effect on the course of popular Irish music history. Its first important transfer was that of urban rhythm & blues, nowhere more crystallized than in the Dublin band Bluesville who with Ian Whitcomb brought it to the top of the American charts in the form of 'You Turn Me On', a snappy hit that signalled the birth of Irish rock.

Again and again American influences were absorbed by musicians and re-created in a Celtic form. Phil Lynott, one of Ireland's greatest rock stars, began his career with versions of Buffalo Springfield songs but then switched to Hendrix, who was his role model in every way. Dylan had a mighty effect on the Irish folk ethic inspiring such as Sweeney's Men to go electric. And what of the San Francisco scene, its festival community spirit easily transferred itself to the Irish progressive era of the late '60s and early '70s. And then of course there's Van Morrison whose U.S. relocation completed the circle in the form of *Astral Weeks*, the '68 East Coast recorded album that defined a whole new area of rock and has survived the decades of change to be rated as the very best of what the genre has to offer. And what of Henry McCullough's guitar contribution to Joe Cocker's Woodstock performance of 1969? Surely history in the making.

When Irish rock went through a turbulent phase during the mid-'70s it was to turn to American country blues for inspiration. When the 'punk' phenomenon took hold Irish youth were more in tune with its New York roots such as the music of The Velvet Underground and Patti Smith. Thus U2 naturally leaned to America, searching for that perfect blend of Irish emotion and American quest that was so perfectly encapsulated in 1987's *The Joshua Tree*. It was no mere chance that Bob Dylan gave one of his career's best performances in Ireland in 1984. With a huge audience, a country setting, and both Van Morrison and Bono in tow his set was crystal clear, magical. Standing ten feet away from him, watching him peel off a heartfelt version of 'It's Alright Ma', my heart leapt. Images of *Easy Rider*, the Vietnam War, civil rights marches of the '60s just flew around my mind and then I understood why this man was considered 'the voice of his generation'.

If U2 were bringing it all back home by collaborating with such as B. B. King, Roy Orbison, and Robbie Robertson, Irish folk musicians were doing likewise in their oeuvre. In the pages of this book you will read about the new acoustic music of Maura O'Connell and Davy Spillane, fashioned out of Nashville strings and Irish traditions. You will also read about the blues of Mary Coughlan and Tríona Ní Dhomhnaill, admirable Oregon ventures into new age. With respected sessionman Philip Donnelly Nashville experienced one of Ireland's great country pickers, himself graduating from his native land's continual love of American bluegrass. The close connection between both musical cultures is obvious when it comes to a group like The Waterboys whose arrival in Ireland in 1986 led to an album that exploded with the delight of rediscovering the ease with which both American and Irish folk merge into a contemporary Irish rock music.

And what of the high American profile of Christy Moore, Enya and Sinead O'Connor? What of the way countless young Irish bands now tour America as a matter of course? What of the radio airplay afforded to new Irish records? And so on and so on. Yes here I am some years after the book was first published still reeling with pride at the way Irish rock/blues/folk has pulled itself away from being considered a mere outcrop of British music and in the process becoming all that is necessarily vital for a living modern music. Though it was a long and sometimes painful creation, this very first bound document on the subject is as much a product of rock music in general as Irish rock in particular. For this reason I dearly want the American people to explore these pages and marvel at how what is ostensibly an American form has had such a long-lasting resonance in late twentieth-century Irish culture.

August, 1989, London.

Preface

It is strange to think after so many years of wrestling with the practical and conceptual problems of putting together a book on Irish rock that it is finally completed. The original inspiration came to me in 1983 when discussing the colourful American and British music scenes of the sixties and early seventies with two friends in a Dublin pub one evening. Having witnessed at first hand the vibrancy of the new Irish music I was intrigued to find out something of what had happened in the past when I wasn't of an age to appreciate it. My companions were much older than me and had played a bit of music in the Dublin of the sixties. They were quite cynical about it, and excepting a slight mention of Ditch Cassidy and *The People*, their attitude was that little of worth had happened. Remembering my childhood days listening to the radio and hearing 'Whisky in the Jar', I immediately experienced a jolt of disbelief. How could they be so negative about their own heritage I thought? That night I went home and scribbled the words 'Tales of a Blue Orphanage' on some paper, and thus began a process far longer than I anticipated.

The stimulus for the book was a combination of curiosity and imperative. I wanted to know about the musical environment in Ireland prior to the punk rage of the late seventies, but I also felt that if somebody didn't take the bull by the horns and go out of their way to gather the information and process it something would be lost forever. The reaction I got from most people when I told them I was writing a history of Irish rock was one of incredulity or indifference. Some thought it would be a very slim volume if accomplished, others said I was wasting my time. Because of the lack of archives and such material, more stated that it was impossible. In fact, this lack turned out to be a blessing in disguise, for I had to meet the activists themselves, the musicians and media people who had shaped Irish rock. One startling interview followed another and soon a clear picture of the beat and progressive rock era began to imprint itself in my mind.

As I met more people who referred me to even more, the research accelerated. One could sense an energy about the book as one listened to people ecstatically recalling their younger days. There were few sad moments, but one rendezvous has to be recalled for its poignancy and that was with Philip Lynott in 1984. I met him in Howth and in Dublin city around the time he was rehearsing *Grand Slam*. He was under a lot of pressure yet found the time to chat to me about the old days and how he wanted to still retain melody in his heavy rock music. He was to die so soon afterwards and in a curious way this book is a testament to his spirit.

From the early eighties to 1987 rock in Ireland underwent significant change. It was more professionally organised, making a larger wave internationally — and of course there was *U2*. Suddenly Ireland was the place where everything was happening, as the British and American music cultures wound down to repetition and video-pap commercialism. Irish rock on the other hand still had that organic element that had made the hippie rock sound of California and London so appealing in the past. But this element was decidedly Irish, something which was drawing strongly from the mystical forces of the country's spirit.

When I started this book that feeling was there, and over the years it has been magnified and through historic occasions like Live Aid and Self Aid it seemed to explode into many people's awareness. After all that has happened, it seems fitting that this document exists to acknowledge all the energy, all the hope and emotions that have gone into the making of Irish rock.

Acknowledgments

My enthusiastic thanks to the following people who were in some way involved in the preparation of this book.

Photographic: Andy Catlin who made the largest photographic contribution to the book. Terry Thorp of *The Irish Times.* Stephen Dixon, Phil Dowling and Cathal O'Doherty of RTE who were collectively responsible for the transfer of rare photographs to better the project. Honest Dave Clifford of *Vox* fame. Steven Averill. All the relevant record companies. Seán Ó Treasaigh. Derek Speirs/Report. Stuart Marshall. Greville Edwards.

Research: All the staff of RTE's record library, particularly Joan Smyth who introduced me to the facilities and endured ceaseless enquiry. RTE producer Bill Keating who grasped the feelings of the project from a very early stage , and stimulated its initial fabrication. The staffs of Irish and English record | companies, too numerous to mention for putting up with my endless queries and constant double checking. Andy Linehan and Paul Wilson at the National Sound Archive, London. John Salter at Pippin for being very understanding. Donal Gallagher at Strange Music. Larry Gogan for providing a substantial amount of information on the 1960s. Terry O'Neill for information on the early seventies. Michael Appleton of the BBC. Tony Bradfield for allowing me access to his *Hitsville* archives. Marcus Connaughton, Deke O'Brien, Danny Hughes, Elvera Butler, Fachtna O'Kelly and George Murray for their contributions. All the following people for some extraordinary interviews—Pat Egan, Johnny Moynihan, Gay Woods, Tim Booth, Tim Goulding, Philip Lynott, Brush Shiels, Alan Dee, Jimi Slevin, Paul Brady, Robbie Brennan and Roger Doyle. Special reference must be made to Brian Downey for his sensitivity and involvement at a crucial stage of the book's development. Ian Wilson and Dave Fanning for their energetic interest early on in the book. Eamon Carr for his belief in the Irish heritage. Jimmy Greeley for being the only one to go into print in his support for the book during its difficult creation. Mary Paul Keane and Seamus Cashman who gave some encouragement for the book during its infancy. Brian Howard at Russells for a protracted but interesting correspondence. Paul Charles for reading the script at one point and taking time to make corrections and suggest changes. Trevor Hodgett of Record Collector for his ground-breaking work on post-Van Morrison *Them.* Finally the legendary rock archivist John Tobler, whose suggestions, opinions and patient good humour helped no end.

Publication: During the long run up to publication of this book many people made promises that weren't kept and went back on the words they gave in good faith. It only required three people to make it possible and they were Lar Cassidy of the Arts Council, and of course Michael O'Brien and Íde Ní Laoghaire of The

O'Brien Press. Also thanks to Pete Hogan for sorting out a few legal matters.

Personal appreciation to my father William Prendergast for his kind understanding and support over the years of preparing this book. Rodney Breen for his superobjective viewpoints, constant critical perceptions and resolute belief in the concept. The Magic City Trash Company, Donal, Kate and Fenella, Olly and Anna, Steve and Louise, Finian, Mary and Con, who all formed the necessary human network of contact during the first writing phase in Croswaithe Park, Dun Laoghaire, between 1983 and 1984. The Holmes brothers for their loyalty. David West for keeping the home fires burning. Louise Foulkes for a truly alternative way of life which enabled me to be more creative. And most of all to Genie Cosmas for her enthusiasm, her artistry and deep conviction in my ability as a writer and as a person.

Special commendation has to go to Fergus Linehan and Joe Breen of *The Irish Times* Arts and Studies department who brought me onto the panel of music writers in 1982 and thus sparked off the writing process that in the end led to this book.

To every individual who helped, no matter how seemingly small the deed or action, thank you very, very much!

ONE

From Beat Music to Progressive Rock

In the beginning you had the showband and very little else. The idea was that Irish audiences wanted entertainment first and last. The showbands dominated every town and city in Ireland. From the early sixties they made fortunes from live appearances, playing 'covers' of standard hits and English Top Thirty material rather than original material. When *The Beatles* started in England, the Irish response was to cover their material within the showband format. There were usually lots of members in the band — eight or ten musicians with set routines, special dances and neat suits. Ballrooms on the circuit were packed out every night by thousands, to hear hours and hours of covers by the showband of the day. It was this popularity that led to their affluence. With their vast resources they controlled the dissemination of popular music throughout the country. Records were a secondary thing to the showband since it was the live event that generated the money. Artistic integrity and creativity were subsumed under the primary motive of profit.

In certain quarters the showband was regarded as a plague. Even though the bands were really professional, played their music very well and put on a good show, there was something missing. In a word, sophistication. There was something very superficial about all the showbands. Tom Jones and solo artists in that vein were their role models. As the bands became wealthier their rules stood over all musicians. If a musician wanted to make a living he or she would, somewhere along the line, get roped into a showband, play every night for good money and that was that. In short, any musical sharpness would be eradicated.

Since the venues, media and record companies were all in the hands of the showbands, alternative scenes had to develop to cater for the new awareness. A simple way of avoiding the showband was not to play the same venues. Around the mid-sixties different venues sprang up to cater for a more interesting music. These were small cavernous clubs called beat clubs and they catered for teenagers switched on to the sounds of the sixties. Records were danced to and bands were avidly followed. The groups became known as beat groups. Their looks and sharp dress style were modern and could be identified with. Around the suburbs of Dublin, and in small clubs in the city, a circuit developed which could play host to these groups and an environment was created for groups to play their own material. As the sixties came to a close a number of groups had developed their own personal style of music. They were able to take on the larger international arena with their musical awareness, and by the early seventies certain Irish bands were playing huge venues all over the world.

The genesis of Irish rock is in no way logical. There was no simple linear development from one type of music to another. More a reaction to circumstances and the effect of the expanded awareness of the sixties when some of the youth decided enough was enough. Even though Brendan Bowyer and the *Royal Showband* provided one of the classiest number one singles in 'Hucklebuck' (EMI 1965), it still didn't satisfy that very special craving for a youth music with its own frame of reference.

BEAT MUSIC

The word 'beat' is a familiar one from the 1950s. Originating in that first period of youth culture in the America of Jack Kerouac, the beat scene was about an alternative. Very much a literary thing initially, the beat generation was all about the roaming pursuit of a greater freedom. Its soundtrack was the folk and rock 'n' roll of the period. It was an alternative to the lifestyle of parents and those who represented the establishment. As the fifties wore into the sixties youth culture became more focused around rock music. In America and Britain small clubs sprang up and hosted groups who played tight rhythm and blues (R & B) music — white groups doing black music in an urban style. (English groups like *The Who* and *The Animals* were in this vein.) These clubs were small and sweaty and packed every night with teenagers. In London the scene was going a speedy hundred miles an hour by the mid-sixties.

The Dublin beat scene developed as an antidote to the showbands. The emphasis was on youthful exuberance, the groups playing all night through the early hours of the morning, while the records played were the latest from the *Stones* or the *Beatles*. In effect this was an underground circuit where musicians could have more freedom. With the emphasis on entertainment, these early groups would still do covers, but of more esoteric material, with a couple of their own songs thrown in.

The first beat group of the early sixties to make an impact was *The Greenbeats* — John Keogh, Mog Ahearne, Brian Lynch and Peter Williams. Now they would do covers but not ones that were known, except for *Beatles* covers. Jerry Lee Lewis, Ray Charles, jazz and R & B were all covered. According to Robbie Brennan, long-standing Irish percussionist, they specialised in 'having every *Beatles* song learned off before it was released'. They built up a fanatical following in the Longford Tennis Club. In 1964 they went to the Cavern in Liverpool to play, under the direction of B. P. Fallon (who described them as the very first Irish beat group).

But it is generally acknowledged that Irish rock started with Ian Whitcomb and *Bluesville*. Whitcomb was born in Woking, Surrey, England on 10 July 1941. Raised there, he went to private schools, eventually crossing the channel to Dublin to relax into the atmosphere of Trinity College. There he met Barry Richardson and Peter Adler. Whitcomb was extremely talented, played piano and sang. He was itching to play music in a live context and after a few experiments on the underground circuit formed *Bluesville* with the following line-up: Barry Richardson (bass), Deke O'Brien (guitar), Mick Molloy (guitar), Ian McGarry (drums) and Peter Adler (saxophone). The band had been going for little more than a year in 1964, but they'd become notorious as the best live act ever seen in Dublin. Whitcomb was a true extrovert on-stage and the tight rhythms of the group exuded all the energy of black R & B. They played faithful versions of unheard-of black music to the teenage audience on the college and tennis-club circuit. In Deke O'Brien's words: 'It was really heavy going at the time. Every second night we'd be at it. In Mount Merrion we would be playing one venue, and Van Morrison's *Them* another, and the place would be black. You couldn't get a car into the area it was that packed.'

Bluesville played really basic dance music with a sharp, tight beat. They really let rip. Specialists in soul, latter-day Tamla Motown, and R & B, the group really worked hard on-stage. Putting musicianship before everything, they were known to spend quite a long time before each concert tuning up and getting their vocal harmonies right. Certain line-up changes did occur but the basic line-up above stayed together. Ian Whitcomb visited America in the summer of '64 taking some tapes of the band with him. In Seattle he met Jerry Dennon, a record executive who listened to the music and signed him to a contract on the Jerden label. Dennon had had considerable success with the likes of *Paul Revere and The Raiders* and spotted Whitcomb's talent. A single was released but it flopped. Back in Dublin, Ian got the rest of *Bluesville* together and hired out the Eamonn Andrews studios. A straight live take to two tracks, 'You Turn Me On' rates as the first Irish rock single of note. Self-penned and done in standard Chuck Berry fashion, the song is an all-time classic. With searing guitar and thumping beat, Whitcomb staggers the vocal in typical *Who* fashion:

> Come on now girl
> You know you really
> Turn me on.

Capitol Records had picked up on a previous song, 'This Sporting Life'(Jerden) by *Bluesville* and continued to show interest in Whitcomb. In Seattle 'You Turn Me On' went to number one and was thus networked on national radio coast-to-coast. By June 1965 it was a Top Ten hit in America. Deke O'Brien considered the whole thing a freak: 'We were all sitting in Dublin and still coming out of school when this happened. The next thing we knew we all had to go to the States. Oh, we all had commitments except Ian who went by himself and nearly became famous. Now he lives in Los Angeles and is the local BBC expert on music from 1884 onwards. You can catch him on TV expounding the virtues of George Formby and the steam ukelele!'[1]

Back in Dublin the other musicians were undaunted and continued to crank out their type of music. Two excellent groups were the result, namely *The Chosen Few* and *The Action*.[2] Led by Deke O'Brien, *The Chosen Few* were specialists in soul, using horns, keyboards and strong riffing in a highly melodic context. Their interest lay in bringing the sweet sounds of Otis Redding, Wilson Pickett, and

Sam and Dave to the beat scene. Following in a more jazzy vein, *The Action* was led by ace face Peter Adler, son of famous harmonica player Larry Adler. Covering esoteric recordings like those of Oscar Browne Jnr., *The Action* played cool jazz-type music, with Adler on vocals and saxophone. Adler was definitely right for the period, with up-to-the-minute hip clothes and dark shades.

From the early sixties to the end of the decade the beat scene thrived. In Dublin it was a frenetic rush between 1964 and 1968 when the clubs, groups and youth all combined to make it really happen. In those four years about a dozen clubs sprang up in the city, a couple more north and south on the coast, and a tennis-club circuit around the outlying urban area. In other towns like Cork, Limerick and Galway, beat clubs also opened up but not on the same scale as Dublin. In the North, Belfast was moving at a faster speed, with a music scene headed by Van Morrison's *Them*.

Beat music was definitely a city phenomenon. In Ireland difficulties arose because of the rural nature of the country. Country folk, unused to the complexities of the city, really enjoyed the showbands. One person described their music as 'great to dance to on a Saturday night — meet a girl, have a few jars — even be lucky enough to meet the person you're going to marry.' It was a business, a danceband business, where music as such was the last priority. These bands dominated the country entirely. An important aspect of their presence was the lack of developed sensibility in listening to music in rural Ireland. The radio was popular, but stereo systems were not in great demand outside the cities. A showband playing locally was much preferred to the weirder strains of music emanating from across the water. Rural people could identify with the showbands. The very young who were mostly disenchanted with that scene favoured the beat groups.

Anything creative came from the groups. They were more intimate and less caught up in the business side. It was true that each group had to make a living from its musical endeavours. Robbie Brennan describes the pattern of playing with a beat group: 'I joined *The Chosen Few* in 1965. It was all hop in the back of the Volkswagen van we had, with the PA and all the gear. We would cover Belfast, Derry, Cork and all the major cities. The money was ridiculous — the average wage for a person was £6 a week, I was getting at least £25 a week. The showbands were huge and making so much money that they could offer any musician between £70 and £100 a week. Somebody reckoned that there were about six hundred showbands in Ireland during the sixties. They made so much money that they are still living off it to this day!'

An important pioneering beat group of the early sixties was *The Chessmen*, with Alan Dee (who played the first Vox Continental organ in Ireland). They started when *The Beatles* started and played both the beat music venues and also the ballrooms. They were fairly dedicated to the beat circuit — even trying out their own songs on country audiences — but they incorporated brass into their set and little by little became more showband oriented. Alan Dee, favouring the beat circuit, left the group in 1966 to form *Alan Dee and The Light*, a highly experimental group which had no guitarist and featured a line-up of organ, bass and drums. Dee himself played sax and organ simultaneously.

Another group dedicated to beat in the early sixties was *The Creatures*, who became noted for playing Dublin's Number Five Club. Reputed to have a really tight, clean sound they toured Germany and were spotted by an American promoter who brought them to the States. Unfortunately, they did not have enough of their own material to do them justice. It was said that when they got to the studio the group were unable to come up with anything new because their writer was still in Dublin! They did a promotional tour of the US with minimal impact.

The general trend among the beat groups was to have a large overlap and interplay of musicians. When a group would break up each member would go off and form his own group. In the many clubs, especially in Dublin, people would freely jam with other artists in rave-ups that would go on into the early hours of the morning. These clubs were non-alcoholic and genuinely aimed at the high-energy atmosphere created by groups playing fast rhythm and blues. The emphasis was on pure fun. The Caroline Club, an old converted cinema in the south coastal area of Dublin, became notorious for its hectic rock nights. It hosted every beat group of the mid-sixties, and one Irish musician remembers: 'It was always getting headlines in the papers ... girls dancing topless on-stage etc. One night an English group, *The Pretty Things*, were playing there, which was very wild — they just played one number for the whole set based on a Bo Diddley-type beat.' The club was watched by the authorities who suspected drugs and orgies to be the order of the day, and one night when *The Chosen Few* were gigging there it was raided by the police. It was accused of having 'shot coffee' freely available to the teenagers. Of course the accusations were bogus, but the bad publicity did nothing for the beat scene.

As the sixties wore on, more and more groups formed and their horizons broadened. What separated the men from the boys was whether a group went away or not — to play the Irish scene meant going around in an inevitable circle which seemed to have no real potential. Even more important was the record contract with a large English or American company. Irish record companies concentrated on the showbands and cared little for the beat group scene. Very few Irish beat groups got record contracts abroad. Some did, and capitalised on it; others fell by the wayside. This early period of the development of Irish rock music was one of slow growth, but by the late sixties things had changed substantially.

Major Irish Beat Groups to 1967

The Action	The Chosen Few	The Movement
Alan Dee and The Light	The Creatures	Orange Machine
Peter Adler and The	The Few	The People
Next in Line	Granny's Intentions	Rockhouse
The Black Eagles	The Greenbeats	The Strangers
Bluesville	The Kingbees	Taste
The Chessmen	The Method	Them
		The Uptown Band

Note: Choice is selective.

1

2

3

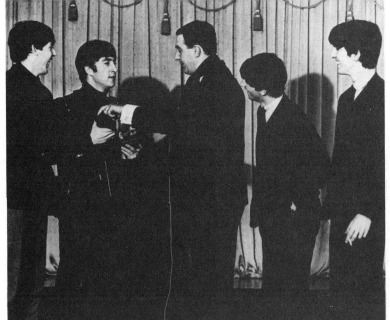

4

1 Brendan Bowyer and *The Royal Showband* on 'The Showband Show' in the early sixties when they were the most exciting showband in Ireland.

2 Ian Whitcomb led *Bluesville* to Top Ten fame in America with the rhythm and blues masterpiece 'You Turn Me On' in June of 1965.

3 *The Chosen Few,* formed shortly after the break-up of *Bluesville,* were a premier blues group — that's Brendan Bonass, Robbie Brennan and Deke O'Brien standing up.

4 *The Beatles,* English beat group extraordinaire, mess about with Paul Russell at Dublin's TV Club in the early 1960s.

5 *Granny's Intentions:* the line-up which cut 'Honest Injun' in 1969. *Left to right:* Pete Cummins, Johnny Duhan, Johnny Hockedy, Pat Nash, John Ryan.

6 *Granny's Intentions:* the shortlived third line-up which laid down only three tracks on the first album. *Left to right:* John Ryan, Pete Cummins, Johnny Duhan, Noel Bridgeman and Johnny Hockedy.

5

6

THE BEAT SCENE — A LOOK BACK

Alan Dee: 'There was an incredible scene at that period. All the clubs were going seven nights a week. If a group wasn't playing regularly something was wrong. If a club wasn't a cellar, well then it wasn't a club.[3] They were all underground and utterly dangerous. By 1967 all gigs were pitched towards the "happening" during the set — something wild at the end of the gig to cause alarm. Every group had a gimmick. Explosions, weird clothes or whatever would be the order of the day. My band used to vie with *The Uptown Band* for a more spectacular ending. One night in the Scene Club my band, *The Light*, ended with clouds of smoke rolling offstage. Since it was a cellar, the smoke started going out on the street, and soon enough the fire brigade were there looking for the fire which passers-by had reported! Things like this were happening all the time.'

Danny Hughes (top Irish DJ of the 1960s): 'I was at school during the midsixties. I loved the music and the whole scene. Everything was going. I decided to get my own place and play my own music to my own friends. There was a room available for hire in Mount Street and the landlady wanted two weeks' rent in advance. I was sixteen at the time ... The minute the club opened it was packed — *packed*! It ran for two nights a week. A new club, the A-Go-Go, opened up and I got the DJ's job there. It all started to happen very fast. I worked in all the clubs where groups like *The Stepping Stones, The Just Five, The Bye Laws, The Method*, and *Peter Adler and The Next in Line* used to play. I worked seven days a week — just to get dressed and be there. The wilder you were the better ... you would stay up until four in the morning with only Coca-Cola and Seven-Up to drink and the places would be stuffed with beat fans who were really into the music. The bands would be booked and other musicians would get up and join in — really electric.

'I would go all over the country doing clubs with groups. When I was up in Belfast I met a guy called Donall Corvin, a real head journalist at the time who wrote a really zany column for a newspaper called *City Week*. Corvin introduced me to a really springing scene. Van Morrison used to hang out with him, and myself and Van became very good friends. He was extremely moody and wore suit and tie and a straight haircut. Anyway, the beat scene was about energy and bands doing really tight guitar solos. This and the showbands were worlds apart. Most people liked cover versions and the showbands played what they knew, wore suits and did little set dances. The beat scene was all about love for the music. It was *The Animals* and *Manfred Mann* on the record deck or say *The Chosen Few* on-stage. This type of music was sacred and no beat fan would go near the showbands'.

Paul Charles:[4] 'In the early days ballrooms were just a primitive progression from barn dances. They were the prime meeting places for men and women who danced to *céilí* bands. Then came a form of band that could put on a show called "the bandshow". Eventually this became the popular showband. A typical showband set of songs would consist of Irish tunes, country and western, and party pieces. As the radio, or wireless as it was called, became more and more popular the showband sets changed. Still the showbands got very big and at one point there were over nine hundred registered in Ireland. *The Clipper Carlton Showband* were the best band musically to ever tour the ballrooms of Ireland and were a "show" band in every sense of the word.

'The ballrooms would not fill up until turfing-out time at the pubs, so the showbands, getting slightly lazy, would get "relief groups" to play from nine until the pubs closed, and this was the breeding ground for the Irish beat/rock scene. Some of these groups, discovering blues, soul, R & B, Tamla and pop, started to build up a following and found other places to play. This was how the club scene in Dublin and Belfast started. It was generally acknowledged that Belfast had a better club scene than Dublin. The Maritime Club in Belfast was an old sailors' drinking club and in the early sixties Van Morrison and a group of friends decided to start a music scene there. As far as Morrison was concerned the version of *Them* which backed him in this club was the only real *Them* that ever happened. The Maritime was later to be called Club Rado, and one after the other some of the best bands to come out of the beat scene played there. [*Them, The Interns, The Wheels*[5], *Cheese* and *Taste* all held down residencies in succession.]

'In Ballymena there was the Flamingo Ballroom where *The Gentry*, a gigging band, would blow everybody to kingdom come especially the English chart groups. They would work everybody up into a frenzy and it was the first time I ever experienced music mania. Also from Ballymena was a guy called David McWilliams who was a great singer/songwriter. He sent a tape to Major Minor records who signed him up and from 1967 onward he recorded four albums for that label. He had an immediate hit with "The Days of Pearly Spencer" which was played to death on Radio Caroline, as every Major Minor record was. [Radio Caroline was the original pirate station set up on a ship in the North Sea by Irishman Ronan O'Rahilly during the first half of the sixties.] The album which contained that song sold bucket-loads but on later records he suffered from over orchestration, an in-house musical director and stiff session musicians. In the early seventies he recorded two albums for EMI. Anyway, the North produced a lot of good music, and clubs like Sammy Hustons and Clarkes in Belfast and the Embassy Ballroom in Derry were all important breeding grounds for the beat groups. It was great fun then and all the groups were always in competition.'

BREAKING THE BARRIERS

No matter what happened in Ireland, a group benefited considerably from overseas exposure. One of the very early groups to get this opportunity was *The People*, who came from Portadown in Northern Ireland. Their speciality was quite heavy psychedelic music, beefed up by guitarist Henry McCullough. After becoming hot contenders on the Irish beat circuit they went to London in 1967 where they were noticed by Chas Chandler and signed to Track Records. Ernie Graham was the vocalist, using a high-pitched, nasal whine to accentuate his singing, while the complete line-up was a foursome with Eric Stewart on bass and Dave Lutton on drums.

Since Chas Chandler was managing *The Jimi Hendrix Experience*, the Irish group would get booked to do tours with a number of well-known bands. *The People* changed their name to *Eire Apparent* and supported big-name English acts — *The Soft Machine, The New Animals,* and of course Hendrix's *Experience*. Eventually *Eire Apparent* made it to the States on a Hendrix tour and the great guitarist was quoted as saying, 'that group, the *Eire Apparent*, are really good.' Certainly they had a gifted lead guitarist in Henry McCullough. In 1968 everything was happening for them, but tragedy struck when McCullough had visa problems in Toronto, Canada, and had to return to Ireland.[6] Mike Cox was drafted in to replace him, and this outfit went on to record an album in 1969 on the Buddah label.

Sunrise by Eire Apparent featured production by Hendrix, and was engineered by his man, Eddie Kramer. The result was real, spacey, acid music in keeping with the mood of the times. The group certainly looks spaced out on the cover — wearing period, patterned robes and the customary frizzy hairstyles. The record commences with multi-phasing, and the listener is whizzed through a maze of pop, country, folk and rock strains. 'Mr Guy Fawkes' is indicative of the whole concept — a ballad song with strings, horns and acoustic guitars folded into electronic explosions. In short, Hendrix went wild on the mixing desk and ended up with a swirling, bubblegum music with no defining quality or direction. Of course it was appropriate for the 'stoney' period it was released in. Producer Jack Hunt did one track, '1026', which was cohesive. Other personnel were such luminaries as Robert Wyatt, Noel Redding, Mitch Mitchell, Gerry Stickells and, of course, Hendrix himself. *Eire Apparent* had broken up by May 1970.

Granny's Intentions

One of the most popular and unorthodox beat groups of the 1960s was *Granny's Intentions*. Hailing from Limerick in the West of Ireland, their immediate musical influence came from America in the form of black soul music and the soft sounds of Tamla Motown. Leading light and constant force was vocalist Johnny Duhan, a prolific songwriter with an authentic deep-throated singing style. The band went through many personnel changes, many musical oeuvres. Their career criss-crossed the map of musical inventiveness, never engaging a single style for too long, but 'careering' into new territories almost every year. For six years *Granny's Intentions* thrilled audiences everywhere. They were in touch with prevailing moods and musical developments.

The original group was formed in 1965 in Limerick. Arriving in Dublin in 1966 they added an organ player and hit the beat club scene. The line-up consisted of Johnny Duhan (vocals), Cha Harren (vocals), Johnny Hockedy (guitar), Jack Costello (bass), John Ryan (Vox Continental) and Guido Devito (drums). By 1967, after spending time in Britain and Germany establishing themselves, the group had been pared down to a five-piece, with one lead singer in Duhan, and Greg Donaghy on drums. They were signed up by Frank Rogers, Decca's A & R man, and based themselves in London. Immediately, success was theirs. Normal gigs were packed out. They played the Speakeasy in London with Jimi Hendrix, Steve Winwood, Brian Jones and Keith Richards from the *Stones*, and Eric Burdon in the audience. English business people like Kit Lambert of *Who* fame approached the Irish group but Brian Tuite, their manager, wanted them to direct themselves to the Irish pop scene and this they did with a lot of razzmatazz and aplomb.

Very influenced by *Sgt. Pepper* and psychedelia, their first single, a 1968 hit, was called 'The Story of David'/'Sandy's on the Phone Again' on Deram, the experimental offshoot of Decca. Their second single 'Never an Everyday Thing'/'Hilda the Bilda' (Deram 1968), an American-style pop song, was an even bigger hit. That year the band became Irish superstars — riots at every gig, their clothes being ripped off by ecstatic audiences invading the stage! The pressure was on the group to become a showband; managers were offering them big money. Meanwhile, Irish showbands covered 'Never an Everyday Thing' up and down the country. John Ryan comments: 'When Conny Lynch from the *Royal Showband* came over to London and offered us a large wage in 1968, we turned it down because it would mean selling out! Brian Tuite wanted us to form some sort of supergroup with *Orange Machine*, which meant becoming a showband. None of this happened because *Granny's Intentions* Mark II folded in 1968 in Ireland.'

Granny's Intentions were never really a pop group. Underneath the surface bubbled a more sophisticated attitude. When the second line-up appeared on the first *Like Now* programme, they did a version of *The Byrds'* 'Eight Miles High' — which was just that! They had a personal arrogance and distinctive character. Certainly they were in tune with the psychedelic drug consciousness of the period and this became more visible in their music and style of dress. The third line-up of the band recruited Peter Cummins from *The Grassband* and Noel Bridgeman from *Skid Row*. They went to London to record the debut album *Honest Injun* in 1969 but, unfortunately, only three tracks were laid down as hassles caused the group to return to Ireland and audition for another drummer and guitarist. This time Gary Moore came in with Pat Nash (ex *The Uptown Band*) on drums. Back in England this version of *Granny's Intentions* put down the other eight tracks. The resultant album was greeted with critically good reviews.

Granny's Intentions: Honest Injun (Deram 1969)

Side One	Side Two
1 Maybe (Duhan)*	1 With Salty Eyes, Dirty Lies (Ryan)
2 We Both Need to Know (Duhan)	2 Fourthskin Blues (Duhan)
3 Goodeye (Duhan)	3 Nutmeg Bittersweet (Ryan)*
4 Fifty Years On (Ryan)	4 I'm Goin' (Duhan)*
5 Susan of the County (Duhan)	5 Heavy Loaded Minds (Duhan)
6 Rise Thenfall (Duhan)	

Personnel

Johnny Duhan — vocals	Pete Cummins — bass, flutes and whistles
John Ryan — piano, organ and harpsichord	Pat Nash — drums and percussion
Gary Moore — electric and acoustic guitars	

Initial three tracks laid down with Johnny Hockedy (guitar) and Noel Bridgeman (drums).

Notice how the writing credits are divided between Duhan and Ryan. The first side is very restrained in an American country style. 'Maybe' features Duhan's deep raspy vocals and is an industriously measured song on the theme of freedom. The American flavour is obvious in 'We Both Need to Know', which is executed in waltz time, and 'Susan of the County', with its bluegrass tone. Side two has an unusual introduction in 'With Salty

Eyes, Dirty Lies' — flutes, acoustic guitar and brass. This is quickly followed by vocals of a fairly pointed nature: 'So you're leaving and you thought you'd be gone, Before I'd got home but I caught you sneaking away.' The band benefited from the production quality on Deram which by this stage had reached a very high standard. Their label favoured much complexity and the group could really indulge themselves. Gary Moore demonstrates the subtle, laid-back side of his guitar personality. 'Fourthskin Blues' touches the psychedelic and recounts group experiences on the road in vivid detail. 'Nutmeg Bittersweet', a song of lost love, is heightened by Pete Cummins's flute and has the air of a film soundtrack from the 1960s. There is something quite abstract about many of the songs, definitely more to them than meets the eye or ear. Overall, the combination of Duhan's unique vocals and the jazzy quality of the music make *Honest Injun* a distinctive contribution to Irish rock. The strange cover was only a sketch drawn by John Ryan because Decca's art department never bothered to do a photo session for it, much to the group's chagrin. On the commercial sea it sank without a trace.

After a couple of months Gary Moore split to be replaced by former *Blueshouse* guitarist Ed Deane. Deane was reputed to be extremely eccentric — playing the electric upside down in the left-hand position, with all the chords fingered in reverse; this gave him his distinctive low-tone sound. Practising in their country cottage in Killala, the group became more 'progressive', favouring avant-garde sounds and less commercial songs. Their career had spanned several important musical changes, many management hassles, a few crashes in their Ford Transit and five different band line-ups. But a certain amount of disenchantment set in, and the group disbanded in 1971.[7]

CHANGES

It was well known that to play music for music's sake in Ireland during the sixties meant compromise. Most of the beat groups were able to enjoy their popularity because of the dearth of bands coming from other countries. But when rock music literally exploded into youth culture in 1967, attitudes began to alter radically. It seemed that in that year young musicians all over the world sang in unison — and crystallised their position in a series of monumental statements. From the obvious *Sgt. Pepper's Lonely Hearts Club Band* by *The Beatles* to the hippie revolution of West Coast California, youth had a voice.

Thinking back on that year, the most important single event in rock music was the coming of age of the electric guitar. Almost single-handedly, James Marshall Hendrix altered the course of rock music history forever when he became a worldwide superstar at the Monterey Pop Festival. His heavy, over-the-top expression turned the instrument inside out. He stretched the whole concept of playing rock music into a primal outburst of total humanity. Never had anybody heard or seen someone play with such ferocity, or feel his music so deeply. Jimi Hendrix was the living incarnation of everything that was 1967. From his extreme psychedelic dandyism to his decadent, luxurious attitude, he was a living embodiment of freedom and the limitless.

While *The Jimi Hendrix Experience* awed and dumbfounded every audience, a fellow three-piece, *Cream*, rivalled them for technical virtuosity. With Eric Clapton on guitar, *Cream* were rated the finest English blues trio of their day.

Before *Cream* most English groups saw the guitar as a rhythm instrument to be played in the context of song structures. If there were lead breaks they would complement melodies in songs. When Eric Clapton started playing with John Mayall in the blues context, he used the instrument in a total way, and when *Cream* were formed in 1966 their music freely explored the uncharted. Instead of putting limitations on the song, they began to jam on-stage, fast building up a reputation for themselves.

Both Jimi Hendrix and Eric Clapton exuded the air of high priests — garbed in a million colours of the rainbow, the stringed sceptre of power dangling from their shoulders. Every rock group from that period onwards had to take the electric guitar into account. English groups *Traffic, The Yardbirds, The Who, Pink Floyd, Ten Years After* all concentrated on guitar-based music, infusing it with different styles. In America there were *The Grateful Dead, The Byrds, The Steve Miller Band* and many more, emphasising the guitar in their music. Guitar-based blues made for long, slow soloing sessions. At festivals and gigs all over the world young people danced to the new 'heavy music'. The guitar was to reign supreme until the late seventies.

The long-term effect of this in Ireland was to bring out a pride in playing music better than anyone else. The beat scene had been very much a garage band phenomenon, with only a few groups making it in the international arena. What dawned on an enlightened few was that to make it one had to be extra special and play one's own material.

In the following list of popular beat musicians of March 1968 are included the names of those young people who decided to stake all for what they believed in — to play their kind of music regardless of the consequences or general criticisms. They understood the importance of the guitar and its possibilities in the rock music of the late sixties. They were Brendan 'Brush' Shiels, Rory Gallagher and Philip Lynott. The resultant bands, *Skid Row, Taste* and *Thin Lizzy*, put Ireland on the international rock map and finally broke the psychological barriers that had restricted Irish rock for so long.

Popularity Poll — March 1968

1	Brush Shiels	11	John Ryan (*Granny's Intentions*)
2	Johnny Duhan (*Granny's Intentions*)	12	B. Twomey (*Sugar Shack*)
3	Pat Nash (*The Uptown Band*)	13	Eamonn Gibney (*Dead Centre*)
4	J. Farrell (*The Movement*)	14	M. Walsh (*The Bye Laws*)
5	E. Durkin (*Orange Machine*)	15	G. Neill (*The Gentry*)
6	Cahir O'Doherty (*The Gentry*)	16	R. Abbott (*Cheese*)
7	Rory Gallagher (*Taste*)	17	P. Lynott (*Skid Row*)
8	Mojo (*The Uptown Band*)	18	M. O'Brien (*Good Times*)
9	Dave Lewis (*The Method*)	19	A. Thunder (*The Movement*)
10	J. Fanning (*The Strangers*)	20	P. Fortune (*Sugar Shack*)

Note: Popularity poll taken from Pat Egan's beat column, *New Spotlight* magazine, March 1968. Of the many seminal groups in Ireland both *Sugar Shack* and *The Method* concentrated on blues. The latter, from Northern Ireland, changed their name to the more flamboyant *Andwella's Dream* and were always labelled 'heavy blues' in the *Cream* vein, favouring the psychedelic style.[8] Acquiring a record deal with CBS UK, they released three albums: *Love and Poetry* (1969), *World's End* (1970) and *People's People* (1971), plus several singles. Eventually they went to the USA. *Orange Machine* were also into psychedelia, scoring an Irish hit with 'Three Jolly Little Dwarfs' (Deram 1968). This was off the first *Tomorrow* LP (*Tomorrow* EMI). They were a very English psychedelic group whose 'My White Bicycle' track was pure '67 chemistry. *Tomorrow's* influence on *Orange Machine* was great, and the latter's version of 'My White Bicycle' was reputed to be terrific in the live forum. Incidentally, *Granny's Intentions* also did a class live version of 'Three Jolly Little Dwarfs'!

RORY GALLAGHER, TASTE AND THE BLUES GUITAR

When most beat groups were doing the elliptical circuit of Ireland, Rory Gallagher was concentrating on bringing his talent to the world. Gallagher's achievement was to develop through all the normal Irish music circles and reach the dizzy heights of international acclaim. His one great asset was clarity. He knew exactly what he wanted and where that ambition came from. Unlike most Irish musicians his inspiration came from the blues — the black American variety from the Mississippi delta where music had served to replenish a tortured spirit.

A complete dedication to the guitar and the blues was a significant ingredient of the greatness which surrounded Eric Clapton and Jimi Hendrix. Rory Gallagher was a contemporary and rates as the third driving force in the electric guitar revolution of the late sixties. While Clapton and Hendrix were heavily into the 'drug culture' and the exotic imagery of the times, Gallagher was a purist. He preferred to play any venue at any time, regardless of the situation. He did not exploit the media or use dramatic gestures on-stage. He was strictly low-profile, and seldom gave interviews.

Whatever his attitude, Gallagher lived his music. He physically embodied the archetypal rock performer of the period. Long, brown hair flowing down as beads of sweat dropped onto his electric Fender. His natural ability coincided perfectly with his environment — long solos, serious, complex lyrics and large festivals. Just by walking on-stage and plugging in his instrument, Rory Gallagher epitomised the world youth consciousness of the late sixties and early seventies. His reputation was so strong that he brought his Irish blues trio to the Isle of Wight in August 1970 to play alongside the greatest rock musicians of an era.

Rory Gallagher was born in Ballyshannon in the north-west tip of Ireland on 2 March 1948. He grew up in the rural tranquillity of West Cork in the south, spending all his early years surrounded by the Irish countryside. The new rock 'n' roll sounds of the fifties made a deep impression on his consciousness as he listened to the radio, and he immediately took an interest in the guitar. At the very young age of nine he acquired his first wooden instrument and started to play for dear life. School fêtes, openings, community events — the young Gallagher played all of them while still at school, his inspiration coming from Doc Watson, Leadbelly and Bob Dylan. He paid his dues early on, drawing on those musicians who had developed in a similar 'bluesy' manner. Always noted to favour skiffle and rock 'n' roll, his teenage determination paralleled that of Elvis Presley on the one hand and John Mayall on the other.

After leaving school Rory couldn't find anyone who shared his strength of feeling about playing one's own music. Since he wanted to play professionally he took a vacant slot in *The Fontana Showband* and played the ballroom venues. Only sixteen at the time, his minimal equipment was upgraded and he did some English clubs with the showband, gaining invaluable experience. Gallagher was all against the rigidities of the showband scene and set himself the task of altering the balance of power. He never liked the idea of having to play Jim Reeves covers, and even when *The Fontana* changed its name to the more beat-oriented *Impact*, he still felt limited.

In 1965 Rory Gallagher took the unprecedented step of forming the first three-piece rock band, with the idea of forcing the barriers. He was joined by the bass player and the drummer from *The Impact*. They chanced their luck in Hamburg, Germany, after being noticed on a Dublin television programme doing an original Gallagher composition 'You Fool Me All the Time'. Since the requirement for most clubs then was the 'four-piece neatly dressed beat group', Rory's vision was to come under the hammer. Gallagher himself has said of this adventure that they 'had to get a friend to pose with a Vox Continental organ' so they could fill the stereotyped image. He tried to keep the group together, but hassly gigs, bad money and a rickety van put paid to the idea, and the group fizzled out in 1966.

Undaunted, the young teenager played around for a while in Cork until *The Axles* showband broke up, leaving musicians at a loose end. Gallagher approached Eric Kitteringham and Norman D'Amery to attempt the blues trio experiment once again. The minute they started to gig, the working name of *Taste* was settled upon. Taking off to Europe, *Taste* worked themselves into the ground on a seven-hour-a-night schedule in Hamburg clubs. Back in Ireland they played around but still encountered the same reactions to their music. Usually Gallagher would be asked: 'Where are the rest of the group?' or 'You can't play with only three guys, that's breaking union rules.' Usually Gallagher would bring in a tambourine player or an organist, but the main thrust was always Eric Kitteringham (bass), Norman D'Amery (drums) and of course Rory spitting the blues.

The first embryonic version of *Taste* lasted until early 1968 and, as a guitar-based blues three-piece, was ahead of its time. Normally if the guitar was accentuated by Irish groups it was done in the context of the 'song'. Gallagher wanted to define his music around the instrument itself — lyrics, bass and drum instrumentals all revolved around the echoing solos of his electric Fender. *Taste* slogged up and down the country in 1967 when the beat scene was reaching a frenzy, and yet their power blues still only netted them £5 a night. It was in some of the rhythm and blues clubs in Belfast that *Taste* were first noticed by Eddie Kennedy, a club owner who recognised their revolutionary potential, and by Van Morrison who became a regular at their gigs.

No authorised recordings exist from this period, but a rock entrepreneur Mervyn Solomon released a selection of half-finished tracks on Emerald Gem discs called *Rory Gallagher: In The Beginning* (1974). This is a batch of songs taped in July 1967 during a regular *Taste* residency at the Maritime Hotel, Belfast. The sound is of a dirty blues, with harmonica and electric guitar played heavy. 'Take It Easy Baby' is a typical long, twelve-bar blues number, but the gritty guitar has

7 *Taste* in 1968 — just barely out of his teens, Rory Gallagher was to lead John Wilson and Richie McCracken to international success.

7

8

9

8 Rory Gallagher, Irish longhaired guitar genius of the 1960s and 1970s.

9 Between 1968 and 1970 *Taste* were the Irish power blues trio par excellence, in the same league as *The Jimi Hendrix Experience* and Eric Clapton's *Cream*.

10 The second line-up of *The Rory Gallagher Band. Left to right:* Gerry McAvoy (bass), Rod de'Ath (drums) and Rory Gallagher (guitar). From 1972 to 1976 Gallagher produced five brilliant blues-based albums with this personnel.

11 Rory Gallagher in fine fettle at the Dominion Theatre in 1984 when he played with Juan Martin and Richard Thompson.

10

character. Gallagher, still only in his late teens, was reaching the same level of technical virtuosity as his counterpart Eric Clapton in England. If this seems doubtful, listen to the fluidity of his playing on 'Norman Invasion' — if you can manage to acquire a copy of this first album.

Finding the Irish grind a dead end, Rory Gallagher set out to find a wider audience. With Eddie Kennedy as manager, *Taste* made the big jump to England in May 1968. Still a three-piece, the line-up was surprisingly different, with Richard 'Charlie' McCracken (bass) and John Wilson (drums) backing the guitarist. McCracken and Wilson had met each other in the *Derek and the Sounds Showband*. John Wilson had briefly played with *Them* before teaming up with McCracken again to form *Cheese*, Ireland's answer to English supergroup *Cream*, in 1967. Rory Gallagher decided that Wilson and McCracken were the most proficient musicans for the second version of *Taste*. Hitting every blues and smoky club in the country, the group built up a legendary reputation as the hardest gigging band on the blues scene, and, since *Chicken Shack*, *Fleetwood Mac* and *Bluesbreakers* were their contemporaries, this was a fertile environment. Spending most of their time sleeping in a banged-up transit van, *Taste* projected a characteristic determination, and when money was in short supply they hit the German scene again.

The inevitable recording contract came from Polydor and their debut album *Taste* was done almost live, recorded on a rudimentary eight-track machine. Very bluesy, the album was indeed rough in comparison to the smooth sounds of say *Ten Years After*, an English blues band of the period, but 'Hail', 'Leaving Blues' and 'Sugar Mama' all had that Rory Gallagher feel.

> I'd rather see a coffin
> comin' right through my front door
> Than to hear you say, you don't want
> me no more . . .
>
> 'Leaving Blues'

The above song is an original of Huddie Ledbetter, or 'Leadbelly' as he became known, a late nineteenth-century Louisiana half-caste, whose speciality was the 'hollerin' blues' or 'work song'. This in itself reflects Gallagher's own perceptions and preoccupation. On another level the album defined *Taste's* forceful, power-blues style in such blasters as 'Blister on the Moon' and 'Born on the Wrong Side of Time'.[9] Release of the album in 1969 made *Taste* the new force in the rock arena. Since *Cream* and *The Jimi Hendrix Experience* were no longer in action, the Irish group were acclaimed as their successors by press and public alike. Within one year of its release 175,000 copies of the record had been sold worldwide.

Accelerating demand for public performance pushed *Taste* farther and farther afield. In autumn 1969 the group toured America with English supergroup *Blind Faith*. This group was an assemblage of superstars from *Cream*, *Traffic* and *Family*, led by the guitar hero himself, Eric Clapton. It was not surprising that Clapton had chosen Gallagher's group as support act, a great sign of respect from one bluesman to another. *Taste* were still very young, but doing America and Canada with the biggest group of the period was a sure-fire golden opportunity.

By 1970 the boys were major headliners in Europe and Scandinavia, and gaining a fanatical following in West Germany. Gallagher summed up his attitude during this period: 'If you know what you want to do and know what you want to play, all the other things are just coincidentals ... the showband experience was very good in that I knew damn well·what I wanted to play — electric stuff. So I knew then what direction I was going in.'

On the Boards (Polydor 1970) is *Taste* at their peak and stands the test of time admirably. In the eleven tracks Gallagher disciplines indulgency and accomplishes a controlled expression. Taking a wide sweep of his talents the album is grounded in rhythm and blues, ranging from 'Railway and Gun' (stylish blues) to 'See Here' (acoustic). The title track is an instrumental of soft jazz music, involving an alto-sax solo by Rory himself. 'What's Goin' On' is a classic heavy song and was to become his most famous opening number in concert. He even did a pop song, 'If I Don't Sing I'll Cry', his voice a raspy blues howl.

The period of rock music that *Taste* emerged through was hectic. Groups formed, achieved stardom and disbanded within months of formation. *Taste* were also part of the festival scene of the times — a period when large open-air events attracted world-class acts in an atmosphere of relaxation and collective enjoyment. When Rory stepped on-stage anywhere, he was greeted with howls of adulation. He was fast becoming the new doyen of the electric guitar. By 1970 he had cut a brilliant album, gone to the States, toured Europe and made it to the Isle of Wight Festival. Here he had played with *The Doors* and *Jimi Hendrix*, two of the sixties' most inspiring components.

Taste were a definitive sixties blues band, second only to *Cream* in terms of three-piece instrumental showmanship. Their set was filmed at the Isle of Wight in August 1970 — all the more significant in that it represented the passing of an era. With Eric Clapton past his prime and Jimi Hendrix's tragic death in September of that year, Rory Gallagher was the only blues guitarist of strength to fill the position of international guitar hero. Indicative of the pace and stress of that period, *Taste* broke up in October 1970. This unexpected move occurred under very mysterious circumstances which in the end had little to do with the music. Unfortunately, business and personal problems had encroached on Rory Gallagher's career.

Taste — live albums released 1971

1 *Live Taste:* Recorded at the Montreux Casino, a very good live album made up almost entirely of blues material. The most prominent cut being 'Feel So Good', a Big Billy Broonzy composition.

2 *Live at the Isle of Wight:* The album cover shows the primitive orange amps and minimal equipment which *Taste* were using for a huge rock festival. The sound quality is atrocious and the numbers poorly performed. *Taste* were obviously at the end of their lease. Redeeming feature is a lengthy version of 'What's Goin' On'.

The Rory Gallagher Band emerged into the twilight of the next decade with a more subdued attitude. Rory had replaced his drummer and bass player with Wilgar Campbell and Gerry MacAvoy, both from Irish group *Deep Joy*. Immediately they recorded an album which broke away from the fuzzy style of *Taste. Rory Gallagher* (Polydor 1971) is varied, more dexterous and even delicate in parts. 'It's You', 'I'm Not Surprised', 'Just the Smile' and 'Can't Believe It's True' are worked acoustic compositions. His lyrics are better, having graduated from gruff howls to such lines as:

> I feel so blue,
> I think I'll wave myself goodbye.
>
> 'Wave Myself Goodbye'

Bringing in Vincent Crane on piano displayed Gallagher's interest in widening the format of his blues style — the down home sound on 'Wave Myself Goodbye'. There's even a country blues sound from his acoustic here and there. Nevertheless, Rory couldn't help letting go on 'Laundromat' and 'Sinner Boy', the hard electric blues tracks. This line-up of the band lasted until June 1972, producing two more records which made the international charts, and carrying the Irishman's electric blues to the four corners of the earth.

At this stage, Gallagher was becoming more extravagant in his playing, more interesting. *Deuce* (Polydor 1971) is another landmark, produced by Rory himself. Opening and closing tracks of both sides are hard rock, simple and to the point. The rest is more experimental — flourishing acoustic displays ('I'm Not Awake Yet'), to picked harmonics ('Maybe I Will'). 'Out of My Mind' is interesting since Rory sings in an American country style with banjo-sounding guitar. Again he used good bluesy lyrics well thought out and heartfelt:

> Wake up in the morning
> it's a brand new day.
> Though it seems the same
> it's different from yesterday.
> Then I envy the leaves and put my cup away. (*Repeated*)
> Runnin' down a country lane lookin' on a field of grain,
> Just to see your smile, makes me feel in love again.
>
> ('Maybe I Will')

By 1972 Rory Gallagher was recognised as undisputed blues guitar hero. May of that year brought him enormous commercial and artistic success with the release of *Live in Europe* (Polydor). 'This is a song by Blind Boy Fuller ... he cut it way back in 1920 or something or other ... Pistol Slapper Blues,' announces Gallagher. For another, with his pronunciation very black, very negro, he picks up a mandolin and strumming like mad, the crowd clapping and stomping, he growls: 'Mama's in the kitchen baking up a pie, Papa's in the backyard ... get a job son you know you ought to try.' 'Goin' to My Home' is the title of this mandolin blues, his theme being leaving home, gettin' a job and feelin' the 'lonesome blues'.

'Thank you, thank you, thank you very much ... Did you everrrrr, did you everrrrr, did you everrrrr, well did you ever wake up with those bullfrogs on your mind. Well did you ever wake up with those bullfrogs on your mind ...' — the intro to 'Bullfrog Blues', the song which has become synonymous with his name. Rory on vocals, guitars, mandolin and harmonica is peaking all over the place.

Just when the seas of superstardom began to roll again, Rory Gallagher switched direction. In June 1972 a new *Rory Gallagher Band* was formed, with Rod de'Ath (drums), Lou Martin (keyboards) and old friend Gerry MacAvoy fretting the bass. Obviously the man was more interested in blues than in the hassle of being public property. Through the three albums of blues music he put down between 1972 and 1974, a sincere desire to embrace its very nature is apparent. *Blueprint* (Polydor 1973) explores the delta blues of Big Bill Broonzy ('Banker's Blues'), the romantic spirit of American folk ('Daughter of the Everglades') and waltz-time music ('If I Had a Reason'). He mixes pedal-steel guitar with strong production overdubs, embroidering 'If I Had a Reason' with an historical mesh of nineteenth-century Americana.

Gallagher had chosen Lou Martin for his interest in blues piano after the fashion of Otis Spann, the great 'spanking' Chicago pianist. Their next record, *Tattoo* (Polydor 1973), re-echoed American roots. Besides its florid cover design, the songs are coated with an 'olden time' film — something of the music hall and vaudeville atmosphere. 'Tattoo'd Lady', 'Cradle Rock' and 'Livin' Like a Truck' are straight heavy rock while 'Who's That Comin' slides in with acoustic bottleneck guitar, transferring quickly to electric. Produced by Rory himself, the album contained another definitive Gallagher tune — 'A Million Miles Away'.

His most important accomplishment of this period was the legendary Irish tour of early 1974. Filmed by Tony Palmer and recorded for posterity, the concerts were indeed Rory Gallagher reaching a new height in his expression of blues. His rendering of Muddy Waters's 'I Wonder Who's Gonna Be Your Sweet Man' and Tony Joe White's 'As the Crow Flies' are erudite versions of American blues originals. As an example of how incredible Gallagher's guitar work could be, 'Walk on Hot Coals' is a fifteen-minute revelation — precision picking, harmonic wah-wah, fuzztone — you name it, it's involved here. The more he plays the more the instrument plays him. It rolls out faster and faster, reaching crests of scintillating hooks and lead breaks. If you want to know why Gallagher is so good, listen to *Rory Gallagher Irish Tour 1974* (Polydor), and remember it's his tenth album and third band.

After a change to Chrysalis Records, *The Rory Gallagher Band* struck gold with *Against the Grain* (1975) — much louder and crisper than earlier recordings, with one side Gallagher compositions and the other a collection of tributes to ageing bluesmen. 'Out on the Western Plain' (Leadbelly) is about the most authentic rural American song Rory Gallagher ever accomplished with a deep, bassy acoustic sound evoking rolling plains, hot sun, and barren townships:

Me and a bunch of cowboys   Com a cah cah yiccie yiccie
rode into Jesse James,   Com a cah cah yiccie yiccie yeah (*sic*).[10]
Me and a bunch of cowboys
rode into Jesse James.

If one closes the mind to the immediate surroundings, sounds of cowboys, horses, campfires, firearms flare up in tune with Rory's picking and booming on the bass strings — gliding from one chord to the other — changing key and bringing you with it, his voice the husky colour of a woodsman.

During the seventies Gallagher's interest in blues went far. Numerous trips to the States brought him into contact with those black artists who had pioneered the genre — Freddie King, Albert King and Muddy Waters, amongst others. Rather than just sit in the audience, Gallagher would get up and jam with the great old men, preferring small, smoky, acoustic clubs to large stadia. His humility and debt-paying to those who inspired him was definitely off the beaten track. An important event was his involvement with Mississippi bluesman Muddy Waters on *Muddy Waters — London Sessions* (Chess 1972), where he jammed to his heart's delight. Stevie Winwood, Georgie Fame, Mitch Mitchell and other sixties musicians all paid Waters a tribute by guesting on the record.

After producing *Calling Card* (Chrysalis 1976), there was another line-up change to make *Rory Gallagher Band* number three. This time Ted McKenna took the drum seat with Gerry MacAvoy still on bass and Rory concentrating on a better-produced, tougher sound with less exploration.

Picture Macroom Mountain Dew Festival in West Cork, mid-June 1978 — blue skies and sun shining high — everyone feeling right for a day of open-air live music — the small town thronging with people, mostly teenagers, drinking, cavorting, making hay in anticipation of Rory Gallagher's appearance. Spanning two decades, his eternal presence on the rock scene drew many admirers, fans and well wishers. A free and open spirit made Rory Gallagher's return to his home town an emotive happening with everyone rising to the version of 'Out on the Western Plain' — the breeze blowing in his hair — jeans, check shirt and battered Fender. A survivor of the heavy sixties, Rory Gallagher had made blues his life-force, a constant in a world of flux, a lifelong source of being:

> I don't know where I'm goin'
> and I don't know where I've been
> and I haven't seen my baby since I don't know when.
> I'm walking down that long road with a smile upon my face,
> broken hearted but people can't see a trace.

('Don't Know Where I'm Goin', *Deuce* 1971)

From May 1978 to March 1981 *The Rory Gallagher Band* toured the world and recorded three albums: *Photofinish* (Chrysalis 1978), *Top Priority* (Chrysalis 1979) and *Stagestruck* (Chrysalis 1980). Heavy rock tracks such as 'Shadow Play' and 'Won't You Follow Me' were very popular and kept the public wanting more. In May 1981 there was a fourth line-up change when Brendan O'Neill replaced Ted McKenna on drums. After the 1982 *Jinx* album on Chrysalis, Gallagher opted to spend much of his time in Europe, appearing only twice in his homeland over the next four years. Despite his absence, Gallagher still has an enormous following and many rate him as the finest blues guitarist of his generation. A new album, *Defender* (Capo/Demon) was released in summer 1987, and showed that none of the old fire had gone. The inclusion of a Sonny Boy Williamson track and the acoustic blues 'Seven Days' assured everyone that his original vision was still intact.

SKID ROW

'Progressive rock was about guys who played their instruments at a higher level than other guys who played their instruments — in fact playing your instrument exceptionally well. Rock was about playing your instrument as well as you can' (Brush Shiels 1984).

Skid Row evolved from the normal Irish beat scene of the mid-sixties. Their unique quality sprang from a difference in attitude — while most groups played safe *Skid Row* not only played unheard-of music but played it in a manner never seen before. The group believed in 'rock progress' and broke away from the restrictions of four-four time, melodic chord structures and balanced composition. Their speciality lay in instrumental virtuosity and bringing this to its logical limit on record and in live performance.

Like *Taste*, *Skid Row* were a three-piece band concentrating on lead electric guitar. They had a definite interest in blues, but unlike Rory Gallagher were not rooted in its character. *Skid Row* were more urban and thus their music had a city quality of concrete and glass. The standard three-piece group of the time had blues roots — Hendrix, Clapton and Gallagher all believed in the spiritual quality of blues — but *Skid Row* had something devilish and strange. Their music worked on awkward patterns, atonality, sharp stops and starts, jagged breaks and ear-splitting drum, bass and guitar solos. They were indeed 'something else'.

The instigator and founder member of *Skid Row* was Brendan Shiels, or 'Brush' Shiels as he became known. Born in Dublin in 1952 he divided his early teens between football and rock 'n' roll. One of his earliest groups was a country-and-western style rock outfit called *Brian Rock and the Boys*. By 1967 he had joined *The Uptown Band*, playing bass. He played the beat club circuit gaining experience and developing his musical technique. Coming suddenly under the influence of the new English musical consciousness of that period, Brush Shiels decided to go out on a limb and form his own group. Humorously entitled *My Father's Moustache*, the group consisted of Philip Lynott (vocals), Noel Bridgeman (drums), Bernie Cheevers (guitar) and Brush (bass guitar). Almost instantly they changed the name to *Skid Row*.

Fired with youth and an enthusiasm for what was happening in rock music worldwide, Brush Shiels opted for experimentation. Between 1968 and 1969 *Skid Row* defied the normal Irish stereotype, playing when they felt like it and whatever music they felt was right. They were known to do strange covers of West Coast American sounds, crazy versions of psychedelic classics like 'Strawberry Fields Forever', or spaced-out versions of Eric Burdon songs. Their attitude was let whatever happen — happen! Brush felt the time was right to get musicians of different backgrounds together and he formed a focal point called 'The Ghetto' in a Dublin beat club, to encourage any musician to play with another, regardless of musical differences. The venue attracted folk and rock musicians in a melting pot of free-form experimentation. Poetic folk ensemble *Tara Telephone* would turn up, while psychedelic acoustic *Dr Strangely Strange* suspended the imagination with their musical abstractions. *Skid Row* would always wrap up the proceedings with say a *Buffalo Springfield* song, while projecting liquid lights and 8mm film of previous gigs as a backdrop. It was all very new and very interesting.

Temporarily recruiting Robbie Brennan on drums and having replaced their guitarist with the very young Belfast-born Gary Moore, *Skid Row* did sessions in Belfast and Dublin in the studio. During the summer of 1969 the outcome of these surfaced in a single on the yellow Song label: 'Misdemeanour Dream Felicity'/'New Places, Old Faces'. If 'Strawberry Fields' affected the course of English rock this *Skid Row* single certainly reflected the change in the Irish context. 'New Places, Old Faces', featuring a very young Philip Lynott on vocals, is furrowed in an acoustic guitar/flute instrumental — it has a melodic, psychedelic quality, evoking meadows, trees and flowers. Taking Dave Brubeck's 'Take Five' beat in five-four time, 'Misdemeanour Dream Felicity' is ear-catching, an acoustic instrumental extending into far off corners. The beat anchors the song while the many sound variations alter your musical perspective. *Skid Row* performed these songs and many others on television in Belfast with English group *The Troggs* and also appeared on RTE's *Like Now*, blowing everyone away in the process.[11] Robbie Brennan comments: '*Skid Row* played very intricate music and would space off in different patterns ... definitely an "acid band" at the time.' This was a band of teenagers opening their minds to the possibilities inherent in the music of Jimi Hendrix, *Pink Floyd* and *The Byrds*.

Philip Lynott parted company with the group during the summer of 1969, a parting prompted by the incompatibility of Lynott's vocalising with the group's growing instrumental sophistication (Lynott quickly formed *Orphanage*, his own travelling band). *Skid Row's* line-up was now reduced to a three-piece with Noel Bridgeman back on the drums, Gary Moore on guitar and Brush, the bassman, taking vocals. This time the group's music leaned in a direction that few groups had thought of, let alone tried. According to Robbie Brennan, they went for 'techno-flash, heavy rock with very speedy, very precise playing — a mixture of ten-minute guitar solos, extremely fast riffs played in unison, bass and drums going full out on one chordal guitar solo. Pre-Mahavishnu jazz-rock songs were just a vehicle for highly involved soloing.' Eric Clapton's *Cream* had developed an instrumental soloing technique but it revolved around the blues. *Skid Row* were on a different plane and rank as one of the first 'progressive rock' groups of the sixties era.[12]

Brush Shiels: 'When *Cream* and Hendrix came along it changed the whole music thing from songs to guitar playing, from singing songs to being virtuosos on your instruments. The whole progressive rock thing came from being an exceptional player. At that time there was a lot of credibility in the blues as done by *Fleetwood Mac* or *John Mayall's Bluesbreakers*. This blues became guitar-oriented and to survive in those days one needed an exceptionally good guitar player. So we had Gary.'

For their inventiveness, *Skid Row* were rewarded with a record contract from CBS, and ended 1969 with a scorcher of a gig in Dublin's National Stadium, with English progressives *Blodwyn Pig* (ex *Jethro Tull* guitarist Mick Abraham's new band), Scottish soul-based *Stone The Crows* and of course *Dr Strangely Strange*. A very unusual line-up, and fondly remembered by many as one of the weirdest concerts ever — very packed, with everyone giving off a spaced-out vibe. It demonstrated the change of attitudes in rock music when all styles, and people from all manner of backgrounds, could coalesce and produce. The interplay between the rural character of *Dr Strangely Strange* and the more urban *Skid Row* was unprecedented, Gary Moore contributing interesting guitar pieces to *Strangely's* live and recorded work.

Skid Row started the new decade by spending sixteen hours a day in the studio working on their debut album. As a sampler to *Skid Row's* heavier style, a single, 'Sandy's Gone' Parts 1 & 2, was released in April 1970 (CBS). The sound is a dense, up-scale, guitar-based blues, and is so long that both sides of the single are taken up with it. *Fleetwood Mac, the* English blues band of the period, played with *Skid Row* in Dublin that year, and their legendary guitarist, Peter Green, rated Gary Moore 'the best guitarist I have ever played with in the world'. Momentum had begun to build as the British music press and underground disc-jockey John Peel picked up on *Skid Row* and, after a succession of managers, Clifford Davis (*Fleetwood Mac's* manager) was brought in to run the group's affairs, and following a stint in America *Skid Row* flew back to Britain to sort out some problems with their album.

Skid (CBS 1970) was finally released in October and entered high on the English album chart. The reaction to the music was surprise and shock — how could a group of seventeen-year-olds produce such a bundle of devastatingly inventive songs? The rock world had never heard a music so piercing, so unconcerned with melody. People had pointed out the importance of English innovators *King Crimson*, but they had coated their off-the-wall notation with sweet melodies and soft cascades.

The main hinge of *Skid* is the staggered solo on any instrument. Disorientation and a 'blackness' is what one feels after listening to the record. 'Mad Dog Woman', 'Virgo's Daughter' and 'Awful Lot of Woman' are exercises in awkward musical composition, very heavy and intricate. 'Heading Home Again' draws on country music for substance — soft bass and electric guitar with a liquid sound. 'Un Co-op Showband Blues' is an excellent put-down of the Irish music scene; really heavy *Skid Row* blues, with biting lyrics by Brush:

> Got a job in a showband
> working like a slave
> six nights and every Sunday
> c'mon and put me on a weekly wage.

The record also contains a long version of 'Felicity' with a more electric application in the mould of the instrumental qualities of English groups *Blind Faith* or *Traffic*. What characterises Skid Row's music is the way notes are left out in a sequence or put in at odd times. The music follows a logical pattern and then turns suddenly at a right angle — streams of notes very close together on the scale involving flats and sharps, punctuated by step-like drum strikes. The complete opposite to pop music, *Skid Row* were definitely a head band, pitching their musical sails to the open seas of the new rock intelligentsia.

So a group of teenagers decided to play music the way they wanted to, irrespective of criticism or financial loss or gain, and in doing so brought their unique ideas to the world. The attitude among a lot of Irish people was that they were weird, and Brush Shiels commented at the time: 'Irish audiences are a hundred percent musically retarded compared to English ones and I think even here [England] we're a bit above people's heads at the moment. In Ireland we are always being asked to play "Oh Well" or "Albatross".' In the autumn of 1970 *Skid Row* were financed with £10,000, and toured in Europe with American blues act *Canned Heat*. Things accelerated for the trio as American dates had them rubbing shoulders with *Ten Years After, Jethro Tull, Frank Zappa and the Mothers of Invention* and *The Allman Brothers Band*. To take a musical vision and carry it so far must have been an incredible experience for a group so young in age. The rise and rise of *Skid Row* was fast, very fast, and audiences everywhere were dumbfounded by their eerie music and artful light shows.

Based in Britain, *Skid Row* spent the first part of 1971 recording their follow-up album.[13] More advanced and technically brilliant than previous Irish rock albums, *34 Hours* was recorded in just that time. Stylistically unique, its twelve tracks spread themselves over the vinyl in a continuous cycle of instrumental peaks. The cover of the record is a de luxe gatefold sleeve in green — a heady picture of a normal *Skid Row* performance with liquid lights flashing, taken from German television's *Beat Club* programme of the time which was a real 'progressive' show by this stage.

Skid Row — 34 Hours (CBS 1971)

Side One
1 Night of the Warm Witch/
  The Following Morning
2 First Thing in the Morning/
  Last Thing at Night
3 Mar

Side Two
1 Go, I'm Never Gonna Let You (incl.
  Go, I'm Never Gonna Let You Part
  2)
2 Lonesome Still
3 The Love Story (Parts 1-4)

The opening cut 'Night of the Warm Witch' is a salvo of drums, guitar and bass travelling at high speed, gurgling in the middle of the track and soloing into infinity. They were getting a violin sound from Gary Moore's guitar by putting it through a Vox volume pedal — a very Celtic violin sound. There is a lack of monotony in this track since the instrumental passages crest over each other, enveloping and developing more interesting noises in return. Two guitars are used on 'Mar', which is very tight and hard-sounding. 'Go, I'm Never Gonna Let You' has Gary going full out on wah-wah pedal, rocking up the sound to a crescendo and then starting all over again when you least expect it. 'Lonesome Still' displays the country music influences *Skid Row* picked up in America from the likes of *The Allman Brothers*. This time Moore uses an 'A' tuning on his Les Paul, playing bottleneck through the Vox volume pedal, resulting in a steel guitar sound; and Noel Bridgeman plays accordion. Produced by Clifford Davis, the album still sounds innovative and deserves to be included in all written work on the history of rock. The music is very far-out in any sense and meant to make the listener hear (and feel) the sounds — awkward, uncomfortable, physical, abrasive, viscous, dynamic are words that come to mind.

'I'd call it controlled freedom. We start together, finish together, but in the middle its more or less every man for himself. *34 Hours* is good, but we plan to keep changing our style — more country, more funk' (Brush Shiels 1971).

In the summer of 1971 *Skid Row* toured America with San Francisco's finest, *The Grateful Dead*, and English blues band *Savoy Brown*. *Skid Row* played the Fillmore auditorium to American West Coast 'hippie' audiences as their album went on general release. Continuing to explore uncharted musical territory, the teenage Irish group absorbed many strains of country rock. Their range became so great that they were reported to have had equitable jamming sessions with world supergroup of the period *Led Zeppelin* in Los Angeles. By the fall of that year *Skid Row* had started work on their third album and everything seemed to be going up and up.

Tragedy struck when Gary Moore walked out on the group in December 1971. 'I left *Skid Row* because I wasn't happy with the music anymore and because I just felt it was time to do something new. I think a lot of the hassle was that *Skid Row* were playing too fast and you can't very well get a good sound when there is too much speed going on' (Gary Moore 1973). Eric Bell from *Thin Lizzy* was drafted in as a temporary replacement for Christmas concerts in London, and eventually Paul Chapman was hired as guitarist, but according to Brush, 'we couldn't get the old telepathy going.' *Skid Row* had pushed into dangerous land, risking the meteoric rise to fame on a strangely uncompromising rock music. As teenagers they travelled the world, gigging constantly with major world leaders in the field. Their epitaph is contained in four splendid singles and two extraordinary albums. By 1972 *Skid Row* in their original format were no longer.[14]

HARD ROCK AND POETRY — THE SOUND OF THIN LIZZY

'Sure do appreciate ye' all comin', especially you, Skinny Lizzy,' drawls the nineteen-year-old black Irishman in a thick Dublin accent. He laughs as the music begins to flow, his voice deepening in tone. A mysterious piano and guitar lend a Celtic mood to the words. Philip Lynott's voice is romantic and endearing — flickering images of an Irish heartland as he slowly repeats, 'won't ye'all come, your faces keep us warm.' There is a far-off, brittle quality to the song, adolescent and fragile. It is *Thin Lizzy's* first ever single, called 'The Farmer'.

When *Thin Lizzy* formed in early 1970 they found a magic formula. Every move, every concert, every song led to more. Their character was defined by the tall, dark Lynott, who had charisma and a voice of pure poetry. They played progressive music with an air of dignity and class. Lynott's lyrical artistry was balanced by Eric Bell's sweetly succulent electric guitar. Bell was a graceful master of tone and colour on the instrument. More ethereal than the blues of Rory Gallagher or the sharpness of Gary Moore, his accomplishment was in subtle understatement.

Thin Lizzy were a three-piece like their predecessors *Taste* and *Skid Row*, but the emphasis this time was on the song. Lynott brought the song back to its prominent position in progressive rock, shunning the over-indulgent soloing of earlier times. He played bass guitar up-front, allowing the other instruments to add to his songs and not overblow them completely. People were tiring of the endless solos and jamming on-stage — *Thin Lizzy* favoured economy and quality. Their appearance on the rock scene of the early seventies was an important signpost to change, while 'Whisky in the Jar' (Decca 1972) contains the most accomplished guitar work of any group from that era.

12 The folk-based seminal *Skid Row* with Brush Shiels, Philip Lynott, Gary Moore and Robbie Brennan (1968).

13 *Skid Row. Left to right:* Brush Shiels, Noel Bridgeman, Gary Moore (notice the sitar).

14 *Skid Row* at the time of their ground-breaking *34 Hours* album in 1971: Gary Moore, Brush Shiels and Noel Bridgeman.

15 Originally *Thin Lizzy* were a four-piece, formed in Dublin during the spring of 1970. In this rare shot we see Eric Wricksen (keyboards), Philip Lynott (vocals, bass), Brian Downey (drums) and Eric Bell (guitar).

16 After six months *Thin Lizzy* were a trio. This is a typical scene in Phil Lynott's flat in Clontarf. *Left to right:* Eric, Brian and Philo; this line-up lasted from 1970 to 1973.

17 *Thin Lizzy* — final tour, London 1983.

15

16

17

Early Days

Philip Parris Lynott was born in the English West Midlands on 20 August 1949 of Brazilian/Irish parentage. Raised in the suburban Dublin of the fifties and sixties, his unorthodox background made him an individualist from the very start. While at secondary school he followed his creative instincts and became the singer with a local band, *The Black Eagles*. In his early teens the rock music of America and Britain excited his imagination, giving impetus to his decision to opt for a career in music. Black soul singers from the States, and white rhythm and blues specialists Graham Bond and Alexis Korner in Britain, were fertile influences.

After gaining confidence in local clubs, playing *Beatles* covers and Top Twenty material, *The Black Eagles* tried the mushrooming beat club scene. Lynott started to make his mark as a choice interpreter of the song, getting numerous support slots with seasoned beat groups such as *The Chessmen*. On drums was fourteen-year-old Brian Downey, initiating a musical relationship that would last for a long time. 'The *Black Eagles* played support to us on a number of occasions. We used to say, "Look at that little black guy in the van, he'll never get anywhere." They were children, but they had something — a certain arrogance' (Alan Dee of *The Chessmen*).

Working their way through the taboos of the Irish music scene, *The Black Eagles* played every type of venue, including bingo halls. The group broke up in 1966, Lynott joining another local outfit, *Kamasutra*. By 1968 Brian Downey had a rejuvenated interest in playing music and joined the blues group *Sugar Shack* with Brian Twomey (vocals) and Dermot Woodfell (guitar). Meanwhile Lynott was going psychedelic with the hugely innovative *Skid Row*. A Tim Rose song, 'Morning Dew' (Tribune), became an Irish hit for *Sugar Shack*, giving the group nationwide recognition. Simultaneously *Skid Row* were experimenting in every possible direction and then, during recording and television appearances, *Skid Row's* Brush Shiels decided that Lynott as lead singer did not suit the band's sound. Forced to quit but determined to make his mark, Lynott started to take bass guitar lessons from 'The Brush'.[15]

During 1969 Philip Lynott applied his voice to the bass and acoustic guitar. The sudden change in rock music internationally fired his instinct to write and play his own songs. In Dublin at this time all manner of musicians would get together and play, and Lynott opened himself up to the folk mainstream, allowing that area to influence his playing, and kept company with *Sweeney's Men* and *Dr Strangely Strange*. Lynott could have been swallowed up by the dross of the ballroom music scene, but he plunged for the narrow ledge of new progressive music. Always enthusiastic, he formed a new group under the working title *Orphanage* which would mix blues, folk and progressive rock.[16] The drum seat was filled by old chum Brian Downey, who had played in *Skid Row* for some gigs, and the theme of the group was looseness and adaptability. They played up and down Ireland in every type of venue, adapting their music to suit any crowd, with Lynott writing and performing his own songs, wearing hippie clothes and putting forth his own version of 'expanded consciousness'.

It was obvious that Lynott had come under the spell of Jimi Hendrix in England. Hendrix was black and powerful, the mainspring of the new psychedelic heavy rock. His whole stance was revolutionary — freedom through release. He exuded an air of spiritual and physical completeness, achieved through a synthesis of sex, psychedelia and music. To the conservative elements of society Hendrix was the emperor of hippiedom, exploding on-stage with the most overtly explicit 'human' performance ever witnessed. He defied all limits, soaring to intergalactic heights on other-worldly music. Philip Lynott similarly defied the compromising nature of the Irish rock scene. He wanted to do his own thing, wear his own mode of dress, speak his own words, sing about his own personal experiences in his own home town. From 1969 to 1970 he did just that — writing beautiful poetry and haunting the smaller folk venues with his imagery. During performances by *Orphanage* in 1970, a young Belfast guitarist named Eric Bell would turn up and enthuse. Fed up with his restricted role in *The Dreams Showband*, Eric wanted more, and Philip Lynott had something unique.

Shades of a Blue Orphanage

During the spring of 1970 the first line-up of *Thin Lizzy* was assembled: Philip Lynott (acoustic guitar, bass and vocals), Brian Downey (drums), Eric Bell (lead guitar) and Eric Wricksen (keyboards).[17] The name was coined by Eric Bell from a children's comic. From day one there was no doubt about their future — they were the most progressive band in the country at the time. Through a booking agency they were offered plenty of gigs in clubs, halls and country venues. Also through this agency the group met Terry O'Neill, who began to manage them. In Dublin they hired a hall to practise in day and night. Philip Lynott began to pour himself into writing, combining his muse with Bell's mesmerising guitar ability. Playing original material with a heavy emphasis on guitar and effects, their attitude was simple: no compromise.

When it came to recording their first single in Trend studios, studio manager John D'Ardis insisted that his song 'I Need You' be done by the group. This rhythm and blues number was executed by *Thin Lizzy* with guitar breaks thrown in; the other side being an unorthodox Lynott composition called 'The Farmer'. The song has an unreal character and begs a dozen listenings. Commercially the single was a flop and, although making steady ground on the live circuit, *Thin Lizzy* were not living up to Lynott's expectations. They would play a support slot in a ballroom, get paid £50, but that was it. Lynott wanted much more.

August 1970 saw the group reduced to a trio, as Eric Wricksen's role in the group had become redundant. According to Terry O'Neill, Wricksen used to play the piano with one hand and drink and smoke with the other! Their following began to grow: 'The people who came to our gigs were the intelligentsia or posers, depending on what side of the fence you were born. If we played the CYMS in Fairview or Dun Laoghaire, these people would fill the hall, so the promoters would book us again. With *Thin Lizzy* the music had to impress the musicians. If we played a cover of a song to please the audience it would be something that was unusual. We used to do a version of Jimi Hendrix's 'If Six Was Nine', since it wasn't a single and would impress our audience' (Phil Lynott).

In October 1970 *Thin Lizzy* played open air, in a festival headlined by English group *Mungo Jerry*, plus Irish acts *Granny's Intentions*, *Blueshouse* and Ditch Cassidy's *White Magic*. By the end of the year several record companies from England were eagerly sending people over to suss out exactly what *Thin Lizzy* were about. Decca were duly impressed and the group were brought over to London to record their first album in West Hampstead. 'We only had a week to record that first album. We were knackered all the time — in at eight in the morning, finish at two, and by the time you'd get to bed you'd have to get up again. We had the set off by heart from rehearsing so much, so it was easy' (Brian Downey). Arriving back in Ireland to continue playing for a living, the group faced all criticism with more zeal. 'Will *Thin Lizzy* ever grow fat?' was one of the headlines that ran in an issue of *New Spotlight* magazine of the period.

All gibes were ended on release of their first album in April 1971. *Thin Lizzy* is the first real hard-core resolution of Irish rock on vinyl. The album cover with its fish-eyed photography of a battered car in a backstreet has a quality, a simplicity. The contents epitomise the music of the period. While *Free* or *King Crimson* were pointing their music into obscure areas, *Thin Lizzy* complemented instrumental aspects with melody. All songs were written by Philip Lynott, mirroring personal experiences with a vivid imagination. The Indian tom-toms play as Lynott recites the words: 'I'm damned indeed comrade, I'm being bombed, and all the people's faces turned Strawberry Blonde'; then a magical guitar sounds, then drums enter, giving the sound a lush ripeness. 'The Friendly Ranger at Clontarf Castle' opens an album of superlative taste and originality.

Thin Lizzy (Decca 1971)

Side One
1 The Friendly Ranger at Clontarf
    Castle (Bell, Lynott)
2 Honesty Is No Excuse
3 Diddy Levine
4 Ray-Gun (Bell)
5 Look What the Wind Blew In

Side Two
1 Éire
2 Return of the Farmer's Son
3 Clifton Grange Hotel
4 Saga of the Ageing Orphan
5 Remembering

Personnel

Philip Lynott — vocals, bass acoustic guitar
Eric Bell — lead guitar and twelve-string guitar
Brian Downey — percussion, drums

Philip Lynott, only twenty-one when this album was released, was a new type of adventurer poet, drawing on a Celtic environment and teenage experiences, the music blasting with a sexual power. 'Honesty Is No Excuse' is an epic acoustic track with soaring vocals. In 'Diddy Levine', his voice has the deep tone of an Irish rambler delivering words of wisdom: 'Inheritance you see runs through every family, who is to say what is to be is any better'. 'Ray-Gun' is a heavy riff piece *à la* Hendrix. 'Éire' opens far off and distant with echoing guitars. It is full of Irish legend and history:

In the land of Éireann
Where sat the high king
Faced with a problem
Dreaded Viking
Gather all the menfolk
Speaking the Celtic tongue
The land is Éireann
The land is young

Stands Red O'Donnell
Fighting the Saxon folk
With Hugh O'Neill
Oh! Oh! Oh! Oh!
All along the northland
They fight bitterly
The land is Éireann
The land is free.

'Saga of the Ageing Orphan', a beautiful acoustic ballad, is obviously an intimate experience, as the consistent imagery of Lynott in relation to 'orphan' and 'farm' sees these words cropping up again and again in his songs; they are very personal words coming directly from Lynott's physical and mental states. The album ends with 'Remembering', a song of first love, enchantment, sadness and nostalgia, backed up by crashing, heavy rock. When Jimi Hendrix wrote songs he combined delicate words with his own power blues, and Lynott similarly achieved a synthesis: 'Hendrix was a very good influence on me as a personality and Eric as a guitar player. It would be ridiculous for a black man fronting a three-piece not to know about Hendrix' (Phil Lynott).

It was the summer of 1971 and *Thin Lizzy* were working Germany playing clubs and doing television appearances. They recorded for the BBC Radio One programme *Sounds of the Seventies* and disc jockey John Peel picked up on their album, giving it much airplay. Commercially the album wasn't selling, but hot shot Radio Luxembourg personality Kid Jensen thought the album was gold dust and played it constantly on the air. Eventually the album reached number one in Radio Luxembourg's 'Hot Heavy Top Twenty'. At this stage *Thin Lizzy* were seen as the most progressive of rock groups, especially among the underground intelligentsia.

They followed up the album with the release of *New Day* (Decca 1971), a four-track maxi single in a gatefold sleeve.[18] This contains Philip Lynott's ode to Dublin: 'How can I leave the town that brings me down, that has no jobs, is blessed by God and makes me cry, Dublin.' One of his most personal songs, its sadness is enunciated by Eric Bell's milky electric guitar work. Through this song one can empathise with the young Lynott's feelings of frustration and love for a city he has to vacate.

Back in Ireland the group headlined a free festival, supported by an out-and-out progressive bill: *Horslips, Elmer Fudd, Gypsy Rock, Supply Demand and Curve, Mellow Candle* and others. Working harder and harder, the group played 'every corner in England, Scotland and Wales ... at it seven days a week ... if you got a day off it was a Godsend' (Brian Downey). Taking a month to record their second album they changed studios and relaxed into it. Improving in their playing ability and looking better at every concert, they finished off 1971 by playing Tramore festival with *Skid Row* and *The Rory Gallagher Band*. The band's belief in their new type of music and freedom had served them well. Technically this concert show-cased the best of Irish rock from that period.

Shades of a Blue Orphanage (Decca 1972) is an historical testament to the early seventies. *Thin Lizzy* are pictured walking through Dublin's St Stephen's Green on a rainy day — a proud threesome. The mauve cover opens out, showing a hazy photograph covered by the words of the title track. Clodagh Simonds (*Mellow Candle*) plays harpsichord and mellotron. This time Lynott's lyrics are less abstract, yet his dense romanticism remains. As one listens to this collection of songs one hears a thoroughly felt experience, every atom of input distilled by sensitivity. Acoustic strums are intertwined with bass/drum leads, intersected here and there by Bell's injected electric guitar.

Thin Lizzy ... *Shades of a Blue Orphanage* (Decca 1972)

Side One
1 The Rise and Dear Demise of the
  Funky Nomadic Tribes
2 Buffalo Girl
3 I Don't Want to Forget How to Jive
4 Sarah
5 Brought Down[19]

Side Two
1 Babyface
2 Chatting Today
3 Call the Police
4 Shades of a Blue Orphanage

The album title is reputed to combine the name of Eric Bell's former band *Shades of Blue* with Phil Lynott's *Orphanage*. 'The Rise and Dear Demise ...' goes full out on instrumental soloing. 'Brought Down' has a vengeful character, utilising a crashing break on acoustic/electric guitars. 'Sarah', an acoustic lovesong, is simpler, sweeter — atmosphere enhanced by the sounds of twittering birds and acoustic piano.

'Chatting Today' holds one's attention with rolling acoustic guitar over Lynott's childhood memories. 'Shades of a Blue Orphanage' extends slowly through a melancholic atmosphere — moody, translucent and incandescent. Lynott's words are embedded in a wavy sea, overflowing with emotion. 'And it's true, true blue and sometimes it reminds me of you', recount childhood with a sense of loss, while 'we used to go over the brick wall and into old Dan's scrap-yard', conveys happier reminiscences. With subtle intelligence he compares his situation to that of an older generation of Irishmen who never had the opportunity to travel outside their small island:

> There's an old photo of Dan
> That I wish you could have seen
> Of him and the boys, poised
> Standing in St Stephen's Green.
> You see they were part of the great freedom dream
> But they were caught and detained
> And they're locked inside the frame of the photograph ...

That was the old Ireland, but the new Ireland is personified by himself and his band.

> But like old, old master musicians
> We kept on wishing
> We were headed for the number one hit country again.

Now based in London, *Thin Lizzy* played and played and played. One day they were recording their third single, 'Black boys on the corner', in Decca's studios. 'We were in the studio and just working out a traditional song for the laugh. Ted Carroll, our manager, takes a liking to it and asks us to put it on the flip side of the single. It was called "Whisky in the Jar" and was dead easy to play. We were into the heavier stuff at the time. A few days later the record company brought us in and told us that the single was going to be reversed, with "Whisky in the Jar" as the A side, because they felt it would chart. When it was released it didn't make any impact. After a while it was a disc-jockey's choice — you could hear it on juke-boxes and at dances' (Brian Downey). Then in February of 1973 the song reached number six in the English singles chart. The electric guitar strikes a battleground fanfare — a full resounding lick — then stops, acoustic guitar enters with full strum, then drums, cavalry-sounding electric guitar, and vocals:

> As I was going over
> The Cork and Kerry mountains
> I saw Captain Farrell and his money he was counting.
> I first produced my pistol
> And then produced my rapier
> I said stand and deliver
> Or the devil he may take yeah
>
> Wept for my daddyo
> Wept for my daddyo
> There's whiskey in the jarro.

'Whisky in the Jar' is a song of passionate love and highway thievery, spirited by Lynott's howling vocals. With Lynott leading the band and Eric Bell's misty lead guitar, *Thin Lizzy* represented the full flowering of Irish rock on *Top of the Pops* as the song goes into every niche in the British Isles. The group were becoming famous very quickly. In Ireland at the time they were the most prominent group — every day on the radio one could hear their hit single. Cool and individualistic, they had stuck to their guns and come out on top.

Continuing to progress, a flamenco-style song called 'Randolph's Tango', with churning acoustic guitars, gurgling bass and Lynott going 'la la la la la', is their next single. Their music was changing, becoming more funky and upfront. 'Well, Phil began to really hit the bass. We did a tour with Slade which went down a treat in 1973 ... We also recorded another album' (Brian Downey).

Vagabonds of the Western World (Decca 1973) is *Thin Lizzy's* last album on that label, and closes their period as Irish envoys of progressive rock. The cover artwork, by Jim Fitzpatrick, is a colour painting of the group in quasi mythological setting and exudes a hippie mentality.[20] Printed on the sleeve is 'The Legend of the Vagabond', a fairly suspect reworking of the old Irish legend of Oisín and the Land of the Young. Produced by Philip Lynott and Nick Tauber, the album mixes heavy bass riffing with a few mellow songs. 'Too ra loo ra loo ra lay' are real Irish drinking words; they are sung by Lynott at the beginning of the title track. 'Little Girl in Bloom' softly relates the experience of a young mother, Lynott's voice emotively grasping the traumatic theme: 'She feels something sacred, she's going to be a mammy soon.' His favourite theme of lost love is reiterated on 'A Song for While I'm Away',[21] every alteration in his voice coming from his soul:

> You are my life, my everything
> you're all I have.
> You are my hopes, my dreams
> You're all I have.

Decorated with keyboards/strings 'A Song for While I'm Away' is the last song of Lynott's 'blue period'. In contrast, the most important track on the record, the sexplosion 'Rocker', realises Lynott's change in direction to a fuller, out-and-out heavy rock style. Rivalling *Led Zeppelin* or *Deep Purple* in terms of power, it's loud, gutsy and phased all over the place.

Thin Lizzy were going through a transitional phase between 1972 and 1973, when they returned to Ireland to play a homecoming tour. The magic three-piece, however, was split by Eric Bell's decision to quit because of poor health, the wear and tear of incessant gigging, and the uncertain political situation in his native Belfast.[22] Friend and former *Skid Row* virtuoso guitarist Gary Moore took his place.

All in their early twenties, *Thin Lizzy* had remoulded the whole essence of Irish rock. Their idea of playing rock music came from a willingness to change, to see what could be done with ideas, words and the electric guitar. Philip Lynott's own version of the blues carried itself side-by-side with a frontier spirit. As the progressive rock of the early seventies reduced itself to simple heavy metal, *Thin Lizzy* became world ambassadors of that style. Few groups had a poet to lead them. Fewer still could offer such heartened inspiration.

THE LATER DAYS

Thin Lizzy cut a single with Gary Moore in 1974 before he too left the group prior to a German tour. Andy Gee and John Caan replaced him on twin lead guitars. Caan was reputed to be more of a record collector than a guitar player, so this didn't work out. 'After this hassle, myself and Phil wanted to jack the whole thing in for good, but we came back to England and got a hall to rehearse for more guitarists. We wanted a certain sound, but few guys could play like Gary. After months and months, Scott Gorham walks in one day. He looked real cool with his long hair, and after a while he was a natural choice. Brian Robertson, a seventeen-year-old from Glasgow, had a great guitar technique so we got both of them' (Brian Downey). Gorham was from California and keen to play the new style heavy guitar rock. The group had been through many management changes, so for financial reasons they signed to Vertigo in the summer of 1974, playing a heavier rock music around England. *Nightlife* (Vertigo 1974) is a turn-about from early work, with a Los Angeles type sound, but it bridges Lynott's music from acoustic roots to '70s hard rock. This record contains 'Still in Love with You', a track which would become mandatory in all subsequent *Thin Lizzy* performances. This is the only song to feature Gary Moore on guitar. *Nightlife* also has piano and acoustic guitars which appear sporadically throughout, giving the record some blues tinges.

The next six months was taken up with more touring, with America the major focal point. 'To go on tour in America you need lots of money; trucks, PA, lighting, drivers, roadies, promotion all cost a lot of money. The record company didn't really give us much that time, so we came back with less than we had when we started!' (Brian Downey). Their next album, *Fighting*, is a real clunker — out-and-out heavy metal with weak lyrics and little inspiration. Whatever the artistic merits, their new music won audiences everywhere, especially the increasingly heavy-rock oriented Reading Festival. By March 1976 their creative juices were ripening; release of *Jailbreak* sustained Lynott's reputation — 'Running Back' and

'Romeo and the Lonely Girl' are sweet soul songs mixed in with bombardments of decibels. 'The Boys are Back in Town' (Vertigo 1976) could be heard in every disco up and down Ireland that year, giving thousands of teenagers music to dance to and words that rolled around your head for days. May of that year and *Thin Lizzy* were international superstars, topping the charts everywhere, touring the world — parties, planes, media — the works.

Their American tour of 1976 was marred by Lynott's sudden downturn in health, and after cutting short and returning to Britain, Brian Robertson was forced to leave due to physical injury. 'Don't Believe a Word' (Vertigo) started 1977 for them as a hit single, full of rolling soul and thumb-slapping bass. *Thin Lizzy* quickly recuperated with the addition of Gary Moore, by then one of the hottest axemen around, and commenced yet another United States trek.

'America was torturous — you'd finish one tour and be immediately booked into another. We would headline in say Los Angeles or San Francisco, but play second to say *STYX* somewhere else. It never slowed down. When we played that time with *Queen* [English flash rock band] we had a holiday in Florida for twelve days. That was cool' (Brian Downey). Deep bass tones and smooth lyrics charted another Lynott composition 'Dancing in the Moonlight' (Vertigo) in the UK during the summer of that year.

Many remember the Dalymount Park Festival of 1977 as Irish rock's hats off to Phil Lynott and his Dublin-inspired rock adventurism. I remember a bill which ranged from *Fairport Convention* through various styles of modern music — the night lit up with light reflecting from his mirror bass — the leather clad Irishman — 'I'm still in love with you' — an emotional return. *Thin Lizzy* were now one of the best live bands in the world, making the higher reaches of world album charts with *Live and Dangerous* (1978). From then on it was a succession of tours, records, line-up changes and numerous projects. Gary Moore came back as guitarist and was duly sacked for not coming to gigs in America. Dave Flett, Midge Ure and Snowy White were some of the guitarists who helped the group. Philip Lynott released a synthesiser-based album *Solo in Soho* with mellower songs than *Thin Lizzy*, who by this time were enormous. 'Yellow Pearl' (Vertigo 1981), a Lynott/Ure song with whirling computer-like electronic overdubs became the theme music for BBC's *Top of the Pops* show. By 1983 the stature of the band had peaked and a world tour was put together as a farewell to everybody. Philip Lynott showed his respect for the original band by featuring Eric Bell and Gary Moore as guest guitarists, as well as an amalgam of all the guitar players that were ever involved with *Thin Lizzy*.

Thin Lizzy — albums

1	*Thin Lizzy*	(Decca (R) 1971)
2	Shades of a Blue Orphanage	(Decca (R) 1972)
3	Vagabonds of the Western World	(Decca (R) 1973)
	Original group: Philip Lynott, Eric Bell, Brian Downey	
4	Nightlife	(Vertigo (R) 1974)
5	Fighting	(Vertigo 1975)
6	Jailbreak	(Vertigo 1976)
7	Johnny the Fox	(Vertigo 1976)

| 8 | Bad Reputation | (Vertigo 1977) |
| 9 | Live And Dangerous | (Vertigo (R) 1978) |

Official second line-up (with Gary Moore popping up here and there): Philip Lynott, Brian Robertson, Scott Gorham and Brian Downey

| 10 | Black Rose | (Vertigo (R) 1979) |

Philip Lynott, Gary Moore, Scott Gorham and Brian Downey

11	Chinatown	(Vertigo 1980)
12	The Adventures of Thin Lizzy (singles compilation)	(Vertigo 1981)
13	Renegade	(Vertigo 1981)

Philip Lynott, Snowy White, Scott Gorham and Brian Downey

| 14 | Thunder and Lightning | (Vertigo 1983) |

Philip Lynott, John Sykes, Scott Gorham, Darren Wharton and Brian Downey

| 15 | Life | (Vertigo 1983) |

Live album featuring all previous *Lizzy* line-ups. (How many guitarists can play at the same time?)

(R) Recommended.

Thin Lizzy — recommended singles

1	The Farmer	(EMI 1970)
2	New Day	(Maxi single, Decca 1971)
3	Whisky in the Jar	(Decca 1972)
4	Randolph's Tango	(Decca 1973)
5	The Rocker	(Decca 1973)
6	The Boys Are Back in Town	(Vertigo 1976)
7	Dancing in the Moonlight	(Phonogram 1976)
8	Do Anything You Want To	(Vertigo 1979)
9	Sarah	(Vertigo 1979)

Philip Lynott spent a lot of time outside *Thin Lizzy* working on various projects between 1978 and 1983. Production, songwriting and music in general occupied him completely after the break up of *Thin Lizzy*, and Lynott's output would have continued to increase if it was not for his untimely death at the beginning of 1986. (See 'In Remembrance of Philip Lynott' p. 000).

Philip Lynott — recommended listening

| 1 | Solo in Soho | (Vertigo 1980) |
| 2 | The Philip Lynott Album | (Vertigo 1982) |

Singles with Gary Moore

3	Parisienne Walkways	(MCA 1979)
4	Spanish Guitar	(MCA 1979)
5	Out in the Fields	(10 Records 1985)

Gary Moore albums since Thin Lizzy

1	Back on the Streets	(MCA 1978)
2	G Force	(Jet 1980)
3	Corridors of Power	(Virgin 1982)

4 Victims of the Future	(10/Virgin 1983)
5 Dirty Fingers	(Jet 1984)
6 We Want Moore	(10 Records 1984)
7 Run for Cover	(10 Records 1985)
8 Rockin' Every Night — *Gary Moore Live in Japan*	(10 Records 1986)
9 Wild Frontier	(10 Records 1987)

AT THE TURN OF THE DECADE

The most important aspect of progressive rock in the Irish context was the longing for a better music and a better scene to play in. 'Musicians playing music because it was a better type music to play' (Brush Shiels). In the English and European context the term had a refinement; here it was used to describe cross-fertilisations between jazz, classical, folk and blues. Musical precision was a prerequisite, keyboards began to dominate and unusual time signatures became the order of the day. Performances were musically excellent, but some bands, like *Soft Machine* or *Van Der Graaf Generator*, brought this to a level of boredom that few people could tolerate — sustaining atonal riffs on guitars and pianos for overly long periods. Of the English groups only those who combined melody with strangeness achieved any level of popular appeal. *Pink Floyd* and *Yes* dazzled their audiences with astonishing innovations in the use of 'visuals'.

In Ireland the scene was less sophisticated because of the limited scope given to any band. What made *Skid Row* so unusual was their ability to produce radically new music in such a limiting environment. At the end of the sixties most of the original beat groups were absorbed into the money-spinning showband scene. One glaring example of this was how *Dickie Rock and the Miami* literally killed off *The Chosen Few* by poaching two of their most talented members in Paul Ashford (vocals) and Fran O'Toole (vocals) with offers of £70 a week!

Some musicians had integrity and continued in their own furrow, playing their own music in their own way. Hair began to come down in length, with bell-bottomed trousers and platform shoes the normal attire for a group in 1970. Equipment began to become more involved. Instead of the tiny Vox AC30 amps, larger Marshall stacks and WEM equipment began to crop up. One observer comments: 'During the late sixties most groups would play say the National Stadium with their equipment set up around them in-the-round so to speak. A lot of gigs were done like that in those days.' The result was that the emphasis turned more towards the quality of the music itself — how to make it more interesting and unusual. In that way rock music had progressed in Ireland substantially.

Below are listed some lesser-known Irish groups from the years 1969 to 1971. Notice the peculiar names, the subtle change to more personalised and characteristic titles as the sixties became the seventies. The lists indicate when the groups first came to prominence.

1969

Anno Domini	Crypt	Ditch Cassidy and the
Bye Laws	Deep Set	News

Doll's House	Mitch Mahon and the	SK' BOO
Druid's Prayer	Editions	Some People
First Edition	Pan Pipers	Taxi
Grassband	Perfume Garden	Wheatstone Bridge
Magic Garden	Purple Pussycat	

1970

Blueshouse	Honeysweet	Reflections
Cromwell	Hot Air Machine	Reform
Crossroads	Julian's Heirs	Smokestack
Dandelion	Ned Spoon	Tomorrow's People
Deep Joy	Originals	Uncle Ham
Executive Suite	Others	Watchtower
Gaslight	Portrait	

1971

Adolf J. Rag	Elmer Fudd	Time Machine
Advent	Fantasy	Tranquillity
Alyce	Gypsy Rock	Under River
Andala	Iron Horse	Velvet Poetry
Bagenal Harvey	Jeremiah Henry	Window
Chocolate Vehicle	Stoney Road	Wormwood
Elas Horn	Stud	

Notes: Some of the groups in the 1969 column featured on an album entitled *Paddy's Dead and the Kids Know It* (Golden Guinea Records) which was an atrocious collection of badly recorded covers. The only redeeming songs are those by *Taxi*, which display originality and an interest in guitar-based blues. *Anno Domini* were a short-lived acoustic rock group likened to Crosby, Stills and Nash. Originally from Belfast, they released one album *Anno Domini* on Decca before breaking up in 1969. *Ditch Cassidy* was a famed Irish soul merchant, who led countless bands with a vocal style of power and class. *Wheatstone Bridge* were into bluegrass music, whilst *Watchtower* were a highly progressive act, using organ and saxophone as lead instruments.

The groups in the 1971 column were pretty eclectic, using acoustic and electric instruments within hard riffing compositions to further the name of rock progress. *Adolf J. Rag* travelled extensively, playing 'heavy' in a three-piece format. *Andala* used a lot of free distortion in the psychedelic mode. *Advent* and *Elas Horn* were harmony- and accoustic-based outfits respectively. *Stud* was formed on the break-up of *Taste* by John Wilson and Ritchie 'Charlie' McCracken. They released a debut album *Stud* (Deram) in May 1971 which was critically raved about in the English rock press. Two more albums of free-form complex music followed — *September* (BASF 1972) and *Goodbye Live at Command* (BASF 1973) — but though technically advanced they were not a commercial success. *Elmer Fudd* were 'a serious riff band' featuring one Philip Donnelly (ex *Gary Moore Band*).

Some people termed progressive rock that which was underpaid and under-played. From 1971 to 1975 every conceivable mix of music was attempted and played. Things became looser and freer. Around Ireland the open air festival came into its own so there were dozens of opportunities for bands to try out something different. The halls and clubs weren't really into these so-called long haired hippies — they brought a 'bad' element to the local communities. The more enlightened organisers went for the open air scene where there was less likelihood of hassle from the reactionary locals. Terry O'Neill, a young manager who had given *Thin Lizzy* their initial push, recounts a scene in county Clare in the West of Ireland:

'I was involved with *Alyce, Horslips, Granny's Intentions, Gypsy Rock* and *Iron Horse*. There was this gig in Clare where English group *The Third Ear Band* were billed but they never played. We were using *Skid Row's* 2000 watt WEM speaker system and thousands of people turned up. There was a big marquee, a huge field, loads of freaks, long hair, minibuses painted all colours, drugs, busts and an ordinary gate and hedge surrounding the field. This farmer owned the field and I got a thousand pounds to pay the bands. Now the bill was *Skid Row, Mellow Candle, Iron Horse* and *Ditch Cassidy's Freak Show*. Anyway the money didn't really go around so I had to get another £150 to pay *Iron Horse* and *Mellow Candle* who were waiting behind me for their money. The farmer was standing there with a crowd of his friends around him — an us and them situation — real gombeen men. He didn't want to pay, of course, so I asked his friends did they trust him. They all said yes, so I collected the money from them in bits and pieces saying if you trust the farmer so much then he can pay you all back later. This was a typical scene in the country.'

The glaring feature of early seventies rock was its drug connotations. The sight of a few hundred 'heads' hitting a festival town was apt to cause hair to stand on end. Basically the whole thing was harmless fun, with marijuana and alcohol consumed to the heavy sounds. An anonymous witness comments: 'There was a very viable hippie community here at the time. They weren't dope fiends but had long hair, good vibes, peace, love and understanding. In those days people would get together and have a few smokes, go down to the beach and groove out, then have a few drinks and sit around maybe listening to records or making music. Some people were reading Timothy Leary and doing experiments with LSD, but not in the serious way that English and Americans were doing it. It was more careful and carefree. Some people would like you to think that everyone was going around in cloud cuckoo land then, but it was the same scene that you have now — just that most problems seemed much more remote.'

Venues for the music got bigger and more involved — Alice's Restaurant, Osibisa's and The Fillmore West all featured whole nights of music from a string of groups appearing one after the other through to the early hours of the morning. Light shows, rock films and theatrical elements made for more interesting environments than the cave-like traditional beat clubs. All situated in the Dublin area they attracted a sweep of bands ranging from far-out English groups like *Hawkwind, Family* and *Capability Brown* to big-name acts like *Horslips* and *Thin Lizzy*. Add to this the growing number of acoustic sessions in pubs and the numerous solo artists who populated them, the burgeoning health food/ meditation/peace scene and the rise in youth consciousness.[23] A thriving environment for all sorts of musical activities, the early seventies produced some strange music.

Horslips started doing the rounds in 1971, touting glitter trappings and a version of Celtic rock. This was initially greeted with catcalls and boos from the musical intelligentsia, but after they'd become hugely successful other musicians followed their example.

Mushroom mixed hippie drug music with Irish traditional tunes played vigorously, and released an album called *Early One Morning* (Hawk) in 1973.[24] Attempting to do something completely new, the record opens with the sound of a clock and waves crashing on the shore. It contains some fine harpsichord, electric guitar, and pipe instrumentals, yet the concept is marred by staying too close to Horslips-style traditional/rock pieces. The cover of the album is a simple drawing of a very large mushroom, a definition of the group and a more than adequate hint at the psilocybin hallucinogen inherent in certain species of Irish mushroom.

The Celtic rock phenomenon spawned a lot of shamrocks on guitars and players, mock Celtic paraphernalia and ridiculously ornate album covers. Consider Belfast group *Fruupp*. After several incipient line-up changes, the group settled down to a working team of Vincent McCusker (guitar), Peter Farrelly (vocals), Martin Foye (drums) and Steve Houston (keyboards). Their years of constant gigging and writing were aptly rewarded when they scored immediate cult success with the release of *Future Legends* (Dawn 1973).[25] Their reputation was based on flamboyant stage performances, medieval trappings, Celtically decorative gatefold sleeves, concept albums and long, involved projects. Definitely in the 'pomp rock' mould, their music was predominantly keyboard based, with grandiose use of harpsichord. Listening to *Fruupp* was close to venturing into the middle ages, yet it was original and highly complex.

The early seventies produced fewer groups than the sixties, but those that did get an opportunity to put their work on vinyl predominated.[26] When *Alyce* went to America they built up a good following in the New York clubs playing electric hard rock with the emphasis on vocal harmonies. Their guitarist was a highly rated young man called Jimi Slevin. Back in Dublin in 1973 Slevin formed *Peggy's Leg* —Jimi Slevin (guitar), Jimmy Gibson (lead acoustic guitars and vocals), Don Harris (drums and vocals), Vincent Duffy (bass) — a group who did semi-classical rock in an all-original format. Highly accomplished, the group demonstrated the subtle art of playing music better than anyone else around. They received many accolades on release of *Grinilla* (Bunch records 1973), a six-track album which still stands up to repeated listenings, featuring long passages of inventive instrumentation — precise, clear and imaginative music. Optimism oozes from every note. 'Just Another Journey' and 'Variations for Huxley' display an ability to play creamy, smooth and structured compositions.

Supply Demand and Curve was Ireland's answer to the hardcore progressives outside the country. Avant-garde and academic, their approach refined many sounds to a synthesis of, as *High Times* paper described in 1973, 'what sounds like folk, what could be called jazz and what leans towards classical'. They would usually perform sitting down, doing their utmost to concentrate on precise fingering of their instruments. During 1973 they were performing such songs as

'Sally Racket' (English folk) and 'Turpsicory', a classical adaptation featuring piano, tenor recorder, cello and bodhrán! Most people compared their approach to John Cage or his famous student John Cale. Structural, serious or celebral, depending on one's frame of reference, they had a definite cult following.[27]

Being able to play one's instrument in a dazzling manner was proof positive of a progressive mentality. Take Joe O'Donnell for example. After stinting with Gay and Terry Woods and English folk rock outfit *Trees*, the Limerick-born fiddler built up quite a reputation for himself. More than a player, he knew everything about the technical aspects of electric violin — using pick-ups, rebuilding old instruments, putting eight-string violins through wah-wah, reverb and oscillating sound effects. His talent stretched to mandolin, six- and twelve-string guitars, plus keyboards. He was obviously 'away-ahead progressive', making a big enough impression to be offered a job with international rock group *East of Eden*.[28] During recording and touring, his violin solos received many plaudits.

Developing Bands (1971 to 1974)

Angel	Human Flesh	Rodeo
Aton	Jack	Sheriff
Bananas	Jonathan Kelly's	Skid Row (sic)
Bees Make Honey	Outside	Sleepy Hollow
Bratt	Keltic Wine	Spud
Brogue	Lotus	Stepaside
Cat's Pyjamas	Loudest Whisper	Sundown
Consort of St Sepulchre	Mellow Candle	Supply Demand and
Cloverhitch	Mushroom	Curve
Dave Prim Band	Naima	Taboo
Eyeless	Peggy's Leg	Wildlife
Fruupp	Pumpkinhead	Zebadee.
Harvest Research	Railroad	
Hot Dusty Roads	Rob Strong Band	

Notes: The list above is not fully comprehensive but gives an accurate picture of emerging groups of the early seventies. While *Horslips, Thin Lizzy* and *Rory Gallagher* were international leaders of Irish progressive rock at this time, most of the groups above played the local Irish circuit.

Eyeless was a three-piece bluesy folk rock outfit. *Mellow Candle* was very folky, with two female vocalists (Clodagh Simonds and Alison Williams), their delicate and poetical music surfacing on *Swaddling Songs* (Deram 1972). More eccentric was *The Consort of St Sepulchre*, who specialised in medieval to renaissance music, their sounds coming from krummhorns, viols, recorders, shawm (a medieval form of oboe), cittern and flutes. *Pumpkinhead* were basically a folk quartet, made up of two American couples based in Ireland.[29] Their debut album on Mulligan records is energetic American folk rock of a high standard — real 'ride-along-in-an-open-wagon' plains stuff, with Irish traditional jigs and reels thrown in. *Hot Dusty Roads* and *Rodeo* were early combos of country rock. *Rodeo* contained Erroll Walsh on electric guitar who went on to form the eternal bluegrass/funk/rock group *Stagalee* with Jonathan Kelly who as Jon Ledingham came to prominence as an above average singer/strummer not unlike Bob Dylan. Utilising many

American and British sessionmen, he then formed *Jonathan Kelly's Outside,* who put down *Waiting on You* (RCA 1973) and later that year *Wait Till They Change the Backdrop* appeared under his own name with the *Sutherland Brothers.* Ledingham's smooth singer/songwriter style surfaced on subsequent solo albums. *Naima* played very tight jazz rock with a line-up of Fran Breen (drums), Andrew Boland (guitar), Trevor Knight (keyboards) and Garvin Gallagher (bass). They built up a strong reputation live, but never recorded anything. *Bees Make Honey* were the first group to play 'pub rock' and were formed with the nucleus of the original beat group *Bluesville* in 1972. They recorded *Music Every Night* for EMI in 1973. Finally the name *Skid Row* appears in this list because Brush Shiels kept different line-ups going during the seventies. Between 1973 and 1974 a whole new *Skid Row* was brought together — Eamonn Gibney (vocals, ex *Alyce* and *Brogue*), Ed Deane (ex *Granny's/Woodsband* on lead electric) and John Wilson (ex *Taste* and *Stud* on drums). Yet again the line-up cracked, and Brush formed a gigging group with Eric Bell in 1974. By 1975 Brush had laid his hands on a magic guitarist in Jimi Slevin (ex *Peggy's Leg*) and *Skid Row* was reborn. Slevin later quit to form his own group and became one of the most highly rated flash guitarists of the seventies.

The turbulence of the sixties wasn't continued into the seventies. Rock music became more segmented and differentiated. In cities the club was replaced by the new American-style discotheque — the flashy, tinsel, dance-oriented venue where live groups and heavy rock were discouraged. Then there were the pubs which came into their own, but because of the availability of alcohol the audiences were different and the atmosphere less hectic than the old beat clubs. The university campus scene became the domain of the progressives, with gigs happening literally every night all through the seventies. The looseness of money and the viability of gigging every night thawed as the recession slowly ate its way through the decade. Still, the open air festival with all its freedom became the mainstay of Irish rock.

With regard to records and record-buying, the public was very much in favour of foreign product. George Murray, owner of one of Dublin's first record chains comments: 'We opened four shops during the sixties, the great Irish showband era. Philip Lynott used to come around to our shop on Ormond Quay, which we'd close on a Saturday for lunch and then come back to find a queue a hundred yards down the road. This was the normal thing during the *Sgt. Pepper* era, but changed during the seventies. Collectors bought a lot of albums and the underground would hang out in the shop. Anyway the showbands used to come in and buy up all their own singles, say 1500, which would be enough to put their record in at number one in the Irish chart. Overall, Irish taste has been very catholic, and middle of the road records were always popular. It was only the progressive underground which bought the interesting records — *Grateful Dead, The Doors* and *Traffic.* Irish records were never a big thing since so few groups made records. I always thought 'You Turn Me On' was about the best of them.'

So, what Ian Whitcomb had started had no discernible end. Groups formed, played and broke up, changed their names, clothes and styles of music. Musicians continued to develop their abilities but on a more individualistic basis, since a highly experimental group found it harder and harder to play live and record continuously. The showbands continued but with less impact. Without certain people, most notably Brush Shiels, the whole idea of improving and developing rock music would not have occurred in Ireland. His group, *Skid Row,* catalysed a whole change in attitude towards playing one's own music in one's own way. They took unthinkable risks and were years ahead of their time. It is safe to say that without the original *Skid Row* the progressive rock phenomenon in Ireland would have been an empty blank.

REMEMBERING NIRVANA

'Nirvana' was the brainchild of a county Waterford man named Patrick Campbell-Lyons and a Greek student called Alex Spyropoulos. Born in 1943 in Lismore, Lyons went to England in 1962 in search of summer vacation work before entering Trinity College, Dublin. He never came back. He was an above-average keyboardist and vocalist, and by chance he met *The Detours* and a group of musicians called *Second Thoughts*. He joined *Second Thoughts* who accompanied *The Detours* on a package trip to the Star Club in Hamburg. Of course *The Detours* were to become *The Who*. After this excitement he split for Sweden in 1965 where he spent over one and a half years gigging with a band called *The Merry Men*.

After that experience he headed back to London where he teamed up with former *Second Thoughts* bass man Chris Thomas to form a song-writing duo. Their second composition 'Finding It Rough' was recorded by *The Everly Brothers* in America, but because of a weak publisher they didn't have much success. Campbell-Lyons was simultaneously studying film production at St Martin's Art College where he happened to meet Alex Spyropoulos and Ray Singer. In 1967 they formed *Nirvana* and immediately decided on classical rock music. Frequent visits to the Royal Academy of Music resulted in the trio persuading a celloist and a French horn player to add their structured training to the rock format. Their progressive attitude was in tandem with the efforts of *The Nice* and *Procol Harum*, and they easily found a recording contract. Island Records' Chris Blackwell took them under his wing and put them on a wage of £60 per week, as he did *Traffic* and *Free* at the beginning of their careers. Their first single 'Tiny Goddess' (1967) was a favourite with John Peel on his Radio London 'Perfumed Garden' programme. Their second, 'Rainbow Chaser' (1968), became a European number one and a British chart hit. It became a definitive acid classic and was out on its own in terms of phasing and orchestration. From there the group became a cult and were viewed as unorthodox and risqué. Their first album, *The Story of Simon Simopath* (Island 1967), was a psychedelic nugget and included the acclaimed 'Pentacost Hotel,' but it was their second, *All of Us* (Island 1968), which made their name, particularly for the inclusion of the aforementioned 'Rainbow Chaser'. Elton John, Jim Capaldi and Stevie Winwood were some of the people involved in the making of the *All of Us* set.

The initial enthusiasm cooled however when Blackwell lost interest, and as the group were flexibly experimental the break from Island records was amicable. *Nirvana* nevertheless had recorded a third album *Black Flower* for the label, but it was left in the can. Eventually it was released in 1974 on Metro Media. Patrick Campbell-Lyons continued to write and work in the record business. Jimmy Cliff had been playing gigs in London and voiced an interest in recording one of Patrick's songs called 'Waterfall'. One day Lyons received a phonecall informing him that his presence was requested in Rio de Janeiro for the annual song festival. Jimmy Cliff had entered 'Waterfall' as his Jamaican entry and both he and Campbell-Lyons as songwriter were invited to Brazil. After flying to Brazil, Lyons as usual did not return to England for over a year. That time was spent in studios producing and dabbling in South American music.

After that experience Lyons spent the next two years as in-house producer for Phillips before going back to vinyl and recording solo albums with friends under the working title *Nirvana*. *Songs of Love and Praise* (Phonogram 1976) and *Local Anaesthetic* (Phonogram 1977) were the results. As a producer, songwriter and teacher, Patrick Campbell-Lyons has worked at a variety of disciplines while his new interests have been film/television scores and special video projects music in the 1980s. In 1983 he recorded his first solo album under his own name in New York and Berlin. *The Hero* by Patrick Campbell-Lyons was released by Shanachie in 1984. Alternatively titled *The Electric Plough* in Europe, it was his first ever Irish release. Lyons is currently realising a compilation of Nirvana tracks from the 1960s and 1970s. The album, on the Impex label, will contain the three original hit songs plus never before heard tracks from the vaults.

CHAPTER
TWO

Folk into Rock

The word 'folk' conjures up people. 'Folk' also conjures up a simplicity in lifestyle — groups of people bonded together over generations. Among such communities certain traditions build up, symbolising strength and togetherness. These attributes are usually found in the folklore and folk music of a people. Folk music is passed from one generation to the next, and re-created with a certain amount of authenticity. One writer describes it as 'the day-to-day music created by the people for the people. It gives form to the democratic ideal. It moves below the mainstream of culture, sustained and altered by small élites.'[1]

Modern living has affected what most people would regard as folk music — somebody playing an acoustic guitar can be labelled a 'folky' when he or she is trying hard to achieve something else. The complexity of modern living has allowed most city people access to all kinds of information including the folkways of other people. Country people are in turn affected by the whirl of the cities in their attitudes towards their own native environment and its traditions. There is a great deal of cross fertilisation between city and country and between one culture and another.

When Bob Dylan started using electric instruments in 1965 he was denounced for betraying the folk stream he had developed within. The Newport Folk Festival of 1965 saw him clamber on-stage with an electric rock band to boos and catcalls from the audience. What had happened? Well, Dylan had been groomed among people who considered pure re-creation of traditional American songs and tunes — on acoustic instruments — a necessity. To those attuned to the academic pursuit of American folk tunes, Dylan had lowered himself into the commercial mire labelled 'pop', as his records went into the charts.

The hotchpotch environment of the late twentieth century bred this purist folk attitude. Folk rock broke the rules, as shown in the reaction to electric Dylan. During the sixties in America this music was called folk rock because, well, here was a folk singer and yet he was using electric guitars, also here was a rock music with a strange attentive quality — one had to listen, even think! It was a new type of sound, one with the articulacy of folk and the virility of rock.

Bringing it all around to Ireland and Britain we observe cultures whose traditions stretch way back into history. Layers and layers of influences have built up, impregnating the mass consciousness of whole populations. Every place has its own definitions and ways of doing things. The unpredictable climate of both countries leads to certain superstitions and myths. Both countries are made up of rural and urban populations living in close proximity. Both countries have strong folk traditions rooted in local and national history.

The rural regions of the British Isles all display their historical roots in local music which can be termed folk music. Irish traditional music has developed in two general directions: the slow air or ballad on the one hand, reflecting the plaintive aspects of life, and the more rumbustious jigs and reels on the other, usually associated with dancing. These have been preserved by musicians and singers down through the generations, embodying the history of the Irish people in different regions of the country.

It has always been natural for folk music to use acoustic instruments, usually handmade and deriving from traditional, local craftsmanship — Scottish border pipes and Irish uileann pipes, for example, differ in construction and sound. Acoustic instruments are more intimate and suit small groups of people. The soft tone of an acoustic guitar, accompanied by flute or mandolin, is a pleasing and relaxing experience.

However, if Bob Dylan hadn't crossed folk with rock, somebody else would have got around to it eventually. The constant mixing of people and ideas prevalent in modern society leads to universal communication. The innovations occurring in rock music in the sixties directly affected the mainstream popular music of the cities, and the folk music of the regions was not left untainted. It is significant that by the late sixties and early seventies a whole host of bands in Britain and Ireland were freely combining the older traditional music with electric instruments, literally driving old songs with a new energy. Combine youth, exuberance and skilful playing with the communicative power inherent in rock, and the results are fascinating. People were picking up on aspects of life that would have been rendered obsolete if left in the older context.

In this chapter, while purist folk musicians will be acknowledged as such, the focus is on those musicians who started as 'folkies' and developed into rock and those who drew on older traditions while being primarily rock musicians.

TAKING OFF WITH SWEENEY'S MEN

It has been said that *Sweeney's Men* were the formative electric folk band — the first purist folk band in the British Isles to involve themselves in electric music. The original line-up contained Johnny Moynihan, Andy Irvine and Joe Dolan, and was formed in Galway during the summer of 1966. They played the local folk circuit until the then leader of *The Capitol Showband*, Des Kelly, involved himself in their affairs and managed the group. They toured Ireland, appearing in ballrooms, carnivals and dances — a more commercial atmosphere than they were used to — and started to release singles. They scored a number one in 1967 with 'Old Maid in the Garret' (Pye), a traditional ballad sung by Andy Irvine.

Dolan was replaced during the summer of 1967 by Terry Woods, an accomplished five-string banjo player and multi-instrumentalist who drew heavily on American folk traditions. Woods was very much in tune with the American folk revival of 1962 to 1968, and his ambition was to sound straight out of North Carolina, holding American folk purists like Clarence Ashley and Doc Watson in high esteem. Johnny Moynihan had garnered a reputation as a true folklorist, going to every extreme to glean verses of songs from older artists. His singing rated him one of Ireland's finest, while he played several instruments, most notably the bouzouki. Andy Irvine was a nomadic Englishman who had picked up many influences in his travels, displayed in his dexterous mandolin ability. Appearing in such folk haunts as the Neptune club in Dublin, this line-up of *Sweeney's Men* started attracting serious attention from the press. Early in 1968 they cut their debut album for Transatlantic. All members of the band were in their early twenties.

Sweeney's Men was recorded in a rudimentary manner and its thin production matches the vein of music pursued. The material was, for the most part, collected in the classical folk tradition, through personal contact with singers and musicians from Ireland, Britain and the United States. Album credits were: Johnny Moynihan (vocals, bouzouki and tin whistle), Andy Irvine (vocals, mandolin, harmonica and guitar), Terry Woods (vocals, six- and twelve-string guitar, five-string banjo and concertina). Standout tracks are Woods's version of 'Housecarpenter', an authentic rough version of a Southern American ballad, and Irvine's heartfelt 'Willy O' Wimsbury', a slow English/Scottish ballad. The album was greeted with critically good reviews in the music press in Britain and Ireland.

By the summer of 1968 Andy Irvine had caught the wandering spirit, and *Sweeney's Men* were reduced to a duo when he departed for Eastern Europe. The electric guitarist, Henry McCullough, then joined, making history by combining his hippie rock background with the music of Moynihan and Woods. McCullough came from Portstewart in Northern Ireland and had played in bands from an early age. He started in showbands like the Enniskillen-based *Sky Rockets* and *Gene and the Gents*, then graduated to the more rock/psychedelic music of *The People* in Belfast. *The People* became *Eire Apparent* and toured internationally with *The Jimi Hendrix Experience* and others. McCullough had seen his fair share of the rock 'n' roll circus, and returned from Canada in 1968 to involve himself with *Sweeney's Men*.

It is said that McCullough was very sympathetic to the folk circuit and used to go on-stage and finger-pick his electric guitar. At the Cambridge folk festival of that year *Sweeney's Men* took the stage with McCullough playing guitar, his hair flowing down, his electric sounds mixing with the work of Terry Woods and Johnny Moynihan. In this embryonic format the band were writing their own material and getting lead reviews in rock papers such as *Melody Maker*. Their enormous potential was short-lived as that line-up stayed together for a couple of months only. But they had paved the way for the likes of English band *Fairport Convention* to electrify pure folk material.

Johnny Moynihan: 'The only recording of that line-up was an RTE programme called "Twenty Minutes of Sweeney's Men", where we sat around a camp-fire of logs, against a backdrop of darkness.[2] We went out in a sociological context to mix styles. There were Eastern and African strains to our music. It was ethnic music with an innovative rock 'n' roll backing. Henry used to play acoustic and electric guitars, tin whistle and even cider bottles. In effect, the polarisation between styles may have been reduced — American and Irish folk

18 *Sweeney's Men,* the band which recorded its debut album in 1968. *Left to right:* Andy Irvine, Johnny Moynihan, Terry Woods.

19 Henry McCullough of *Sweeney's Men,* the formative electric folk band, in 1968.

20 *Sweeney's Men* in action. *Left to right:* Johnny Moynihan, Andy Irvine, Terry Woods.

21 *The Woodsband,* 1971. *Left to right:* Terry Woods, Austin Corcoran, Gay Woods, Pat Nash, Ed Deane.

20

21

music pooled, with Henry putting funk into it. Henry would just pick up on traditional tunes and they would come out in his playing. Anyway, one night we were playing in Dublin and after the gig Henry jumped in a car and drove like mad to catch the end of a John Mayall concert elsewhere. This told us what direction he was headed in, and when he was offered the job with Englishman Joe Cocker he naturally gravitated towards it.'

Even if the line-up was short-lived it was influential; McCullough played bouzouki on his own composition 'A Mistake No Doubt', while Woods's 'Brain Jam' and Moynihan's 'Standing in the Shore' were stage favourites. Terry Woods and Johnny Moynihan continued on and recorded a second album without McCullough in 1969. *Tracks of Sweeney* (Transatlantic) is a complex deviation from the rigid academicism of the previous album. The record would have been dynamite if McCullough had appeared on it.

Tracks of Sweeney (Transatlantic 1969)

Side One	Side Two
1 Dreams for Me (Woods)	1 A Mistake No Doubt (Woods, Moynihan, McCullough)
2 Pipe on the Bob (Trad. arr. Woods/ Moynihan)	2 Go By Brooks (Cohen/Woods)
3 Brain Jam (Woods)	3 When You Don't Care For Me (Woods)
4 Pretty Polly (Trad. arr. Woods/ Moynihan)	4 Afterthoughts (Woods)
5 Standing in the Shore (Trad. arr. Woods/Moynihan)	5 Hiram Hubbard (Trad. arr. Woods/ Moynihan)
	6 Hall of Mirrors (McCullough/Woods, Moynihan)

This is a fully-fledged, cohesive work, containing mostly self-penned material, with arrangements of traditional pieces reworked in modern vein. Terry Woods's material is provocative, especially the acoustic rhythms achieved on 'Brain Jam' and 'Dreams for Me'. On 'Pretty Polly' he sounds very much like the early Dylan, with that raspy vocal inflection suiting the topic of the song — murder. Even if the album is wholly acoustic, the feel of the songs part-written by McCullough is livelier, and indicates the direction of the band if their career hadn't ended so abruptly in 1969.[3]

STEELEYE SPAN — HARK! THE VILLAGE WAIT

After the demise of *Sweeney's Men*, Terry Woods involved himself with a roving group called *Orphanage* (see Chapter 1). As its name suggests, the unit was a musician's shelter, allowing for a variety of styles and cross-overs. The idea was to travel around Ireland playing a bit of blues and a bit of folk on electric and acoustic instruments, picking up musicians here and there. Its mainspring was a young Philip Lynott, who had brought poetry to the acoustic music of *Skid Row* and liked the company of folk players, spending some time in the late sixties haunting Dublin coffee houses and bars with an acoustic guitar.

Terry Woods and his wife, Gay, had grown up in Dublin, maturing within the purist folk clubs. Gay made her debut when she was aged fifteen at the Neptune club, a popular hang-out for folk artists from Ireland and abroad. Prior to *Sweeney's Men*, Gay and Terry had sung together around the British Isles and they continued to do this in 1969. It is important to point out the release of *Fairport Convention's* second album *What We Did on Our Holidays* (Island) in the same year. The English band had fully embraced the eclecticism flooding popular music with their debut album in 1968. This new record, however, contained a perfect blend of contemporary electric music, sung and performed in a folk vein. If *Sweeney's Men* had set a trend in Ireland, here was its natural successor. *Fairport Convention* would become more solidly folk based as their career progressed.

Tragedy struck the *Fairports* when they lost drummer Martin Lamble in a road crash in 1969. Their bass player, Ashley 'Tyger' Hutchings, met Gay and Terry Woods and, tired of the setbacks with *Fairport*, suggested an electric folk band. He deeply appreciated the Woods's wide-ranging repertoire and abilities. Gay and Terry were interested in having old friends Andy Irvine or Johnny Moynihan involved, but instead Hutchings recruited Tim Hart and Maddy Prior, a folk duo from St Albans who were extremely popular at the time. This collection of English and Irish musicians brought differing backgrounds and attitudes to their collective music. Retiring to a country house in Wiltshire, the group called themselves *Steeleye Span*. By 1970 they had rehearsed enough material to record their first album. *Steeleye Span's Hark! The Village Wait* is a definitive album of traditional folk material moulded by rock instrumentation.

Steeleye Span — Hark! The Village Wait (Mooncrest 1970)

Side One	Side Two
1 A Calling-on Song	1 All Things are Quite Silent
2 The Blacksmith	2 The Hills of Greenmore
3 Fisherman's Wife	3 My Johnny Was a Shoemaker
4 Blackleg Miner	4 Lowlands of Holland
5 Dark-eyed Sailor	5 Twa Corbies
6 Copshawholme Fair	6 One Night as I Lay on My Bed

Personnel

Gay Woods — vocals, auto-harp, concertina and bodhrán
Terry Woods — vocals, mandola, five-string banjo, acoustic and electric guitars, concertina and mandolin
Maddy Prior — vocals
Tim Hart — vocals, electric guitar, electric dulcimer, fiddle and harmonium
Ashley 'Tyger' Hutchings — electric bass
Dave Mattacks and Gerry Conway — drums

The range of traditional songs originating from all over the British Isles indicates the knowledge of the performers. The gel of instrumentation gives the album a subtle atmosphere, while the songs sustain a rustic quality of age. Gay and Terry Woods's contributions are excellent, especially the former's sweet vocals, which matched Maddy Prior's, note for note. Here is a perfect example of intersecting folk traditions, electrified. While the whole album is consistently bright, 'Dark-eyed Sailor' and 'Lowlands of

Holland' are precisely honed exercises in electric folk. It is with 'Lowlands of Holland' that the album strikes its richest vein and embellishes the traditional song with enough modern rock texture to deserve the title folk-rock. While Maddy Prior's vocals are sung in olden idiom, Gay Woods's voice is more modern. Terry Woods's electric guitar shimmers on every beat while Hutchings's bass and Dave Mattacks's drums square off neatly. This is the fully fledged dive into folk-rock, producing a piece of music rooted in its own singularity and to this day unmarred by time.

It is not unusual for band tensions to result in excellent music, and, according to Gay Woods, the recording of the first *Steeleye Span* album was a traumatic experience. While the Woods were contributing a fair slice of the material, the rest of the band reaped the accolades. The second the last note was struck the group disintegrated. Gay and Terry returned to Ireland leaving *Steeleye Span* in England to fight its way through a patchy career of continual hassles with personnel and uneven music. The Woods teamed up shortly afterwards with psychedelic folk band *Dr Strangely Strange*, who impressed the couple with their theatrical flair and out-and-out weirdness. Taking on a tour of Holland, Scandinavia and Belgium, internal tensions yet again led to the Woods breaking away to pursue their embellishments of traditional folk on their own terms.

THE WOODSBAND

It seemed that once the dust had settled, the true artistry of the Woods could develop. Contracting themselves to Decca's Greenwich Gramophone Records, the duo released an album of sparkling quality and exhilarating music. *The Woodsband* shows musicians at a pinnacle of maturation giving full vent to the term folk rock. Gay's vocal abilities shine. Terry's guttural inflexions summon the true character of the traditional material. The re-arrangements are spectacular, while the electric instruments, especially Ed Deane's slide guitar, give the work an all-over strength.

The Woodsband (Greenwich Gramophone 1971)

Side One	Side Two
1 Every Time	1 Dreams
2 Noisy Johnny	2 As I Roved Out (trad.)
3 January's Snows (trad.)	3 Promises
4 Lament and Jig (incl. 'Valencia Lament' and 'Apples in Winter' trad.)	4 Over the Bar (incl. 'The Road to Athy')

Personnel

Terry Woods — mandola, concertina, acoustic and electric guitars, bass guitar and vocals
Gary Woods — concertina, autoharp, dulcimer, bodhrán and vocals
Ed Deane — electric/acoustic/slide guitars and bass guitar; harpsichord
Pat Nash — drums and other vocals
Plus:
Austin Corcoran — bass guitar on 'Promises' and 'As I Roved Out'; acoustic guitar on 'Dreams'
John Ryan — organ on 'As I Roved Out'; acoustic guitar on 'Dreams'
Tony Reeves — bass guitar on 'Every Time' and 'Noisy Johnny'

Ed Deane had cut his musical teeth with Irish sixties pop band *Granny's Intentions* and his guitar work on this album gives the collection an edge, a sharp exciting quality. 'Every Time' opens the album with his sliding guitar and Terry's raspy vocals, giving an American touch to the overall mesh of acoustic guitars and drums. Gay comes into her own on 'January's Snows', which uses the tune of the well-known Irish traditional song 'She Moves through the Fair'. Harpsichord and mandola give it a rural feeling. Her sweet vocals are evident throughout, coming up trumps on 'Promises', which includes piano and a subtle smattering of electric guitar. The traditional pieces are finely spun among the original material — 'Over the Bar' is an instrumental piece which alternates its rustic quality between acoustic and electric guitars.

Certainly, Terry Woods had achieved his ambition of authentically mixing several styles of folk music. His strong American leanings ride easily in this mix of Irish and English traditional sounds and words. Top that off with the electricity and drive of the other players and the results are eight structured pieces of original folk-rock unequalled by any other performers.

The band played mostly in Britain and Holland, occasionally dropping back to the home country. By 1972 Gay and Terry decided to settle permanently in the pastoral surroundings of county Meath where time would be spent in simple ruralism, providing inspiration for more music. Gay Woods remembers: 'I wasn't very much into the business side of things, since Terry would do that. I would just sort of look out the window. The natural environment was beautiful.'

After changing labels and realigning themselves, the duo produced *Backwoods* (Polydor) in 1975, an album much hailed for its complex sound and smoother production. The record contains a swell of self conscious, personalised accounts of life in Ireland. 'The Hymn' became synonymous with their style — a large-sound format, with Gay and Terry taking alternate vocals to slide/electric guitar backing. While 'Dublin Town' (Gay) is a sincere autobiographical acoustic ballad and 'The Fair' (Gay) hearkens for pastoral peace, the album's strength lies in only one track, 'Dunlaven Greene', a traditional Terry Woods foray into electric folk with perfectly executed finger-picking electric guitar.

Instrumentation on *Backwoods* is lush, with violins, congas and drums augmented by Ed Deane's electric guitars, Joe O'Donnell's electric violins and the classically trained Mike Giles (former drummer extraordinaire with the ingenious *King Crimson*). Other musicians were also recruited for the sessions, but the work fails to match the freshness and innovation of their first solo album or the early *Steeleye Span* work. Yet the ground had been firmly ruffled, and Terry and Gay had brought a whole new approach to mixing folk and rock styles. Their attitude can be summed up in the following quote from Gay: 'Terry was always very sharp towards the lazy attitude of a bunch of boring musicians standing there and playing deadpan traditional tunes to audiences who had paid good money. We wanted to do something more. Something special.'

Note: Gay and Terry Woods continued to produce material, but in a more middle-of-the-road American vein. Albums listed below show the group progressively going into fully fledged rock music. Gay Woods formed *Auto da Fé* in 1980, a theatrical new-wave band, garnering national acclaim in public performances.

Gay and Terry Woods — *The Time is Right* (Polydor 1976)
Gay and Terry Woods — *Renowned* (Polydor 1977)
Gay and Terry Woods — *Tenderhooks* (Mulligan 1978)

THE PSYCHEDELIC FOLK OF DR STRANGELY STRANGE

During the 1960s two young Scotsmen revolutionised the whole idea of folk music. By combining a crossover of international styles and instrumentation with uniquely brilliant song compositions, Mike Heron and Robin Williamson forged themselves a place in history. Calling themselves *The Incredible String Band*, the pair played a music that in 1967 was drenched with the acid visions and cerebral utopias of a generation steeped in psychedelics.

Williamson and Heron brought a mystical wisdom to the nationalist folk music idea — taking Scottish traditions and mixing them with styles from around the world, combining Scottish pipes, Indian sitars and dozens of other instruments. Williamson's brilliant vocalisations and authority in mythology and folklore brought such a texture to their music that by 1968 *The Incredible String Band* were the rave of the popular media. Their *Hangman's Beautiful Daughter* album of that year (Elektra) broke all barriers, with its awesome song structures and carnival variety. On this Williamson plays fifteen acoustic instruments, including water-harp, oud and chahanai.

The response in Irish terms came in the form of *Dr Strangely Strange*, a highly creative free-form folk group, comprising Tim Booth, Ivan Pawle and Tim Goulding. Their stage debut in 1968 was, fittingly, supporting *The Incredible String Band* in Dublin. *Dr Strangely Strange* brought an intellectual and lyrical consciousness to their music. This music grew out of informal, friendly sessions where any musician could drop by and add something to the mix. Their records broke new ground in terms of a self-conscious lyricism which was a direct result of psychedelics. More than that, for the first time we had Irish musicians who wrote truly autobiographical lyrics which mirrored their lifestyle, environment and experiences.

The evolution of *Dr Strangely Strange* was unusual. Tim Booth, born on 6 September 1943, came from a country background in Kildare and had been exposed to music through the piano playing of his mother. He enrolled in Trinity College, Dublin, during the sixties and as a counter to academicism took up painting and the guitar. Tim Booth: 'There was a lot of disposable income around at that time — one could drift, play a little music and get by without worries. I could earn ten bob a night playing the local folk circuit. During my last year at college I struck up a friendship with an Englishman named Ivan Pawle [born 17 August 1943], who was a serious guitarist and singer.'

In 1965 Booth graduated and went to apply his graphic ability in the advertising world. Still with his ear to the ground, he was quite affected by electric Dylan and the first *String Band* album of 1966, which in his own words was 'a major breakthrough for folky musicians; it had a certain spontaneity and joy.' This kept him playing music with Ivan Pawle, doing small gigs all over the place with friend/musician/dancer Brian Trench.

Tim Goulding (born 15 May 1945) also came from a rural background. Nurtured on classical music, he grew up in Enniskerry, County Wicklow, but went to boarding school in England. By the late sixties he had returned to Ireland to pursue a painting career, while he played tin whistles, recorders and fiddle on the side. He had known both Pawle and Booth, and it was in a house in Mount Street, Dublin, that *Dr Strangely Strange* took shape. This house was owned by Goulding's girlfriend, Orphan Annie, and it became known as The Orphanage, as all three used to live there on and off and a stream of musicians and artists was always passing through. Interestingly, Ivan Pawle was very close to the *String Band* and both Robin Williamson and Mike Heron used to come over from England to visit. Goulding himself remembers vividly when Williamson was in the house demonstrating his new 'October Song', which was later to appear on *The Hangman's Beautiful Daughter* album.

With all these connections and influences the music of *Dr Strangely Strange* flowered. Tim Booth remembers: 'We just got together and started writing and playing music — those were early hippie days and there was a great sense of freedom from everybody.' While the cool, relaxed atmosphere of the Orphanage continued, *Dr Strangely Strange* played the local circuit, a circuit which couldn't really cater for the band's brand of folk eccentricism. Tim Goulding: 'The ballrooms only catered for the superficial showbands, whereas folk-rock, especially our music, was limited to the likes of pubs or the literary societies like those in Trinity College.'

When Tim Booth moved to a house in Sandymount in 1969 it became known as the second Orphanage and continued to attract musicians and friends in a freely creative atmosphere. The mixture of art, music and outside influences represented the lifestyle of a generation. People like Gary Moore and Philip Lynott both hung out in the Orphanage. The importance of this represented itself in Moore's later contributions to *Dr Strangely Strange* on record and in concert — Lynott's first band was called *Orphanage* and *Thin Lizzy's* second album was titled *Shades of a Blue Orphanage*.

Dr Strangely Strange wanted to spread their wings, and sent tapes of their music to Joe Boyd in England. Boyd had helped establish the first successful folk rock label, Island, by producing such artists as John Martyn, Nick Drake and *Fairport Convention*, but wasn't initially taken with *Strangely's* music. Tim Booth recalls what happened next when an American, Bernard Stollman, picked up on the band: 'Yes, he ran a very famous off-the-wall record company (ESPDISC) which had *The Fugs, The Gods* and *Sun Ra* on its roster. He came over and threw all these contracts about, but said he was going to sell his record company. We got back to Joe in Britain and he changed his tune: "Come over to London and I'll record you".' *Dr Strangely Strange* signed, and made their way immediately to London, where they recorded their debut album for Island Records.

Kip of the Serenes was recorded in a day and a half, and laid down without overdubs. The cover of the album shows the group sitting with their instruments and robes, on the banks of the Dargle river in county Wicklow. That the photo had been taken by a close friend of the group showed that they wanted to be as individual as possible.

22 Tim Booth (1969) was the first
Irish lyricist to paint a surreal picture
of life in Dublin. His 'Donnybrook
Fair' has passed into legend.

23 Tim Booth in 1984 — fresh,
young and increasingly interested in
film-making and animation.

23

24 Englishman Ivan Pawle found Ireland inspiring, and stayed to play electric folk innovations (1969).

25 Tim Goulding left the *Strangelys* in 1970 to meditate in a Tibetan Buddhist monastery in Scotland. He eventually resumed painting fulltime, turning his back on the rigours of the music business.

26 *Dr Strangely Strange* in 1970; following in the footsteps of close friends *The Incredible String Band,* they forged an identity based on a fantasmagorical lyrical consciousness. *Left to right:* Ivan Pawle, Tim Booth, Tim Goulding.

Dr Strangely Strange — Kip of the Serenes (Island 1969)

Side One	Side Two
1 Strangely Strange but Oddly Normal (Pawle)	1 A Tale of two Orphanages (Booth)
2 Dr Dim and Dr Strange (Goulding)	2 Strings in the Earth and Air (Pawle)
3 Roy Rogers (Booth)	3 Ship of Fools (Goulding)
4 Dark Eyed Lady (Pawle)	4 Frosty Mornings (Pawle)
5 On the West Cork Hack (Goulding)	5 Donnybrook Fair (Booth)

Listening to this record now, one can't help but smile at the sweet naiveté of the music. All instrumentation is acoustic and the slow, discordant, free-flowing structures change key several times. Vocals are spoken or sung over the pipe, whistle and guitar sounds. 'Strangely Strange but Oddly Normal' sets the tone of the album, while Ivan Pawle's 'Dark Haired Lady' and 'Strings in the Earth and Air' are more refined and show his guitar-playing ability. On the lyrical side, the album is a departure from previous Irish recordings, since the words recount experiences in a stream of consciousness technique. 'A Tale of Two Orphanages' represents the band's lifestyle, while 'Donnybrook Fair' is the band's tour de force. The song shows their attitude towards the Irish showband by the use of the word 'cretin' and the line 'lead the pikemen from the rear', which cleverly alludes to the regressive side of showbands and certain forms of nationalism.

> The mighty cretin showband
> lead the pikemen from the rear
> and nobody sees the unicorn
> quietly standing there.

The unicorn is obviously the new enlightenment of the new generation. The folk-rock of *Dr Strangely Strange* certainly had a new lyrical consciousness, an incisive poetical wit and perfect autobiography.

The band, in Tim Booth's words, 'had come over from Ireland with long hair, good vibes and no money'. They acquired a van and a manager, playing the university circuit at seventeen shillings and sixpence a day. Being on Island, the band got the opportunity to open for certain groups — like Sandy Denny's *Fotheringay* — who were involved in folk rock music. Travelling in Europe they built up their stage craft, recruiting drummer Neil Hopwood at a gig in Wales, where they simply invited someone from the audience to drum for them. With hindsight, *Dr Strangely Strange* were very much in the psychedelic tradition, drawing on quizzical, medieval imagery, dress and words, fusing these elements with a wider consciousness whilst purveying a sense of decadence. All *very* sixties. Tim Goulding recalls the band 'playing a medieval scene in Guildford where we brought books of madrigals to perform during the concert and dressed up in suitable robes.'

The band travelled back and forth, taking time off the road to pursue other interests and relax in the country. Their second album *Heavy Petting* was recorded in Britain and Ireland, and shows the group toughening up their easy sound with drums and electric guitars. In many ways the album is stronger than the first and uses the talents of several folk and rock musicians who were around at the time.

Dr Strangely Strange — Heavy Petting (Vertigo 1970)

Side One	Side Two
1 Ballad of the Wasps (Goulding)	1 Gave My Love An Apple (Booth)
2 Summer Breeze (Booth)	2 Jove Was at Home (Pawle)
3 Kilmonoyadd Stomp (Pawle)	3 When Adam Delved (Pawle)
4 I Will Lift Up Mine Eyes (Goulding)	4 Ashling (Booth)
5 Sign on My Mind (Pawle)	5 Mary Malone of Moscow (Goulding)
	6 Goodnight My Friends (Pawle)

Personnel

Tim Goulding, Tim Booth and Ivan Pawle, assisted by the following musicians:
Dave Mattacks — drums
Gary Moore — electric guitar
Andy Irvine — mandolin
Brush Shiels — electric bass

Gary Moore and Brush Shiels obviously took some time out from *Skid Row* to assist in the recording of this album. Its essential rock orientation is punctuated with the playing abilities of musicians working in different areas. The free-flowing *Strangely* style gets more eclectic as the album features blues, country and even gospel elements. It's as if the band wanted to play everything at the same time. It all comes together on Ivan Pawle's 'Sign on My Mind' — the best cut on the album and *Dr Strangely Strange* at their peak. This is a long, extended piece of musical inventiveness, opening with the usual *Strangely* meanderings — pipes, whistle and acoustic guitar. As the slow pace of the beat picks up with Dave Mattacks's subtle drumming, Gary Moore comes in with a deft piece of 'stoned' guitar picking which is, in Tim Booth's words, 'easy on the beat'. This delightful sound is capped off with the well-seasoned mandolin playing of Andy Irvine. The track is a true melting pot of folk rock, a great slice of the late sixties, early seventies, hippie idiom.

This album demonstrated a need in the band, to use Tim Booth's words, 'to rock 'n' roll'. Even though the album was good, and in many ways a breakthrough, the florid packaging marred its impact. The record sleeve probably rates as the most extravagant piece of design work ever — opening out with several layers, containing words and information in ancient script. Tim Booth again: 'We are graphic designers and the record company insisted on Roger Dean doing the record sleeve — he was just starting off and this was the period when double, even triple albums with crazy sleeves were the rage. We weren't into all the folds and messy artwork. Anyway, the album got a multiple release worldwide and the record company were satisfied.'

The band continued to gig in Europe, becoming a stage favourite and something of a cult attraction. This was the time of progressive rock, when volume was cranked up and up, and monolithic tours were the order of the day. With gruesome aberrations like *Blodwyn Pig* or *Wynder K Frog,* bands were more bombast than substance. The Irish band would go on-stage and play at a quarter the volume, eventually building up their sound in layers. They attracted special attention from the rock press and built up a substantial following. Tim Booth comments: 'We would go on after *Skid Row* had blown the heads off the audience, and tone things down a bit. Since Gary Moore was the guitarist in that band he would join us on-stage and play his electric guitar in a sympathetic way. Since we had all lived with each other, we were open to one another's influences. Gary would play sweet guitar with us which suited our easy style.'

Later in 1970 Tim Goulding decided to quit the group, finding the rigours of touring a debilitating factor on his inspiration. He returned to Ireland to continue painting, eventually finding spiritual peace in a Tibetan buddhist monastery in Scotland. The rest of *Dr Strangely Strange* joined forces with Gay and Terry Woods, playing a short tour before obvious differences in musical direction split the band up. Tim Booth recalls: 'At this stage we were being offered plenty of concerts; even a gig in Poland was on the cards. By this time, however, it was no longer a pleasure to do it, musical differences between ourselves and the Woods being too great, so we all called it a day. In retrospect it was a very eventful era musically as well as socially. We played some strange and bizarre venues and experienced a lot on the road. English bands like *King Crimson* were definitely pushing the state of the art at the time, and we in our way were a new Irish band who had broken the mould and become more or less successful abroad.'

During the late sixties, early seventies period, *The Incredible String Band* acknowledged their associations by featuring *Dr Strangely Strange* on an album titled *Changing Horses* (Elektra 1969). Furthermore, Robin Williamson covered 'Strings in the Earth and Air' (from *Strangely's* first album *Kip of the Serenes*) on his second solo album *Myrrh* (Elektra), released in 1972. In 1973 the group undertook a reunion tour of Ireland, playing all over the country. Tim Booth continued his interest in graphics and music, contributing to various endeavours. All three original members of the band decided to modernise the original material in a 1980s vein, adding synthesisers and electronics to fill out the sound. Select appearances in 1982 saw the band in fine style, a newly polished version of 'Donnybrook Fair' going down a treat. Certain takes were put on tape and used for the soundtrack of a short animated film by Tim Booth called *The Prisoner*, based on a poem by W. B. Yeats. With Gary Moore on guitar, the music was recorded in full Dolby stereophonic sound, a first for an Irish film, and still proving the innovatory aspects of *Dr Strangely Strange*.

THE DELICATE RHYTHMS OF TÍR NA nÓG

Sonny Condell (born in Wicklow, 1 July 1949) came from a rural, farming area, spending most of his early childhood listening to rock, folk, jazz and classical music. Both his parents were seriously interested in classical music. *The Beatles* influenced Sonny to compose songs as a youngster. Leo O'Kelly (born in Carlow, 1950) started playing music when still very young, joining local beat group *The Word* at only fifteen. Playing guitar, O'Kelly joined the more lucrative showband circuit with *The Tropical Showband* before settling down with the highly acclaimed folk group *Emmet Spiceland*. Sonny and Leo crossed paths at small venues up and down the country and decided to form the duo *Tír na nÓg* in the late sixties.

Sonny had found the polarity of larger venues a bit excessive: 'We weren't into the excesses of hard rock music of the time, while the pubs featured mostly ballad groups. The extremes were either the heavy rock of *Skid Row* or cabaret shows. We went for the small folk clubs, places like the Coffee Kitchen or the Universal were great. Music would be listened to intensely, and people would come along as spectators one week and the next week they'd have formed a group. It was a very fervent time when bands like *The Incredible String Band* had deepened lyrical awareness.'

Sonny had already recorded a successful single on Song Records, called 'Look', yet tired quickly of the poor attitude of native Irish record companies. Having played the rounds in Dublin as *Tír na nÓg* in 1969, Leo and Sonny decided to head for the UK in 1970. Arriving in Britain, the pair immediately hustled small gigs, where they added hand drums and other ethnic instruments to their twin acoustic guitar playing. They built up a solid reputation in progressive music circles, and were snapped up by Chrysalis Records on the strength of one demo tape. Since Chrysalis had been formed as an offshoot label to Island — its prime aim to sport the more adventurous progressive rock acts, notably *Jethro Tull* — *Tír na nÓg* found themselves on large tours constantly playing to excited audiences.

Sonny Condell: 'It was very exciting and we had great fun indeed. We met a lot of people through tours — *Jethro Tull, Procol Harum, Cat Stevens* and *Steeleye Span*. We did one very long tour with *Jethro Tull* ... people would come for a rave-up with the eccentric Ian Anderson and the rest of the band, and we would play our guitars quietly, building up the rhythms slowly until we reached a frenetic level of playing — a very chunky sound. We also played with the astounding *Caravan*, who were extremely meticulous about their music.' Both *Jethro Tull* and *Caravan* were major innovators in the early seventies progressive music scene — *Tull* from the ebullient showmanship angle and *Caravan*, who were literally the first rock group to mix jazz and pop flawlessly.

Tír na nÓg took their music immensely seriously, and when it came to recording the first album it was done in the relative country seclusion of a small studio in High Barnet. Bill Leader, who had involved himself with a lot of English folk music, produced the record. When they were making *Tír na nÓg* Sonny and Leo utilised only acoustic instruments, but demonstrated a complex artistry in the manipulation of the recording studio itself.

Tír na nÓg (Chrysalis/Island 1971)

Side One	Side Two
1 Time is Like a Promise (Condell)	1 Boat Song (O'Kelly)
2 Mariner Blues (Condell)	2 Our Love Will Not Decay (Condell)
3 Daisy Lady (O'Kelly)	3 Hey Friend (Dolan)
4 Tír na nÓg (O'Kelly)	4 Dance Of Years (Condell)
5 Aberdeen Angus (Condell)	5 Live a Day (Condell)
6 Looking Up (O'Kelly)	6 Piccadilly (O'Kelly)
	7 Dante (Condell)

Personnel

Sonny Condell — acoustic guitar, moroccan pottery drums, jew's-harp, tablas and vocals
Leo O'Kelly — acoustic guitar, dulcimer, electric bass, tin whistle and vocals

The ethnic quality of the music comes from the mix of instruments and the simplicity of the songs. The sound is contemporary, both artists drawing their inspiration from personal experiences. While the general feel of the album is pastoral, Tír na nÓg manage to convey an all-over vision. 'Mariner Blues' is the first important song — ear-catching acoustic patterns resonated by the use of phasing. Here we see the production studio being used to accentuate the intimacy of folk music. In 'Tír na nÓg' itself, the group rework the old Irish myth, making it available to a whole new audience through the recorded medium.

The other songs are more personal. 'Hey Friend' is an exercise in the chunky playing typical of a live performance, but 'Piccadilly' is something very special, a song about London that uses swirling cello and violins to recreate the fleeting nature of Piccadilly Circus. The effect is a result of using phase effects on the natural sounds — the innovative use of electronics with acoustic sounds. The results give a mysterious quality to the music. The album was enormously well received on the British market, logging up healthy sales and giving the group a solid reputation. On the home market the album was never given the optimum boost, despite pleas from Sonny and Leo, and the potential was lost.

Tír na nÓg continued to play regularly on their own tours and supporting other bands. Sonny Condell talks about the attitudes of the group at that time: 'We had what would be called a religious dedication to our music — very professional and ambitious. Even though the hippie thing was going on at the time, we didn't go in for the lifestyle or values it had — socialising in London, doing the clubs and drugs and things. It was a time when bands got huge recording contracts. They would have the whole image — lots of clothes, instruments and piles of speaker stacks to pump out the sound at the big festivals on the usual long tours. Bands like Curved Air were very much in that vein, the era of progressive rock I suppose. The problem with most of these groups is that their music lacked substance, like waterflies when you took all the pomp away. We would put loads of energy into our sets — using only microphones the sound was great from just two pairs of hands. I would play all sorts of hand drums, including African sets. Anyway, the album really did quite well — at a time when people were attuned to hearing unusual music.'

On the second album, Tear and a Smile (Chrysalis 1972), Tír na nÓg continued to develop their technique. This album shows a marked change from the delicacy of the first, with the emphasis on strong percussion and strange compositions. Certainly the music is more rock oriented. The record reflects divisions in musical direction, the purely acoustic numbers definitely coming out on top. 'Down Day', 'The Same Thing Happened' and 'When I Came Down' are memorable. The group also earned themselves a considerable reputation for live appearances, playing mostly with Jethro Tull, swapping headlines with Supertramp and so forth.

In the following year, 1973, they toured the United States with Procol Harum and Steeleye Span, a memorable excursion. That year also saw them make a timely appearance at the Sligo Folk Festival, sharing an appropriate stage with Fairport Convention, The Chieftains and burgeoning rock/traditionalists Horslips. Obviously their experiences had strengthened their music and this was readily apparent on their third album Strong in the Sun (Chrysalis 1973), a different kettle of fish for which the sound quality was widened and more overdubs used. Matthew Fisher

(*Procol Harum* organist) produced the album with panache, and the overall effect is another leap in the direction of full-blown rock.

The record opens with 'The Wind Was High' (O'Kelly), a fully rounded, booming, acoustic love song, with flutes in the background. This is followed by 'In the Morning' (Condell), another love song of exquisite quality. Then suddenly the music changes with 'Lost Love', a really chunky sound with twangy acoustic guitar, a psychedelic slice of rolling brilliance in the vein of *Tomorrow's* 'My White Bicycle'. Images of cliffs and swooping seagulls in a bright blue sky are in apt psychedelic mould. It ends with a gong crash straight into 'Most Magical', a real rock number. This is dotted with keyboards and strange sounds. By the end of the first side we are into heavy rock with 'Whitestone Bridge' (Condell), an electric guitar song about crossing a bridge on their American tour. The title track by Leo O'Kelly was released as a single and is a valid attempt at a pop song, with nice keyboards and vocal harmonies. A strange album which could not be easily classified, it did not fare well on the market.

By the summer of 1974 both Leo and Sonny had tired of the exhausting pace they had set themselves. Seeing the limitations of continuing as *Tír na nÓg*, each decided to go his own separate way. Sonny Condell returned to Ireland to continue playing and writing, embarking on the second phase of his prolific career.

From Tír na nÓg to Scullion — the Acoustic Rock Fusions of Sonny Condell

By the mid-seventies Mulligan records had established itself as a local Irish independent label. Having released records with the Irish traditional group *The Bothy Band*, the label was interested in the experiments that Condell was doing. During 1976 Sonny Condell and a mixture of other musician friends got together and worked out a selection of songs and music that would make up the content of what still stands as Irish rock music's most important crossover album.

Sonny Condell — Camouflage (Mulligan 1977)

Side One	Side Two
1 Camouflage	1 Movie of You
2 Moondust	2 Why Do We Fight
3 Red Sail	3 Leaders of Men
4 Down in the City	4 Backwaterawhile

Personnel

Sonny Condell — acoustic guitar, percussion, saxophone and vocals
Jolyon Jackson — keyboards and cello
Greg Boland — acoustic and electric guitars and electric bass
Fran Breen — drums and percussion
Ciarán Brennan — acoustic bass
Brian Dunning — flutes
Paul Barrett — trombone
Rosemary Taylor — backing vocals

27

28

27 Sonny Condell doing a special for
RTE television in 1977, at the time of
Camouflage'.

28 *Tír na nÓg:* Sonny Condell *(left)*, Leo
O'Kelly *(right)*. They brought acoustic
rock to a new level in the progressive
music environment of the 1970s.
(Photo used on their first album.)

29

29 *Tara Telephone* was Eamon Carr's *(centre)* grand homage to the spirit of Jack Kerouac and Allen Ginsberg. *Left to right:* Peter Fallon (percussion), Eamon Carr (vocals) and Johnny Fean (guitar).

31

30 *Horslips* in the early seventies in full regalia and with coloured back-projections. *Left to right:* Barry Devlin ('shamrock' bass), Charles O'Connor (electric mandolin), Eamon Carr (drums), Johnny Fean (electric guitar) and Jim Lockhart (keyboards).

31 Barry Devlin, Charles O'Connor — *Horslips'* Live in Action was a spectacular show.

32 *Horslips* in 1979, showing a change in dress sense and a haggard, road-weary look.

The record is an enveloping mist of free exploration, a surging fog of Irishness which is full of light timbres and shading melody. All instruments stay away from the middle key, moving in classical and jazz areas, meshing the sound in a melodic pattern. 'Red Sail' features an extended flute piece by the renowned Brian Dunning, a jazz virtuoso whose cascading sound dips and rises in the overall mix. Sonny Condell's experiments with overlaid acoustic rhythms reach a zenith on the exemplary 'Down in the City', a song which has become synonymous with his talent.

Away from the rock 'n' roll circus of the early seventies, Condell continued to thrive in his native country. Developing his 'rock music with acoustic roots', he went into a long series of jamming sessions which resulted in the formation of *Scullion*, and the release of a debut album in 1979. *Scullion* (Mulligan) uses an eclectic range of musicians and instruments, but the highly ambitious project seems in hindsight to be directionless. Condell's own compositions range from the familiar pastoral themes to labour struggles, and even James Joyce's *Ulysses* gets the treatment. The poetical lyricism of the work and the addition of countless numbers of musicians to the band nucleus of Condell, Philip King and Greg Boland led to a smothering confusion. Philip King's version of John Martyn's 'John the Baptist' is the brightest cut and became a stage favourite.

John Martyn himself was drafted in to produce the more satisfactory *Balance and Control* (WEA 1981). The sound is smoother and the compositions more forthright. With fewer outside musicians there was more room for the group as a unit to breathe and the album yields another distinctive Condell ruby in 'Eyelids into Snow'. *Scullion* continued to embellish their acoustic rock on the 1983 album *White Side of Night* (WEA) which has an electronic flavour and contains two more Sonny Condell gems in 'Evil' and 'The Actor'. The following year the group suffered serious personnel changes with the departure of both Robbie Brennan and Philip King. Magically, this calamity was put in the shade by the sudden return to Ireland of Leo O'Kelly who instantaneously united with Sonny Condell in a rejuvenated *Tír na nÓg*. 1985 was a surprise year for folk rock fans as the duo toured Ireland and released an infectious modern-sounding single titled 'Love Is Like a Violin' (Tir).

Despite numerous setbacks, *Scullion* were fated to stay together and after making their respective apologies, Sonny, Greg Boland, Philip King and Robbie Brennan put their energies into the making of an album which liberally mixed folk, rock, reggae, jazz and Eastern music. *Spin* (Dara 1986) is *Scullion's* toughest and most muscular set to date. Greg Boland's guitar work seems to reach a new vocabulary of expressiveness while the song compositions and production are certainly those of the eighties rock band. After hearing the painfully beautiful 'Sign of Madness', or the emotive ballad 'Coming Back Soon', or even the outwardly pop-oriented 'Carol', one couldn't deny the eclectic maturity of *Scullion's* music.

Repeatedly in broadcasts and analysis, Sonny Condell has been ignored as an important Irish musician. His low-profile, folky stance cloaks his personality and conveys timidity. Yet Condell has been experimenting with acoustic rock music since the seventies and his work in the progressive era, coupled with his jazz/folk experiments on *Camouflage* and with *Scullion* make him one of the most inventive musicians ever to emerge from Ireland.

THE SNAKE'S FAREWELL TO THE EMERALD ISLE
HORSLIPS — A TALE OF MYTHOLOGY, CELTICISM AND ROCK MUSIC EXTRAORDINAIRE

When *Horslips* broke into mainstream consciousness with their first single 'Johnny's Wedding', they invented a whole new genre — Celtic rock. This single put them in a class of their own. Here was a piece of music which unashamedly mixed Irish traditional sources with rock. The group did not replace traditional with contemporary styles, however, but achieved the uncommon mix of being able to play both strands side by side. They started where nobody had started before, sweeping away all competition with one song, 'Johnny's Wedding' (Oats), in March 1972.

The bane of most rock musicians was that Irish traditional music was too rigid in its format. Moreover, the attitude of most older artists was aloof and purist, staying in their own cliques and treating the newer forms of youth music with suspicion. The sight of a number of long-haired, weirdly-dressed youths with electric guitars was enough to make the older traditionalists reel. If this was the new breed, then the older music was more holy, more sacred and not to be tarnished with the electric beast.

Horslips were part of a younger generation who understood the communicative power of the electric medium *and* the potency of their Celtic ancestry. They appeared at the right time and were to have one of the most colourful and successful careers of any rock group from the early 1970s.

Horslips merged together, as a meeting of like spirits and minds, at the beginning of the seventies. It was a fortuitous and fertile experience, a real fusion of literary and musical abilities. Eamon Carr had lived his childhood in Kells, county Meath, a place of ancient Irish historical significance with its burial grounds, castles and monasteries. Having picked up on poetry and literature, he travelled as a teenager in Europe — a case of 'did a Jack Kerouac very young ... got a sort of beat scene in Barcelona together'. Floating through Britain, Carr decided to set up a poetry-reading workshop in Dublin. This was 1969 and the sixties had inspired a free spirit. Working beside potters and artists in a small mews-type building, Eamon Carr and a friend, Peter Fallon, set out to stimulate literary activities through readings, magazines and other publications. The workshop picked up on the writing of international artists, and published anyone from Marc Bolan to Allen Ginsberg in a quarterly magazine called *Capella*.

Dipping into old Irish myths, the workshop produced another quarterly broadsheet *The Book of Invasions*, the subsequent title of a *Horslips* album. At the same time as the flowery folk of *Dr Strangely Strange* emerged, Eamon Carr decided to experiment with poetry and music. He and Peter Fallon, along with a couple of guitarists, called themselves *Tara Telephone* and toured Ireland. Female vocalists, viola and other instrumentation were not uncommon in this unusual formation, which became known as *The Tara Telephone Revue*. After this, Carr joined an advertising agency, where he met graphic designer Charles O'Connor.

While O'Connor had been at Middlesborough Art School, he had developed his interest in Irish traditional music, playing concertina, mandolin and fiddle. Coming to Ireland to work in graphic design, he played in local traditional bands, honing his craft. At the same time, a bright young guitarist called Johnny Fean was hotting up the Shannon area with his fiery brand of playing. Fean was fascinated with all styles of playing, working them out on banjo, harmonica and guitar. He was reputed to have spent one summer with old-time traditionalist Ted Furey, just learning old Irish tunes. Another musician, Jim Lockhart, had a master's degree in environmental studies and a championship tin whistle accomplishment. His enthusiasm for jazz and folk impressed Eamon Carr as much as his multi-instrumental talents, which were fiercely expressed on woodwinds and keyboards. Carr also met Barry Devlin in the advertising world, a man from a literary background (master's degree in English, gained in Northern Ireland), whose interests lay in songwriting and the bass guitar. This motley crew of men in their early twenties became *Horslips*.

The group of friends started to produce their own material and took the Irish charts by storm with 'Johnny's Wedding' in March 1972.[4] Quickly establishing their own Oats label, the band settled on a policy of working through the Irish rock music scene before venturing abroad. They even managed to pack out all the ballrooms, once the sole province of the showbands. Just seven months after the release of their first single, *Horslips* released their debut album to an ecstatic new audience. Here was a band that had gone out on a limb with its own independent record label, without large company backing, realising a majestic stroke with a first album of unique and innovatory genius. *Happy to Meet, Sorry to Part* develops a whole new tapestry of references, charting new territory in its music. Along with all this richness, the record came in a strange, accordion-shaped sleeve, designed by the band themselves. The sales were runaway, the reviews ecstatic.

Horslips — Happy to Meet, Sorry to Part (Oats 1972)

Side One	Side Two
1 Happy to Meet ...	1 Furniture
2 Hall of Mirrors	2 Ace and Deuce
3 The Clergy's Lamentation	3 Dance to Yer Daddy
4 An Bratach Bán	4 Scalloway Rip Off
5 Shamrock Shore	5 The Musical Priest
6 Flower Among Them All	6 Sorry to Part
7 Bim Istigh ag Ól	

Personnel

Jim Lockhart — keyboards, concert flute and vocals
Johnny Fean — electric and acoustic guitars
Barry Devlin — bass guitar and vocals
Eamon Carr — drums and bodhrán
Charles O'Connor — electric and acoustic fiddle, mandolin, concertina and vocals

Album recorded in Rolling Stones mobile studio in Ireland, October/November 1972.

Horslips achieved a very special synthesis on this album. 'Shamrock Shore' intersperses tight guitar flourishes, militaristic drumming and acoustic instruments, with Irish traditional airs. Phasing and electronic underscoring are imaginatively used in 'The Clergy's Lamentation'. 'Happy to Meet' starts with the wheezing, coughing and spluttering of a typical traditional barroom session, but quickly switches to electric music. The formula peaks in 'Furniture' with its long, tricky, guitar passages, embroidered with flutes and percussion. This track is a maturation of the *Horslips* synthesis, and a pointer to what could be expected on the next album, *The Táin*.

Eamon Carr: 'This album was a collection of bits and pieces that we all had worked on for a while. As far as we were concerned there was no such thing as a real Irish rock tradition until the mid-sixties. With people such as *Granny's Intentions* or *The Greenbeats* you saw something happening. Even still, people were more interested in what was coming from Britain or the States. Our wish was to provide an essentially Irish rock music, something distinctly our own, to galvanise each style with the other. We felt it was very important to convey our Irishness — a sense of our own identity and our heritage. In modern terms, people look to comic-book characters and identify with those. We were saying: Well, look at our own myths, which are full of riches. People could pick up on aspects of our music and look again at Ireland. Since our work had the rock context, most young people could relate to it immediately and learn a lot about Irish folklore as well.'

During their first hectic year the group was approached by the Abbey Theatre to provide music for a stage adaptation of a native Irish fable 'The Táin'. *Horslips* were immediately challenged by this idea, which they developed over the next year. Taking the conceptual flow inherent in tracks like 'Furniture' from their first album, the band wove the myth into their music, sustaining the whole tale through a record of devastating clarity. If the myth was a watershed in Irish history, the album was one in terms of Irish rock. *Horslips* again struck gold.

The Táin

The 'Táin Bó Cuailgne' (Cattle Raid of Cooley) is the centrepiece of a cycle of Ulster heroic tales. Dating from 500 BC, the tale refers to the conflict between the forces of the ancient Irish provinces of Connaught and Ulster over the possession of a prize bull. Maeve, the queen of Connaught, wants to own the famed brown bull, or *'Donn'*, to outmatch her husband's magnificent white bull. The sleeve notes carry the following quotation: 'We Irish should keep these personages much in our hearts, for they lived in the places where we ride and go marketing, and sometimes they have met one another on the hills that cast their shadows upon our doors at evening' (W. B. Yeats, March 1902).

Horslips — The Táin (Oats 1973)

Side One	Side Two
1 Setanta	1 Cú Chulainn's Lament
2 Maeve's Court	2 Faster than the Hound
3 Charolais	3 The Silver Spear
4 The March	4 More than You Can Chew
5 You Can't Fool the Beast	5 Morrigan's Dream
6 Dearg Doom	6 Time to Kill
7 Ferdia's Song	
8 Gae Bolga	

Personnel

Jim Lockhart — flute, whistles, Uileann pipes and vocals
Eamon Carr — drums, bodhrán and percussion
Barry Devlin — bass and vocals
Charles O'Connor — fiddle, mandolin, concertina and vocals
Johnny Fean — banjo and vocals

All compositions by Horslips.

The record is a perfectly executed concept album from start to finish. The group took great pains over the creation of the music and the resultant work sounds disciplined and complete. Watery electric sounds ebb and flow while traditional Irish sounds punctuate throughout. The normal Irish climatic conditions — wind, rain and drizzly weather — come across in electronic patterns.

Each song recounts a passage from the myth. In 'Charolais', flute solo and electric guitar feature prominently with the refrain:

> champions and the seven sons
> are going to take away the Donn

'Ferdia's Song' relates the battle between champions Cúchulainn and Ferdia while flutes and whistles accentuate the sadness of the theme:

> But Ferdia just grinned
> and shook his golden hair.
> Everything I do is ringed about with fantasy.
> But Ferdia just laughed
> and shook his silver spear *(flutes)*
> and fell . . .
> To battle again. *(electric guitar)*

> *(Break, all instruments, then enter whistles).*

On every refrain the instrumentation spins a web of Irish emotions, climate and nuance. 'Fool the Beast' layers vocals, flute, electric guitar and violins, one after the other on each verse. The most successful track on the work is 'Dearg Doom', a showcase Celtic rock song with a tight dance beat and uilleann pipes being used as the lead instrument. Their use of the traditional tools of pipes, tin whistle or bodhrán is so good that both public and folk purists had to acknowledge the coming of a new force.

Concert appearances were thronged with thousands of Irish youths eager to witness the music which so perfectly reflected their living environment. *Horslips* made their Irish appearances major events, making intelligent use of Celtic stage props. They commanded considerable respect since all album covers, sleeve notes and stage designs came from their own imaginations. Moreover, they mixed, pressed and distributed their own records so as not to allow major record companies to dilute their all-over Celtic vision.

Horslips had proven the worth of the home market and, with due success behind them, 1973 was the year of their first British tour with *Steeleye Span*.

Another huge response here prompted the band to sign a distribution deal with RCA. International and British release of *The Táin* was lapped up. The group was ready to conquer the world. Exhausting tours of Europe followed and the band wrote material loosely based on the travels of Turlough Carolan, the late seventeenth-early eighteenth century blind Irish harper. The strain of this period was apparent when the material finally surfaced on their next album *Dancehall Sweethearts* (RCA 1974), a weak effort compared to its predecessors. Both conception and content are strained, the album cover portrays the group in tired, unhealthy condition, while the sleeve notes jibe, 'believe it or not these tracks have traditional airs concealed about their persons.' One redeeming factor is 'King of the Fairies', a solid Celtic rocker.

Since the group was now involved with a large record combine this new album required a world tour to promote it. The lads found a ridiculous pace being cranked up to cover America and Canada. Early records had gained a cult status in the States and the band found a willing audience on that side of the Atlantic. Eamon Carr reflects on the strange tour: 'I remember going into the head office of RCA in New York and it felt like a gigantic doctor's waiting room, very automated and plastic. On the wall was a roster of artists which was crammed from top to bottom with country artists — Felton Jarvis and the like. At the very, very bottom, were leading rock people David Bowie and Lou Reed, and *Horslips* were even lower down. It took us weeks to get into the States from Canada — sitting delirious in a Toronto hotel room waiting to get visas to play America. We took a real moral hammering on that tour, arriving back to Ireland Christmas of 1974 having lost thousands.'

Having experienced the demand of the world rock music scene, *Horslips* were left, according to Carr, 'deeply confused and well addled'. The group retired to cottages in the Irish countryside of Tipperary, working out songs and relaxing. The results were made available on *The Unfortunate Cup of Tea* (RCA 1975), an album displaying more rock music and less adventurous pieces. The cover shows the group attempting to push a green monster into an old fashioned Irish cabin where two people are drinking tea. Foisting a new creature on traditional attitudes, the album makes hazy allusions to symbolism and the Holy Grail. Bar the incoherence, the album contained one exemplary piece of *Horslips* music in 'The Snake's Farewell to the Emerald Isle'. This instrumental piece of distant guitar and flute saw the group return to the genius of earlier work.

Their sojourn in Ireland during 1975 proved to the band that it was better to work in the native environment and use their own record company, Oats. The end of that year resulted in a more satisfactory acoustic album in *Drive the Cold Winter Away* (Oats 1975). The album is in true folk vein, with tunes conveying original traditional leanings and a knowledge of European varieties. The cover is a tongue-in-cheek look at the 'shamrocky' image of Ireland.

Horslips — Drive the Cold Winter Away (Oats 1975)

Side One

1 Rug Muire Mac do Dhia (medieval arrangement of traditional carol with Gaelic words)

2 Sir Festus Burke/Carolan's Frolic (celebratory Carolan tune)

3 The Snow that Melts the Soonest (English tune)

4 The Piper in the Meadow Straying (hornpipe)

5 Drive the Cold Winter Away (*Playford's Dancing Master* 1651)

6 Thompson's Cottage in the Grove (Reels)

7 Ny Kirree Fo Naghtey (Sheep 'neath the Snow — a Manx carol)

Notes adapted from album sleevenotes.

Side Two

1 The Crabs in the Skillet
2 Denis O'Connor (Carolan tune)
3 Do'n Oíche i mBeithil (That Night in Bethlehem)
4 Lullaby (instrumental with Victorian lyrics)
5 Snow and Frosts are All Over
6 Paddy Fahey's (Céilí pieces)
7 When a Man's in Love

This was something the band had always wanted to do — a simple folk album, a collection of personal favourites. The album pursues the themes of Christmas and winter, and was designed by the band as a collector's item. It was a pleasurable return to form.

The next year the band used the Rolling Stones mobile studio to record a tour of Ireland, the sometimes chaotic results surfacing on *Horslips Live* (Oats). By now *Horslips* had earned themselves a distinctly underground reputation. They had subverted the normal attitudes toward rock music in Ireland, subtly using traditional roots to make people realise that Irish rock music had its own identity. They saw themselves as part of the tremendous groundswell of Irish youth awareness at the time, an attitude which left an indelible mark on the musical environment. In every respect, *Horslips* were going to play second fiddle to no one.

Realising their creative strength again on home soil, the time was right for a more ambitious, conceptual *Horslips* album, and the *modus operandi* of *The Táin* was returned to. 'This time the project was to embrace the birth of Celtic consciousness in Ireland, a staggering objective on paper while in musical terms a feat and a half' (Eamon Carr). In a twelfth-century chronicle called 'The Book of Invasions', the pre-Christian colonisation of Ireland is recorded. The race who inhabited the country were reputed to have mystical powers and be learned in all things. They were known as the Tuatha de Danann. After a long occupation they were banished from the land. *Horslips* called their ambitious project *The Book of Invasions — A Celtic Symphony* (Dick James Music 1976). The album displays the group's ability with large conceptual endeavours, and the soft Celtic rock music makes its impact. Picking up on such a valid contribution, Dick James Music distributed the record in Britain, where it charted.

Horslips — The Book of Invasions, A Celtic Symphony (DJM 1976)

Side One
Movement One (geontraí)

1 Daybreak
2 March into Trouble
3 Trouble
4 The Power and the Glory
5 The Rocks Remain
6 Dusk
7 Sword Of Light
8 Dark

Side Two
Movement Two (goltraí)

1 Warm Sweet Breath of Love
2 Fantasia (My Lagan Love)
3 King of Morning, Queen of Day

Movement Three (suantraí)

4 Sideways to the Sun
5 Drive the Cold Winter Away
6 Ride to Hell

'In old Ireland there were three principal categories of song called *geontraí, goltraí* and *suantraí* — the joyous strain, the lamenting strain and the sleep strain' (*Horslips*).

When the surrealist artists of early twentieth-century Europe redrew the map of the world they enlarged the normal size of Ireland many times — a place of mythology, magic and many uncertainties. *Horslips* created this vision on record, their nature being to play around with rock and traditional tunes, merge them by accident and experiment with them. Their earlier work had done this in a simple style and by *The Book of Invasions* they had grown much more sophisticated, making it their *magnum opus*. Never again would they achieve the beauty of 'Fantasia (My Lagan Love)' or the earthiness of the reworked 'Drive the Cold Winter Away'. In concert, the stage sets included Celtic circles and designs, the work of Charles O'Connor, merging the theatrical element with rock. Tours were highly prosperous.

The *Horslips* experiment was successful primarily as a result of the literary and musical awareness of its members. Eamon Carr was a self-taught percussionist, yet his sleeve notes and lyrics were thoroughly researched. The creative mix of the group would usually spark on the road in between concert stints.

Their next phase of European and American tours affected the band fundamentally, dividing it into separate camps with disparate aims. Their next album, *Aliens* (Oats 1977), reveals the band creatively stifled. It is a suspect package of songs reflecting the fate of the immigrant Irish in the America of the mid-nineteenth century. The intensive tours of the US and Europe had weakened group morale and the record was a rushed job. 'Stowaway' and 'Ghosts' are sensitive, acoustically flavoured tracks, while the rest of the album is straight guitar rock.

Their concert schedule intensified further, and the group was dissatisfied with *Aliens*, which most felt lacked the former magic. America had tainted some members of the band with a liking for a densely produced West Coast sound. The band was hugely popular in upstate New York, Rochester, Boston, Buffalo, Washington, Philadelphia, Cleveland, Chicago and San Francisco. Eamon Carr ruminates: 'Well, Barry Devlin wanted to do most of the next album and he was highly impressed with the American music scene of the time. The band was under a lot of pressure so we went ahead with the idea of *The Man Who Built America* [Oats 1978]. The style had changed — no fiddle, no flute, no mandolin, no concertina nor whistle. It was just guitar rock and American guitar rock at that. We did for the first time get a fine big production sound with Declan Doherty, a guy who'd produced Gerry Rafferty.'

Barry Devlin and Jim Lockhart were highly impressed with this album while other members looked on it as the Achilles' heel of the group's career. They again dizzily toured America, arriving back to record their last studio selection in *Short Stories Tall Tales* (Oats 1979) — more bland music with the exception of 'Rescue Me', an acoustic folk tune, proving that their worth lay in Celtic roots. A farewell live set, *The Belfast Gigs* (Oats 1980), put an end to the *Horslips* saga.

In ten years *Horslips* had achieved great recognition for their innovations. They had defined Celtic rock and their records contained enough lasting music to fill subsequent compilation albums. Even though they roved around the world, the group based themselves in Ireland and recorded all their material either on home soil or in Britain. In 1982 Eamon Carr, Charles O'Connor and Johnny Fean worked together again on a new concept: the last witchburning to occur in Ireland. Going under the new title of *The Host*, the trio produced a modern electronic album on the theme of Brigit Cleary, a reputed changeling, burned as a witch by her own family in late nineteenth-century rural Ireland. To this day the spirit of *Horslips* remains intact and it is a credit to the group that nobody since has equalled or emulated its unique contribution to Irish rock.[5]

THE ETHNIC MAGIC OF CLANNAD

Clannad was formed in 1970. Reared in the Irish-speaking district of Gweedore, county Donegal, the five members of the group were related and touted a strong national element in their music, an element which went as far as singing most compositions in Irish and using Irish as much as possible in their work. In effect, *Clannad's* music was unorthodox in that it freely mixed folk with jazz and classical idioms. Spending the next few years playing all over Ireland, they quickly earned a reputation for having a lucid experimental style from which emanated a youthful energy and a potent Celticism.

By 1973 they had enough material and experience to feel confident in the studio. The outcome was *Clannad* (Philips), an album of folk and self-penned material, featuring quality instrumental solos and the distinctive vocal abilities of Máire Ní Bhraonáin. Her harp playing also features, while flutes, double bass and acoustic guitars give *Clannad* their characteristic sound. This sound centres on the low, soft tones of upright bass, bongos and other percussion, balanced with twanging guitars and the lead vocals. 'Níl Sé ina Lá' (a Donegal drinking song) and 'Brian Boru's March' (a tune reputedly from the Battle of Clontarf 1014) are full of instrumental virtuosity. A version of 'Morning Dew' (by American folk singer of the sixties Tim Rose) gives *Clannad* an affinity with English contemporaries *Fairport Convention, Pentangle* and *Steeleye Span*.

By their next album *Clannad 2* (Gael-Linn 1974) the group had progressed to a point where the ethnic pride of their work was powerful enough to deflect any criticism levelled at them by the purist element in Irish folk music. Still qualifying as their *magnum opus*, this album is an exemplary document of Irish folk-rock, complete with extensive sleeve notes on origins of songs, full Irish lyrics and the group represented by their Irish names. A statement on the use of the Irish language in songs and on albums, here was a young group in their twenties combining their heritage with the electric rock of the 1970s.

Clannad 2 (Gael-Linn 1974)

Side One	Side Two
1 An Gabhar Bán (old Irish tune)	1 Dhéanainn Súgradh (Welsh tune)
2 Eleanor Plunkett (Carolan tune)	2 Gaoth Barra na d'Tonn (Irish tune)
3 Coinleach Ghlas an Fhómhair (Irish tune)	3 Teidhm Abhaile Riú (Irish match-making song)
4 Rince Philib a Cheoil (dance tune)	4 Fairly Shot of Her (Irish jig)
5 By Chance It Was	5 Chuaigh Mé na Rosann
6 Rince Briotánach (Breton song)	

Personnel

Máire Ní Bhraonáin — harp, vocals
Pól Ó Braonáin — flute, guitar, bongos and vocals
Ciarán Ó Braonáin — acoustic bass, guitar, piano and vocals
Pádraig Ó Dugáin — guitar, mandola and vocals
Noel Ó Dugáin — guitar and vocals
Also:
Donal Lunny — bodhrán, guitar and moog
Micheál Ó Domhnaill — guitar and vocals
Robbie Brennan — drums

The response this album draws is to listen again and again to the soft strains. 'Eleanor Plunkett' has the clear influence of a harpist, while 'Chuaigh Mé na Rosann' features the medieval tones of the harpsichord. 'Dhéanainn Súgradh' is an odd tune — vocal harmonies are used in fast tempo to conjure up a workaday feeling (the song was used by Welsh weaver women to complement their work). This gives way to a crisp acoustic/electric break, with drums and flutes filling out the sound. *Clannad*, unusually, implement flutes and harp as prominent lead instruments on 'Fairly Shot of Her', an Irish jig. 'Coinleach Ghlas an Fhómhair' sets the album in perspective; roughly translating to 'autumn stubble', the song charts the escape of two lovers from their homes. Over a slow beat the emotive vocals are sung passionately by Máire Ní Bhraonáin, while bass and guitar are plucked sensitively in the background.

Ar choinleach ghlas an Fhomhair	On the green stubble of Autumn
a stóirín gur dhearc mé uaim	my love I first saw you.
Ba dheas do chos i mbróig	Warmly neat your shoe clad feet
's ba ró dheas do leagan siúil.	and wonderful your nimble gait.
Do ghrua ar dhath na rósaí	Yellow gold the colour of your cheeks
's do chuirníní bhí fite dlúth	and tightly woven your curly hair.
Monuar gan sinn 'ár bpósadh	Sadly I long for our wedding night
nó 'r bord loinge 'triall' un siúil.	on the ocean deep in a ship full sail.[6]

The whole is earcatching and contemplative, and Robbie Brennan contributes sensitive percussion. The result is *Clannad* at their best. The pronunciation of the words displays the native Irish inflection, something which singled *Clannad* out as incomparable. Their next move was to take their bounty abroad where young audiences were waiting and willing to appreciate the forwardness of their vision. This period in their career was more intensive, with concerts becoming a mainstay.

By 1976 the group was showing signs of tedium, and *Dúlamán* (Gael Linn), their traditional album of that year, featured little in the way of rock music. Staying on the European concert circuit, the 1978 live set, *Clannad in Concert — Swiss Tour* (Ogham), is again mostly acoustic, but the ten and a half minute version of 'Níl Sé 'n Lá' features instrumental passages of strength. Their jazz and classical roots shine through the upright bass playing of Ciarán Ó Braonáin and on all guitar pieces. Spending most of their time between Europe and Ireland, *Clannad* took advantage of their mobility to try out Conny Plank's prestige continental recording studio in Köln. The largely conceptual *Crann Úll* (Philips 1981) is the usual stylised folk-rock of previous albums and most tracks are fairly predictable with the exception of 'Ar a Ghabháil 'n' a' Chuain Damh', a tempestuous song, full of energetic vocalising, instrumentals and a strange, twangy guitar.

Indicative of their usual pace, *Clannad's* tour schedule for 1982 included concerts in the major cities of Europe, with special emphasis on Holland, Italy and Austria, the latter featuring a debut televised concert at the Vienna Concert House. Their vinyl output, however, continued to be unstriking, with *Fuaim* (Tara 1982) making little impression in terms of material or delivery. Recorded in Dublin, the added clarinet and saxophone and lush production technique detracts from the ethnicity of the group. This album introduced another family member to the public in Eithne (later spelt Enya) Ní Bhraonáin, who sang and played keyboards.

In hindsight, *Fuaim* was a product of a group in the transitional stages of their career. Having brought their rustic gaelicism to its logical limits, *Clannad* became interested in the technical possibilities of the recording studio and in particular the application of the 'prophet' synthesiser to vocals. In truth, something very special was in the air — a magical, mercurial music from the very annals of Celtic mythology, something atmospheric, moody, sage-like and historical. Yes, *Magical Ring* (Tara 1983) is all this and much more. It combines the character of Irish folk with electronic wizardry and produced *Clannad's* first British Top Five chart entry in 'Theme from Harry's Game'. This album was *Clannad's* second peak in nine years and they acknowledged the certitude of their original inspiration with a new version of the best song from *Clannad 2* 'Coinleach Ghlas an Fhómhair', the quintessential Irish folk ballad.

By this stage *Clannad's* climactic music had earned them quite a reputation with film and television producers eager for new quality soundtrack material. Swiftly they were commissioned by Independent Television to do the soundtrack for a new series of programmes based on the myth of Robin Hood. The resultant album *Legend* (Tara 1984) is a thick fog of electronic slices that are contemporary in sound but somehow lack the depth of previous compositions. It was at this juncture that a lot of people questioned *Clannad's* obvious deviation from their original folk roots. In reality, Máire, her two brothers and two uncles never were a traditional folk band in the specific sense. Having been surrounded by parents and relatives who were more interested in jazz than Irish traditional music, *Clannad's* early work was eclectic to say the least. In fact *Beatles, Rolling Stones* and Joni Mitchell songs translated to Irish were part of their initial repertoire back when they performed for the locals in the family pub in Gweedore. This element was to find its fullest expression on their next album *Macalla* (RCA 1985).

Produced by English avant-garde keyboardist Steve Nye, this record saw *Clannad* achieve a distinctive fusion of their Gaelic personality with modern rock. Even if the record opens with the atmospheric sounds of moving rocks, crashing waves and ancient chants; it quickly moves through jazz on 'The Wild Cry' into pop with 'Closer to Your Heart'. It is on the fourth cut, 'In a Lifetime', that *Clannad* become unashamedly a rock band, as Bono Vox of U2 lends his soaring emotionalism to the melancholy of Máire Ní Bhraonáin's sweet voice. *Macalla's* state-of-the-art sound production is punctuated only once by an acoustic folk number, 'Buachaill Ón Éirne', a traditional song delivered in Irish. This song stands out as something very special and it is true to say that *Clannad's* largest contribution to Irish rock is the way they have managed to transcend the limitations of the use of the Irish language by the sheer beauty of their sound.[7]

TRANSITIONS

One of the most important aspects of the 1960s and 1970s was the way in which folk music underwent a radical transformation at the hands of young musicians. Those who initiated this change and pioneered electric folk were imitated, then drawn upon and involved in later projects. During the seventies, two record labels, Tara and Mulligan, were set up to promote the development of Irish ethnic music, and both labels used their facilities to allow musicians of mixed skills to put their music on to vinyl. The emphasis was on 'difference', while maintaining a certain Irishness. The results were interesting.

Mulligan released *Midnight Well* (1977) when rock music was undergoing an important transformation — punk rock in England and Ireland — yet the album was greeted with applause and enthusiastic reviews. The album is a collection of American-style folk songs with what must be the most wide-ranging group of musicians ever to play on a crossover record. Just look at the following list.

Donal Lunny (Mulligan founder) — bouzouki, fiddles and bodhrán
Thom Moore — vocals
Janie Cribbs — vocals
Gerry O'Beirne — six- and twelve-string guitars
Ciarán Ó Braonáin — double bass
Martin O'Connor — Anglo concertina, button accordion
Kevin Burke — fiddle
Fran Breen — drums, percussion
Robbie Brennan — percussion
Shaun Davey — string machine, electric piano
Jolyon Jackson — piano, cello
Pat Farrell — electric guitar
Garvin Gallagher, Brian Masterson — electric bass
Keith Donald — alto saxophone
Paul Barrett — trombone
Dave McAnamey — piano
Greg Boland — acoustic guitar

With this cauldron of styles and influences the album sustains a consistent quality throughout. An adventurous project, with members of *Pumpkinhead*, *Clannad* and *The Bothy Band* rubbing shoulders and enjoying themselves. Yet the mix is not exceptional and compares poorly with the innovative work of previous groups. Still on crossovers, that year also produced the first symphonic Celtic concept album in Joe O'Donnell's *Gaodhal's Vision* (Polydor 1977). The work spans classical, jazz and rock, and charts the journey of the Milesians from Egypt to Spain and thence to Ireland. The orchestral nature of the music conveys the atmosphere of the history, with flutes, violins and percussion forming the basis

33 *Clannad,* from Gweedore, county Donegal, were
the most Irish of folk groups to bring Celtic music
from its roots into the splendour of the electronic
age.

34 Máire Ní Bhraonáin of *Clannad.*

35 *Clannad,* the epitome of Gaelic mysticism.

36 Paul Brady in the ballad group *The Johnstons,*
sometime in the 1960s.

37 Brady's involvement with pure folk music took
up thirteen years of his life.

38 Paul Brady: in 1986 his return to rock 'n' roll was
celebrated with the immaculately played *Back to the
Centre.*

36

37

38

of the structure. Unfortunately, the overall effect is 'pomp' rock, with nice solos and instrumentation doing little to ease the bombast. The only redeeming feature of this album is the final cut, 'Poets and Storytellers', which develops into something very special when Rory Gallagher applies a searing, fast-fretted guitar sound to the mix.

Despite such laudable projects it was still a fact that purist Irish traditional musicians were very wary of rock and its eclectic nature. Particularly the older, more conservative element, who were apt to discount the playing abilities of the younger generation. It was not until two highly influential musicians established their careers that Irish traditional music could embrace rock music with confidence. Their names were Paul Brady and Christy Moore.

PAUL BRADY — THE YOUTH WHO WAS INCLINED TO RAMBLE

One of Ireland's best-loved performers, singers and songwriters, *Paul Brady* has managed to live through a varied selection of musics from rock to folk to Irish traditional and back to rock again with increasing respect. Born in Strabane, county Tyrone, on 6 May 1947, Brady spent his early youth attending boarding school in Derry. By his own admission there was little in his childhood that would have led anybody to expect him to choose a musical career. Yet his parents, both teachers, were good singers and piano players, something which encouraged the youth to be an avid radio listener.

At the age of seventeen, *Paul Brady* left Strabane to attend university in Dublin where he started a course in Irish and French. It wasn't long before he became entranced by the beat music of the early sixties: 'Within a few months I had gone to see a lot of rhythm-and-blues groups that were beginning to become popular in Dublin. One night I went to a concert in the Crystal Ballroom and there were four bands playing: *Bluesville, The Greenbeats, The Inmates* and *The Semitones. The Inmates* had a guitar player called Brendan Bonass, who played a left-handed guitar and I thought this was very good so I wanted to be in a band.' Brady had brought an electric guitar and a small amp with him from Tyrone and after pestering a number of groups was taken on by *The Inmates* as vocalist/rhythm guitarist. They changed their name to *The Kult* and Brady played the local beat circuit. After this he joined *Rootsgroup* and eventually founded his own outfit, *Rockhouse*, playing keyboards and singing. This was shortlived, as pressure from college and parents forced him to 'quit rock-'n'-roll' and go back to his studies.

After a summer vacation he returned to Dublin and began playing solo acoustic blues around the ballad lounges and folk clubs. Very soon the young Brady came into contact with traditional Irish musicians like accordion player James Keane, who opened his eyes to the quality of pure folk music. In early 1967 the ballad group, *The Johnstons*, had a number one Irish hit single with the Ewan MacColl song 'The Heart of the People'. They had noticed the serious way in which Paul Brady applied himself to traditional songs so they invited him to join the group in June of that year. This was the start of an involvement in folk music that would persist for the next thirteen years of Brady's life.

At the time *The Johnstons* were a major-league folk group who were popular worldwide for their perfect harmonies and clear renditions of traditional songs. They also did cover versions of material by Joni Mitchell, Leonard Cohen, Jacques Brel and Ralph McTell. It was in 1969 that they got their first big break when they based themselves in London and suddenly received lots of media attention. With Brady on twelve-string acoustic guitar, mandolin, tin whistle and vocals, *The Johnstons* had three prosperous years in England with a total of six albums released on Transatlantic. By this stage Brady had begun writing songs for the group to perform and in 1971 *The Johnstons* played the Philadelphia Folk Festival. They were greeted with rave reviews in *The New York Times*, *The Philadelphia Enquirer* and newspapers nationwide. A decision was made to locate in New York and the band made the rounds of the record companies. Just as they were about to be signed by Columbia Records the energy crisis hit the record industry and ruined their chances. *The Johnstons* kept going by playing folk haunts like The Gaslight, Cafe Wha and Folk City, but the impetus had been lost. In 1974 Paul Brady got a fortuitous letter from Irish uilleann piper Liam Óg O'Flynn asking him to join *Planxty*, then the most important Irish traditional music group in Western Europe.

The reasons why Brady joined *Planxty* were complex. In his own words: 'Basically I got turned off rock 'n' roll in the early seventies, particularly the American West Coast. I hated *The Doors*, I hated *Love*, I hated *Jefferson Airplane*, I hated *Buffalo Springfield* and I hated *The Grateful Dead*. The West Coast scene was all nonsense, all tripping and flower power, just people who were crazy. In my head I was completely into traditional music and that way of looking at the world. Here were real people playing real music and that for me was reality.' So Brady came back to Ireland in 1974 to join Christy Moore and *Planxty* and follow the pure vein of Irish traditional music. After only two months Christy Moore left and the line-up was Brady, Liam Óg O'Flynn, Andy Irvine and Johnny Moynihan (the latter two having played together before in *Sweeney's Men*). After touring Europe, Britain and Ireland, the group split apart in late 1975 leaving Andy Irvine and Paul Brady to pursue a highly interesting project.

The fact that Irvine and Brady were young, innovative musicians working in traditional folk circles attracted a lot of attention from the younger generation. After a trip to Rockfield Studios in Wales the duo released what was to be the most commercially successful and critically acclaimed modern folk album of the decade. *Andy Irvine/Paul Brady* (Mulligan 1976) is a blissfully simple album of ethnic songs from Britain and Ireland, played on the most colourful range of acoustic instruments ever heard in traditional music. Things like the harmonium, the bouzouki, the cittern and hurdy-gurdy give the music a cosmopolitan character. Even though Irvine and Brady sported long hair and looked almost like hippies to their contemporaries, they had succeeded in transforming traditional music into something palatable to everyone.

For Brady there followed a long period of collaboration with older Irish traditional musicians. An album was done with Matt Molloy and Tommy Peoples for Mulligan. Then he did four fiddle-based records with Tommy Peoples, Andy McGann, John Vesey and Kevin Burke between 1976 and 1978. It was at the end of this hiatus from the commercial music world that Paul Brady came back to prominence with *Welcome Here Kind Stranger* (Mulligan 1978), a collection of folk songs recorded in the sophisticated environs of a multi-track studio. This time he utilised the facilities of the recording studio to give traditional music the 'kind of backdrops and rhythmic qualities' that one would normally find in rock music. The arrangements are quite modern and songs like 'I Am a Youth that's Inclined to Ramble' and 'The Lakes of Pontchartrain' were huge successes with the public and established Brady as one of the pre-eminent acoustic musicians of his generation.

As far as the young Tyrone man was concerned the time had come to go back to rock 'n' roll: 'I was always a musician who was going to work through the medium of rock music to express myself, but for a long period in the seventies I took a left turn up a whole side-road of folk music. When I came out of that I carried with me a whole experience which I could incorporate into rock.' Recruiting guitarists Jimmy Faulkner and Arty McGlynn, along with bass player Tommy Moore, keyboardsman James Delaney and Fran Breen on drums, Brady ensconced himself in Windmill Lane Studios, Dublin, to record his debut rock album *Hard Station* (WEA 1981). This time the music is hard-edged and exciting, with a biting collection of songs that display originality in the rock format. Although the 1981 release of the record was lapped up in Ireland, internationally the album was mismanaged by Brady's record company, WEA, who refused to release it in America. Wanting desperately to succeed abroad, Brady complained vigorously to Warners who promptly dropped him from the WEA label. He quickly secured another recording contract with the 21/Polydor group, who re-released *Hard Station* in 1982. Curiously, a re-mixed version of the record also surfaced on both WEA and Polydor the following year, placing four different versions of the same title album in the record stores.

The problems with *Hard Station*, coupled with the lack of record company support for touring abroad, caused Paul Brady much heartache in the early eighties: 'that was the low point of my career; the failure of *Hard Station* to make any serious impact outside Ireland and Britain caused me a lot of problems. I felt I didn't want to face a lifetime of touring around the Irish circuit, doing the same thing again and again.' He needn't have worried, for his stature as a first-class songwriter was beginning to make waves abroad. When Latin American musician Carlos Santana covered 'Night Hunting Time' it wasn't going to be the last time that internationally famous artists sang Brady's songs. Despite feelings of resignation he pushed onward and released the album *True for You* (Polydor) in 1983, a record which utilised a cool American production technique and the crystal clear guitar playing of Englishman Phil Palmer. Criminally neglected by both public and critics alike, the album is one of Brady's most complete statements on the value of folk rock convergence and yields a riveting example in 'Trouble Round the Bend'.

Obviously, Brady had something very special which appealed to established world music stars, for American soul singer Tina Turner covered his song 'Steel Claw', while UK rhythm and blues artist Dave Edmunds did 'Busted Loose'. Yet Polydor did not handle *True for You* with any kind of enthusiasm and Brady found himself in the unenviable position of having to start all over again. Working in the rock world was proving to be quite a different kettle of fish to the folk environment basically because of the intense competitive and commercial perspectives of large record combines. Brady simply bided his time and played gigs in Britain and Ireland with a working unit of Phil Palmer (guitar), Kenny Craddock (keyboards) and Ian Maidman (bass). A session at the Half Moon, Putney, London, in April of 1984 was recorded for posterity and issued by the Demon label as *Full Moon* in that year.

One important ingredient that Paul Brady had to find was a musical environment which would allow the pure, spontaneous element of his folk roots to shine through. His attitude to recording can be summed up by the comment: 'The essence of what I do can be done simply on acoustic instruments like the piano and the guitar, I don't need fancy technology to tart up my work because I'm a spontaneous performer. The first time I do something is always the best.' A deal was duly made with Phonogram Records and with the help of Eric Clapton and Mark Knopfler Brady set about the task of creating a rock album that was a true reflection of his spirit. After some false starts he finally succeeded and *Back to the Centre* (Mercury 1986) ranks as his finest achievement to date. *Back to the Centre* was recorded in three British studios and boasts a back-up group of twelve top-notch musicians, including Clapton on electric guitars, drummer Larry Mullen Jnr of rock band *U2,* and American protest singer Loudon Wainwright III. Brady plays acoustic and electric guitars, piano and electric keyboards, percussion, bouzouki and of course, the tin whistle. The record contains four compositions of outstanding craftsmanship. 'Deep in Your Heart', a song about the pain of separation, utilised a double melody line of great complexity, backswept by the heavenly atmospheric guitars of Eric Clapton and Phil Palmer; 'The Homes of Donegal', a traditional song of Bridie Gallagher's, is rendered tastefully with subtle acoustic guitar and synthesiser treatments, proving that Brady was still very much aware of folk music; 'Follow On' is a warm, slow ballad, which advises the inhabitants of troubled lands that peace can be found in hope and love; and, most strikingly, in 'The Island' Brady sensitively encompasses such topics as the Middle East war, the sectarian strife of his native Ulster and the dubious faith put in freedom dreams and hippie idealism. More than this 'The Island', with its simple guitar/piano accompaniment carries with it a message of optimism and humanity:

> Up here we sacrifice our children
> To feed the worn-out dreams of yesterday
> And teach them dying will lead them into glory ...
>
> But hey! Don't listen to me!
> 'Cos this wasn't meant to be no sad song
> We've heard too much of that before
> Right now I only want to be here with you.

So, in 1986 Paul Brady achieved his ambition of being a highly respected rock musician of stature. He became much sought after by the media and recorded a brilliant acoustic session for BBC alternative disc jockey Andy Kershaw as well as appearing on BBC television's rated 'Old Grey Whistle Test'. Here one saw a confident Brady performing 'Back to the Centre' and 'The Island' in addition to playing some of the most exquisite classical guitar ever heard on the show. Indeed, Brady had arrived, as witnessed by his top billing at a summer festival beside the river Lee in Cork. Getting top slot at such occasions was something he was by now used to, but the fact that international superstar Chris de Burgh was not granted this spot, playing second to the Strabane man, signified Paul Brady's position as a giant of both Irish folk and rock.

Bob Dylan has said of him that 'He is one of the few musicians worth getting out of bed in the morning for', and Eric Clapton and Tina Turner have expressed a heartfelt desire to include some of his best songs in their repertoires. When Lilian Roxon wrote about American folk-rock artist Tim Buckley, she commented, 'There is no name yet for the places he and his voice go' — at present, no better words could be used to describe the voice of Paul Brady, except that it conveys manifold emotions while drawing on a profound sense of his Irish heritage. On his fourth rock album with folk overtones, *Primitive Dance* (Mercury 1987), Brady has continued on his merry way without inhibitions. In every sense, Brady characterises a unique spirit in Irish music, that of a pure folk child who has just discovered the heart of rock 'n' roll.[8]

CHRISTY MOORE — THE HEART OF THE COUNTRY

It would be fair to say that the arrival of Christy Moore on the folk scene changed the entire history of Irish traditional music. From the early seventies onwards, he strove to give it back its energy and vitality without losing the perspective of its original purity. By slowly building up a reputation for authenticity and faultless performance, Moore attracted larger and larger audiences to his music. In so doing he broke down the barriers between the old and the young, the purists and the innovators. Through his popular appeal people were able to come to terms with the place of foreign and electric instruments within the Irish traditional sound. Moreover, he continues to be one of Ireland's great folk singers, whose understanding of the value of old songs in a new format, and new, living songs in an old format, is unique.

Born just after the Second World War in Newbridge, county Kildare, Christy Moore grew up listening to the great pipe and drum marching bands, so much a feature of that province. Exposed to the raw sounds of Irish traditional music played in a country environment, the young Christy found it easy to be enthralled. Even though music was his first love, economic necessity directed him from school into the so-called safe world of white-collar employment, and Moore started work as a bank clerk at the beginning of the sixties. His spare time was taken up with practising the acoustic guitar and bodhrán, learning the odd traditional tune, and sitting in on pub sessions frequented by more established veterans.

His life was abruptly altered by a protracted bank strike in 1966 which forced him to seek a living elsewhere. Like so many of his forefathers, Christy Moore took the inevitable boat to England and there started performing professionally around the then blossoming folk circuit. This experience helped him to appreciate the huge range of folk music from Britain and America that had hitherto been unavailable to him. He, in turn, impressed folk purists with his depth of knowledge of Irish folk and it wasn't long before the enthusiastic Irishman persuaded some of his fellow countrymen that the time was right to give the dusty native Irish traditional scene a taste of what was happening in the UK.

Returning to Ireland in 1970 Christy Moore began enlisting the help of some highly creative young players who could share his vision of a new folk music, rich with new textures and treatments. Soon he was joined by Donal Lunny (acoustic guitar/bouzouki), Andy Irvine (mandolin) and Liam Óg O'Flynn (uilleann pipes), who comprised the core unit of musicians on the historic breakthrough album *Prosperous* (Tara 1972). Recorded live in Rynne's stately Georgian house in Prosperous, county Kildare, the album turned the heads of a nation quickly forgetting the value of its own heritage. It had a spontaneity, a certain youthful exuberance and enough original ideas on presentation to make people realise that Irish traditional music had to change. If the group had only recorded the album's opening track 'Raggle Taggle Gypsies/Tabhair Dom Do Lámh', that in itself would have been enough. Starting with the humorous line 'There were three ould gypsies standin' at my hall door', the song gathers a fast pace until it magically turns into a type of classically flavoured Irish instrumental. Donal Lunny engineers the skilful transition to the second tune. *Prosperous* also features Bob Dylan's 'Tribute to Woody' and Woody Guthrie's 'Ludlow Massacre', showing that Christy Moore had taken heed of the American protest movement of the sixties. A version of 'James Connolly', learned from *Sweeney's Men* member Johnny Moynihan, and a re-written version of 'I Wish I Was in England' display Moore's strong understanding of Irish history, something that would become more important as time went on.

After *Prosperous*, Christy Moore took the core unit of Irvine, O'Flynn and Lunny to form *Planxty*. In 1973 they released the legendary black album, simply called *Planxty*, on Polydor and solidified their burgeoning reputation. The best cut on the record is a well recorded studio version of 'Tabhair Dom Do Lámh'. After two more albums Moore tired of the expectations of a public who wanted him to simply reel out the old material. In 1975 he went solo and began devoting himself to radical social and political concerns. He became the most outspoken musician working in Ireland on the issue of Irish unity, and supported the republican movement to the hilt. Still, his 1977 solo *Christy Moore* (Polydor) album contained enough traditional material performed with vigour to please his fans. He continued to work with old friends Donal Lunny and Andy Irvine as well as a varied selection of Ireland's up-and-coming young acoustic musicians. In 1979 *Planxty* re-formed to much national enthusiasm, but as far as the rock audience was concerned Christy Moore was a scruffy folky who drank large bottles of Guinness on-stage and perspired through a bushy, unkempt beard and sleeveless vest as he sang. There was something still very traditional in his appearance that alienated the rock audience, particularly during the frenzied era of punk music.

Andy Irvine, one of Moore's old associates in *Planxty*, was to point towards a new direction in traditional music. On his *Rainy Sundays . . . Windy Dreams* (Tara 1980), Irvine utilised a mixture of East European folk strains with polymoog synthesiser, electric bass, bouzouki and soprano saxophone. Bringing jazz elements and electronic ideas into traditional music was a departure and one that Christy Moore embraced wholeheartedly when he founded *Moving Hearts* in February 1981. The reaction to a jazz/rock/traditional ensemble was surprisingly positive and the release of the album *Moving Hearts* (WEA 1981) saw it reach the number one slot in the Irish charts. It was another watershed album for Christy Moore, for at the time it was the biggest-selling native Irish album ever released, and it catalysed an entire new direction in folk-rock. The calibre of his fellow musicians was without precedent. *Moving Hearts* were: Christy Moore (vocals, guitar and bodhrán), Donal Lunny (electric and acoustic bouzouki, synthesiser and vocals), Declan Sinnott (lead guitars), Eoghan O'Neill (bass and vocals), Davy Spillane (uilleann pipes and low whistle), Keith Donald (tenor and soprano saxophones) and Brian Calnan (drums and percussion).

Moving Hearts is a superlative debut album in a new type of musical genre. It has a lush Celtic personality, grilled over with uilleann pipes and bouzouki, backed up by an atmospheric jazz bass and saxophone sound. Its songs are a selection of covers dealing with a wide range of political issues like war, emigration, exploitation, internment without trial, espionage, torture and so forth. One of Christy Moore's most beautiful ballad versions is that of J. Gibbs' 'Irish Ways and Irish Laws', a song that emotionally draws on eight hundred years of Irish suffering at the hands of foreign invaders and pleads for a return to the innocent Irish life of Celtic times. A version of new-wave artist Phil Chevron's 'Faithful Departed' also shows that Moore is very much a man for all generations, someone who does not see age as a barrier to communication. The album also features quality traditional dance instrumentals 'McBrides' and 'Category', plus the moody, shifting landscape-like 'Lake of Shadows'.

Moving Hearts showed that Irish traditional music could produce musicians who were as aware and innovative as rock musicians. Christy Moore's attitude at the time was: 'There is no difference between a folk and a rock musician. What kind of music you play is not going to decide who you are. There is a different aura from these two musics, rock is very high-powered while the music scene I come from was never very high-powered. I was playing for a long time without any amplification although I don't find it any more difficult to sing with a six-piece band than by myself with a guitar. The uilleann pipes particularly excite me and it was a desire to use them in a rock context and to sing with bass and drums that caused the band to come about. Donal Lunny's primary interest was one of musical arrangement while mine was a vocal involvement.'[9]

In their incipient stages *Moving Hearts* were very much perceived as an overtly republican group. Yet this pigeon-holing overshadowed the group's musical excellence and led to lack of airplay, record company support and financial rewards. Organised as a co-operative, the band found it harder and harder to get their message across. After *Dark End of the Street* (WEA 1982), an album which produced the dreamlike Declan Sinnott track 'Let Somebody Know', Christy Moore left the group to pursue a different avenue with *Planxty* and to play solo. Surprisingly, the rest of the group kept going and recruited Mick Hanly on vocals, releasing *Moving Hearts Live* (WEA) in 1983. Very little financial support was given to the group and though the music was boosted by the addition of young singer Flo McSweeney, circumstances forced disbandment in 1984. A farewell concert saw Christy Moore return to the fray for one last jubilant Dublin show. This fortunately wasn't the end of the *Moving Hearts* story. During 1985 an enlarged line-up of the group recorded an entire album of instrumental music called *The Storm* (Tara). With Noel Eccles (assorted percussion), Matt Kellaghan (drums) and Declan Masterson (uilleann pipes), the central unit of Donal Lunny, Davy Spillane, Eoghan O'Neill and Keith Donald together wove a masterpiece of a record. Side One is taken up with a series of jigs and reels that soar on contrapuntal riffing between Spillane's pipe and whistle lines and Donald's saxophones and complex percussion sounds. Side Two contains three phenomenal pieces in 'Finore', a lilting ballad piece memorable for Keith Donald's bass clarinet work, 'Tribute to Peadar O'Donnell', which reveals the young Davy Spillane to be the most expressive contemporary uileann piper and low whistler in the land, and the elegiac 'May Morning Dew', where again Spillane's low whistle playing is both profoundly melancholic and optimistic. The latter became the most-played Irish traditional tune on Irish radio, featuring as a signature tune for late-night RTE Radio 2 programme 'Night Train'.

What of Christy Moore? After he left *Moving Hearts* his work seemed to regress to a basic ballad framework utilising just simple acoustic guitar behind his soft Irish brogue. His 1983 solo album *The Time Has Come* (WEA) saw him treading water by compiling a series of bland covers of folk material as well as regurgitating old stuff like 'Lanigan's Ball' and 'Faithful Departed'. What gives the record some merit is a version of his brother Barry Moore's 'Section 31', an attack in rock style on the Irish censorship law governing transmissions of interviews with members of illegal organisations like the IRA. The project also showed Moore's continued association with Donal Lunny, who co-produced and arranged the album. Lunny, Declan Sinnott and Christy grouped together down in Lakelands Cottages, Killarney, county Kerry for the next opus — the highly successful *Ride On*, recorded for WEA in March of 1984. This is a crisp selection of wide-ranging songs, two of which were written by Northern Irish republican internee and Member of Parliament Bobby Sands. Compositions by W. B. Yeats, Pearse Turner and Barry Moore are also featured. The record's best moments are the slow, almost *Pink Floyd*-like 'Ride On', a version of Johnny Duhan's powerful anti-Reagan song 'El Salvador' and Christy's highly comic tale of the most popular of Irish summer music festivals 'Lisdoonvarna'. The following year's *The Spirit of Freedom* (WEA) travels similar terrain, but is more outspoken in its republican, anti-imperialist stance. The martyred Bobby Sands seems to dominate the record. This time Donal Lunny went for a thin production style. However, the acoustic guitar playing on *The Spirit of Freedom* is piercingly captivating, as exemplified by its virtuosity on 'No Time for Love'.

In the modern era Christy Moore represents the stubborn face of Irish folk music, one that can be equally at home in a traditional tavern or on a huge stadium rock stage. His most significant contribution to Irish rock is that he gave the work of Irish traditional musicians that sense of glamorous aura that had for so long been the province of rock music. His second 1985 album *Ordinary Man* (Demon) is a splendid collection of folk material involving old *Planxty* cohorts Arty McGlynn, Donal Lunny, Andy Irvine and Liam Óg O'Flynn as well as ex-*Clannad* lady Enya Ní Bhraonáin and *Skid Row* drummer Noel Bridgeman on

39 Christy Moore and Adam Clayton *(U2),* at political press conference, August 1983.

40 *Moving Hearts'* farewell concert, November 1984. *Left to right:* Christy Moore, Flo McSweeney, Mick Hanly and Donal Lunny.

41 Enya Ní Bhraonáin — creator of Ambient folk music for the 1980s.

42 Mary Black.

43 Maura O'Connell — the Irish 'rose' of the new acoustic music.

44 Mary Coughlan — Galway 'queen' of folk-rock-blues.

41

42

43

44

accordion.[10] In 1987 *Unfinished Revolution* (WEA) was released — an album that cloaks the heavy seriousness of its lyrics in a smooth modern, almost middle-of-the-road sound. But again it conveys a sense of differently fresh perspective on a culture that few other folk singers could hope to emulate. Some may label Christy Moore a dyed-in-the-wool republican folk singer, but history shows that he engineered the fusion of traditional folk, jazz and rock. For a former heavy-drinking, emigrant Irish busker that isn't such a small accomplishment.

THE CONTEMPORARY SCENE

What has happened to Irish folk rock in the recent past is part of an ever-changing process of maturation. This process has made Ireland a fertile land of exploration and experimentation for all types of musicians wishing to gravitate from acoustic music to rock or vice versa. For example, *Stockton's Wing* had long been respected for their staunch traditionalism. Group members were considered to be some of the best players in the country and had distinguished themselves at several Fleadhanna Ceoil. When they added an electric rhythm section to their banjo, mandolin and fiddle sound, they automatically widened their appeal. This was proven by the popularity of their first rock-type album *Light in the Western Sky* (Tara 1982). Or consider the work of Kevin Burke, long one of Ireland's most distinctive of traditional fiddle players whose *If the Cap Fits* (Mulligan 1978) and *Up Close* (Green Linnet 1984), albums kept within the strict boundaries of old Irish folk while exploring the use of Eastern notation, electronics and exotic instrumentation. Or even think about Philip Lynott's two forays into folk-rock, the first, with the legendary Terry Woods, called 'Tennessee Stud', a single which begins with Woods's characteristic Appalachian banjo picking and then suddenly blows into a real Lynott rocker; the second with *Clann Éadair* entitled 'Tribute to Sandy Denny' (Crashed 1984), a simple ballad sung with intense emotion by Lynott, which laments the passing of one of England's greatest folk singers, *Fairport Convention's* Sandy Denny. These few instances represent a new-found vision in Irish folk-rock, a vision which has stimulated more and more musicians to vary their styles as new ideas become apparent.

Enya (Eithne) Ní Bhraonaín
Even though Eithne Ní Bhraonáin played assorted keyboards and sang on *Clannad's* fifth album *Crann Úll*, it wasn't until 1982's *Fuaim* that the youngest sister of Gweedore's most famous musical family got proper billing as a bona-fide member of the group. By that stage tensions were beginning to make the twenty-year-old, classically trained Eithne wish she had stuck to her original ambition of becoming a piano teacher. *Clannad* wanted a new manager, David Kavanagh, but Eithne was quite happy with the old Dublin team of Nicky Ryan and his wife, Roma. So Eithne left and went to live with the Ryans in their sixteen-track studio home. Here she worked on keyboards and started to compose vocal melody lines that had a traditional Irish character mixed in with a texture akin to Ambient music. Using such equipment as sampling keyboards and drum machines, Eithne was supported in her search for a new career by

former *Clannad* manager Fachtna O'Kelly, who felt she could write film soundtracks. After putting some of her music down on tape Eithne was introduced to famous English film producer David Puttnam, who immediately commissioned her to do the theme music for a French film, *The Frog Prince*. Now that her career was going international, she re-spelt her first name phonetically as Enya for the benefit of those not conversant with Donegal Irish.

Maintaining her association with Irish folk, Enya did some sweet backing vocals on Christy Moore's *Ordinary Man* LP in 1985. She also spent time between London and her Dublin home laying down the music for a six-part BBC television history of the Celtic peoples. The BBC were so excited by her contribution that they released the soundtrack as Enya's first solo album. *Enya* (BBC Records 1986) ranks as the very first Ambient folk album to be released by an Irish musician. Accompanied by *Planxty* uilleann piper Liam Óg O'Flynn and guitarist Arty McGlynn, Enya uses her voice, an acoustic piano, a drum machine and several electronic synthesiser instruments to literally paint a soundscape of Celtic times. Unlike many rock or pop records, this allows the listener to drift through its atmosphere without pressure. 'Aldebaran' sounds like an inter-galactic theme tune, 'Bard Dance' seems like a children's nursery rhyme of ancient Ireland and 'Epona' involves synthesised Irish harp lines! If this kind of experimenting smacks of sacrilege to a lot of folk purists, the album is well balanced by Enya's *Clannad*-like vocals on 'I Want Tomorrow' and Liam Óg O'Flynn's faithful slow air 'The Sun in the Stream'. The fact that Enya Ní Bhraonáin overdubbed her voice at least a hundred times and utilised the English, Irish, Scots, Welsh, Latin, and French languages to achieve a perfectly authentic sound proved her credentials as a new Irish composer of serious intent.

Mary Black

When Mary Black's third album *Without the Fanfare* (Dara) was released at the beginning of 1986 it signified another new direction for Irish folk-rock — that of the adult-oriented market. The music is smooth, pleasant, almost bland in quality, but is differentiated by the rich singing and floating melodies of a woman who could be equally at home performing in a rural Irish pub or at a North American barndance, or even in a smoky London jazz club. The record is certainly bolstered by the inclusion of *Moving Hearts* men Eoghan O'Neill, Donal Lunny and Declan Sinnott as well as the experienced drumming and percussive craft of Noel Bridgeman. Sinnott's velvety production and tasteful guitar-playing also feature. Mary Black started her career singing with her two brothers in a pub in Castlebar, county Mayo. She made two folk albums before she was noticed by Christy Moore, who covered one of her songs on his 1981 album *Christy Moore And Friends* (RTE). After teaming up with *Horslips/Moving Hearts* guitarist Declan Sinnott, Mary produced her debut album *Mary Black* (Dara 1983), a record of traditional, contemporary and jazz music. After an Irish tour with Declan Sinnott, she joined the inventive Irish traditional band *Dé Danann* with whom she recorded an album and toured America and the British Isles. After two highly acclaimed albums of pure Irish folk, *Anthem* with *Dé Danann* and her own *Collected* (Dara), both in 1985, Mary Black became a respected figure in Irish music, one who had proved her ability as a talented multi-faceted artist. It was the recording of *Without the Fanfare* that cemented her reputation as an all-rounder — the record combined rock, pop, traditional, jazz, middle-of-the-road and bluesy elements with professional aplomb. Some criticisms of her work would be that it's too safe, too old fashioned and dependent entirely on other people's songs — songs which seem to harp on about the vagaries of love affairs. Some might find her over romantic, others find her sound too polished, too superficial and too derivative for their taste. Detractions aside, the angelic voice of Mary Black, and the quality of Declan Sinnott's guitar work, on *Without the Fanfare* are without fault. After a final American tour with *Dé Danann* in August 1986, Mary Black decided to re-unite with her three brothers and sister for the October 1986 album *The Black Family* on Dara Records.

Mary Coughlan

Since the days of the formidable Rory Gallagher, Ireland had not been known as a country that produced blues musicians, that is, until the arrival of Mary Coughlan on the scene. A blues singer of great talent, Coughlan was catapulted to fame by the release of her debut album *Tired and Emotional* on Mystery Records in the autumn of 1985. She brought the entire tradition of black American blues vocalising to Irish folk rock, with an outlook that mixed politics with sociology, anger with humour. Being a liberated woman in a country that openly restricted women's rights gave Mary Coughlan all the material she required to plough the depths of the blues, to rightly re-invent the genre to suit her times.

Born Mary Doherty, she grew up during the heady 1960s in Galway town in the West of Ireland — a town quickly succumbing to the left-wing idealism of the international counter-culture. After being thrown out of school she did some nude modelling for a short while before emigrating to London to embrace hippie mysticism and its accompanying drugs, marijuana and LSD. After a spell as a road sweeper she returned to Galway, settled down and got married. Her interest in music was stimulated by the success of local traditional band *De Danann*, and specifically the singing of Dolores Keane. After trying out the pure Irish folk she realised that she would never make the grade and promptly changed to the raspy blues of her idols Billie Holiday, Ella Fitzgerald and Bessie Smith.

Still very much a conventional Irish housewife, Mary Coughlan decided in the late seventies to throw off the stereotyped role and live dangerously instead. Heavy drinking, smoking pot and throwing pints of Guinness over male musicians who took exception to her style of folk-blues, made her a local *cause célèbre*. Over the years, she was aided in her quest for a personalised blues style by Dutch musician Eric Visser, a guitarist/producer/songwriter of some note who had come to Galway to study pure Irish traditional music. Coughlan was also a strong defender of women's rights and became a fervent believer in natural motherhood, divorce and abortion, freedoms greatly restricted by the power of the conservative Catholic Church.

Finding the strain of leading a schizophrenic existence intolerable, Mary Coughlan separated from her husband in 1983, and with her three children dived headlong into the music world, a move that would change the history of folk rock in Ireland. After paying her dues through some tough gigging, she entered a talent competition in Salthill, Galway, and came a disastrous second. This failure pushed her into action and within two weeks Mary Coughlan, Eric Visser, Keith Donald of *Moving Hearts* and a bevy of Ireland's leading session musicians on assorted accordions, synthesisers, brass and percussion recorded the breathtaking *Tired and Emotional* album in Greenfields Studios, county Galway.

The record is a truly original concept from an Irish woman. Coughlan could express a range of personalities, from that of a little girl in the bossa nova styled 'Lady in Green' to that of a tough, world-weary mamma on 'Country Fair Dance'. Her sensuous pronunciations are more than just coquettish posing, for she expresses a socially aware perspective, one that has fully experienced the voyeurism of men, the problems of being sexually open in a hypocritical country and the never-ending drunken bar scenes so much an integral part of Irish life. Eric Visser's shady production and unusual minor key acoustic guitar are vital features of *Tired and Emotional's* attractiveness. A variety of sources identify the songs — New Orleans and Chicago jazz, Irish traditional music, black gospel hymns, Spanish and tango dance rhythms, Irish and American country forms and of course Billie Holiday, whose ghost can be clearly discerned on 'Meet Me Where They Play the Blues' or 'Nobody's Business But My Own'. The album's most succulent creation is 'Mamma Just Wants to Barrelhouse All Night Long', a rippling concoction of smouldering guitar and early hours blues.

Given the radical nature of Mary Coughlan's art, the self-financed album was, at first, turned down by all the major Irish record companies. Of course nobody could ignore *Tired and Emotional* for long and when industry man Jackie Hayden heard it, he set up a label for Mary Coughlan called Mystery, and released the record with the help of WEA. It soared to the top of the Irish charts and sold 20,000 copies within a year. The woman herself increased her notoriety by publicly calling for the legalisation of cannabis and by participating in the pro-divorce lobby during the referendum of 1986. Mary Coughlan was seen as a wild, foul-mouthed, tough female who would have nothing to do with traditional Irish sentiments and dangerously avowed a new liberty. She was a breath of fresh air both to Irish folk-rock and to society as a whole.

The release of *Ancient Rain* (Mystery) at the end of 1986 solidified her following and saw her move to a more vibrant rock base. On this album electric bass, electric guitar and *Scullion's* drummer Robbie Brennan give her music a stronger personality, and Keith Donald is still there on saxophone. Moreover a spine-chilling a capella version of 'Strange Fruit', a song that had historically become synonymous with the work of Billie Holiday, is blues at its very extreme.

Mary Coughlan had lived on the very edge, become a national star, appeared at Ronnie Scott's famous London jazz club and even supported archetypal black American bluesman Robert Cray all in the space of one glorious year. Her 1987 output continued to be of a high calibre with a single 'Ride On' (Mystery), involving the high-powered uilleann piping of Davy Spillane, and an album *Under the Influence* (Mystery/WEA), which affirmed her standing as the sole inventor of Irish folk rock blues.

Barry Moore

Most people associate the name Barry Moore with his older and more famous brother Christy Moore. True, Barry wrote the controversial 'Section 31' and the poignant 'City of Chicago' which Christy made famous. He also penned 'Remember the Brave Ones' which *Moving Hearts* popularised, but Barry Moore has been making his own definitive mark on Irish folk-rock since 1976. Unlike most Irish folk musicians he commenced his career by writing his own songs and from the age of twelve practised the guitar as much as possible. Since his local Newbridge College did not appreciate his lifestyle, particularly his hard drinking, he was expelled, but quickly found a place in Trinity College, Dublin. His love for acoustic music soon diverted him from his studies, but the traditional Dublin folk clubs did not take kindly to a musician who wrote his own folk material, so Barry Moore took the familiar boat abroad. His first album of personalised folk, *The Treaty Stone* (Mulligan 1978), created certain waves of interest in Europe, so Barry settled in Holland with saxophonist Eamonn Murray, where he eventually put down a second album. *No Heroes* (Ruby 1982) is an acoustic rock gem, full of human experience and intimate understandings. Still, his wild lifestyle drained him considerably and he wasn't able to capitalise on the positive critical reaction to his work. When he returned from Holland he unfortunately contracted a rare condition called tendonitis, which abruptly put an end to his music. After giving up his drinking and smoking, Barry Moore joined a younger rock outfit *Red Square* and became a leading voice at human rights benefits. His name was always appearing on posters for anti-nuclear gigs and he wrote many songs against the idea of siting nuclear stations or bases in Ireland. Having left *Red Square*, he succeeded in throwing off the mantle of Ireland's most depressing folk singer-songwriter, instead charming his audiences with a sober variety of neatly executed acoustic compositions. He still continued to write songs for his brother Christy, but in 1987 Barry Moore became very much a force in his own right.

Maura O'Connell

Coming from an Irish country background in Ennis, county Clare, Maura O'Connell first aired her vocal chords with Irish traditional group *Dé Danann*. After many successful international performances, she left to pursue a solo career in the autumn of 1983. Her American travels had brought her into contact with the bluegrass and country music of the southern states where *Dé Danann* caused quite a stir. Acoustic musicians in Nashville were blown out by the immaculate playing standards of the group, and wanted to be involved. Maura O'Connell liked the idea of bringing the Tennessee element into her brand of folk, so with the help of Philip Donnelly on all manner of guitars and ace side-man Bobby Whitlock on a variety of keyboards, she organised the recording of *Maura O'Connell* (Ogham 1983) in Nashville and Dublin.[11] This trans-Atlantic project is a lucid amalgam of country rock, American folk-rock, straight rock, some gospel tinges and even swing. Banjos, mandolin, auto-harp and tenor saxophone season the album, which was a real first for an Irish traditional singer. The best of the American recordings is a version of 'My Lagan Love', a plaintive folk song made even more evocative by the added wirey slide-guitar of Phil Donnelly. 'Saw You Running' and 'All of Me' were both recorded in Dublin; the first features the fiddles and uilleann pipes of *Stockton's Wing*, while the second is a bluesy jazz number recorded with Jimmy Faulkner's *Hotfoot* band.[12]

Maura O'Connell, with her infectious enthusiasm and crystal voice, had brought two traditional areas together and pushed them through a kaleidoscope of sounds. Nashville, always considered something of an anachronism in the face of experimental music, succumbed to a phenomenon called 'new acoustic music' during the eighties and had to take heed of such leading players as Mark O'Connor (violins/fiddles), Bela Fleck (banjo/guitars/mandolin), Jerry Douglas (dobro) and Edgar Meyer (arco bass). They, in turn, were open to combining their histories with those of Ireland's new folk artists and since Maura O'Connell was as comfortable with the Nashville sound as she was with her native music, a collaboration was proposed. Produced by Bela Fleck and arranged by Edgar Meyer, Maura O'Connell's second album, *Just in Time* (Ogham/Polydor 1986), was recorded at the Nashville Sound Connection. Despite a fair selection of Irish and American musicians, and a set of strong songs, the music veers strongly away from rock and could have been much tougher. Interesting aspects are the combination of Irish and American folk on Thom Moore's 'The Scholar', the inclusion of Paul Brady's 'Crazy Dreams', the powerful playing of Eric Clapton guitarist Albert Lee on 'Another Morning', a version of 'I Will' that is on a par with *The Beatles'* original and the incorporation of swing jazz in the tunes 'New Orleans' and 'Just in Time'. Even if Maura O'Connell's music was not exactly folk rock, her lasting contribution lay in the creation of a new dynamic fusion of Irish folk music and American ethnic music — something with a lot of rock potential.

Tríona and Micheál Ó Domhnaill

Best known for their work with Donal Lunny's traditional *Bothy Band*, Tríona and Micheál Ó Domhnaill had, since the break-up of that aggregation in 1979, followed diverse paths of explorative folk music. Both had found a greater diversity on the American scene, where many Irish folk musicians were making substantial livings and reputations. Micheál, an expert traditional guitarist, tin whistler, singer and keyboardsman, teamed up with fiddler Kevin Burke, and toured the US, before forming *Nightnoise* with American Bill Oskay. They released an eponymous debut album of classical/jazz/traditional music on the Windham Hill label in 1985 — a label that was a leading light in America's 'new age music' boom. Tríona had first gone to Nashville, but found her feet among the Irish music circles of Portland in the far north-west of America. Soon she formed a group, *Touchstone*, with Claudine Langille, Skip Parente, Zan McLeod and Mark Roberts. Their music was very lively and fresh — a potpourri of Scots, Breton, Irish and American folk, capped with an open rock sensibility. On *Jealousy* (Green Linnet 1984), Tríona Ní Dhomhnaill's spirited approach to contemporary folk can be discerned by the electric surge of the title track, the Joni Mitchell style of the self-penned 'Lonely Wanderer' and the compositional inventiveness of the instrumental 'Invisible Wings'. Tríona is a vocalist and keyboardist of unique ability, whose sound seems to come from the very bowels of Ireland. As an arranger and songwriter, she began to be noticed by the American music world and such country stars as Emmylou Harris, Dolly Parton and Linda Ronstadt expressed interest in her songs.

With all that going on, brother and sister were bound to meet up, and with the Scots brothers Phil and Johnny Cunningham *Relativity* was formed in 1985. Retiring to Phil's hotel in the Inner Hebrides, the four put their heads together and re-arranged a lot of traditional material to suit themselves. *Relativity* (Green Linnet 1985) is an unusual record in that it unselfconsciously treats folk music the way rock musicians treat their sources — as things to be re-formulated and embellished. *Relativity's* best contribution to Irish folk-rock is the track 'An Seanduine Dóite', where Tríona Ní Dhomhnaill goes jazz, pop and progressive all in one glorious flash.

The Pogues

The Pogues were the first ever group to play traditional folk music and punk rock combined. More than that, they represented a rough eighties version of a strain of Irish folk music that was dirty, violent and steeped in the hard-drinking culture of Ireland's working classes. They also appealed to Ireland's expatriate class, those who down through the generations believed that the streets of foreign countries were paved with gold and all too often found themselves in worse circumstances abroad, and lost themselves in sentimental alcoholic reveries. They posed a significant threat to the conservative element of Irish folk, most ostensibly the balladeers who saw their undisciplined approach as heresy. But most importantly they resuscitated the career of one of Ireland's greatest folk innovators, Terry Woods.

The Pogues began their life in North London in 1983 when Shane MacGowan, Jem Finer and Spider Stacey started singing and playing rebel songs in local pubs. They even busked for a while before being joined by accordionist James Fearnley and drummer Andrew Ranken. Jem was a London Jew who loved Irish trad. and played a mean banjo. Spider Stacey was a cockney lad, who loved Irish tin whistling. MacGowan was Irish and had been reared in Tipperary by a mother who was a prize-winning Irish folk singer. Showing an early talent for writing, he was sent to Westminster public school in London, but was expelled for bad behaviour. This rebellious streak brought him, through a succession of labouring jobs and bad experiences of London street life, to the era of punk rock and a band called *The Nips*. Realising that his local North London Irish enclave needed an injection of some ethnic vitality, Mac Gowan created *The Pogues*.

With the Irish-blooded Cáit O'Riordán on electric bass, *The Pogues* began to attract large crowds to their variety of washboard rock 'n' roll folk punk. It wasn't long before Irishman Dave Robinson spotted them and contracted the band to his Stiff label. Their first album, *Red Roses for Me* (1984), is packed full of drinking songs, seafaring paeans and emigrant verses. The performances were shambolic, and the group sounded like a pack of drunken Irish louts let loose in a studio. Public reaction was one of indignation, but English rock musician Elvis Costello liked them enough to have them as tour support and produce their first chart single, the sentimental 'A Pair of Brown Eyes'. As their notoriety spread, *The Pogues* began to play more concerts and after many festival appearances in England came to Ireland in June of 1985 to play the Cibéal Arts Festival in Kenmare. Re-enter *Terry Woods* into the history of Irish rock.

Woods's earliest experiments with folk-rock in the sixties and seventies had shaped the history of the genre, but lack of commercial viability had led him to give up on music and work in a factory. Living in obscurity in county Meath wasn't what Terry was cut out for, so he did some solo gigs and worked with Philip Lynott on the memorable 'Tennessee Stud' (Stud 1980) single. A regular at summer festivals around Ireland, Woods was still deeply committed to playing ethnic American folk music within an Irish context and was reputed to be one of the few living five-string banjo players capable of using the little-known clawhammer percussive strumming technique. Woods was impressed by *The Pogues'* irreverent attitude and they in turn were in awe of his abilities. So Terry Woods joined the group, along with Philip Chevron on guitar, and *The Pogues* became an increasingly native Irish phenomenon.

Yet 1985 was a year of fierce criticism for the band which was considered by the British press to be led by 'a toothless moronic pisshead' and to play 'streams of whiskey' instead of music. They fared no better on Irish radio where a B.P. Fallon special had them faced by the press and some hard-core Irish traditionalists who threw insults and expletives at the group. Whatever inroads *The Pogues* were making on traditional folk notions, there was still a strong conservative element that wanted them to disappear off the face of the earth. Popularity meant that the reverse would happen. In August 1985 their second album *Rum Sodomy and the Lash* (Stiff) was released and the critics had to eat their words, as Shane MacGowan proved himself to be a songwriter of some originality. Both 'The Sick Bed of Cúchulainn' and 'The Old Main Drag' draw on images of Irish degradation abroad; the first deals with alcoholism, the second with male prostitution. MacGowan showers his listeners with vulgar language and a music that is a sandwich of American ethnic, Irish traditional, punk rock and Scottish folk styles. A superlative version of Ewan MacColl's 'Dirty Old Town' is included. Although Terry Woods hadn't joined when the album was recorded the addition of Tommy Keane on uilleann pipes makes a significant difference, as exemplified by the beautiful Cait O'Riordan ballad 'I'm a Man You Don't Meet Every Day'.

At the beginning of 1986 *The Pogues* were voted Britain's best live act and skipped to America in the spring to do a riotous set of concerts in Boston, Baltimore, Washington and New York. Here Cait O'Riordan showed signs of disaffection — she would eventually leave and marry Elvis Costello. Before she was replaced by Daryl Hunt on bass, two important recordings were made. The first a four-track EP on Stiff titled *Poguetry in Motion* (1985), which displayed more care in recording and produced another important MacGowan composition in 'The Body of an American' — a look at the strong prejudices, hypocrisy and empty sentimentality of a certain element of Irish Americans. A point to be noted was that the band explicitly refused to support the actions of the IRA and those that financed them. The second important vinyl release was *Haunted* (MCA 1986), a three-track affair that incorporates some of the soundtrack for the Alex Cox film portrait of the sordid lives of punks Sid Vicious and Nancy Spungen, *Love Kills*. The title track is a complete change in direction for *The Pogues* towards acoustic rock. The rest is even more interesting: 'Hot Dogs', an adrenalin-rush punk song seems as unexpected as the melancholy of 'Junk Theme', a hard-driving folk-rock instrumental where Terry Woods really gives it his all on the

45 Cait O'Riordan, Berlin, 1985.

46 The elusive Terry Woods.

47 Philip Chevron, formerly of *The Radiators,* joined *The Pogues* in 1985.

48 Shane MacGowan in Dublin, winter 1986, recording 'The Irish Rover' with *The Dubliners* for their twenty-fifth anniversary.

49 Freddie White — an Irish perspective on the American tradition of singer-songwriter music.

45

46

47

48

49

111

banjo. Woods had obviously found his niche and made a considerable impression on the group's musicality since he played mandola, cittern, concertina, bagpipes and the banjo with equal brilliance.

Highly rated by Christy Moore and containing one of Irish rock's most important musicians, *The Pogues* are a peculiar adjunct to Irish folk rock. They brought with them a schizophrenic style that could be at home with Irish traditionalism while insulting its backwardness. Musically, they fell into a lot of camps at once and even had enough appeal to make the pop charts. When they came to Ireland near the end of 1986 to record with *The Dubliners*, it was as a sign of respect for a ballad group that had popularised Irish traditional music worldwide for twenty-five years. The project drew a lot of media attention and it was not surprising that a collaborative single, 'The Irish Rover' (Stiff 1987), sold in large quantities.

Freddie White

One of Ireland's most durable singer/acoustic guitar performers, Freddie White became famous for doing excellent cover versions of American artists such as Frank Zappa, Lowell George, and Randy Newman. During the seventies his interpretation of Guy Clarke's 'Desperados Waiting for a Train' alone boosted his career and attracted a substantial audience. It was his association with *Clannad* and the recording of *Freddie White Live on Tour 1978* (Mulligan) with them that dragged him from the relative obscurity of the folk clubs to a higher platform of popular recognition. *White's* background was a mixture of folk, rhythm and blues, blues and rock. Born in Cobh, county Cork, in 1951, he came from a musical family that had strong jazz leanings. By the sixties he was involved with a beat group, *The Krux*, who went on to support Rory Gallagher. After this he played solo folk blues in Cork and was very influenced by the then burgeoning folk-rock of English artists *Pentangle* and *Fairport Convention*. Freddie White found it difficult to rest easy and spent the early seventies vacillating between local bands, the European busking circuit and even tree surgery. His most important move was to de-camp to Dublin, where he fell in with the influential *Sonny Condell* and *Scullion*. He found his niche in the acoustic folk clubs of the capital, which were always full of eager patrons and in 1978 formed *The Freddie White Band* with Philip Donnelly on lead guitar. White was invited by *Clannad* to do acoustic support for their 1978 tour and his charismatic performances coupled with a professional debut album established him.

Much criticised by the so-called intelligentsia for doing cover versions, Freddie White has nonetheless satisfied that need in Irish folk-rock to have an Irish perspective on the American tradition of acoustic singer/songwriter music. With the addition of harmonium, mandolin, brass and electric instruments *Do You Do* (Mulligan 1981) is a much rockier effort, and by *Long Distance Runner* (Tara 1985) White was writing his own songs and involving the substantial abilities of *Moving Hearts*. A highlight of the album is Maura O'Connell's and Flo McSweeney's whooping background vocal harmonies on 'Love Like Blood'.

THREE

Van Morrison

Within the rock world the name Van Morrison causes controversy. To those not familiar with his work, his small, squat five-foot-six-inch frame and square, mute features convey little glamour or attraction, rather a sense of brooding or smouldering intent which doesn't fall into simple categorisation. Whatever Morrison is as a human being, he is not just a pop icon. Whatever excesses the rock 'n' roll circus of the 1960s produced, Van Morrison stands way above those weaknesses. It is well known that he doesn't like the media and rarely gives interviews. His articulacy has always been through his music — an awesome body of work which covers over twenty years of dedication and which, hooked into the rhythms of experience, is a distilled vision of rare genius.

A product of the Second World War generation, Van Morrison was born in Belfast on 31 August 1945, the only son of a musical family. His mother was a respected jazz singer, who loved gospel and country music. His father was a staunch appreciator of the blues and collected thousands of recordings of American black artists such as Bobby Bland, Muddy Waters, Ray Charles and John Lee Hooker. Christened George Ivan, the young Morrison was brought up a Jehovah's Witness, and coming from working class stock he had little in the way of easy options as a child; the emphasis was on self-sufficiency not on self-indulgence. He started writing poetry at eleven and while at Orangefield Secondary School took music lessons and practised hard at night. At the age of twelve he was involved in local skiffle bands and by his thirteenth birthday could competently play guitar, harmonica and the saxophone. Morrison knew what he'd have to do: 'Some people are brought up on jam, I was brought up on Leadbelly and heads like that. I was nervous, but y'see man I got these depressions and I had to sing about them.'

In 1959 he quit school to start his musical career in a local showband, *The Monarchs*, a guitar/harmonicas combo who aped the American rock 'n' roll hits of the period. Morrison was eager to see a change in their repertoire to rhythm and blues and to this end brought his saxophone into the band. Belfast audiences were not yet ready for this type of raw sound and Van had to supplement his meagre earnings with stints as a window cleaner. Wanting to make the big-time, *The Monarchs* ventured to Scotland and then London where they were recognised in jazz circles and promptly sent to Germany to play the armed forces clubs of Heidelberg, Frankfurt and Cologne. Here Morrison fell in with black GIs, who understood his love of the blues, and also met some black musicians. Jamming sessions ensued and *The Monarchs* were at their best doing versions of Ray Charles and James Brown standards for the American soldiers. After a year of seven-hours-a-night, seven-days-a-week gigging, the band returned to Belfast and fell asunder. Morrison wanted a hard-core rhythm and blues group so he went to London in 1963 to try and get support, but hastily returned to Belfast within weeks. Even though he had paid his dues early, the music scene did not return his hard efforts, so Van had to support himself for a while with manual work. By the winter of 1963 he had met a young guitar player, Bill Harrison, whose group *The Gamblers* were into doing rhythm and blues. The legendary *Them* was born.

Van Morrison's original *Them* line-up was: Billy Harrison (guitar), Eric Wricksen (piano), Alan Henderson (bass) and Ronnie Millings (drums). They set up a residency in Belfast's Maritime Hotel, where they excited audiences with a tight, taut rhythm and blues sound, augmented by Morrison's clipped vocal inflexions. The energy of the sessions came from a sharp mix of American folk-blues, rhythm and blues, and electric rock 'n' roll. Certainly the band were brimming with youth and anger, while Van Morrison couldn't try hard enough to express himself. The songs went into extended jams — a trouncing, thudding music, ferocious in its delivery. They were quickly noticed by music businessman Mervyn Solomon, who contacted his London-based brother Philip to come over and manage the group. Contracts were signed and *Them* joined *The Rolling Stones* on Decca Records' recording artists' roster.

In the summer of 1964 the eighteen-year-old Morrison and his scruffy rhythm and blues band went to London where they started working on material in Decca's recording studios. After sorting out their sound, they recorded 'Baby Please Don't Go', a Big Joe Williams composition, and 'Gloria'. 'Baby Please Don't Go' is definitive mid-sixties rock music — frenetic guitar, sub-psychedelic, with a weedy organ, and ploughing the strength of the blues with that typical 'goin' down to New Orleans' phrase. Morrison's nasal intonation and harmonica top a mix which features a young Jimmy Page on electric guitar. Recorded with the help of American soul producer Bert Berns, the song was to be B sided with 'Gloria' — a clutter of ranting, stomping rage, which Morrison said worked better in twenty-minute versions. 'Gloria' became synonymous with the group and later became a hit for American band *The Shadows of Night*, and was subsequently covered by *The Doors* and Jimi Hendrix. 'Baby Please Don't Go' (November 1964) was fuelled in its progress up the charts by its adoption as signature tune for British pop programme 'Ready Steady Go'. In fact *Them's* performances on this show were pretty raw, sweaty and primitive, even by label mates *The Rolling Stones'* standards. All this exposure meant that the single reached number six in the UK charts and made a considerable mark in the States. By February 1965 Van Morrison was definitely on course.

This was a fast period in the music world. Both the media and Philip Solomon were eager to hype an image for *Them* of dark intentions bulging with guts, tension, menace and a hint of mystery, while the chunky rock poet and shouter extraordinaire consolidated the situation with the glamour of narcissistic delinquency. The scowling *Rolling Stones* had already made world headlines with a ruffian image and dirty riffs, but they were way ahead of *Them* in terms of cohesion. *Them* were up against stiff competition and what was worse they had a bad relationship with the hard-nosed Phil Solomon; they were constantly arguing among themselves and fell out countless times with their record company. Not surprisingly, their career was to be fairly problematic.

The next single 'Here Comes the Night' reached number two in the British charts in April 1965. Looking back, the song is a weak white version of what black musicians had been doing for years. It certainly didn't give any indication of what Morrison was capable of doing. Yet, it gave him the freedom to record two albums with *Them* and various session musicians, which between them would indicate his potential and future direction. During the remainder of 1965 *The Angry Young Them* (1965) and *Them Again* (1966) were recorded for Decca with the help of future Led Zeppelin axe-man Jimmy Page. Morrison was displeased with the results and *Them* went through several line-up changes before embarking on an American tour in the summer of 1966.[1] After playing Los Angeles with *The Doors* and *Love*, the group disbanded in financial disarray, leaving Van Morrison in a state of confusion and permanent suspicion of the record business.

When one looks at the thirty or more songs that *Them* cut between 1964 and 1966, a continuity in style and expertise is obvious. Clearly, Morrison was developing his vocal technique, while his jazz leanings were perceptible in the arrangements. 'Mystic Eyes' (1965) starts off with a wailing harmonica solo and then slows down like a train, only to be picked up by a frenzied vocal/guitar solo: 'One Sunday morning we went walking down by the old graveyard. . .', then guitar sneaks in. This song came from an experience of seeing children in a graveyard: 'The bright lights in the children's eyes . . . the cloudy light in the eyes of the dead . . . 'n' Mystic Eyes happened.'[2] 'One Two Brown Eyes' (1984) uses a trippy guitar needle while Morrison repeatedly vocalises the word 'hypnotise' over and over until it becomes pure sound. Again the seeds of future fruition are apparent in his vocal style.

In 'You Just Can't Win' (1965), his phrasing is performed over a slowly strummed guitar with cymbals and tambourine. Similar to *The Animals* in mode, the song gave vent to Morrison's early compositional talents:

> One more coffee, one more cigarette
> One more morning trying to forget
> If I had the chance to join your dance
> I wouldn't like to bet your game is something yet . . .

Morrison uses clear vocal intonations to hammer home the meaning, his clipped vocals resonating as he utilises his voice as an instrument. The period of teenage sax playing was being put to innovative use. 'My Lonely Sad Eyes' (1966) is a very powerful acoustic guitar number. Morrison's range covered skiffle, blues, rhythm and blues, jazz, bluegrass and rock 'n' roll. You name it, Van had it. Just listen to the rumbustious piano on 'Bad or Good' (1966) or the spooky piano of Peter Bardens on 'If You and I Could Be as Two' (1965). One realises that it was the authenticity of the emotions with Van Morrison, not the style of the times or weak fashion trends. If some numbers were too like Mick Jagger and company

50 A sense of brooding or smouldering intent that doesn't fall into simple categorisation — Van Morrison at the start of an illustrious career.

51 In 1964 Decca described *Them* innocently as a group of 'five young Irish boys'. In reality, Van Morrison's crew were known to be the most menancing and trouncing white rhythm and blues band on the English club scene.

52 One of the greatest rhythm and blues bands of all time — *Them*, with Van Morrison, the tousle-haired blond youth *(centre, back)*.

51

52

for comfort, others bore little resemblance to anything ever heard. Angst born of a city existence, the frustration of constraint, ecstasy and agony all in one package, Morrison at twenty was treading the dark path of Robert Johnson and Bob Dylan, communicating the piercing emotions of an outsider and the harsh reality of alienation.

Morrison's version of Dylan's 'It's All Over Now Baby Blue' (1966) was something of genius. To instil the original with even more emotion was hard to do, but he did it. With sparkling guitar and piano, he restrains and controls his voice to get the maximum impact from Dylan's cutting words, resulting in an aural burst of sadness and haunting invocation. Even more important was his version of Paul Simon's 'Richard Cory' (1966).[3] It opens with the tightest acoustic guitar and electric guitar sounds that *Them* ever played, and Van spits out the words in a belligerent way. The song portrays social inequality and surprisingly doesn't end as the original does with

> So my mind was filled with wonder
> When the evening headlines read that:
> 'Richard Cory went home last night
> And put a bullet through his head.'[4]

but continues with Morrison improvising on the refrain with acoustic guitar strums:

> But I, I, I work in his factory
> And I don't dig the life I'm livin'
> And I don't dig my poverty.
> And I wish that I could be
> And I wish that I could be
> Aaaaaaand I wish that I could be
> Richard Cory!
>
> Aaaaaaand I wish that I could be
> I wish that I could be
> Aaaaaaand I wish that I could be
> Just like Richard Cory
> Just liiiiiiaaahhhhhhkeeeeee,
> Richard Cory
> Richard Cory
> Richard Cory
> Richard Cory.

The ending conveys a great sense of the underdog, while the musicianship and the arrangement are potently pristine.

Throughout the *Them* period, Van touched on his essence with vocalisations that let loose a demon. Brass and acoustic instruments were used to add feeling and nuance and some songs were arranged in jazz vein. Yes, he was definitely a man of rare talent who had started pretty young. With 'Hey Girl' (1966) we glimpse the style that would predominate in later years. Flute, piano and guitar summon up an evocative mood, slowly drawing out lyrics in a drifting nostalgia. It's far too short, though, but Morrison would do something about that in the future. Songs like 'I'm Gonna Dress in Black' (1965) and 'I Put a Spell on You' (1966) summon the demon of the black blues. 'Turn on Your Love Light' (1966), like 'Gloria', was a stage favourite and conveyed on record the trouncing nature of the band live. 'I Feel Alright' utilises the familiar vocal clipping technique — just listen to any Decca sampler and you'll get the picture.

It was a simple twist that led *Them* on the road to eventual disintegration, leaving Van where he had started, back in his Belfast homeland. He wasn't the type to ignore band and management hassles, yet he wanted to express himself according to his own standards and not someone else's. He was caught between two stools: his personal vision and the commercial market. American producer Bert Berns had produced some of his earlier work and saw the enormous potential in the man. Berns was into the soul groove, working with such performers as *The Drifters* and *The Isley Brothers*. He was so successful that he could afford to set up his own Bang/Shout label and promptly sent Morrison his air fare to New York and an advance on four singles. Back in the studio Van was again expressing himself on vinyl. The results once more proved his suspicions of the music business as they turned out to be just a patchy collection of songs aimed at the charts. 'Brown Eyed Girl' is a very pop-oriented soul single which skated into the American charts at number five in May 1967. 'Spanish Rose' is in a similar mould yet the flamenco guitar and up-tempo beat was just right for the period. Morrison's true fervour was well down in the mixes.

The eight tracks he recorded were released in an appropriately psychedelic package called *Blowin' Your Mind* (Bang 1967). Morrison saw this as a deceitful move since most of the arrangements and playing were, to his mind, unfinished. The work contains Hendrix-like guitar solos, fuzzy organs and rough percussion. The songs are short and allow him little free rein to explore his personal technique. One track, however, stands head and shoulders above the rest. This is the ten-minute 'T.B. Sheets', a song of painful frustration in the face of the agony of acute illness, his strongest and harshest creative accomplishment from this period, unbelievable in a young man of twenty-one.

'T.B. Sheets' commences — a weedy organ tunes up, smouldering drums and rhythm guitar come in from behind, a whispering, shrill harmonica has an impending tone:

> Now listen Julie baby it ain't natural
> for you to cry in the midnight.

The girl is very ill with tuberculosis and at night it becomes terrifyingly claustrophobic, 'In the wee small hours long for the break of dawn'. His sense of helplessness and indignation, as a visitor to her sick bed, pierces through the crying sound of harmonica and guitar. His own terror comes over in his fearful vocal, accentuated by screaming guitar:

> Hah! So open up the window
> and let me breathe ...

He gasps insanely on these lines, you can literally feel his pain. He continues as the tempo increases:

> ... lookin' down on the street below
> and I cried for you, honey.
> The cool room, Lord! the fool's room
> The cool room, Lord! the fool's room
> I can almost smell your T.B. Sheets
> I can almost smell your T.B. Sheets
> On your sick bed, on your sick bed
> I gotta go
> I gotta go ...

The song is a complete exorcism of a harrowing experience, and shows that Morrison was destined for much more than mere pop music.

Van took a break from the city and moved out to Cambridge, Massachusetts, with his fiancée, Janet Planet. There he hung out in clubs and met black rhythm-and-blues musicians. He even performed the odd time, his music moving more towards acoustic jazz than contemporary pop. Having refreshed himself he returned to New York to record more for Berns. The results were again below his genius and the new album, inappropriately titled *The Best of Van Morrison* (Bang 1967), was bolstered by the inclusion of five tracks from the first Bang album. The only new song of consequence is 'Backroom', which displays Morrison's strong point as an intuitive vocal improviser — his voice seems more forward than on previous recordings and the acoustic guitar hums like a bird. Another album was scheduled to come out of Morrison's association with Bang, but it was abruptly halted by Bern's death from a heart attack in December 1967. Morrison struggled on and played East Coast clubs with Tommy Kilbania (bass) and John Payne (flute), but he was robbed in the process by unscrupulous opportunists. His efforts to convey his unique vision had hardly been allowed to bubble to the surface, but he was writing at a fierce rate, goaded on by his poverty and seemingly hopeless situation. Despite all he had been through, Van Morrison had the future clearly in mind and knew that he could turn his past experiences into something worthwhile.

ASTRAL WEEKS

Finally, Joe Smith, president of Warner Brothers, recognised Morrison's potential and signed him to a new contract. This time everything was in order and Van was allowed a free hand in the recording of one of the most extraordinary albums of all time, *Astral Weeks*. The eight tracks breathe with life remembered, tasted, visited, revisited, renewed, anguished and melted, finally liberating themselves in a stream of vocal/acoustic improvisations. An album of enchanting beauty and deep understanding, it drew an emotional reaction from anyone that heard it. The album is a milestone in contemporary rock music, an everlasting masterwork.

Indicative of how chance can operate to produce results that days of application cannot yield, *Astral Weeks* was recorded in the hot summer of 1968 in an astonishing two days. The tracks themselves were put down live in two eight-hour sessions, and sound natural and automatic. The individual songs are supported by a range of stringed instruments, giving the aura of a musical plain stretching through jazz, classical and folk. The human strength of Morrison's vocals coasts evenly in tune with the instrumentation. The lyrics themselves are pure poetry and single Van Morrison out as a true genius.

The songs flow into one another, each within the acoustic folds of the following professional musicians, handpicked by Morrison himself: Jay Berliner (guitar), Richard Davis (acoustic bass), Connie Kay (drums), Warren Smith (percussion and vibraphone), John Payne (flute and soprano saxophone).

Morrison's voice is the central force, while the other sounds act like pigmentation on canvas, conveying mood in hue and colour. The tapestry of swirling sounds is controlled by the acoustic bass, which acts as a lead instrument — an innovation in itself. From the very opening, the bass playing of Richard Davis stands out, driving the emotion with a plucking freedom. The acoustic guitar comes on next and we are quickly drawn into an aural reverie:

> If I ventured in the slipstream
> between the viaducts of your dreams
> Where immobile steel rims crack
> and the ditch in the back road stops
> Could you find me, would you kiss-a-my eyes
> And lay me down in silence easy
> To be born again
> To be born again . . .

This, the title track, implores an understanding of the creative spirit — to allow oneself to let go, to trust in feelings. Morrison begs understanding from someone, be it lover or some other person. His voice is given full stretch as the flutes and strings build up in the background and he wails: 'Theeere youuu gooo, standing with a look of avarice.' His indignation increases as he expands the image, then images collide one after the other as the instruments sail around in free association. The first verse is repeated again, then the song drifts upward on the imploring tone of the following lines:

> To be born again
> In another world, darlin'
> In another world
> In another time
> Got a hormone high
> I ain't nothing but a stranger in this world
> I'm nothing but a stranger in this world
> Got a hormone high
>
> In another land
> So far away

> So far away
> Way up in the heavens
> Way up in the heavens
> Way up in the heavens
> Way up in the heavens
> In another time
> In another place
> In another time
> In another place
> In another time
> In another place
> In another time
> In another place
> And another face ...

He laughs, hums and vocalises satisfaction as the piece reaches a climax. The song feels like a complete exorcism of feeling through the medium of music. The rhythm slows, the acoustic guitar is picked, the bass drones, and Van breathes satisfaction. One is taken aback by its power.

The next song, 'Beside You', is a full, reflective hallucinatory vision of childhood innocence and discovery. The subject has often been described as Morrison himself as a child, but the song is so dramatic as to involve any listener in its emotional vortex. The acoustic guitar is played in classical mood but slowly, very, very slowly. The vocals again involve the listener in a landscape of tone and vacillating feelings. This time we are in the past — backstreets, narrow roads, darkness, church bells:

> And all the dogs are barkin'
> Way out on the diamond studded highway
> where you wander.
> And you roam from your retreat and view ...

Morrison looks back on the illusory freedom of childhood and youth, then the emotions swell as the song gets deeper and deeper, and the flutes and guitars pick up on the intensity. In the following lines the way 'breathe in' and 'breathe out' are sung is uncanny:

> You breathe in, you breathe out
> You breathe in, you breathe out
> And you're high on your high-flyin' cloud.
> Wrapped up in your magic shroud as ecstasy
> surrounds you.

The album comes down from these heights for the fast 'Sweet Thing'. The upright bass hits a faster beat, the guitar work is swifter and the percussion more shrill. The song is lighter in tone. He hollers, 'And I will never ever ever grow so old again', thankful that 'you shall take me strongly in your arms again'. This flight over, we are returned to Belfast for the next reminiscence, 'Cypress Avenue' — a wealthy area of tree-lined grace where Morrison found certain inspiration. The guitar is slower and contains what would become a trademark in later work — the upswing strum charging the chord. Again we are hearing experience relived. 'I may go crazy before that mansion on the hill', while 'inside shakes like a leaf on a tree'. The mood is autumnal with 'leaves' an ongoing image imitated by strings. The frenetic music is in some ways too harsh, the lyrics slightly obscure, but considering the intensity of the work this is hardly surprising.

What is difficult to imagine is that Van was only twenty-two when *Astral Weeks* was recorded. The album portrays a man whose deeply felt experience has led him to a total expression in words and music. The eight songs are divided between the two sides of the album 'In the Beginning' and 'Afterwards'. The second side opens with a happy song performed with high energy in the midst of some very up-tempo jazz music. 'The Way that Young Lovers Do' is a free celebration of the joys of young love — how all the simple things are deeply moving, and how every gesture and detail is amplified. The feeling of dancing, merry-go-round fun is inherent in the carnival tone of the brass and horns. It's a definite break from earlier tracks — more exhilarating and lighter in tone.

The shift in reminiscence continues with the slower 'Madame George' — a completely mystical piece of writing. The circular spiritual nature of the work is at its most prominent in this song. The various images are uncannily complex and direct us to question our whole view of our own and other people's lives — how small fragments contribute to new directions, or how some small observation can catalyse a whole new realisation. Morrison doesn't answer any questions, but puts his very soul on view, so that the listener can appreciate his or her own experience in the light of a fellow human at one with the natural cycles of living. The song is the most refreshing on the album and continues the uptone of deliverance:

> Down on Cypress Avenue
> With the child-like vision creeping into view
> The clicking clacking of the high heeled shoes ...

A potent sexuality is present in this song, yet the meaning hangs elusive as the stream of images follow one after the other like a film. Then he mentions Madame George, who personifies hidden sensuality — something a young child knows instinctively will involve him in the future:

> you're gettin' weaker and your knees begin to sag
> you're caught out playing dominoes in drag
> The one and only Madame Joy [sic] ...

Childlike guilt — dressing up in women's clothes at play — surfaces when the older woman enters; her name is pronounced mistily as Joy, which is literally the effect of her presence.

The images seem to paint a picture of sexual encounter; the decor of late nineteenth-century parlours is strongly evoked. He repeats words with a trance-like lisp: 'the love the loves the love the loves the love the loves the love the loves the love the loves the loves to love the love the love the love'. He bids farewell to the dream-like vision, setting the whole song in perspective with the words: 'in the backstreet ... down home ... say goodbye'. The upright bass and strings hold the emotion; words, repeated memories flood his mind as the song fades out and the exorcism is completed.

The next song is more direct and obvious. 'Ballerina' is a simple love song. But for this writer the last track of *Astral Weeks* is the most distinctive. 'Slim Slow Slider' is a deeply moving portrait of a woman mercilessly addicted to heroin, caught up in the negative aspects of the city and the subversive nature of the drug. This song reveals Morrison at his most objective — a clear insight into the predicament of a fellow human in pain. The sadness of the lyrics is drawn by the blue tinge of slow guitar, bass and the atmospheric flute-like quality of the soprano saxophone:

> Slim slow slider
> horse you ride is white as snow.
> Slim slow slider
> horse you ride is white as snow.
> Tell it everywhere you go.
> Saw you walkin' down by Ladbroke Grove
> This morning
> Saw you walkin' down by Ladbroke Grove
> This morning. [*laughs*]
> Catching pebbles for some sandy beach
> You're outta reach ...

The words hang in the air with crystal candour. The opening contains a double cryptic image: the fairytale idea of a woman on a horse, but the word 'horse' is also the slang term for heroin, which of course is a white powder. The repetition of the lines makes one remember them; then they are bonded by the piercing tone of 'Tell it everywhere you go'. The narrative continues:

> Saw you early this morning
> With your brand new boy and your Cadillac
> Saw you early this morning
> With your brand new boy and your Cadillac
> You're goin' for something
> And I know you won't be back.
>
> I know you're dying, baby
> And I know you know it too
> I know you're dying, baby
> And I know you know it too
> Everytime I see you
> I just don't know what to do.

A grim picture, and one that was the truth for many during the late sixties and early seventies, especially those in the music business. The meaning is clear from the words — sordid elements of conspicuous consumption (Cadillac), superficial relationships (brand new boy) and the endless search for more pleasure. The song ends abruptly with 'I just don't know what to do', all instruments just ratcheting down the scale and a conga drum slapping into fade. It's the shortest song on the album, the most unusual and a piece of pure empathy. Thus Van Morrison made his intentions clear and the reaction was one of pure admiration for a work of such intensity. The album was one of the finest ever realised, and continues to sell years after its release. *Astral Weeks* will never be strait-jacketed by time or style because it still manages to possess a unique all-over vision of incomparable unity and strength.

AFTERWARDS . . .

Van Morrison contends that he was starving when *Astral Weeks* came out and, because of its complexity, the album wasn't an immediate huge commercial success. Still in New York, he spent the next period gigging and concentrating on new songs. After finding musicians that reached his standards, he set about recording the follow-up album *Moondance* (Warner Brothers) in late 1969. The sound is more direct and tighter than on *Astral Weeks*, using less meandering improvisation and more distinct structures. More instruments are used, with brass being the dominant feature. The following range of musicians were hand-picked by Morrison: Jack Schroer (alto and soprano sax), Colin Tillton (tenor sax and flute), Jeff Labes (piano, organ and clavinette), John Platania (lead and rhythm guitars), Gerry Malaber (drums and vibes), John Klingberg (bass), Guy Masson (conga drum), Emily Houston, Judy Clay and Jackie Vardell (backing vocals).

Van Morrison himself produced the record with his own strident acoustic guitar providing a powerful rhythm. This time we get ten tracks, starting off with 'And It Stoned Me', a mellow acoustic piece with horn sections tightly arranged in a lush spatial sound:

> Me and Willy standing there
> with a silver half-a-crown
> Hands are full of fishing rods
> With the tackle on our backs
> We just stood there getting wet
> With our backs to the fence
> Oh the water Oh the water Oh the water
> Hope it doesn't rain all day
> And it stoned me to my soul
> Stoned me just like goin' home.

This again is childhood remembered, but with more clarity and gusto, as he recounts the simple pleasure of boys fishing. Acoustic guitar, horns and piano pop up here and there. 'Moondance' itself is clearly a healthy song about romance. Lovely rippling jazz piano, smooth guitar and terrific arrangements made this track easy material for radio and film use. Morrison was now entering mainstream consciousness with music well up to his personal standards and finely distilled:

> It's a marvellous night
> for a moondance.
> With the stars up above in your eyes.
> A fantabulous night to make romance
> 'Neath the cover of October skies ...

One significant element of Morrison's voice was its proximity to the sound of the saxophone. This element has been observed by others, and springs directly from his early interest in the instrument. With 'Moondance', each instrument is given a passage in turn — piano, sax, flute and of course the vocals, which are inflected before the end of the song like a horn. The style was to become Morrison's trademark and is developed throughout the album.

'Caravan' has a jumpy drum/sax beat directing the emotive vocals. It's the kind of song that stays in your head for days, and in live performance it became a vital hook in his repertoire. 'Into The Mystic' closes the first side and brings us back to the tone of *Astral Weeks*. A lovely light guitar strum, the light bass, electric guitar and drums preside over words of sweet melancholy, as we are carried away on the man's happiness. Morrison considered this period to be an important break from past hardship. This is clearly reflected in 'Brand New Day' where he sings:

> I've been used, abused and so confused
> And I didn't have nowhere to run ...

Further images of 'hands tied behind my back', or 'shoved out on the railway track', suggest a harsh, alienating experience. But there is an exalted hopefulness on the album and nothing is quite so stunning as the saxophone sound after the line 'when the foghorn blows' on 'Into the Mystic'. We know that the man is doing what he always wanted to do, with the dexterity and subtlety to match his emotion. This album brought him critical and commercial success and set him firmly on his path.

More settled and relaxed, Morrison had by this stage moved to Woodstock with his wife and friends. He was more laid back, so his music loosened up and became less intense. He was playing a lot more live music, yet his recorded work suffered. 1970 and 1971 also saw the release of two relatively minor works, considering the scope of his abilities. There was less concentration, more spontaneity and more free experimentation in his work of this period.

Van Morrison: His Band and the Street Choir (Warner Brothers 1970) is an unfortunate follow-up to his awesome work of the late sixties. The looseness of the twelve tracks is 'boppy' and carefree, with little intensity — Van was simply having fun. The band line-up is: Jack Schroer (alto, baritone and soprano saxophones, piano), Keith Johnson (trumpet and organ), John Platania (lead and rhythm guitars, mandolin), John Klingberg (bass), Alan Hand (piano and organ),

Dahaud Elias Shaar (drums, percussion, bass clarinet and backing vocals), Van Morrison (vocals, guitar, harmonica and tenor sax).

The sound was again of session jazz standard, with some of the best musicians in the country. 'Domino' opens the album with a raunchy sax sound (it became a 1970 US chart hit). The album has some good flashes — 'I've Been Working' with its fast horns and acoustic guitars catches a happy vibe with the line 'Set my soul on fire'. 'I'll Be Your Lover Too' is a black and sultry song, with beautiful classical guitar playing. 'Gypsy Queen' is a very strong combination of sax, vocals and acoustic guitar, while 'Sweet Jannie' is a blues number with a Claptonesque electric guitar. The album cover is atrocious and the sleeve notes worse. Morrison wasn't pleased with the results, which in truth were confusing — some fine songs but in the end no cohesion.

Tupelo Honey (Warner Brothers 1971) saw him go deeper into the country music of the Americas. Just before this album he played with *The Band*, who were American ethnic rock to the hilt. Since they were all fine musicians, Morrison involved himself with their 1971 album *Cahoots* (Capitol). He went to San Francisco for *Tupelo Honey*, displaying the amount of freedom he had within the American rock music scene, still in its flowery affluence. Here Morrison tried another experiment by re-jigging his musicians and going more country. With the usual brass and acoustic range he added pedal steel guitar and more drums. The album cover shows Morrison with his wife, Janet Planet, on a farm and the contents of the record are happy and playful, mirroring their country lifestyle atop a forested mountain in San Rafael, Marin County, California.

'Wild Night' and 'Straight to Your Heart' are speedy rushes of happiness, and the general air of the album is sweet simplicity and connubial bliss. 'Tupelo Honey' itself is an acoustic ballad with a definite touch of earlier mastery and became Van's personal, in-concert, favourite for years to come. Even though Morrison was not completely satisfied with the album as a whole, it sold a third of a million copies and charted worldwide. Busy jamming and doing impromptu gigs with the likes of John Lee Hooker and Ramblin' Jack Elliott, Van began to regain his confidence as a live performer. He also had a studio built in Marin County and set up his own 'Caledonia Productions Company' in order to free himself from some of the more unscrupulous people operating in the music business at the time. Over the next two years his personal life was to be shaken by the break-up of his marriage to Janet Planet, a period which caused a lot of emotional scarring. Not surprisingly his next album of music was to reflect his angst-ridden state.

St Dominic's Preview (Warner Brothers 1972) is the third great Van Morrison album. The blue condition of the man is evinced on the blue cover — sitting on church steps in San Francisco in front of blue doors, wearing blue jeans and strumming his acoustic guitar. The whole album is acoustic-flavoured and contains the usual host of prime session musicians.

'Jackie Wilson Said ...' opens the record in fine burlesque fashion. The next song, 'Gypsy', compares his own aloneness with that of the nomadic race. With saxophones coaxing the nuance that the piano and acoustic guitar bring, the song reaches its initial crescendo:

54

53 A happy and contented man, Van Morrison on his brief visit to Ireland in 1973.

54 Van Morrison as solo performer in the early 1970s. No other Irish rock artist would hold on to fame for such a long time.

55 Van Morrison at the Lisdoonvarna Folk Fair in the summer of 1983. His performance gathered rave reviews all around.

No matter where you wander
No matter where you roam
Any place you lay your hat
You know that's home ...'

Sweetest sound of two guitars
Round a campfire bright ...

The change of tempo and sweet guitars summon the demon in Van Morrison.
Like Dylan, he sings and writes much better songs in states of depression than
happiness. With the acoustic guitar as his driving instrument the album reaches
its first peak on the eleven-minute epic 'Listen to the Lion'. Again we are pulled
into his burning emotion, again we are part of a free flow of images. Repetition is
the key factor as every line builds up and up and up:

All my love was tumbling down . . .
I, I, I shall search my soul
I, I, I shall search my very soul
I shall search my very soul for the lion . . .

This is phrased and repeated over and over again. It is close to the acoustic blues
of *The Rolling Stones* on *Sticky Fingers*, similar in the way the guitar work has that
same frightened tension. The song bubbles with slow rage; Morrison is
wounded but strong. The guitars are in tune with his pain. He just lets the music
take his spirit wherever it wants to go and the result on this track is in the same
vein as *Astral Weeks*.

After getting through the first side, it is hard to imagine that this is the same
man who put down the previous *Tupelo Honey* and *Street Choir* albums. 'St
Dominic's Preview' itself is a tour de force.

Cleaning all the windows
Singing songs about Edith, dear soul
And I hear blue strains of no regrettion
Across the street from Cathedral North o' Down
Meanwhile back in San Francisco
Trying hard to make this whole thing blend ...
It's a long way from Buffalo
It's a long way from Belfast city too ...
This time you bit off more than you can chew
As we gaze out on, as we gaze out on
As we gaze out on, as we gaze out on
St Dominic's Preview ...'

Note his reference to the boyhood odd job of cleaning windows and the
interleaving of several aspects of his complex experience. It is definitely in the
'stream' mould, with dreamy connections impossible to just think up. Look at the
hatchet meanings in the following lines:

All the orange boxes are scatterin'
Against the Safeway supermarket in the rain
And everybody feels so determined
Not to feel anyone else's pain
No one makin' no commitments
To anybody but themselves ...

This is a cutting indictment of consumerism to rival any Dylan song. It continues to increase in complexity, trundled along by strong sax and drums. It tallies flags and emblems while throwing in the strange line 'Where every Hank Williams' railroad train just cry', invoking more blues. The song continues auto-biographically, listing his own experiences with record companies: 'And they's flying too high to see my point of view,' he spits.

To say that Van Morrison communicates directly through his music is in itself enough — no need for mythology or image building, the usual trappings of commercialism. When Mick Jagger conceived the phrase 'sixties rock was built to last', he could have had Morrison in mind. When the first acoustic guitar strains of 'Almost Independence Day' trap our attention we know instinctively that the piece has that touch of genius. Over ten minutes long, the song is a soft musical stream hinging on magical chops of the acoustic guitar. It swells and gushes, yearning for our attention. Slowly, like a wave breaking on the shore, the song develops with slow drums and horns making their entry:

I can hear them calling
way from Oregon
I can hear them calling
way from Oregon
And it's almost, Independence day.

His voice arcs on the words 'hear' and 'way', and the music unfolds slowly with the lines:

I can hear the fireworks
I can hear the fireworks
I can hear the fireworks
Up and down the San Francisco Bay ...
I can hear them echoing ...
I can see the boats in the harbour
Way across the harbour
Light shining out
Light shining out
In a cool cool night
In a cool cool night ...

The words are enunciated through his attack on the acoustic guitar: the words 'up and down' have the guitar strings reverberating strongly; 'I can hear them echoing' has the instrument being literally strafed along the fretboard. His emotion and feeling take over and he loses himself in the expression. It's unadulterated muse from the depths of his soul. He continues to repeat the line 'way up and down the line' over and over again, allowing the double bass, horns, drums and bass to describe the music. Near the end he attacks his guitar so sharply that one is taken aback by the way the strings almost jump out of the speakers. 'Almost Independence Day' counts as Van Morrison's best work from his middle period.

Still in America he was working fast, and 1973 saw him capitalise on his artistic freedom. Early in that year came *Hard Nose the Highway* (Warner Brothers) which hit harder at society in the lyrics, while maintaining perfectionist musical standards. Horns, strings, piano, guitars, bass, vibes and the Oakland Symphony Chamber Choir give the album the dimensions that Morrison was itching for all along. The eight songs cover a large expanse of insight and experience. Songs of love, deceit, history and nature. It is a very complex work indeed. The beautiful 'Wild Children' acknowledges the post-war generation:

> We were the war children
> Born 1945
> When all the soldiers came marching home
> Love looks in their eye
> Tennessee Tennessee Williams
> Let your inspiration flow
> Let it be around when we hear the sound
> When the springtime rivers flow
> When the rivers flow
> Rod Steiger and Marlon Brando
> Standing with their heads bowed on the side
> Crying like a baby thinking about the time
> James Dean took that fatal ride, took that ride.

This breaks into an instrumental jazz piece with soft lead piano and guitar. He airs his feelings about American capitalism with 'The Great Deception', indicting all participants in the process: 'plastic revolutionaries take the money and run', 'rich rock singers with Cadillacs', 'love city', 'Hollywood', even the art world for making fortunes from the work of artists who died in poverty.

> Did you ever, ever see the people
> With the teardrops in their eyes
> I just can't stand it, stand it no how
> Living in this world of lies ...

This year was an important one for Morrison. He took all his musicians on the road to perform throughout Europe and America, for by now a huge audience was waiting to catch a glimpse of the living legend. The people who had stuck with him all along made up the *Caledonia Soul Orchestra*, and the live concerts were so perfect that the resultant live album *It's Too Late to Stop Now* (Warner Brothers 1974) is a goldmine. Morrison looks happy and strong on the cover and insert photos show a man who instinctively knows that what he has is very special. The double album is made up of cuts from London and California shows and sounds better than a studio record. For those not familiar with the man's work it is an essential purchase as its eighteen tracks chart the very best of his career. The sustained quality of playing makes the album a landmark in live recording, disqualifying rock music's lazy notion that this type of venture never works properly.

The live version of 'Into the Mystic' is better than on *Moondance*, while 'Caravan' reveals his style in all its inflexion and innuendo. 'Cypress Avenue' gets a brass treatment and blues originals are covered with suitable respect. Willie Dixon, Sonny Boy Williamson and Sam Cooke are all given special dedications. 'I Believe to My Soul', by Ray Charles, is a remarkable tribute to a man who had inspired Van to take the plunge into music. The 1973 tour showed that Morrison had achieved his musical ambition while his fame brought a physical freedom that he had never had. Only twenty-eight years of age at this time, he decided to return to Ireland for a holiday with his new girlfriend. His cult status in his native country was enormous. Absent since the mid-sixties, his colossal musical feats were legendary. Van Morrison had a mystical aura, and, since many Irish people had never seen their hero, this was as good an opportunity as any.

OBSESSIVE INDIVIDUALITY

In October 1973 he spend three reflective weeks in the south of Ireland. The national television service RTE were eager to satisfy demands from the public that he be given air time. Indicative of Morrison's attitude to the media is the way he handled his appearance on television. 'Talk about Pop', featuring an exclusive programme on Van Morrison, was originally to be two hours long. The final version was only half an hour. What happened in between? Bill Keating, the programme producer, talks about the incident: 'The first meeting with Van Morrison to discuss the programme details was in a Howth restaurant. We had to wait for a very long time, until he had finished his dinner and other things, before he would see us. He was very arrogant and demanded a grand piano and other instruments to be arranged in the studio. Also, a lot of his entourage had to be present during the filming. When we finally got him in the studio he tinkered around for the whole duration, failing to settle at any one thing. He never played the piano and didn't talk very much. Most of the footage was useless with the exception of certain bits where he played some acoustic guitar songs.'

He returned quickly to America to record his next album in his own Caledonia recording studio. While this was a sudden departure from Ireland, the country had given him enormous inspiration and the resulting *Veedon Fleece* (Warner Brothers 1974) was a return to the mystical acoustic style of *Astral Weeks*. The strange cover shows Morrison kneeling with two Irish wolfhounds, a photograph taken by Tom Collins in Ireland, and the album comprises slow, moody pieces of abstract quality. The instrumentation is very sparse while the songs transmit his emotional responses to Ireland. Mercurial and abstract, it stands as Van Morrison's fifth work of true genius.

The first side is soft and delicate — slow songs of Irish romanticism with strings and woodwind instruments caressing Morrison's low vocals. 'Fairplay' mentions Oscar Wilde. 'Linden Arden Stole the Highlights' is about an Irish American. 'Who Was that Masked Man' tells of the period of highwaymen. On the latter he raises his voice to sound like a black soul singer. 'Streets of Arklow' closes the first side with a warm reminiscence centred on acoustic guitar and full-blown flute.

The second side commences with the more direct 'Bulbs', a song of forceful vocals and up-tempo rhythms. 'Cul de Sac' and 'Comfort You' follow in country flavours. 'Come Here My Love' is a surprisingly short melancholic love song. The final cut is the flute/strings-based 'Country Fair', an Irish mystical appreciation, a loosening of images remembered, a regeneration of experience past, a slow exorcism, a cyclical perception — a musical metamorphosis from human state to spirit. The abstraction of this album makes it more ethereal than *Astral Weeks* and to this day it remains enigmatic and distant.

JAZZ — THE TRUE ESSENCE OF VAN MORRISON

When Morrison played Dublin in 1974 he appeared at the Olympia Theatre with a scaled down unit called *The Caledonia Soul Express*.[5] The reaction was one of incredulity, but the reviews were positive for he had at last deigned to actually perform in his native land. The falsity of most people's perceptions was made clear. If one thinks of his attitude to the media, it is obvious that he wanted no part of the rock scene image, building fashion-conscious superficiality. He was indeed a jazz composer, skilled in his craft, who only wanted to produce perfectionist music. Like jazz men John Coltrane, Miles Davis, B.B. King, to name but a few, the quality came first, all the other candyfloss second. No wonder the man had little time for interviews and television appearances.

During the early seventies a very short television special was made from a flawless concert at London's Rainbow Theatre. The project was purposely commissioned by his record company, Warner Brothers. An authentic document of perfectionism and control, the film portrays Morrison at a performing peak. Relayed on RTE, and on BBC's 'Old Grey Whistle Test' several times, the footage was sheer excellence — Morrison quavering behind the mikestand, his orchestra perfectly synchronised, the music sultry and intense. The sound was jazz, not rock. The film revolved totally around the music and it was to become the most important visual document of his career.

Morrison confirmed his individualism by showing up at the Montreux Jazz Festival (summer 1974) without the usual *Caledonia Express*, but with Jerome Rimson (bass), Dallas Taylor (drums) and Pete Wingfield (keyboards) to form a jazz/blues jamming quartet. After appearances in Germany, Holland and at Knebworth Fair, plus a well received North American tour, his career became a puzzle to most outsiders, since little was heard or seen of him for a very long time. This gave rise to the usual false stories, sightings and speculations. His mystical aura grew once more. Meanwhile, Morrison was just redirecting himself after spending all of his youth working very hard for a living. He declined to appear publicly, devoting himself to studio experiments. The first, an album titled *Mechanical Bliss*, recorded with the Montreux Jazz line-up, received avid previewing in early 1975, but the work never saw the light of day. Another, a soul-oriented project, recorded late in the year in California, also got the hammer. Morrison's standards were uniquely high and went well beyond the confines of simple rock, where material gets cranked out indiscriminately. He guested on some people's albums though, his acoustic guitar, harmonica and saxophone giving the likes of Bill Wyman (of *The Rolling Stones*, who recorded *Stone Alone* in 1976) a taste of musical craftsmanship.

Besides small outings of this nature, Morrison had seemingly had enough of the music business. He had enrolled a solid team of accountants, lawyers and management, setting up his own production company in the process. He spent almost an entire year living life on his own terms — going where he liked, doing things that pleased him. He was also genuinely fatigued from the road. Most people didn't want to acknowledge his mere humanity and his, by any standards, strained transition from childhood to young adulthood. His physical appearance, indeed, belied his thirty-one years.[6]

American ethnic rock group, *The Band*, staged a retirement concert, The Last Waltz, in San Francisco at the Winterland auditorium on Thanksgiving Day, November 1976. This event was a tribute to those who had survived the sixties, and included a cast of legends: Bob Dylan, Neil Young, Joni Mitchell, Eric Clapton, Muddy Waters and Van Morrison. It was a very special tribute to an era of eclectic experimentation. Also on the bill was a gutsy blues singer named Dr John, or Malcolm John Rebennack. A catalytic influence on the young bands of the sixties, Dr John had involved himself with New Orleans bluesmen during the 1970s. Later known as MacRebennack or 'The Night Tripper', he developed his own unique soul/gospel sound. He had made an important impression on Morrison.

A Period of Transition (Warner Brothers 1977) is a collaboration between Morrison and Dr John. The usual collection of accomplished session musicians assist on an album of redirection. It has a more rocked-up sound but with a flat gospel quality. Here is real southern blues with that black tinge. Low saxophone features throughout and the downhome influence of Dr John on keyboards dominates the overall effect. Its plodding slowness and slight variety make this one of Morrison's minor contributions. He was indeed altering his perspectives — but to what end?

The answer came in 1978 with *Wavelength* (Warner Brothers), an album of tight up-tempo rhythms, catchy riffs, danceable songs and straight rock music. With Peter Bardens on synthesiser, keyboards and Roland horns, and a very strong rhythm section, the album is a pulsing adventure in quality rock. More cohesive and taut than the expansive work of *Veedon Fleece* or *Astral Weeks*, the album made a positive impact on the public, displaying Morrison as an artist of substantial resourcefulness. The title track is powerful, with bubbly synth sounds and high-pitched soul vocals spinning faster and faster, accompanied by the tempo of guitar and drums rolling along at a dizzying pace. 'Natalia' is an addictive creation, a Morrison 'pop' masterpiece whose sound is his salute to the new technology and its possibilities.

Even though Morrison had re-affirmed his position as a major league rock star, the late seventies were years of increasing anxiety for him. Firstly, his relationship with the media had gone out of control and after a series of disastrous confrontations with the English press and radio, Morrison found it increasingly more difficult to communicate at this level. Secondly, his live performances were erratic and after the unusual jamming sessions on American television and in English clubs during the 1977 transition year, Morrison decided to support the *Wavelength* album with an arduous autumn/winter tour of America, Britain and Ireland.[7] With a five-piece backing group which included Herbie Armstrong, Mickey Feat and Pete Bardens, Van Morrison commenced the US performances in good form, but by the time he got to the New York Palladium his temper was boiling because of poor sound conditions. After a few songs he cancelled the rest of the American dates and headed for his birth-place, a town that hadn't seen Morrison playing live in well over a decade.

The Belfast concerts of January 1979 were to bring all of Van's problems to a head. His arrival was sensationalised out of all proportion. The English press were flown in for a series of ugly and pointless interviews. Tickets were being sold at outrageous prices and, while efforts were being made to salvage Morrison's tarnished image, his excellent relationship with WEA Records was ruined by a press release relating to the previous New York Palladium fiasco. After playing Dublin he went to England where the media took their revenge and overly criticised his Hammersmith Odeon gig. Obviously a change of direction was crucial and Morrison retired to California to immerse himself in a new album.

Becoming more optimistic and gathering pace he quickly released his twelfth album *Into the Music* (Phonogram) in the summer of 1979. Basically one of easy listening music, the record has a lot more instrumentation than previous albums. Things like mandolin, viola and straviola encounter the usual acoustic brass while added trumpets and piccolo make for a strange sound. The inclusion of Robin Williamson (ex-*Incredible String Band*) on penny whistle and Ry Cooder on slide guitar show that Morrison was seeking to widen his musical dimensions even further. Albeit exploratory, *Into the Music* appealed to a wide spectrum of people and not surprisingly 'Bright Side of the Road' became an instant hit and an automatic radio choice.

COMMON ONE

The cover of Morrison's next album, *Common One* (Mercury 1980), showed the man walking peacefully up a country hillside, thus imbuing the project with a certain sense of mystery. Rumours were again rife that he was studying ancient philosophies, comparative religions, spiritual healing ideas and even educating himself in the precisions of English literature. A lot of these gained credence on the release of *Common One* which could only be described as a magical fountain of spiritual and aesthetic concerns. With a crack band of blues, jazz and rock side-men, Morrison vacated California and opted instead for the south of France where the album was recorded in ten straight working days during February.

Common One features four extended tracks of mood music with flute and flugelhorn playing eerie roles. 'Haunts of Ancient Peace' is Morrison streaming again — a song which flows subtly between vocal, slow bass and saxophone nuances. 'Summertime in England' seems to reach back into the past glories of English and Irish literature and merrily celebrates the spirit of T.S. Eliot, William Wordsworth, Samuel Coleridge, William Blake, W.B. Yeats and of course the 'streams of consciousness' of James Joyce over its incandescent fifteen and a half minutes. This ebbing, meandering song is Morrison's tribute to a frame of mind that had established his own genius on *Astral Weeks*. At the end he beckons to the listener to 'listen to the silence', one that can only be heard in rural environments such as hillsides, river valleys, country roads and so forth. This sheer joy with nature and its quietude is continued on 'When the Heart is Open', an absolute corporeal flood of images and feelings. Morrison's almost translucent vocal seems to literally spill out through a glittering ambience of vibes, bass, guitar and horns. The manifest talent of Van Morrison oozed from this album and one couldn't help but be emotionally moved and aesthetically stimulated.

The fact that Morrison had gone beyond the confines of previous work seemed to escape most critics who seemed intent on damning *Common One* for its supposed boredom, quasi-mythologising and self-indulgence. Van ignored the bullshit and retired to Mill Valley, California, a perfectly satisfied man. After a long rest period he went back on the road, but this time only to play a few scattered club venues around San Francisco. Instead of being involved in the rock-'n'-roll circus, Morrison seemed to relish learning about Celtic history and hanging out in Irish traditional music bars on the West Coast with old Irish buddies Herbie Armstrong and Phil Coulter. The latter were also involved in Morrison's new album project which was completed in Sausalito, California, near the end of 1981. Flushed with a new-found enthusiasm for his heritage and Irish folk music Morrison was in high spirits, but instead of going deeper into the terrain of *Common One*, he chose to subject his muse to the rigour of well-produced rock. *Beautiful Vision* (Mercury 1982) is a concise bundle of horn/drum-oriented songs. 'Celtic Ray' has the Irish texture of uilleann pipes, while 'Dweller on the Threshold' and 'Aryan Mist' are part-inspired by the book *Glamour — A World Problem*, by Alice Bailey (Lucis Press, London, 1950).

> So many people goin' down
> to the river to get clean ...
> The fog of illusion
> the fog of confusion, honey
> It's hangin' all over the world.
> Gurus from the East gives you the West
> Do they lift you up ...
>
> (Aryan Mist)

His lyrics remain that bit shadowy. Recurrent childhood images of trains and railways are incorporated into a selection of songs which journey through physical experience and unknown areas of spirituality. Mark Knopfler plays guitar on 'Aryan Mist' and on the track 'Cleaning Windows', which is a clear piece of autobiography for Morrison. A fast rock beat underpins the highly descriptive lyrics:

Jimmy Rogers on the radio ... lemonade ...
blowin' sax at the weekend ...
I'm a workin' man in my prime cleanin' windows
Heard Leadbelly and Blind Lemon
on the street where I was born
Sonny Terry and Brownie McGhee and Muddy Waters
think I'm a rolling stone ... Kerouac ...
What's my life ...

Again Van Morrison doesn't forget his background nor the experiences that seem to have haunted him throughout his career.

After a series of international performances and a good, positive reaction from the media, Morrison decided to take up residence in the quaint surroundings of West London near Holland Park. Rumours abounded that he was mesmerised by cult beliefs and semi-religious teachings such as those of Gurdjieff, Rosicrucianism and Scientology, but he refused to give anything away. The fact that he was near Ireland and probably homesick but had to live near his business operations proved too obvious for a lot of journalists, who revelled in gossip to fill their columns. He was also searching for musicians and recording facilities to match his mood. It is known that he got a friend to drive him around Ireland so he could personally call on musicians and chat to them about future projects.

Released in the spring of 1983, *Inarticulate Speech of the Heart* (Mercury) is another quality product of well produced, deeply expressed, mystical music. With flute, uilleann pipes and acoustic guitar, the album has an Irish traditional folk character most resonant on the instrumental tracks like 'Celtic Swing' and 'Connswater'. This was an enduring development that would dominate Morrison's work over the next while. The feel of the record is very 'modern' and he succeeds in colouring and texturing his mental 'scapes with the electronic technology of the eighties. The only track which seems regressive is 'Rave on John Donne', in that it covers similar ground to *Common One*, but this scatting rendition of great poets is more accessible and was to become one of Morrison's most popular concert pieces.

The successive series of sold-out shows at Belfast's Grand Opera House provided enough good music to enable Phonogram Records to release an album selection early in 1984. Its nostalgic mood features high points from Morrison's mystical past, but its best track is a paced version of 'It's All in the Game' which includes a distinctive lipped saxophone riff. Obviously the climate of Western Europe was giving Van a lot of stimulus and in July of that year he appeared unannounced on-stage with Bob Dylan at a giant outdoor rock festival staged on the banks of the river Boyne in Slane, county Meath. After hours of great performances by *In Tua Nua*, UB 40, *Santana* and Dylan himself, the concert seemed over when Dylan came back on-stage accompanied by an acoustic guitar-carrying Morrison. To the delight of the crowds they did some old favourites, including an historic version of 'It's All Over Now Baby Blue'. Renewing his Last Waltz experience with Dylan obviously chuffed Morrison no end and he even allowed himself to be interviewed with Bob backstage. Conducting the interview was the relatively inexperienced Bono Vox of *U2* and when it appeared in *Hot*

56 Van Morrison duets with Bob Dylan on 'It's All Over Now Baby Blue' at the
historic Slane Castle concert of 1984.

Press magazine some weeks later it revealed hardly anything about two of rock's greatest living enigmas. Bar a few sentences on the influence of *The McPeakes* and *The Clancy Brothers* on their music and the poor recording facilities they had to put up with during the sixties both Morrison and Dylan answered Bono's enthusiastic questions with a typical series of 'yeahs' and 'nahs' and other such monosyllabic utterances. Of all the media confrontations of Morrison's career this one could have been lengthy, informative and unusual if handled by an experienced interviewer.

Early in 1985 Van surprised everyone with *A Sense of Wonder* (Mercury) which contained some unusual compositions and was again steeped in an Irish atmosphere. Produced by Morrison himself, the album not only features the tight instrumentation of some of the best jazz sessionists around, but also the folk rock of *Moving Hearts*. One can hear Davy Spillane's uilleann pipes echoing throughout the moody title track and the entire group are allowed to let rip on Morrison's fast-step traditional instrumental, 'Boffyflow and Spike'. The record is a basket of surprises, as Morrison also includes dedications to some of his black heroes in Ray Charles's 'What Could I Do' and Mose Allison's 'If You Only Knew'. The latter's weedy organ and rhythm 'n' blues accent could be from any *Them* album while the bitter lyrics contain some of the finest put-downs of the music business ever put to vinyl. The record is one of great contrasts and some reviewers found it inconsistent. 'Evening Meditation' is a lovely lilting instrumental accompanied by the scatted humming of Morrison, but this spiritual feeling is abruptly altered by the inclusion of 'A New Kind of Man' which sounds straight out of *Tupelo Honey*. The album does have its weak points and the use of a lengthy William Blake extract on 'Let the Slave' sounds more pretentious than convincing, while the trivial pop structure of 'Tore Down à la Rimbaud' seems a trite way to empathise with literature's greatest Symbolist writer of the nineteenth century.[8]

NO GURU, NO METHOD, NO TEACHER

Looking back it seems that the incohesive nature of *A Sense of Wonder* was a result of Van Morrison's strivings for a new kind of expression, one that could accommodate his different perspectives and increasing maturity. That album was, in a way, a hats off to the various elements of influence that had formed such a part of his creative output since the mid-sixties. For two years he had been writing material for a new LP that would, on release, clearly define his contemporary viewpoint and significantly remind people that the mind which had created *Astral Weeks* was still capable, eighteen years later, of producing a work of equal brilliance.

Recorded over seven months in California and London, *No Guru, No Method, No Teacher* (Mercury) arrived in the summer of 1986 and once again Van Morrison was hailed as a musician of enormous stature and ability. Consisting of ten precisely cut slices of artistic perfection, *No Guru* is an homogeneous crystallisation of an intensely complex personality. What distinguishes this output from Morrison's other work is its use of classical arrangements where instruments like cor anglais, classical guitar, oboe, grand piano and strings contour the vocals to provide a chamber music effect. On top of this the delicate feel of the music has a vaporous Irish character that is difficult to pinpoint, but is still very much an important ingredient of the album's attractiveness. 'Got to Go Back' coolly evokes a nostalgic and loving attitude to his homeland as, accompanied by Kate St John's oboe, Morrison remembers his days at Orangefield School, gazing out the windows and dreaming about going home and playing Ray Charles records. The song continues to place Ireland and the past in the context of a healing place and Morrison sums up his feelings of dislocation neatly in the lines:

> I've been living in another country
> That operates along entirely different lines
> Keep me away from porter or whiskey
> Don't play anything sentimental
> It'll make me cry ...

'On the Warm Feeling' has a soul/gospel quality — a simple song of spiritual wonder wrapped up in Richie Buckley's plaintive soprano sax lines, it intimates Morrison's sensitivity towards even the simplest of life's events. Musically, the transcendent mood of the song is made complete by the addition of the gospel-like vocal harmonies of Bianca Thornton, Jeanie Tracy, June Boyce and Rosie Hunter. 'Foreign Window' is characterised by sharp classical guitar playing but lyrically is quite opaque. Here Van conjures up memories of 'T.B. Sheets' in terms of phraseology, but the suffering victim this time seems to be himself, his life aligned with the romantic despair of the poets Byron and Rimbaud. More optimistic than 'T.B. Sheets', 'Foreign Window' resolves the inner turmoils of the artist by rejoicing in the power of faith and the Lord to replenish a life of misery. The most important aspect of *No Guru, No Method, No Teacher* is its Christian overtones and even though Van Morrison denied having any strong affiliations to organised belief systems, including Scientology, the album itself conveys a whole-hearted re-assessment in the light of a new-found personal Christian ideology. This aspect finds its strongest expression in 'In the Garden', which in parts is powerfully evocative of *Astral Weeks* in its use of the images 'wet with rain', 'beside you' and 'childlike vision'. Compositionally it takes the ballad structure, underpinned by delicate piano (Jeff Labes), simple bass (David Hayes) and acoustic guitars (John Platania and Chris Michie). The song interestingly follows the ideas of 1968's 'Beside You' to a similar conclusion of re-birth with a loved one, but went much deeper towards a spiritual metamorphosis in its closing lines:

> No Guru, no method, no teacher
> Just you and I and nature
> And the Father and the Son
> and the Holy Ghost
> In the garden wet with rain ...

No Guru also has its lighter moments. 'A Town Called Paradise' opens up with the killer lines: 'Copycats ripped off my songs, copycats ripped off my words,

57 Morrison in 1987 — his *No Guru, No Method, No Teacher* album showed that he was still an artistic force to be reckoned with.

copycats ripped off my melodies.' In later interviews Morrison explained their meaning by railing against Bruce Springsteen, Paul Brady and Bob Seger for ripping off his style. It is true that Van Morrison was one of the first true singer/ songwriters in rock and had pre-dated the seventies' explosion of solo artists, but his music is very different from the traditionally influenced folk work of Brady and the working man's stadium rock of Springsteen. None of their music has the jazz or complex arrangement qualities of Morrison's best work. 'A Town Called Paradise' isn't that bitter anyway and its uptempo funky sound mirrors a joyous feeling of rapture exemplified by the lines: 'We're gonna jump for joy ... we're gonna swing around' again reminiscent in texture of *Astral Weeks'* 'The Way Young Lovers Do'. 'Tír Na nÓg' is also buoyantly happy and benefits from a swirling string arrangement by Jeff Labes. Here Morrison is exultant in his portrayal of re-birth through mythologised love and the powerful Christian faith of Ireland. Again the link with *Astral Weeks* is obvious in the line, 'Many many many times you kissed mine eyes.' The inclusion of a song titled 'Here Comes the Knight' is obviously a tongue-in-cheek reference to his early career but this composition confidently speaks in chivalrous medieval terms about the eternal quality of love. Morrison's interest in W.B. Yeats is proven by his altering of the great Irish poet's epitaph 'Cast a cold eye, On life, on death. Horseman, pass by!'[9] to 'Here comes horsemen through the pass, They say cast a cold eye on life on death.'

'Thanks for the Information' is the album's loudest cut, driven by Baby Trunde's thudding drums. It is also Morrison at his most bitter, literally pulverising the music business and castigating the media with lines like: 'Oh never give a sucker an even break. When you're onto something it's a dime in a dozen people start coming out of the woodwork.' Thankfully this attitude is short-circuited by the follow-up tune 'One Irish Rover', an elegiac but contented little song that puts Morrison's wandering spirit in the context of Irish emigration. The final track, 'Ivory Tower', is in some ways out of synch with the rest of the album because of its overt popness. Morrison claimed, in later interviews, that the song is about a working class man's position, the false images that the public had of his own situation and the realistic sacrifices that everybody has to make in order to live. On close inspection 'Ivory Tower' is much more an introspective analysis of Morrison's own development from working class roots to isolated rock figure and the problems of alienation that such a radical transition can cause. Musically it is lightweight and unadventurous and *No Guru, No Method, No Teacher* could have benefited from its exclusion. Regardless of this minor flaw, Van Morrison's 1986 album is one of his very best — one that exhibits a fresh approach in its classical sound, and has a lyrical vision that is on a par with *Astral Weeks*.

Subsequent press interviews with Morrison proved to be disappointing as he continued to criticise the media and downplay his own importance as a musician. Throughout his career Van Morrison has found the interview situation a difficult one to handle and rarely if ever opens out his character in this way. But a look at the contents of *No Guru* would inform any individual with enough concentration about all he or she would need to know of its maker. It's quite probable that Morrison's only adequate method of communication is through his music and that his gift for spontaneous creativity is something even he cannot properly understand. Whatever he says in interviews about it just being a job is obviously contradicted by his lyrical associations with the great writers and poets of the past. His passionate denunciations of the music business are equally contradicted by his continued involvement in it. Finally, his statements concerning his aversion to live performance are contradicted by impeccable concerts and the late 1986 European series saw Morrison playing material from all aspects of his career for up to three hours at a time.

Putting the media element aside, Van Morrison's contributions to Irish rock heritage are immeasurable. He was the first Irish musician to define a unique style that had a profound effect on the evolution of American rock. He showed that an Irishman could take on the corporate music business of the sixties and seventies and win. After the fads of British and American music disappeared into the past Van continued to develop his abilities and always produced music that demanded respect from all corners of the spectrum. His music has always managed to cut through the superficialities of pop or the more unsavoury aspects of rock, and communicate itself directly to a huge listening public who are ever eager to hear more. His greatest achievement has been in harnessing the mystical side of his Irish personality and transfusing it into a music that is all at once a Celtic mixture of folk, blues, rock, jazz and classical forms. Van Morrison defies categorisation; he is a law unto himself, a visionary and a complete artist.

In 1987 Van Morrison released the intriguing *Poetic Champions Compose* (Mercury). This time the most interesting aspect is the extensive use of instrumental tracks. These pieces, in particular 'Spanish Steps' and 'Allow Me' see Morrison exploring jazz saxophone in a way he had never done before. 'Spanish Steps' is breathtaking — drifting string sections hover over a Morrison alto sax line that is all of Miles Davis but more. The root tune is that of Rodrigo's 'Concierto De Aranjvez' which Davis and Gil Evans had attempted to rearrange on *Sketches of Spain* (CBS 1960). Here Morrison finely fuses classical arrangements with his particular style of jazz. The closing track, 'Allow Me', equally builds on Davis but is again Morrison's unique vision. In between is a selection of songs that muse on themes such as mystery, death, loneliness, happiness and the greatness of thinkers of the past, including Socrates and Plato. 'Alan Watts Blues' is a jaunty rock track with some nifty guitar playing by Mick Cox. 'Sometimes I Feel Like a Motherless Child' is a traditional blues number rearranged in incomparable Morrison fashion. Underneath beautifully slow and brooding brass and string waves (courtesy Fiachra Trench) one hears Morrison contemplating the loneliness and constraint of life's struggle and his awareness of the kingdom of heaven at hand. What makes this song is the simultaneous ratchety guitar melody and African drumming that subtly trot their way underneath it all. Mysticism is exemplified by the instrumental 'Celtic Excavation', literally a sound film of the physical and spiritual atmosphere of Ireland or Scotland. Morrison proves that he is not simply a rock artist, but has no problem in merging jazz, classical, blues, skiffle, country rock and anything else that pleases him into an homogeneous work that tastes entirely of his own magic.

C H A P T E R
FOUR
Modern Music

While the 1960s had seen a cohesive development in rock and popular music culture, particularly in Britain and the USA, the 1970s saw a gradual divorcing of the music from the general culture that had given it birth. When all the dust had settled on the revolutionary decade that was the sixties, rock and popular music splintered into fragments during the seventies. Worldwide, the decade was inaugurated by the awesome sound of British band *Led Zeppelin*, whose music was a gargantuan derivative of blues and basic rock 'n' roll. Jimmy Page — hippie guitarist, star child, cosmic personality and appropriately described as orchestrating 'a somnolent wake for the battered remains of the first psychedelic era' — led the group to international superstardom.[1] The early seventies also saw the culmination of English progressive rock in that groups like *Pink Floyd, Yes* and *King Crimson* reached hitherto undreamed of levels of technical sophistication and musical adventurousness. On top of all this one also had the English 'art rock' phenomenon, where the likes of David Bowie and *Roxy Music* combined a progressive music with 'glam' theatrics and a liberal attitude to creativity. Unfortunately, such auspicious beginnings were not to be capitalised upon.

In truth, these groups were merely an oasis in a quagmire of banality. By the mid-seventies rock and popular music were dominated by the horrid 'glitter rock' spectacle. Here rock music reached the height of indulgence, decadence and superficiality. Luminous trappings, fur coats and other glitter paraphernalia adorned stars like Gary Glitter and Elton John. The traditional fun of making rock music and playing concerts was now not enough, since such glitter stars demanded large private jets, huge limousines and expensive hotels. In America there was a 'teeny-bop' movement, with heart throbs such as David Cassidy and *The Osmonds* being mobbed everywhere they went. Certain artists of this era, like Marc Bolan, kept faithful to their musical roots but for the most part popular music and particularly the charts were dominated by vacuous images.

By the mid 1970s progressive rock had reduced itself to sheer out-and-out 'heavy metal'. What had at first been an interesting and intelligent development in the use of the electric guitar was picked up on and turned into the cliché of 'cock rock'. The electric guitar as a glaring sexual substitute was played, and played, and played into the ground. Bands like *Aerosmith* from the US and *Deep Purple* from the UK started the ball rolling and the heavy metal scene just grew unabated throughout the seventies, maintaining a mass appeal regardless of other trends.

Into this maelstrom of varying musics throw the rise in popularity of the singer/songwriter and the growing interest in black music. The latter was exemplified by the growth of jazz-rock fusion, the influx of reggae music with its rhythmic emphasis from the West Indies, and the rise of funk and disco music as the mainstay of New York nightclubs. In fact, however, there was no clear movement in music as there had been during the *Beatles* era, and more importantly nothing substantial which seemed to ground itself in an international rock culture. Everything was indeed fragmented. This dissociation of rock music from youth culture led to an overriding feeling of dissatisfaction and boredom among the young. A lot of the musicians of the sixties had by this time become the rock establishment, a group of people who had become precisely what they had set out not wanting to be — from singing about hippie freedoms to owning huge corporations did not seem to make much sense, especially to those who had bought the records and gone to the concerts. The indulgences of early to mid-seventies rock and popular music were reacted to violently by working class youth in Britain, where in 1976 *The Sex Pistols* took the world by storm by releasing the punk rock anthem 'Anarchy in the UK', immediately catalysing a whole wave of vitality in rock music worldwide, an energy release unprecedented since the days of Beatlemania. It was against this backdrop of activities that Irish rock music literally started all over again.

TURBULENCE

The large wave of rock music which had coasted throughout Ireland during the late sixties and early seventies had abated by 1975. The emphasis on long guitar solos, musical complexity and conceptualisation in rock had suited the period of increasing economic wellbeing and optimism among people, particularly the young. The hippy period, as it had been named, was slightly decadent and the music suited a 'laid back' attitude. Albums in those days were listened to very carefully and the record sleeves were pored over at great length. A certain cohesiveness in lifestyle was necessary for enjoying hippie music and this necessary ingredient did not sustain itself throughout the 1970s. Add to that the expense of putting the music itself together. Equipment, amplification, transport, venues, recording facilities and all the other odds and ends that went into the business of playing music were always a big hassle and costs were ever-increasing. By the mid-1970s the severity of economic conditions had rendered the old form of progressive rock redundant.

There were, of course, exceptions. Guitarist Jimi Slevin, an inheritor of the sixties guitar-based style, continued to play vigorously up and down the country without a care in the world. Definitely forming a vital bridge during the lean mid-seventies, Slevin became a number one live attraction and the most popular home-based guitarist. After breaking formidable ground with the classical rock oriented *Peggy's Leg*, he was enrolled in *Skid Row* for a brief phase before forming his own *Jimi Slevin Band* in 1975, the hottest band in the country at the time. I can remember hundreds of long-haired youths descending on a large Dublin park on a summer's day in 1976 just to hear Slevin play. It was the time of flared designer trousers and open-necked shirts, and Slevin personified enough energetic freedom for young people to identify with.

Slevin changed the name of his group to *Firefly* in 1978 and cut the record *Getting There* for EMI in 1978. A mixed album of guitar music, the tracks 'Magic Lands' and 'Wouldn't It Be Nice' are prominent displays of Slevin playing at his inspired best. Deciding to level off and work on his own, Slevin spent many years conceiving his first solo project which was finally released in 1982. *Freeflight* (Céirníní Cladaigh) is a masterwork. Jimi plays electric and acoustic guitars including a twelve-string, mandolin, tin whistle and percussion. Trevor Knight is on keyboards. The music involves a series of classical guitar introductions and uilleann pipe passages. The track 'Children of Lir' uses an echo effect to evoke the atmosphere of the Irish outdoors — the feeling of being out on the highland reaches, gulls circling overhead as dawn cracks through the mist and water slaps against the shore. Recorded in Slane Studios in county Meath, an area rich in mythology, the record is a perfect swan song to the idealism of the hippy rock culture. Here Slevin manages to transcend the limitations of that culture by summoning forth the more aesthetic side of his own background and melting it with the traditions of his Celtic environment. Even though the guitar is still utilised as a basic tool for development, Slevin's use of the instrument is never indulgent or histrionic. For these reasons *Freeflight* was and still is one of the most essential of Irish rock albums.

Going back to the mid-seventies it was pertinent that the musical sophistication of progressive rock saw itself transferred into the resurgence of interest in folk music. Folk music had always attracted the kind of people who had the concentration to sit back and enjoy a session. The music was part and parcel of a social tradition where the music came first and renditions of songs old and new had to be accurate. When Donal Lunny set up Mulligan Records in 1976, with the aim of facilitating the dissemination of 'music for music's sake', he inadvertently encouraged the changes which had occurred in rock to happen in folk. The idea was to produce new music by Irish artists with a bias towards innovative acoustic folk. The fruits of this and other happenings in the folk scene have already been discussed but what has not been pointed out is that progressive rock in Ireland did not die out but metamorphosed into a healthier form of new folk rock.

What of rock music itself? On a general level there seemed to be little new music of substantial worth to cause any enthusiasm. Irish rock groups that were most prominent in 1975 were really from the old school of sixties and early seventies music. Bands like *Master Hare, Light, Homegrown* and *Cromwell* were regular faces on the national gigging circuit, but most people wanted a change, something more intimate with some kind of vitality. This energy was to find its first outlet in the growth of a phenomenon called 'pub rock', which was rock stripped of all dross and just played for sheer enjoyment. Initiated in England by Irish group *Bees Make Honey*, and at the time more or less ignored by the rock establishment, this trend was without doubt the first sparkling of a simpler, more basic rock sound which was eventually to find its feet in a stronger form by the late seventies.

STRIPPING THINGS DOWN

Bees Make Honey were the first Irish group to get back to the roots of playing rock 'n' roll. Their idea was simply to entertain, to produce music with a sweaty energy — hit chords in four-four time — and create a dance atmosphere that was uncomplicated and unpretentious. *Bees Make Honey* were a product of the Irish beat scene of the 1960s. The originators of Irish beat, *Bluesville*, in part formed the new group: Deke O'Brien (guitar and vocals), Mick Molloy (guitar and vocals) and Barry Richardson (bass and vocals). Ruan O'Lochlann, a London-based photographer, quickly joined on piano, guitar and saxophone, while Bob C. Benburg from Los Angeles made up the five-piece on the drum kit.

After writing songs and rehearsing them in the country, the *Bees* tried out a small pub in Finchley, North London, called the Tally Ho. Even though it was famed for its jazz sessions the venue was crowded after a couple of weeks with people eager to enjoy the simple informality of the music. *Bees Make Honey* broke every pub in North London and Kensington within a few months, supported in their efforts by English bands *Eggs Over Easy* and *Brinsley Schwarz*. Deke O'Brien summed up the situation in one sentence, 'You could get a tour circuit going without venturing outside London — no getting involved in big transports, PAs and that shit.' They secured a recording contract with EMI Records and toured France, England, Germany, Holland and Ireland. Their high-energy rhythm and blues proved highly attractive to those bored with the heavy sounds of the early seventies and their first album *Music Every Night* was greeted with some interest.

Released near the end of 1973 the *Bees* debut LP is a healthy, off-the-beaten-track collection of tight, soul-based numbers which have little to do with the drowsy hippie past. Tracks like 'Knee Trembler' and 'Caledonia' have a certain vitality and living essence rarely heard in the music of the dinosaur mega-bands roaming the world at the time. However, from then on continuous line-up changes damaged the group's chances and they were considered by their record company and the press to be imageless. Fran Byrne played drums from *Music Every Night* onwards, and the last formation of the group had Ed Deane on guitar. Unfortunately, the failure to capitalise on the good impressions made by the raw gutsiness of their music led to disbandment in 1974, while recordings made for Dick James' Music and EMI never saw the light of day.

Soon after, Fran Byrne joined the English group *Ace* who topped the American singles charts with the song 'How Long' (Anchor 1974). Deke O'Brien continued to play and sing, despite past problems. *Nightbus* became his working band in 1975 and included Jimmy Faulkner and Dave McHale, whose funky leanings coalesced nicely with Deke's typical rhythmic playing. A sign of the changing times was their involvement in a round tour of Ireland called The Falling Asunder Review. The idea was simply to bring more energy to what can only be described as a flagging music scene. Significantly, the tour used minimum expense and maximum enthusiasm, including volatile performances from new Irish groups *The Boomtown Rats* and *Cheap Thrills*. *Nightbus* released one album on the Mulligan label in 1976 before breaking up and reforming as the much acclaimed *Stepaside*. Brendan Bonass (guitar and vocals), Paul Ashford (bass and vocals), Dave McAnamey (piano) and Robbie Brennan (drums) joined Deke in a formation that played rock with country and funk influences. Having quickly established a strong Dublin following they toured England with *Graham Parker and the Rumour* and proved that they were an important ingredient of the 'new wave'. Their version of the rhythm and blues standard 'Good Morning Little Schoolgirl' became an anthem and they were always in demand as a concert group. O'Brien quit in 1978 to devote his time to setting up the Scoff recording label in order to encourage, sponsor and develop new Irish talent. *Stepaside* continued on as a four-piece and eventually released the album *Sit Down and Relapse* on their own Sidestep label in 1980. By now the music had been upgraded to high quality, smooth, middle-of-the-road stuff, but it definitely lacked the bare roots of Deke O'Brien's rhythmic sensibility.

O'Brien had done a lot for Irish rock and could be credited with laying the foundation stones for the entire new wave of music that would appear in Ireland and the UK in the late seventies. His involvement with *Nightbus* in the Falling Asunder Tour in August of 1976 was significant in that the entire happening became a watershed in Irish rock, heralding a new era. The music heard on this tour was stripped down and ready to go and didn't require the enormous stage props and complex thematic imagery of traditional rock to be effective. It spoke to an audience in an earthy vocabulary, and to a large proportion of the youth action was what was needed in rock music not complacency. Deke O'Brien's example did not go unheeded and other musicians quickly became aware of the enormous energy potential inherent in playing the new rock music.

THE BOOMTOWN RATS

A setting: A large football stadium in Dublin on a very hot Sunday in August of 1977. Dalymount Park is packed with a bevy of fans in anticipation of the day's conglomeration of rock bands. The bill is topped by *Thin Lizzy* who, along with *Stagalee* and *Fairport Convention*, represent the old, established rock music scene. *Graham Parker and The Rumour* are indicative of the new wave of rock groups coming out of England. Irish groups *The Radiators from Space* and *The Boomtown Rats* are a new breed of highly aggressive, straight down the line, 'punk' bands. This one-day festival is much more than a concert — it's an interfacing of rock music from two very, very different generations.

The Action: It's early in the day and *Fairport Convention* are just finishing off a fairly tepid set of folk rock. *Stepaside* perform an easygoing selection of soft rock numbers, but there is something in the atmosphere, something very different from the usual laid-back vibe at a summer outdoor bash. It's the afternoon now and the sun is high. One knows that *The Boomtown Rats* are around somewhere because of the large cloth backdrop with their name on it billowing from above the stage. The band hit the boards with a bang — a six-piece, led by a gangling, scrawny maniac called Bob Geldof, they launch into the most basic form of animal rock ever heard in Ireland. Jumping, leaping and trouncing around the stage, Geldof spits out an angry stream of lyrics about everyday life in the streets, about life as it's seen from the poor backyards, about youth in a recession-ridden land. Everyone in the audience has caught the sentiments. As one song finishes the next begins, the finale of one being the introduction to another. There seems to be no let up on the fast drum rolls, the screeching, hammering guitars and the thrash, thrash, thrash of ranting noise. Pete Briquette, the bass player with a crew-cut hairstyle, squats low down with his

58

58 After breaking formidable terrain with the classical/rock-based *Peggy's Leg,* Jimi Slevin enrolled in *Skid Row* for a brief period before forming his own band, *The Jimi Slevin Band,* in 1975.

59 *The Boomtown Rats* in February 1977 when they signed with Ensign.

60 The pub rock *Boomtown Rats* coming out of hippiedom to embrace punk. *Left to right:* Pat Cusack, Gerry Cott, Johnny 'Fingers' Moylett, Bob Geldof, Gary Roberts and Simon Crowe.

59

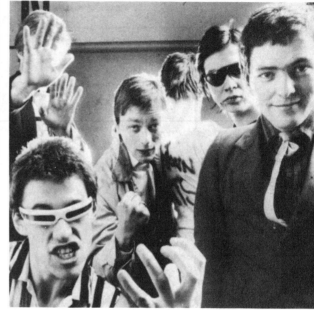

60

61 Bob Geldof doing the splits at Dalymount Park in August of 1977.

62 *The Boomtown Rats,* 2 November 1977. *Left to right: (back)* Simon Crowe, Gerry Cott; *(front)* Johnny Fingers, Pete Briquette, Bob Geldof, Gary Roberts.

63 Bob Geldof performing during the *Rats* In The Long Grass tour 1984.

instrument, grins idiotically at the audience and spends the entire performance speedily frogging his way from side to side across the stage. The music is fast and furious, played with a certain intensity and disdain as if saying 'Wake up everybody, you've been asleep too long.' 'Looking After Number One' is the band's first single and during their spot they distribute it free. The song is the climax of the set and includes a marvellous Chuck Berry guitar break by Gerry Cott. Keyboardsman Johnny Fingers cuts a funny look with his black spiky hair and odd pyjamas. Geldof leaps up and down as he gets into the song: 'I don't want to be like you, I don't want to be like you. I want to be like, I want to be like, I want to be like — ME!' That's it — the crowds are left stunned and baffled. No one can believe that rock music could release so much pent-up energy and feeling. *The Boomtown Rats* have just started a revolution.

A Story

Bob Geldof was described in 1977 as 'a gangling, frenetic, high-intensity type with two days' stubble and a spiky haircut.'[2] Born in 1952, he grew up in Dublin. As a teenager his egocentric ways were fuelled by the moral and physical straps of Irish Catholicism. While at boarding school he was given to playing guitar, an interest usually resulting in corporal punishment by his so-called mentors. He even rejected their priestly authority by writing to China and procuring a bundle of communist material which included hundreds of Little Red Books for distribution. After failing his final school examinations, he started working in photography. Successive jobs lasted only a few months at a time — things like airbrushing photos in London, teaching English in Spain, or working as an underground journalist in North America were formative experiences. After returning to Dublin he wrote a few bits and pieces for the *New Musical Express*, but the situation led to growing dissatisfaction, frustration and disaffection with a social and economic environment that seemed to hold out little or nothing for the young.

In those days Bob Geldof might have been classed as an unemployed waster by many, but he always had a deeper interest in the spirit of the blues and its music. He could play blues harmonica and acoustic guitar (upside down and with his left hand) as a teenager and his involvement with the Irish Blues Federation, dedication to promoting interest in the blues, had certainly proven his worth. He had been instrumental in bringing over the legendary Champion Jack Dupree and was a great enthusiast of the pre-war, American country blues of Son House and Robert Johnson. Now living in the south Dublin coastal town of Dun Laoghaire, Bob decided it was time to go back to music rather than sink into the growing dole queue glut. He had met other musicians who were in a similar situation, so they decided to give rock 'n' roll a bash. After several rehearsals and a string of dubious names such as *The Nightlife Thugs, The Boomtown Rats* came into being in November 1975. Geldof had culled the band title from Woody Guthrie's autobiography *Bound for Glory* and the full line-up consisted of Gerry Cott (lead guitar), Gary Roberts (rhythm guitar), Simon Crowe (drums), Pete Briquette (bass), Johnny Fingers (keyboards) and Bob Geldof (vocals).

Doing folk rock, funk, country-blues or other cross pollinations popular at the time could have been an easy option for *The Boomtown Rats*, but they struck out and aligned themselves with the growing pub rock insurgence. The Much More Music gigs at Dublin's Moran's Hotel were famed for their musical intensity and it was here that *The Rats* became a much talked-about band. Outside Dublin the country was still highly respectful of showbands and easy-listening performers, and Bob Geldof's bunch were greeted with distaste when they appeared in local dancehalls. With journalist Fachtna O'Kelly as manager, the group spread its wings and went to Holland to perform. Even though Amsterdam was still very much a hippie haven *The Rats* were able to get places like The Milky Way and The Paradiso jumping with their raw energy. Back in Dublin with only £40 to their collective name, a couple of hours were paid for at the Eamonn Andrews Studios and four tracks were demoed. The spur to this move came when the group saw English new wave band *Eddie and the Hot Rods* play in Dublin, and since *The Rats* were getting lots of public attention with their rough rhythm and blues sound, they felt they could do better. Fachtna O'Kelly and Bob Geldof then set off for London with the tapes in hand, determined and committed to getting a recording deal.

Winter 1976 and the pair were walking down London's Dean Street, and just by chance they met Chris O'Donnell (*Thin Lizzy* manager) coming out of a doorway. O'Donnell swiftly proceeded to organise a meeting between them and Nigel Grange, the A&R man with Phonogram Records. The tapes were listened to and everybody started jumping. Contracts were wafted in front of their faces because songs like 'Riot in Cell Block Number Nine' and 'Barefootin'' had that fundamental and seemingly lost killer feel of fifties rock 'n' roll. Very soon *The Boomtown Rats* became the hottest property in London, simply because the record business sensed a vital connection between the streets and their music. Fachtna O'Kelly: 'We tried to be a bit cagey and go round to a couple of other record companies like Island and Virgin. Richard Branson in Virgin and Nigel Grange had had this battle to sign *10CC* and Nigel had won. There was again a constant stream of phone calls between them for *The Rats*.' Offers were made by both parties, including a £20,000 bid by Virgin, but the group held out for more. Eventually, in February of 1977, Phonogram Records settled a contract with £740,000, one of the highest fees ever paid for a new band. Through their Ensign and Mercury labels, Phonogram would handle the bulk of the *Rats'* recorded output throughout their career. But up to 1980 Mulligan Records acted as the group's label on the home turf.

Back in Dublin, Bob Geldof was quickly becoming the most media-involved rock personality of all time. Sprawling all over the stage, shouting his mouth off at every turn, appearing regularly on television, radio and in newspapers — his was the garrulous voice of a bored, disgruntled and angry youth. Far removed from the fifties variety of angry young men, this time the anger was directed onto the pavements and into the concert halls. It was significant that Geldof's rise to fame coincided with that of Johnny Rotten in England, but unlike Bob, Rotten and his *Sex Pistols* were excessively nihilistic, verging on the dementedly violent. Geldof in contrast had charm, wit, intelligence and an ability to communicate his radical opinions in a likeable fashion. He hammered Irish conservatism and proved to the nation that anyone could do what they wanted, that is, if they wanted it badly enough. Moreover he could back up his behaviour and attitudes with a version of reality that had the consensus of the young, and was therefore viable. This aspect of the new wave was, indeed, the most important phenomenon to hit rock music since *The Beatles*.

'I just knew that we could do better than what was happening, but I wasn't interested in country rock, I wasn't interested in funk rock, I wasn't interested in jazz-rock. I wasn't interested in the self-indulgence of musicians who played fifteen-minute guitar solos, and then spent half an hour tuning up' (Bob Geldof, 1977).

Settling in the English provinces, *The Rats* built up their set to a considerable standard, before hitting London in June 1977, the blitzkrieg summer of punk. With American bands *Talking Heads* and *The Ramones* doing a stormer of a tour at the time, *The Boomtown Rats* got themselves onto the bill and made a hit with the rock newspapers. Irish rock personality B.P. Fallon was hired as press agent, and exercised his suave talents to get an atmosphere of excitement bubbling amongst the media people. *Tom Petty and the Heartbreakers*, affluent, cool-looking, American new wavers, were also causing a stir in London. *The Rats* played four gigs with *Petty:* Edinburgh, Cardiff, Aylesbury and The Rainbow in London. Using spray cans, large wallpaper strips and lots and lots of imagination, the tour turned out to be an assault on the values of bourgeois rock music.

At each gig *The Boomtown Rats* were in evidence — their name scrawled on walls, hung from steeples, sprayed in subway tunnels, in a defiant street manner reminiscent of the Dadaist movement of the early twentieth century. 'Rats eat Heartbreakers for breakfast' was what greeted passengers who disembarked from the underground train at Finsbury Park, nearest station to The Rainbow. The concert was too much, with Geldof shouting at the end of his set, 'It doesn't matter a fuck whether you clap or not 'cos we're coming back for an encore.' And they did.

In August of 1977 *The Rats* released their first single record 'Looking after Number One' (Mulligan/Ensign). It made the BBC Radio One playlist in Britain, distinguishing the Dublin brigade as the first punk rock group to crack the invisible force that up to then had meant pap all day long on Britain's highest-profile pop radio channel. Their debut album, *The Boomtown Rats* (1977) on Mulligan and Ensign also hit the record racks and it had a devastating effect in terms of cover design, content and sheer audacity. The sleeve portrays Geldof in a large plastic bag, clawing his way towards the viewer through a murky green environment. The music is sheer white heat rock 'n' roll, accompanied by sneering vocals delivered with a maniacal intensity. 'Joey's on the Street Again' portrays derelict urban violence and the problems of modern city alienation. The pumping beat of 'Neon Heart' shivers the spine with a brute simplicity. 'Close as You'll Ever Be' is a nice touch in that it is Geldof's compliment to the rhythm and blues style of *The Rolling Stones* who, in a lot of ways, were *The Boomtown Rats* of the sixties. The group had made a big impression and that first LP would form an important part of the iconography of the new wave, punk rock era.

The Outcome

Going back to Dalymount Park, *The Boomtown Rats* were then joined on stage by Charles Shaar Murray, then rock journalist for the *New Musical Express*. A real fan, he even danced around and played a bit of harmonica. Significantly, he would cover the rise of the group to international stardom over the coming years. After that gig *The Rats* headed for Manchester where they did a spot on the historic 'Marc Bolan Show'. It was in television that Bob Geldof really found his medium; being a natural 'personality' he played up to all its shortcomings and advantages. It was not surprising that *The Boomtown Rats* were the first punk rock group to appear on 'Top of the Pops'. 'Most of the acts for that programme would wander in and do their thing. Bob actually involved the audience; he would rap with them and ask them for their help to make a song good and would give out all these flags for them to wave. Usually the band exploded on-screen!' (Fachtna O'Kelly).

The Boomtown Rats caught the sensibility of the times and expressed their own feelings, agitations and ideas. In November 1978 they became the first Irish rock group to achieve a number one single's placing in the UK charts. 'Rat Trap' (Ensign/Mulligan) was an angry song which summoned forth images of high-rise living and city ghetto squalor. Geldof's lyrics were this time more sophisticated than earlier rantings and conveyed a distinctive insight into glaringly obvious social problems of everyday life. The second album, *A Tonic for the Troops*, (Ensign/Mulligan 1978) still had the thrashing quality of earlier days but its release also showed a different side to the group. None could resist the melodic character of the track 'I Never Loved Eva Braun', which climaxed with the sounds of acoustic guitar strums and military-style whistling. In performance, the band maintained 'punk' characteristics and during a rendition of 'Rat Trap' on 'Top of the Pops' Geldof took great pride in ripping up pictures of John Travolta and Olivia Newton John (the duet whose single *The Rats* had toppled from the number one chart position).

In Britain and Ireland *The Rats'* raison d'être was easily understood, but in affluent America punk rock had different connotations. When the band appeared in the States the rock establishment there immediately went on the defensive. Record executives from their American music company, Columbia, were freaked out by their performances and Geldof made the situation worse by shooting his mouth off at record company receptions and other functions. However, in New York the band were greeted with enthusiasm because that city had always nurtured the punk ideal, specifically from the *Velvet Underground*/Andy Warhol sixties, and Geldof's troupe just added to that tradition of wild, feedback-ridden, jagged, atonal and anarchic music. Outside the Big Apple though, the country wasn't really amenable to such an hysterical approach, but *The Boomtown Rats'* first US tour did end on a high note. Their last concert was scheduled to take place at a place called Frederick's of Hollywood, a ritzy boutique which specialised in mail-order kinky underwear! Columbia Records objected to the idea and refused to take out protective insurance for the band or get involved in a promotional scam of giving away 150 free tickets on the local radio stations. Regardless of obstacles the gig turned out to be a success. Television sets were piled up in the display windows of the boutique and large loudspeakers were placed on the roof. When the band began to play they created such a ruckus that every LA punk in the vicinity made a bee-line for the shop and the streets became crowded. The incident caused so much disruption that all the American TV channels ended up carrying live reports of what happened.

Soon after, Bob Geldof went to Atlanta, Georgia, on a record company promotions trip for the band. There he wrote the song 'I Don't Like Mondays'. In August 1979 this became the second successive number one UK hit single for the Irish group. The track has an orchestral dimension and the lyrics are a passionate and fulsome interpretation of something that Geldof had heard in the Columbia offices in Atlanta — a radio story about the plight of a young girl who, alienated by her environment, used a rifle given her as a present by her father to kill some of her schoolmates. Asked why she did it the girl replied sardonically, 'I Don't Like Mondays'. Geldof was shocked by the event and his song was an emotional reaction to the thoughtless materialism and indiscriminate use of firearms in the USA. Not surprisingly the single was banned there.

Bob was well aware of the limitations of the punk ethos that had fuelled the group's progress thus far. If the band continued to play rough-and-ready their career could easily turn into a parody. Their fourth album, *Mondo Bongo* (Ensign 1981), is a strong musical effort and shows that *The Boomtown Rats* were capable of much diversity. A mixture of funky jungle rhythms, reggae, thrash rock, synthesiser sounds and acoustic guitars the record has a strong lyrical content too. Lines like 'I was reading in New Zealand about Ian Smith, I was thinking they were lucky to be rid of that shit' from 'Another Piece of Red' are typical. Another song, 'Banana Republic', is a sharp and witty put-down of the social/ political state of Ireland, its religious characteristics and sectarian problems: 'Banana Republic, set to go . . . police and priests, forty shades of green, sixty shades of red.' Again Geldof saw fit to honour *The Rolling Stones* by including a high-adrenalin version of one of their old hits in 'Under My Thumb'. The album showed that *The Boomtown Rats* were more than just punk poseurs, out for the quick money, and was in effect a serious attempt to communicate the pernicious consequences of imperialism at home and abroad.

The eighties saw the group spending more time away, visiting such far off places as India, Thailand, Hong Kong and Singapore. Whilst his media profile continued to be high, Bob Geldof's involvement in Alan Parker's 1982 production of *Pink Floyd's* film *The Wall* placed him in a very controversial position. The film, conceived by Roger Waters, covered strange, chilling psychological territory, including such unsavoury topics as war, paranoia, fear, death and other equally harrowing experiences graphically portrayed to the backdrop of *Pink Floyd's* large-scale musical canvases. Bob played Pink, an ageing sixties rock star caught in a trap of drug excess and decadent hopelessness. The combination of Gerald Scarfe's hatchet-like caricatures and certain fascist symbols unfortunately made the final effect rather distasteful. It's interesting to note that Geldof's role here was similar to that of Mick Jagger's flaking rock idol in Donald Cammell and Nicolas Roeg's 1970 film *Performance*. Indeed, Geldof had always been close to Jagger in his singing style, stage antics and general stance of rock 'n' roll rebellion and his acting debut made this similarity all the more obvious.

By 1984 the curious position of being an original new wave group who also had pop sensibility began to lose its novelty effect for a public eager for continuously new stimulation. *The Boomtown Rats* found themselves an anachronism in a situation of ever-accelerating trend changes. Neither *V Deep* (Mercury 1982) nor *In the Long Grass* (Mercury 1984), their last two albums, showed signs of any inspiration or growing sophistication and it was not surprising that the charismatic Geldof felt more relaxed making another feature film. This time he acted the role of a pool hustler, hungry for a slice of the big-time, in Les Blair's atmospheric *Number One* (1984). It was at the end of this year that the aforementioned similarities with Mick Jagger ended, for Bob Geldof suddenly decided to re-focus his energies on helping the less well-off peoples of famine-stricken Africa. The forces that had eroded *The Boomtown Rats'* confidence and made their situation untenable were the very forces that made Geldof strike out and invent the historic relief schemes Band Aid and Live Aid (see Coda). Based on a moral imperative, his work in this area raised the tatty rebel from Dublin to world celebrity status, fêted by statesmen, royalty and public alike. His subsequent British knighthood, the writing of his autobiographical bestselling book, *Is That It?* (Sidgwick & Jackson/Penguin 1986) — the first work of its type to become a school text — and his subsequent double marriage to English rock personality Paula Yates have all become the stuff of legend.

Even though Bob Geldof saw it as his duty to administer his Aid Trusts, he was first and foremost a musician. 'Music is something that I want to do for the simple reason that I don't get a sense of achievement or satisfaction out of anything else except out of writing songs; good, bad or indifferent, whatever other people might think.'[3] After the excitement of Live Aid, Geldof wanted to continue with *The Rats* but certain resentments had set in and the other members did not want to become simply a backing band to a huge world-famous star. Wranglings continued, but Bob decided on a solo career and took himself off to Los Angeles to record an album in the summer of 1986. This coincided with his involvement in the special concerts for Amnesty International, where he and Dave Stewart (from English band *The Eurythmics*) made a surprise appearance at the LA Forum, where they did a choice version of Bob Marley's 'Get Up Stand Up'. Stewart also helped Geldof produce his album with Rupert Hine and others like Eric Clapton, Alison Moyet, Midge Ure, Omar Hakim, Jools Holland and Jimmy Iovine turning up in the studio to lend a hand. Released on 28 November 1986 *Deep in the Heart of Nowhere* (Phonogram) was reviewed severely by the critics but was, on reflection, a very healthy comeback by someone who was out of commercial music-making for two years.

Rising orchestral-sounding crescendoes had always been a feature of Geldof's better moments with *The Rats* and *Deep in the Heart of Nowhere* is chock-full of them. Sometimes these epic motifs sound a bit heavy-handed and it is when they are less in evidence that the record really works. Eric Clapton's assured guitar playing is a highlight throughout and adds perfect finishes to 'August Was a Heavy Month', a reggae-based tune, and to 'The Beat of the Night', a hypnotic African-type lament. The anthemic 'This Is the World Calling' is one of Geldof's most original compositions, and the title track consists of an emotional, acoustic guitar ballad that could have been much longer. Considering that it was done quickly and by a man that had spent at least a year of sleepless nights, the album is a far better rock/pop product than any of the critics allowed.

Having satisfied his need to make music, Bob Geldof embarked on a world tour with some of *The Rats* in tow. The rift hadn't been entirely mended though and Simon Crowe, with Johnny Fingers, busied themselves in Dublin with the setting up of a new group, *Gung Ho*. Over the years *The Boomtown Rats* slowly dissolved but during their incipient period they had provoked a radical change in the rock music consciousness of mid-seventies Ireland. Back then, they were the innovators of Irish punk style and their rise to prominence was quickly followed by an explosion of bands with similar attitudes. This point alone singled out *The Boomtown Rats* as a decisive factor in the evolution of modern Irish music.

The Boomtown Rats — discography

1	Looking after Number One/Born to Burn, Barefootin'	(Ensign, August 1977)
2	Mary of the Fourth Form/Do the Rat	(Ensign, December 1977)
3	She's So Modern/Lyin' Again	(Ensign, May 1978)
4	Like Clockwork/D.u.n. L.a.o.g.h.a.i.r.e.	(Ensign, June 1978)
5.	Rat Trap/So Strange	(Ensign, October 1978)
6	I Don't Like Mondays/It's All a Rage	(Ensign, July 1979)
7	Diamond Smiles/Late Last Night	(Ensign, November 1979)
8	Someone's Looking at You/When the Night Comes	(Ensign, January 1980)
9	Banana Republic/Man at the Top	(Ensign, November 1980)
10	Elephant's Graveyard (Guilty)/Real Different	(Ensign, January 1981)
11	Go Man Go/Another Piece Of Red	(WEA*, August 1981)
12	Never in a Million Years/Don't Talk to Me	(Mercury, November 1981)
13	House on Fire/Europe Looked Ugly	(Mercury, February 1982)
14	Charmed Lives/No Hiding Place	(Mercury, June 1982)
15	Nothing Happened Today/A Storm Breaks	(Mercury, August 1982)
16	Tonight/Precious Time	(Mercury, February 1984)
17	Drag Me Down/Icicle in the Sun	(Mercury, May 1984)
18	Dave/Hard Times	(Mercury, November 1984)
19	A Hold of Me/Never in a Million Years	(Mercury, January 1985)

*Ireland only release.

Albums

1	The Boomtown Rats	(Ensign 1977)
2	A Tonic for the Troops	(Ensign 1978)
3	The Fine Art of Surfacing	(Ensign 1979)
4	Mondo Bongo	(Ensign 1981)
5	V Deep	(Mercury 1982)
6	In the Long Grass	(Mercury 1984)

Bob Geldof — solo

Singles

1	This is the World Calling/Talk Me Up	(Phonogram, October 1986)
2	Love Like a Rocket/Pulled Apart by Horses	(Phonogram, January 1987)
3	I Cry Too/Let's Go	(Phonogram, June 1987)

Albums

1	Deep in the Heart of Nowhere	(Phonogram 1986)

64

65

64-66 Bob Geldof performing during the *Rats* In The Long Grass tour 1984.

67 Paula Yates and Bob Geldof — during the *Rats* rise to popularity, they made an outrageous pair.

66

67

I'm gonna put a Telecaster
through the television screen
'Cos I don't like what's going down.
I'm gonna put a Telecaster
through the television screen
'Cos I don't like what's going down.
I got the right, I got the right,
I got the ticket and the buck stops here.

(From 'Television Screen' by *The Radiators from Space*)

Following fast on the heels of *The Boomtown Rats* was Philip Chevron's *Radiators from Space*, whose first brace of singles and debut album cemented the punk ethos in Ireland. Chevron played lead guitar and sang, the rest of the band included Stephen Rapid (lead vocals), Peter Holidai (vocals, guitar), Marc Megaray (bass, backing vocals) and Jimmy Crashe (drums, backing vocals). Young and vitriolic, their first LP, *TV Tube Heart* (Chiswick), was released in October of 1977. An angry, fast blast of three-minute songs, spat out with a defiant confidence, its thirteen tracks target media conditioning as the prime evil of modern urban life. Delivered with a rough-and-ready adolescent speed frenzy, the likes of 'Television Screen', 'Prison Bars', 'Sunday World' and 'Enemies' are adrenalin rock 'n' roll of the first order. With their leather jackets, short hair and seemingly pugnacious stage presence the band became notorious almost over night. This notoriety was made worse by the fatal stabbing of a member of their audience at a punk rock gig at University College Dublin in the summer of 1977. They were at the very apex of the violence that made punk such a real happening, and that unfortunate incident had less to do with them than with the atmosphere of the times.

The Radiators from Space were a garage band of incomparable stature during the late seventies. Their songs made mincemeat of the rock press, political and social figureheads, and the system in general — a system that to a lot of youth held out only a future of dead-end jobs, or worse, permanent unemployment. They inspired countless individuals to make their own stand by showing that the barriers to progress could be decimated by sheer persistence alone. They continually played live music, anywhere and everywhere, and avoided the compromising situation of having to kowtow to a large record company by releasing their vinyl on the small independent Chiswick label (founded by former *Thin Lizzy* manager Ted Carroll).

The feel of *The Radiators'* music was very pertinent at the time, but the origins of punk rock lay outside Ireland. Take a wily Englishman named Malcolm McLaren and consider New York during the mid-seventies. The edgy, abrasive and simplistic music of a new wave of bands is causing consternation but attracting a lot of youth attention. Bands like *Television, The New York Dolls* and *The Ramones* are seen regularly battering out their primitive tunes. McLaren managed *The Dolls* and in the metropolitan environment of New York he absorbed as much information as possible about street culture, city music and sexual preferences.

Transferring his activities to England, he opened up a high-priced, youth fashion shop in London's King's Road called Seditionaries. It sported a range of sado-masochistic leather apparel and other tacky paraphernalia, in designs taken from what McLaren had seen in the underground New York clubs. This so-called 'bondage' dress started to become popular on the streets, and in late 1975 he brought in a group of juvenile delinquents to wear his styles, play a rudimentary rock music and wreak havoc on the establishment.

This group, *The Sex Pistols*, erupted in a manner unlike any other in the history of rock. From their first single, 'Anarchy in the UK' (EMI), released in December 1976, their music was a crunching attack on all that was held sacred. Their playing ability was so minimal that most people referred to their output as noise, and noise it was, but a noise that had never been heard at such a level of rage. In 1977 their scorching second single 'God Save the Queen' (Virgin) hammered the British establishment and consequently got itself banned and to number two in the charts. Concerts were shambolic, riotous affairs, record companies were taken to the cleaners, while television and radio stations were used, abused and dragged through the dirt. The vicious Fleet Street tabloid press even got a kicking from Johnny Rotten and the rest of the McLaren tribe, who manipulated sensationalist coverage at every turn. Their first album, *Never Mind the Bollocks, Here's the Sex Pistols* (1977) on Virgin, entered the charts at number one, but had to be sold in a brown paper bag. It was this opening up of the hypocrisies of society that resulted in the term 'punk rock' being used.

The most important aspect of rock music has always been its proximity to youth. The feelings and general attitudes of youth develop the mode of rock most in demand. It happened in the sixties with the hippie movement and just ten years after the psychedelic summer of love came its opposite, with the streets of London crawling with the violent energy of punk. The economic climate helped formulate the situation, and with only prospects of 'stagflation', recession and growing redundancies staring teenagers in the face, what was there to do? Feelings of bitterness led to an upsurge in youth fascism, because, of course, it was easier to blame the immigrant Indians, Pakistanis and blacks who had come to England in the booming sixties. The political establishment was getting the definite thumbs down for the simple reason that it had no decent solution to the post-industrial decay which had set into the woodwork of British society. The frustrations of English youth were grandly alleviated by the coming of *The Sex Pistols*, whose projected rock 'n' roll subculture suitably embraced working class and more importantly the unemployed's value systems. In the world of punk, the price of admission was to have a semblance of anarchy. Little money was necessary, since scruffy clothes were the standard uniform and the emphasis was on do-it-yourself style, do-it-yourself records and other such adventures. Even though there were violent incidents on the streets and in the concert halls, most of the anger bubbling in people's veins was transferred into the music, the dyed hair and the bondage clothes.

English punk was more than just another form of rock; it transgressed the idea of music as a form of entertainment and became socially and politically vital. Once the thrashing new music had bombshelled its way into the popular charts, the floodgates were opened to all who had the required venom to do likewise.

Punk rock and its idealism spread out of London and into the regions, firing imaginations hitherto starved of stimulus. The recession had hit the industrialised regions of the UK like a malicious sledgehammer. Towns whose livelihood had centred on traditional industries like shipbuilding, coalmining and textiles, suddenly found their once-secure cosiness broken by closure, redundancy and depression. It was no wonder then that their youth populations took to punk rock as an obvious cure-all for this adversity. It was a way of getting back, a way of feeling marvellously exhilarated.

Even though *The Sex Pistols* collapsed on their first American tour, just within two years of their formation, their legacy to music and youth culture was manifold. In England punk demolished the opaque, bloated beast which seventies heavy rock had turned into. It also encouraged the propagation of dozens of independent record labels whose function was to get as much youth music onto the streets as possible without fuss. (One of the first independent labels, Stiff, was co-founded by Irishman David Robinson. After purchasing one of Eamonn Andrews's old recording consoles, Robinson brought it over to London and installed it in the basement of the Hope & Anchor Pub, where he recorded new wave bands such as *Elvis Costello and the Attractions, Graham Parker and The Rumour* and *Ian Drury and the Blockheads*. Dozens of other groups joined the label which became highly popular in the late seventies.) Punk laid a positive foundation for youth co-operation and inter-racial mixing, since groups like *The Clash* had embraced black music early in 1977 and continued to utilise it on successive albums. It also demonstrated the importance of women as equals in the business, capable of excellent new music — for example Siouxie Sioux of *The Banshees*, who had started with *The Pistols*, went on to become a major star. Once its nihilistic and violent aspects had been displaced, punk rock acted as a positive cleansing agent. Through the late seventies and into the eighties English musicians concentrated their abilities in a clearer atmosphere, one that was refreshed and alive. New music of a fascinating and unusual quality began to filter through the British independent music scene and yet again it was possible to conceive of the idea of 'rock progress'.

NORTHERN IRELAND

The fundamental problem of English involvement in the history of Ireland had never really been settled. The peculiar situation of the six counties of Northern Ireland remaining part of the United Kingdom, as a result of the Treaty of 1921, was to lead to growing tensions in the province. Political and religious intolerance among its divided Catholic/Protestant population developed into insurrection and continual violence throughout the seventies. This, on top of the recession, meant that the punk ideal was seen as a way out for the young — a way to counter the bombs, bullets, riots and crumbling situation. Why not meet the violence with a violent, raucous music of your own creation? Why not voice the feelings and opinions of those who lived through the ceaseless terror every minute of every day through the jagged barrage of punk rock? It was the only way that a lot of people could be heard.

When Terry Hooley set up Good Vibrations Records he instinctively tapped into the electricity on the streets. His tiny Belfast shop resembled the chaos of its environment — records all over the place, recording facilities behind the shop, and always full of ardent youth, hanging-out and enthusing over the latest crackly agit-pop release. Hooley saw that here was something that gave young people hope, something to be actively involved in and committed to.

The first major band to get off on Good Vibrations was *The Undertones* from Derry, with Feargal Sharkey (vocals), Damian O'Neill (lead guitar), John O'Neill (rhythm guitar), Mickey Bradley (bass guitar) and Billy Doherty (drums), Formed in 1974, they paid their dues in the local rhythm and blues youth club. Their founder member, Billy Doherty, noticed Feargal Sharkey in a local competition which the latter had won for his sweet renditions of traditional songs. When they got together the group immediately had that rare musical magic of a unique sound, a sound whose strongest quality was Sharkey's goldenly-pitched vocal chords. Their greatest impetus came from the release of the *Pistols'* 'Anarchy in the UK', which put a stamp on the kind of music they would play — fast, hard-driving, punk rock, with a touch of pop melody thrown in for good measure. The release of their debut four-track single, 'Teenage Kicks' (1978) on Good Vibrations, shot them into the public consciousness, especially as it caused the most credible disc jockey in England, John Peel, to become their biggest fan. Well known as a staunch supporter of the punk movement, Peel adopted the group as his favourite band of all time and never tired of enthusing about their aggressive pop sensibility. It wasn't long before other DJs picked up on the band and the general consensus was that John O'Neill's lovely lyrics and Feargal Sharkey's delectable voice were some of the best things to come out of the punk scene.

Even when they charted their early singles, the group found it difficult to dive into the world of stardom. They were such individualists, believing so strongly in the forcefulness of punk ideology that they insisted on holding down their day jobs in Derry whilst performing their music on the BBC's 'Top of the Pops'. After doing the usual slog of profile-making tours and continually entering the British record charts, *The Undertones* went fully professional and signed to a large international record company. John Peel continued to support them as his favourite 'underground' group and would play their records three at a time back-to-back, whenever he could get away with it.

Their first two albums on Sire, *The Undertones* (1979) and *Hypnotised* (1980), were not much more than singles collections, with some extra tracks. By their third album, *Positive Touch* (Ardeck 1981), the band had outgrown the adrenalised adolescent lyrics and youthful playfulness of their early work and chose instead to envelop themselves in a pop/psychedelic style similar to that of the 1960s. Songs like 'Julie Ocean' and 'Forever Paradise' are very far from their original punk pop, and on the whole the album sounds similar to an aural bowl of fruit with its weedy synths, liquidy effects and almost burlesque feel. 'Forever Paradise' in particular comes across as a moulding of 1968 *Beatles* with *The Velvet Underground* plus a snatch of *H.P. Lovecraft* (a cult American psychedelic group from the sixties). *The Undertones'* last album for Ardeck, *The Sin of Pride* (1983), saw them furrowing deeper into the sixties sound and one can easily identify aspects of soul, *The Beach Boys* and *Love* among the assorted sax, trumpet, violin and cello instrumentation. The music is of a rich, colourful quality and has an optimism not discernible in the 'post industrial punk' of say English contemporaries *Crass* or *Killing Joke*. Tragically, *The Undertones'* maturing artistry was short-circuited by financial problems and shortly after the making of *The Sin Of Pride* they disbanded.

More intense than *The Undertones* was Belfast group *Stiff Little Fingers*, who during the punk era assimilated the repercussions of the constant street violence and projected them into a dense barrage of 'shell-shock rock'. Founded by singer/ guitarist Jake Burns with Henry Cluney (rhythm guitar), Ali McMordie (bass guitar) and Brian Faloon (drums), the *Fingers'* music had a specifically sustained aggression which made concert appearances emotionally unsettling experiences, especially in their home town. Forming their own Rigid Digits label, they leased their early single releases out to Geoff Travis's Rough Trade independent unit in Britain. These were packaged in controversial covers which, for example, reproduced photos of explosives ('Suspect Device' 1978) or a British Army marksman on duty ('Alternative Ulster', Rigid Digit 1979). The latter song became their anthem and historically ranks as the first exact crystallisation of how the youth of modern Ulster felt about their traumatic situation:

> We ain't got nothing
> but they don't really care
> they don't even know you know
> They just want money
> we can take it or leave it . . .
> They say they're a part of you
> that's not true you know
> They say they got control of you
> and that's a lie you know
> They say you'll never be free . . . be free
> What we need is an Alternative Ulster.

This first-rate protest composition opens with the sound of strafing harsh guitars, then, as the other instruments break into a crescendo and the drums go thump, thump, thump, Burns's throaty voice shouts the lyrics in contempt and defiance. Their intentions are simple: to communicate the fact that people could live their own reality without having to subsume their personalities to a mass politic. Large record companies showed little interest though. Chris Blackwell of Island dropped them after they had been signed up by his A&R department. Their music proved itself when *Inflammable Material* (Rough Trade 1979) was picked up by a unanimous eighty thousand fans, zooming it into the English album charts at number twenty. Again, it was John Peel who gave the group that necessary radio airplay and bona fide recognition. After demonstrating initial reluctance, Chrysalis signed them up, and *Stiff Little Fingers* went on to play many concerts and to chart subsequent singles. They will always be remembered, however, as the most provocative side of Belfast rock during the late seventies.

On a smaller scale, Terry Hooley's Good Vibrations proved a healthy catchment organisation for dozens of smaller punk outfits who wished to get

68

68 *The Radiators from Space* — first publicity picture 1977.

69 Stephen Rapid leads *The Radiators from Space* at Dalymount Park in 1977. As well as a steamroller of a set their performance was memorable for Rapid's falling off the stage at one point.

70 Jake Burns of *Stiff Little Fingers* during a house-burning set at Liverpool University, March 1980. The *Inflammable Material* album had by this stage sold nearly 100,000 copies.

71 *The Undertones* were the sweetest rock 'n' roll group to come out of the new wave. Feargal Sharkey is front left (1983).

69

70

71

their rantings onto vinyl. *Rudi, The Outcasts, Ruefrex, The Moondogs, X Dreamysts* and *The Tearjerkers*, all combined pop characteristics with a trench-like barrage of noisy guitars. *The Moondogs'* 'She's Nineteen' (Good Vibrations), or *The Outcasts'* 'Self Conscious Over You' (Good Vibrations) are period examples of what Northern Irish punk was all about — personal, soft vocals delivered against the backdrop of violent music, brittle youth growing up in the war zone. *Big Self* started their career belting their instruments and shrieking ('Snakes and Ladders' Reekus), but quickly fell in love with the rhythms of reggae music. When any of these groups came to Dublin they demonstrated the harsh side of reality, giving harder, more vehement performances than most of their southern counterparts.

THE REPUBLIC

When registered against the punk activity of the UK, the early music of *The Boomtown Rats* and *The Radiators from Space* was very much in context. After laying their cards on the table with *TV Tube Heart* (Chiswick 1977), the latter spent a good year refining their sound and making it more complex. Abbreviating their name to *The Radiators* they released their second album *Ghostown* on the Chiswick label in 1979. This is a magnificent record, one which takes the basics of punk into a different dimension entirely. Full of inspired and memorable urban images its ten songs evoke a sense of young adulthood coming to terms with life in, and away from, Dublin — a city fast succumbing to decay as a result of the recession. Produced by Tony Visconti, the album also features the use of brass, piano and strings. The opening cut, 'Million Dollar Hero', has a speedy assurance and is full of rich saxophone passages. 'Let's Talk about the Weather' is more rootsy; starting with a simple crash/bang effect, it takes off on a terrific rhythm and blues guitar solo, reminiscent of the best of Chuck Berry. Other tracks sometimes remind one of early *Beatles* or *Yardbirds* albums, and in terms of technique alone *The Radiators* had come a long way since their garage-band days. 'Kitty Ricketts' seems to draw its inspiration from James Joyce's 'Nighttown' scenes in *Ulysses*, so redolent is it with the sounds of bar-room piano and the music hall. Finally, an example of Philip Chevron's fine songwriting talents comes in the form of 'Song of the Faithful Departed'. Here the rising, threshing nature of the music gives vent to an emigrant's view of Ireland, recalling such images as 'the greasy tills', 'the Sundays', 'the Sacred Heart pictures', 'the green grass', 'the holy water and rosary beads' and of course the 'whiskey in the jar' of the homeland.

For the most part the punk activity in the South was less pointed, less defined than in the UK. The environment wasn't as harsh as the post-industrialised state of Northern Ireland or England. Even if one did see collections of youth gathered around the streets of Dublin, attired in the latest punk gear, the serious social and political implications of punk rock were diluted by its transference to the easy-going Republic. Nevertheless, what it did stimulate was a willingness among the young to play any kind of music just for the sheer hell of it. In the South it was, without a doubt, in its musical rather than political buzz that punk had its greatest thrust, producing new bands, new venues and a fresh generation of enthusiasm.

One band, *The Vipers*, cut 'I've Got You' for Polydor Records — a simple, naive, adolescent, punk tune — and tried to break the London scene with little success in 1978. Two years later, Paul Boyle's sugary warblings surfaced on 'Take Me' (Good Vibrations/Energy), a weedy, endearing punk pop tune. There were dozens of other young musicians driven on by the impetus of punk and the surge of band activity that spread through Southern Ireland in the late seventies was on a par with the golden days of Irish beat and progressive music. In February 1979 the first punk festival proper was staged in Dublin's Project Arts Theatre. Titled Dark Space — 24 Hours, it was supposed to be headlined by Johnny Rotten's new group *Public Image Limited* from Britain, but they never made it. Compered by John Peel, it boasted a motley collection of new Irish talent such as *D.C. Nien, Zebra, The Modernaires, U2, Revolver, Protex, Rudi, The Virgin Prunes, Rocky DeValera, The Letters, The Vipers, The Boy Scoutz, The Vultures* and *The Atrix* as well as English punks *The Mekons*. That year also saw the release of a punk-style compilation album *Just for Kicks* on Kick Records. A hotch-potch of new music, it ranged from the fifties-sounding rock 'n' roll of *Rocky DeValera and the Gravediggers* to the infectious reggae music of new roots band *Zebra*. The latter were Ireland's first reggae group, racially mixed and prominently benefiting from the Rastafarian nasal intonations of their white lead singer, Pete Dean. As proof of the beneficial catalysing effect of punk on Irish rock, one only had to listen to their track 'Silent Partners', a song with a reggae character as authentic as any West Indian roots music.

The Atrix were quite unusual in that they played a type of minimal keyboards-based version of 'pomp' rock which had a lot of the qualities of punk. Their song 'The Moon is Puce' (Mulligan 1979) became a minor Irish hit and was, in hindsight, a great period piece of Irish new wave music. Another popular band of the period were *The Bogey Boys*, basically a three-piece, guitar-based rock group with a piercingly simply live sound; their treatment of punk was best exemplified by the single 'Friday Night' (Polydor 1979). And then, of course, there were *The Blades*. Originally a three-piece comprised of Paul Cleary (vocals, guitar, bass), Lar Cleary (guitar) and Pat Larkin (drums), their reputation stemmed from continually high-standard exhilarating performances and leader Paul Cleary's soul-based pop melodies. Formed in 1977 they were determined to make it on their own turf and differentiated themselves from a lot of other bands by showing a complete disregard for the attractions of going abroad. Their pulsating force was craftily captured on a series of vital singles. 'Ghost of a Chance' (Energy 1981) was one of the greatest rock tracks to come out of punk — a song of frustrated anger, sung in pure harmony to the fine rhythms of bass, drums and guitar. It didn't have long technical solos or flashy virtuosity, but it did have a clean energy, the energy of a group of north Dublin working-class kids who saw punk as a way forward, a way to attain something that was in some ways better. *The Blades* were never derivative, but incorporated an early sixties sound and dress style (neat Mod-type black suits) into their hammering, positively non-violent version of punk rock. After a continual hard slog around Ireland, the line-up changed in 1982 to founder Paul Cleary being supported by a new rhythm section of Brian Foley (bass), Jake Reilly (drums) and some additional brass players.

72   72 Paul Cleary of *The Blades*. They
used the new space forged by punk to
play a controlled pop music.

73 Post-industrial atavism, the reality
of punk in the late seventies.

74 The doyen of punk, Johnny
'Rotten' Lydon *(second from left),* with
Stano *(extreme right)* and friends in the
Ormond Hotel, Dublin, on one of
Lydon's frequent trips to Ireland to get
away from the intensity of the London
music scene. In 1980, on a visit to see
his brother's group the *4 Be2's,* Lydon
ended up in jail after being involved in
a pub brawl.

74

The other interesting aspect of punk in the South was that it changed young people's attitudes towards getting involved in rock music. Up to then music had been seen, in general, as a serious career choice, something that required dedication. Punk meant that one could make music on a whim and then do something else. Dozens of groups answered the call of punk by picking up instruments, banging out their adrenalinised noise and then vanishing as quickly as they had come. *D.C. Nien* were an outfit who mixed a menacing skinhead image with a harsh guitar sound. Unexpectedly they released a home-made cassette package of rugged tracks in 1980 called *The Red Tapes*, copies of which were surprisingly distributed by the band themselves. From its intelligent, communist-style packaging, to the pointed music inside, *The Red Tapes* represented the healthy 'anyone can do it' attitude of the punk ideal. (Subsequent to this the band myopically turned their backs on what were credit-worthy beginnings and tried to become commercial by adopting a funk/dance approach to their music. The disastrous results of this sudden change appeared on the album *Radio* [Polydor 1982], which was released under the equally atrocious new band name of *The Tokyo Olympics*). Another short-lived group was *The Pop Mechanics*, who produced the best new wave debut single of its time in 'Soldier Boy' (Polydor 1982). It features clipped acoustic guitar strums mixed in with whistles, tough bass lines and drums plus an English-accented vocal that lies somewhere between David Bowie and Paul Weller. Like countless others they followed up their one and only masterpiece by disappearing into obscurity.

In the South, punk also meant that there was an alternative to the conservative middle-of-the-road and country and western music scene which, after the progressive sixties and early seventies, had come back to monopolise venues, record companies and record shops all over the country. (For example: In Cork, Elvera Butler through her Downtown Kampus gigs and fledgling Reekus label brought outsiders Five Go Down to the Sea and Microdisney into the fray.) The punk attitude led to independence on all fronts. More groups wanted to play music. More studios opened up to facilitate the growing demand for recording. Independent record labels developed to give an alternative distribution to the results. Alternative record shops sprang up to enable the product to be sold and a horde of fanzines took shape to cover the thriving outcrop with glee. Even if the punk activity was sporadic and incohesive in the South, compared to Northern Ireland and Britain, it did shake up the infrastructure of Irish rock into reassessing itself in the light of the new activity.

Punk's detractors were quick to criticise its inherent violence and dismiss its music as moronic. It was easy to do this if one didn't understand the general importance of punk to post-industrial cities. In Dublin the tribal element of punk came out in the collective uniform, the clan-like street posing and the mass homage to bands who reflected this audience. The atavistic characteristics that accompanied the more extreme forms of punk had obvious violent tendencies. Such was its volatile nature that hard-core groups like *The Pretty* and *The Nun Attax* encouraged a senseless and mindless violence at concerts. Yet this was the exception rather than the rule in the South, and most groups communicated punk's implications through the music. *The Threat's* 'Lullaby in C' (Web 1980) epitomised punk's ability to represent the harshness of de-industrialisation as a barren landscape where humans forage like animals amongst the debris of concrete and metal. *Chant Chant Chant's* 'Quicksand' (Setanta Peig 1981) was in similar territory—a clang-bang mutation of rock that was such a critical attack on the words 'harmony' and 'melody', it sounded like desolation revisited.

To conclude, the value of the punk years to Irish rock was that in the long run they gave it a new context, a new reference point to jump off from. It's interesting to note that after punk happened in Britain it became fashionable for socially concerned writers like Simon Frith and Dick Hebdige to debunk the movement, to say it had become absorbed into mainstream culture and that it was no longer a vital force. On the superficial side they may have been right but in retrospect they were blind to the enormous amount of new groups, new musics and general new directions that occurred in rock culture as a result of punk. It was an inspiring movement and one that led certain Irish groups to create music of such import that they ended up not only changing the history of rock in Ireland but the history of rock all over the world. Such a group was *U2*.

The Proceeds of Punk — Essential Cuts 1977 to 1983

Singles (Note B sides included only if of good quality)

	Group	Single	
1	*The Atrix*	The Moon is Puce	(Mulligan)
2	*The Atrix*	Treasure on the Wasteland	(Double D)
3	*Berlin*	Over 21/Waiting for the Future	(Charisma)
4	*The Blades*	Hot for You/The Reunion	(Energy)
5	*The Blades*	Ghost of a Chance	(Energy)
6	*The Blades*	The Bride Wore White/Animation	(Reekus)
7	*The Blades*	Revelations of Heartbreak	(Reekus)
8	*The Blades*	Downmarket	(Reekus)
9	*Big Self*	Surprise Surprise	(Reekus)
10	*Big Self*	Don't Turn Around	(Reekus)
11	*The Bogey Boys*	Friday Night	(Polydor)
12	*The Bogey Boys*	Death of a Clown	(Chrysalis)
13	*The Camino Organisation*	Human Voices	(Reekus)
14	*Chant Chant Chant*	Quicksand/Play Safe	(Setanta Peig)
15	*Five Go Down to the Sea*	Knot a Fish (EP)	(Kabuki)
16	*Katmandu*	I Can Make the Future/Australia	(Spider)
17	*Kissed Air*	Kariba/Kissed Air	(Kabuki)
18	*Kissed Air*	Out of the Night/Change of Attention	(Kabuki)
19	*Kissed Air*	Kawaraya (12inch EP)	(Kabuki)
20	*Microdisney*	Pink Skinned Man/Fiction Land	(Kabuki)
21	*The Moondogs*	She's Nineteen/Ya Don't Do Ya	(Good Vibrations)
22	*The Moondogs*	Who's Gonna Tell Mary/Overcaring Parents	(Good Vibrations)
23	*The New Versions*	Like Gordon of Khartoum	(Mulligan)
24	*The Outcasts*	Just Another Teenage Rebel	(Good Vibrations)
25	*The Outcasts*	Self Conscious over You/Love You for Ever	(Good Vibrations)

26	*The Peridots*	Open Season/Calm	(Optional Goods)
27	*The Pop Mechanics*	Soldier Boy	(Polydor)
28	*Protex*	A Place in Your Heart/Jeepster	(Polydor)
29	*The Radiators from Space*	Television Screen	(CBS)
30	*The Radiators*	Let's Talk about the Weather/Hucklebuck	(Mulligan)
31	*The Radiators*	Song of the Faithful Departed/They're Looting in the Town	(Chiswick)
32	*The Radiators*	Kitty Ricketts/Ballad of the Faithful Departed	(Chiswick)
33	*Revolver*	Silently Screaming	(Rockburgh)
34	*Rudi*	Big Time	(Good Vibrations)
35	*Ruefrex*	One By One/Cross the Line, Don't Panic	(Good Vibrations)
36	*The Shade*	6.05	(Independent)
37	*Some Kind of Wonderful*	D'You Read My Letter/Sleighbells across the Sahara	(Reekus)
38	*The Starjets*	War Stories	(CBS)
39	*The Starjets*	Ten Years	(CBS)
40	*The Sussed*	Don't Swim on the East Coast	(Dead)
41	*The Tearjerkers*	Murder Mystery	(Back Door)
42	*The Threat*	Lullaby in C/High Cost of Living	(Web)
43	*The Vipers*	I've Got You	(Polydor)
44	*The X Dreamysts*	Money Talks/I Don't Wanna Go	(Polydor)

Extended Play Singles

	Title	Group	Track
1	The Boddis	*Big Self*	Concrete Curtains
		The Departure	Stop
		Chant Chant Chant	What Do You Know
		The Peridots	Precious Blood
2	Room to Move	*The Outcasts*	Cyborg
		Shock Treatment	Belfast Telegraph
		The Vipers	Take Me
		Big Self	Snakes and Ladders

Cassettes

	Group	Cassette	Publisher
1	*D.C. Nien*	The Red Tapes	(D.C. Nien)

Note: *All the above tracks feature the most interesting strains of minimalist rock music to come out of punk. Each song has an individual quality which holds one's interest. For example* **Some Kind of Wonderful** *adds a highly Eastern flavour to their hot equatorial sound,* **The Peridots** *combine acoustic guitar with thick electronic pulses, and* **Berlin** *use a traditional, wall-smashing rhythm.*

Albums

1	*The Atrix*	The Atrix	(Scoff 1981)
2	*Belfast Rock*	Compilation	(Good Vibrations 1978)
3	*The Bogey Boys*	Friday Night	(Chrysalis 1979)
4	*Just For Kicks*	Compilation	(Kick 1979)
5	*Kaught At The Kampus*	Compilation	(Reekus 1981)

6	*The Nerves*	Notre Demo	(Good Vibrations 1981)
7	*The Outcasts*	Self Conscious over You	(Good Vibrations 1979)
8	*The Radiators From Space*	TV Tube Heart	(Chiswick 1977)
9	*The Radiators*	Ghostown	(Chiswick 1979)
10	*The Starjets*	God Bless the Starjets	(CBS 1979)
11	*Vinyl Verdict*	Compilation	(Scoff 1981)

Discographies
The Undertones

Singles

1 Teenage Kicks/Smarter than You/True Confessions/
  Emergency Cases (Good Vibrations 1978)
2 Get Over You/Really Really, She Can Only Say No (Sire, February 1979)
3 Jimmy Jimmy/Mars Bars (Sire, June 1979)
4 Here Comes the Summer/One Way Love/Top Twenty (Sire, July 1979)
5 You've Got My Number/Let's Talk about Girls (Sire, October 1979)
6 My Perfect Cousin/Hard Luck Again, I Don't Wanna See
  You Again (Sire, March 1980)
7 Wednesday Week/Told You So (Sire, June 1980)
8 It's Going to Happen/Fairly in the Money Now (Ardeck, April 1981)
9 Julie Ocean/Kiss in the Dark (Ardeck, July 1981)
10 Beautiful Friend/Life's Too Easy (Ardeck, February 1982)
11 The Love Parade/Like That (Ardeck, October 1982)
12 Got to Have You Back/Turning Blue (Ardeck, February 1983)
13 Chain of Love/Window Shopping for New Clothes (Ardeck, April 1983)
14 Save Me/Tearproof, I Know a Girl (Ardeck, April 1986)

EPs

1 Love Parade: Like That, You're Welcome/Crisis Of Mine,
  Family Entertainment (Ardeck, November 1982)
2 The Peel Sessions (January/February 1979): Listening In, Family
  Entertainment/Billy's Third, Here Comes the Summer (Strange Fruit, December 1986)

Albums

1. The Undertones (Sire, June 1979)
2. The Undertones (new sleeve plus extra tracks) (Sire, October 1979)
3. Hypnotised (Sire, April 1980)
4. Positive Touch (Ardeck, May 1981)
5 Sin Of Pride (Ardeck, November 1983)
6 All Wrapped Up (compilation) (Ardeck, March 1983)
7 Cher O' Bowlies (compilation) (Ardeck, May 1986)

Stiff Little Fingers

Singles

1 Suspect Device/Wasted Life (Rough Trade, June 1978)
2 Alternative Ulster/78 r.p.m. (Rough Trade, January 1979)

3 Gotta Getaway/Bloody Sunday	(Rough Trade, May 1979)
4 Straw Dogs/You Can't Crap on the Radio	(Chrysalis, October 1979)
5 At the Edge/Running Bear, White Christmas	(Chrysalis, January 1980)
6 Nobody's Hero/Tin Soldiers	(Chrysalis, May 1980)
7 Back to Front/My Fire Coalman	(Chrysalis, July 1980)
8 Just Fade Away/Go for It	(Chrysalis, March 1981)
9 Silver Lining/Safe as Houses	(Chrysalis, May 1981)
10 Listen/Listen 2	(Chrysalis, January 1982)
11 Bits of Kids/Stands to Reason	(Chrysalis, August 1982)
12 Talkback/Good for Nothing	(Chrysalis, April 1982)
13 The Price of Admission/Touch and Go	(Chrysalis, February 1983)

EPs

1 The Peel Sessions (September 1978): Johnny Was, Law and Order/
  Barbed Wire Love, Suspect Device (Strange Fruit, September 1986)

Albums

1 Inflammable Material	(Rough Trade, July 1979)
2 Nobody's Heroes	(Chrysalis, March 1980)
3 Hanx (Live Album)	(Chrysalis, September 1980)
4 Go For It	(Chrysalis, April 1981)
5 Now Then	(Chrysalis, October 1982)
6 All The Best (compilation)	(Chrysalis, January 1983)

U2 — CRYSTAL FLIGHT

U2 have long passed into the mythology of rock history. Unexpectedly, and without precedent, they have managed to bring an Irish rock spirit all the way from Dublin to the four corners of the earth, and write it big on the hearts and souls of everyone they touched. It is not because of their musical virtuosity that *U2* has become the most important rock group of the late eighties but simply because they have understood that music's primary function is as a communicative experience. The feeling of communion that is wrought between an artist and an audience has always been the very kernel substance of rock and popular music — be it the early jazz of New Orleans, or the Mississippi delta blues, or on up to the rhythm and blues of Chicago, or across to the New York 'bop' years and Billie Holiday, or even further along the road to the rock 'n' roll of Chuck Berry, Little Richard and Elvis Presley, or the folk rock of Bob Dylan, or across the Atlantic to skiffle, *The Beatles, The Rolling Stones* and the British blues boom, or back across the Atlantic with the great British Invasion, the West Coast sound and *The Doors*, or the electric Jimi Hendrix at Woodstock, or the seventies thunderous heavy rock of *Led Zeppelin*, or the singer/songwriter era of Neil Young, Stevie Wonder and Joni Mitchell, or the multifarious anger of punk, or the mass appeal of Bruce Springsteen and *U2* in the eighties. Trickling down the years, rock and popular music has always celebrated that feeling. It suffuses dreams, ambitions, ideals and emotions in one chord, one note, one musical point that no words can ever describe. It is this ecstatic point of communion that most music thrives on, but to touch the world and at the same time represent the very maturation of a rock culture as young as Ireland's, that is something very special indeed.

To get a proper perspective of *U2's* career it is necessary to go back to the punk rock years of Dublin in the late seventies. It was in 1977, when spearheading English group *The Clash* came to play Trinity College that punk made its first real impact on Dublin's youth. As a result of this occurrence young people took to the streets, adopted the tattered dress style, graffitied walls, formed bands and made up the heaving crowds at the few venues that would present the new rebellious music. Trinity College was the archetype of these venues — a centre of sorts, it played host to the intense claustrophobic spontaneity of the times. New wave and punk groups were attracted to the university in droves, eager to showcase their raw but vital talents in front of an appreciative audience. It was in Trinity's small, underground Buttery bar that I first saw *U2* — a band of inexperienced teenagers, who played basic rock music with basic instruments. Their sound was a mess, their stage act all over the place and their songs inaudible. Yet it was clear that they did not indulge the chaotic devices of punk or its accompanying visual shocks.

Amidst the hit-and-run atmosphere of the times, *U2*, unlike a lot of other bands, played an emotionally connecting music, one that made an effort to reach its public. The ephemeral side of punk laid waste to dozens and dozens of smash-and-grab groups who, after packing everything into a few short years, just disappeared leaving only a vacuum and broken debris in their wake. *U2* were different because from the outset they didn't just take the superficial safety-pins of punk style, dress them up into the uniform of a band and push it down people's throats, but like English contemporaries *Wire, Joy Division* and *The Durutti Column* used the space afforded by punk to forge a new identity for rock. Lead singer Bono put it succinctly when he condemned the cash-in aspects of punk with the words, 'There's a lot of Johnny Rotten's bastard children running the streets . . . they've been sold into bondage.'[4]

The origins of the band were a complex thread of chance, inspiration and sheer commitment. It all started when environmental health officer and part-time optician Larry Mullen told his son that he would have to play with other musicians if he was to make an impression on the world as a drummer. Mullen Jnr took up the drums as a hobby after failing as a piano pupil at Dublin's College of Music. He was only nine at the time but was sure that he had a future as a drummer if only he was allowed to follow his instinct. After two hard years of technical drum training he joined a military-style fife and drum band, but persisted in doing things his own way. He was even thrown out of another drum band, *The Artane Boys Band*, for not wanting to follow scored music and for having long hair! The wayward Mullen insisted on playing to *Rolling Stones* and David Bowie records at home, even doing a stint at jazz training before he followed his father's advice and formed *U2* in late 1976. He was only fourteen at the time.

Mullen was lucky enough to be able to put together a group from fellow pupils at his Clontarf day school. After advertising his wish to form a band, seven hopeful individuals turned up in Larry's kitchen one day. Of these it was apparent that guitarist David Evans (later known as The Edge), bassist Adam

Clayton and forceful singer Paul David Hewson (later known as Bono Vox) would be his partners. They were all older than Mullen and though radically different in personality, the idea of being in a rock band appealed to everyone's sense of adventure. Evans, the son of a Welsh Methodist engineer, was born in 1961 and had spent his early childhood in Barking, east London. His father's move to Dublin stimulated an interest in music and he took up the guitar when only eight years old. By the age of fifteen, Dave Evans was already an accomplished player with a concentrative application and dedication to his instrument that was rare. Adam Clayton was also born in southern England, his father being a Royal Air Force pilot. After living some of his young life in Kenya he travelled to Dublin with his family at the age of eight because his father switched flying jobs to Aer Lingus Airlines. A true rebel at sixteen Clayton bunked out of a restrictive boarding school and headed for Pakistan, where he revelled in a hippie lifestyle. Arriving back to Dublin with a long kaftan coat, unkempt, curly hairstyle and a chain-smoking habit, he took up his place at Larry Mullen's school, determined to break all the rules. He acted like a hip rock 'n' roll cat and had a bass guitar and amp to match. It didn't seem to matter if he could play the instrument or not, for he looked right and that more than anything impressed Larry Mullen.

Paul Hewson was the most unusual of the four. Born 10 May 1960 in north Dublin, he was the second son of an inter-denominational marriage, his mother being Protestant, his father Catholic. The latter was a true individualist, a free-thinking socialist who added to his life of post office work interests in acting, painting and the music hall. Hewson lived a quiet life, picking up the acoustic guitar at thirteen, until the tragic death of his mother two years later. This unleashed the demon in him and Hewson took to the Ballymun streets and became an angry tearaway. Some of the gangs he was in pretended to be musicians with imitation instruments, but the call to join a real group soon gave him a better outlet for his aggression. He also brought with him a strong belief in Christianity and the potency of godly faith. Within days he had taken over leadership of the band and rehearsals were allowed to take place on school premises.

It would be a mistake to think that it was all plain sailing for U2 from this point on. Firstly, the reality was that the group was not yet able to play properly nor did it have a definable group sound. Secondly, irregular rehearsing and parental pressure to do well at school examinations meant that U2 evolved in fits and starts. By 1977 enthusiasm seemed to be waning as far as Hewson and Evans were concerned, and it was really only Adam Clayton who saw the career potential of the band. It was Adam's inevitable expulsion from school that strengthened his resolve and even though the academically bright Evans felt happy to follow his scholarly leanings and Hewson was heading for a degree course at University College Dublin (UCD), Clayton forced the group to try and break the local music scene. As time went by other factors added impetus to the band. When Hewson's application to UCD was rejected because he did not have the necessary entrance qualification in the Irish language, prospects in the conventional job-market seemed slim. On top of this, the failing Irish economy was throwing more people out of work every day so Evans and Mullen saw no

75

76

77

75 *U2* at the beginning of their career: '*U2* is an Irish expression, we don't want to leave.'

76 Bono, Larry, The Edge and Adam in 1979. They had just released their debut single 'Out of Control'.

77 *U2* in Kilmainham, Dublin, 1981. They had just released the masterly *October* album.

78 Bono Vox emotionally celebrates the Campaign for Nuclear Disarmament, in Dublin on 5 June 1982.

79 Bono and girlfriend, Alison, at the CND rally, June 1982.

80 Keith Donald *(Moving Hearts)* and Adam Clayton *(U2)* at a political rally about abortion and the Irish constitution, August 1983.

80

reason for not allowing Adam to have his way. As self-appointed manager, Clayton hustled gigs at places all over the country. Having adopted such awful names as *Feedback* and *The Hype*, but settling for the more attractive *U2*, they came into contact with the surge of inspirational activity that was punk rock, and in April 1978 had their first big breakthrough when they won a national talent competition sponsored by Harp Lager. Adam's perseverance had paid off and the local press as well as a man named Paul McGuinness began to take notice.

McGuinness, who was involved in film production work at the time, had always had an interest in rock music and dreamed of finding the right group to manage. When he met Adam and saw *U2* live he was impressed by their on-stage chemistry and particularly Bono Hewson's efforts to reach his audience. McGuinness also sensed a rare commitment in the group to each other as individuals — even if they were musically a disaster at this stage, they wanted to stick together and try and make a go of it. Not wanting to rush headlong into things, a six month 'period of inspection' was agreed upon — if McGuinness didn't feel that the band were right for him after six months, or vice versa, there was no obligation on either side to continue the relationship. McGuinness threw himself into his new role as manager with relish and soon *U2* were given heavy orders. More rehearsals, more gigs, better stage clothes and a realisation that the music business was as hard as any other toughened up their attitude to what they were trying to do.

The events of 1978 were a great confidence booster at a time when the group were much criticised for their lack of musical professionalism. Outside their small coterie of devoted fans *U2* were considered to be another amateur punk combo who would go as quickly as they had come. But they refused to go away — every week at an assortment of venues like the Dandelion Market, the Baggot Inn, McGonagles and the college campuses, the name *U2* would appear alongside the other young hopefuls on bill posters, doggedly playing the circuit, determined to dent the consciousness barrier. The more they played, the more experience they got and every gig showed an increase in attendance. The McGuinness partnership was sealed and *U2* became a five-man operation. Often the band performed with close friends and avant-garde group *The Virgin Prunes*, and throughout 1979 the slogan 'U 2 can be a Virgin Prune' became a familiar one around Dublin.

In February of that year they played Dark Space — 24 Hours, one of Dublin's earliest punk festivals. Compere and chief spokesman for British and sometimes Irish new wave music, disc-jockey John Peel, found *U2's* performance lacklustre and uninspiring, predicting little future for the group. Later that summer, I saw them play an open-air gig in the cricket grounds of Trinity College. Their music was fuzzy but they gave it all they had and the set steam-rollered along with a gut enthusiasm. Bono was hopping all over the place, clutching the mike like there was an electrical bolt running through his veins. Still, audience comments were derisory to say the least, some people even tossed half-full pint glasses from the balcony bar that overlooked the stage towards the group in the hope that they might get off quicker. Thankfully by the time they had got to appearing on RTE's 'Our Times' programme, *U2* were beginning to play better and both television crew and viewers were impressed by their hard-driven but economical sound. Another plus was the fact that Paul McGuinness had organised a singles deal with CBS Ireland and in September the first *U2* record was released. Titled 'U 2 3', its contents were selected by listeners of Dave Fanning's RTE Radio 2 rock show after he, with the band present, aired a demo session tape one evening inviting the public to make the choice — the vibe was that 'you too can be involved'. The three tracks 'Stories for Boys', 'Out of Control' and 'Boy/Girl' are adolescent creations, patchy, inchoate, with lyrics hysterically shouted by Bono. The 'Boy/Girl' cut is the best of the lot and shows The Edge to be an exciting guitar player not afraid to use phase pedals and sustained chops to get the required effect.

Things started to move quickly for *U2* as their first record attracted a positive, thumbs up response from public and critics alike. In December they made their first trip to London to play some club dates. Though the concerts were usually half-empty the rock intelligentsia were knocked out by the group, entranced by Bono's spontaneous streams of emotion on-stage and his ability to improvise lyrics in and around the bold instrumentation. The early months of 1980 saw the release of the second *U2* single 'Another Day' (CBS), which helped to hallmark their sound as progressive vocal-based, hard-edged rock and took them away from the limiting punk pigeon-holing that their music had been treated to up to then. Paul McGuinness continued to work hard for them and in March they were signed to Island Records in London. Island boss Chris Blackwell announced enthusiastically that '*U2* are the label's most important signing since *King Crimson*.' Interestingly, McGuinness had secured an unusually artistically free deal for the band in that the record company had to accept what they produced as final.

The band had to work very hard in 1980 if they were to make good their new-found opportunity. No less than three more singles and a full album would be recorded in Dublin by *U2* for Island that year. Unlike other Irish groups who were involved with English record companies, *U2* made a firm decision to stay in Ireland and not hightail it across the Irish Sea and settle in Britain. Granted, they could afford to stay at home at a time when the ferry boats were stuffed with emigrants, but if they had left then it is possible that fame could have been theirs much sooner. Bono's attitude at the time was: 'We had the chance to leave the country when we signed the recording deal with Island Records but we are still here because basically the roots of the group are in Dublin. Living in London it is possible to get blown up too quickly and finally blown out. You can get swallowed up and it becomes difficult to see yourself objectively. *U2* is an Irish expression, so we don't want to leave. Obviously, we will have to go away for long periods but our home is here.'[5]

The group were using Dublin's Windmill Lane Studios for their recordings and as their status improved so would that of the studios. Up-and-coming English producer Martin Hannett, who had made a name for himself producing Manchester neo-realist band *Joy Division*, came in to produce the third *U2* single '11 o'Clock Tick Tock'. Even though he gave their characteristic sound a more pointed surface, the track is cluttered and over-fussy, saved only by Edge's layered guitar riffs. The B side, 'Touch', is much better — a sharp, rhythmic but catchy little rock tune. The next single, 'A Day Without Me' was a vast improvement on its predecessors, probably because a new producer, Steve Lillywhite, was recruited. The relationship immediately clicked and Lillywhite was able to strengthen *U2's* boyish and thinnish music with an epic strength. The song also featured the memorable Bono line, 'Starting a landslide in my ego, looked from the outside to the world I left behind ...'

Lillywhite stayed on to produce the group's debut album *Boy,* which turned out to be a cracker. Hastily recorded and in some places quite brittle, the record nevertheless has a powerful resonance which feeds off Bono's relentless passion. Its eleven tracks work as a storybook of fragile experiences and observations written and sung by a youth whose fast-growing maturity would soon leave an indelible stamp on Irish rock history. The opening song (and fifth *U2* single) 'I Will Follow' is an heroic effort by any standards and at last *U2* could feel confident that as musicians they had something to offer. Beginning with a 'one, two, three, four' count, a guitar can be heard scraping as if in the distance, then comes a tinkle of bells, a cracking of drums and the line 'I will follow' shrieked by Bono, who continues in episodic fashion to evaluate past feelings with lines like: 'A boy tries hard to be a man, his mother takes him by his hand. He stops to think, he starts to cry. Oh why!' sung against a powerfully charging drum/bass lock. The atmospheric watery break in the middle of the song, a feature that really makes the composition, was achieved by adding the sound of rattling milk bottles and a knife scraping bicycle-wheel spokes to the mix. Lillywhite wasn't afraid to experiment and in a lot of ways he opened up the group to the possibilities of what could be achieved in a modern recording studio. *Boy* is a rush of sparkling subtleties fuelled by Bono's vocals which are allowed to dive and echo against a stormy sea of sound. Full of contrasts, the album can be hallucinogenic and impressionistic like on 'Shadows and Tall Trees', or gushingly plaintive, almost holy, like on 'Into the Heart'. The latter is mostly instrumental — brooding bass from Clayton and cliff-cut guitar chords from Edge which build up to Bono empathetically evoking the wonder of lost childhood with the lines: 'Into the heart of a child, I stayed awhile, yeah I can go back. Into the heart of a child, I stayed awhile, yeah I can go back. Into the heart of a child, I can smile, I can go there ...' Another song, the angry 'Electric Co.', though lyrically obscure is obviously a protest, and it transpires that Bono wrote it because a depressed friend had been cruelly mistreated through the use of electric shock therapy. The album seems to resolve its roaring tensions in 'The Ocean', whose soft and endearing tone summons up aural images of gurgling waves and ships at sea. Lyrically, the song is the most poetic of the selection and the words are worth reproducing in full:

> A picture in grey, Dorian Grey,
> Just me by the sea.
> And I felt like a star,
> I thought the world could go far,
> If they listened to what I said.
>
> The Ocean, the Ocean
> Washes my feet
> Splashes the sole of my shoes.

When I looked around,
The world couldn't be found
Just me by the sea.

The release of *Boy* in October 1980 was to be *U2's* first big test on the international market. Paul McGuinness shrewdly judged that it was better for the band, young though they were, to jump in at the deep end and do a major tour. Getting as many support slots as possible, McGuinness mounted an exhaustive schedule that covered first Europe, then the East Coast of America and then back to the UK. It was a make-or-break situation, but it worked. The American dates went down a storm and were so successful that three more months of Stateside work were in order. Their assault on the American imagination resulted in *Boy* making the billboard charts (with the altered, more abstract sleeve design) and the press marking them as 'the next big thing'. Even the pillar of American rock, Bruce Springsteen, made a point of going backstage at one of their concerts to give them his personal accolade. Unlike countless Irish rock bands who saw England as the be-all and end-all of a career, *U2* made a fortuitous decision to look westwards and placed great emphasis on their American audience — even if, in the beginning, it meant losing vast sums of money. By the summer of 1981 the *Boy* tour was over and *U2* were now seen as a nascent force in international rock music, one that people could look to for hope and inspiration. For Bono Vox, *U2* was much more than music, it was something with a message: 'We want our audience to think about their actions and where they are going, to realise the pressures that are on them but at the same time not to give up.'[6]

OCTOBER

Back in Dublin the four members of *U2* were having personality problems. The evangelical Bono, taciturn Edge and reserved Larry Mullen (who was still recovering from the sudden death of his mother, killed in a traffic accident in 1978) were all getting involved with biblical spiritualism and had an association with the Irish Charismatic movement — a doctrinaire Christian sect which preached re-birth through God. In contrast, the older and more hedonistic Adam Clayton, who saw nothing wrong with drinking, smoking and soft drugs, was little interested in spreading 'the word' and more intent on developing the rock 'n' roll band he had worked so hard for. Whatever the tensions, when it came to getting down to the music they always turned up to rehearsals on time, put as much as possible into their work and Paul McGuinness was happy enough to exclaim, 'There's no waste here.'

The pressures probably added much to the recording of their second album, *October*. Having lost a satchel full of new song lyrics on the previous tour, Bono was in a tough situation of having only three weeks in which to write new material before going into the studio to record. With Steve Lillywhite again at the Windmill Lane controls, there were only three weeks of allotted recording time to complete the project, and in October 1981 the record was released to mixed and sometimes derogatory reviews. Looking back, the LP was a great leap forward for *U2*, for while *Boy* was very much in keeping with the new wave/

alternative music of the time, *October* was a singular invention — at once Irish, spiritual and progressive.

The rusty, grainy quality of the cover, a tasteful photo of the group taken in the heart of Dublin's docklands, evokes the natural calm of an Irish autumn. Inside, the contents are a bundle of contrasting creations, some cacophonous, some wailing, others as still as lake water. Bono's hounding, spiritually expressive vocals spill outward as if into a large fortress of misty autumnal sounds. Exaltation pours from 'Gloria', the opening track, in which Bono quotes from a Latin prayer the line *'Gloria in eo domine, Gloria exultate'*. Here, amid the stormy drums and thick bass lines, Edge's Gibson Explorer guitar seems to push many boundaries as it sails, slides and ratchets in all directions. The ferociously delivered 'I Threw a Brick through a Window' also sees The Edge intensely grinding his instrument, this time to get a ripping/smashing effect which, undercut by a heart-throbbing bass line and flailing drums, enhances the inner confusions and desperation of the lyrics. 'Stranger in a Strange Land', a song which recounts Bono's feelings of alienation in America, keeps up the severe attack of the record as does the speedy, locomotively tumbling 'Rejoice', a song in which Bono sketches the importance of change as that which comes from within (a surprisingly mature sentiment from one so young). 'I Fall Down' is similarly charged musically — acoustic guitar, bumping bass, shimmering cymbals all combine to give a waterfalling, splashing effect to the hastily rendered, emotional but confusing lyrics.

October also offers placidity and calm. The title track is more classical, even choral in nature. Edge's church-like piano motif introduces and sustains a simple lyric by Bono which implicitly contrasts the dying leaves of autumn and the vacillations of history with the eternal being of God. Short and sweet, it is the most beautiful and effective song of the selection. 'Scarlet' is another soothingly quiet track; this time Larry Mullen's cluttered military-style drum rolls and Adam's strong bass add to Edge's sharp guitar strokes and piano tinkles to build a cathedral-like sound around Bono's repetition of the word 'Rejoice'.

As a whole, *October* may have seemed fragmented, bitty, even bombastic to some critics but it repaid many listenings and each song when isolated always had something distinctively attractive about it. 'Tomorrow' seems to sum up all that U2 wanted to say and achieve at the time. An openly ambitious piece of music it is helped along by the deep Celtic pepper of uilleann pipes, courtesy of Vinnie Kilduff (later of *In Tua Nua*). As the song opens a sound like a boulder moving in the background can be heard. Bono's slowly sung words then appear, words which hinge on subconscious images of his mother's death. As the tempo picks up the song's atmosphere is one of divine, almost mythological quality. Flickerings of hills, rivers and other aspects of the Irish countryside easily flood the imagination of any sensitive listener. The climax comes with the full release of the group collected behind the beseeching words:

> Will you be back tomorrow
> Open up, open up to the Lamb of God,
> to the love of He who made the blind to see.
> He's coming back, He's coming back.
> I believe Him, Jesus coming . . .

Regardless of critical misgivings over the viability of *October* as a *de rigueur* modern rock album, *U2's* popularity placed it at number eleven in the British album charts. As a live band they were now very much in demand and after a sell-out tour of the UK they hit American again to round off 1981 in style. It would have been easy at this stage for the young troupers to ease off and relax their pace, but Paul McGuinness sensed that *U2* could only improve through continuous work. In January of 1982 they played the Royal Dublin Society's main hall to its first ever capacity stand-up audience. Then it was back to the States for a fourth tour. This opened in New Orleans where they performed an unusual concert atop a nineteenth-century Mississippi riverboat. Fans were greeted to the spectacle of four Irish guys busily banging out their soaring version of rock 'n' roll as the stage chugged merrily downriver. It was on these Stateside treks that *U2* had the opportunity to come to grips with their music, improvising, extending and exploring their sound as the situation arose. It was also the best way to practise.

The way *U2* were changing, musically speaking, was to bode well for their future. In a strange way their music had more in common with the rhythm and blues of the 1950s and the palpable guitar-based sound of the 1960s than with the synthesiser-filled work of their contemporaries. Excepting the interesting and worthwhile work of those at the very fringes of the alternative music scene, the early 1980s saw the emergence of the image-conscious, new romantic movement in Britain. With their shallow lyrics and synthetic instruments these individuals began to dominate the popular music scene, carrying on as if, in the words of one writer, 'punk never happened'. *U2* combined the best elements of old music and the new without ever falling into parody or caricature. The emphasis was on the vocals as the lead instrument and this allowed The Edge to paint the overall sound with rhythmic guitar pigments. Bono's voice would sometimes get very ragged from shouting on-stage and it was continually Edge who saved the day with his atmospheric guitar craft.

(As an aside it's interesting to note Edge's use of the instrument at this time. His Fender Stratocaster or Gibson Explorer would be fed via a switchbox into two amplification systems, each one set at a different level. The amplification systems were made up of two Memory Man echo-units linked to two separate old fashioned Vox AC30 amplifiers. The powerful sound pulses which this arrangement produced were in some ways better than having platforms of Marshall stacks fed by tens of wah-wah and fuzz pedals. It was an economical innovation with simple technology and very in tune with the better side of the minimalist new wave.)

WAR

U2's only vinyl release of 1982 was the single 'A Celebration' (Island) in March. Done between concert commitments, it suffered from a hasty execution and was interesting only for its B side, the superbly ironic 'Trash, Trampoline and the Party Girl', a song whose most striking image is that of a girl desperately trying to find something beyond a superficial party world. Musically, the song's banjo-style acoustic guitar adds a new dimension to the *U2* sound. Still a stronger live group than a recording one, they continued to tour, and after America a special set of European showcase appearances were lined up. Near the summer news filtered through that Ireland's most durable rock magazine, *Hot Press* was having financial difficulties and that a benefit *cum* fifth birthday festival would be held somewhere in the country. It seemed fitting that U2 play their part, for it was *Hot Press's* Bill Graham who had championed the band in their early days and introduced Adam Clayton to Paul McGuinness. Furthermore, *Hot Press* had continually supported the group even through the down periods when nothing seemed to be going right. The time was right for U2 to return the favour.

I can remember the heat of that summer July day as Punchestown racecourse shimmered in the spanning green of the eastern midlands. Rory Gallagher was the main attraction, and as well as U2 and a new rock group named *Eugene*, there were to be some surprise guests. The clear blue skies were dotted with small aircraft, part of an aerobatics display that would entertain the crowds between sets. As the planes circled, the sun's rays would intermittently flash off their bodies, lighting them up like luminous beacons. *Eugene* gave an energetic and sprightly performance, but U2 stole the show. Bono, as per normal, climbed all over the loudspeakers and trestling, going out of his way to reach and uplift his audience. People just stood, staring, mesmerised by U2's music. Afterwards, parachutists descended from gaily coloured planes which trailed cloudy blue, red and purple smoke from their tails. During Rory Gallagher's heavy guitar set the backstage area became crowded with numerous press and road crew (myself included), all indulging in drugs of one sort or another. As lines of cocaine were sniffed and joints inhaled, Philip Lynott and Paul Brady appeared from nowhere to join Gallagher on-stage for an unanticipated jam session. With people coming and going, jostling each other to get a piece of whatever action was going down behind the stage, I remember seeing Bono, arms folded, standing aloof, the rest of the group behind him. A disdainful look covered his young face as he coldly watched the indulgent activities of what to him were associated with the old ways of rock music. The situation must have appeared trite in contrast to the previous day's special inner city concert that U2 played for the poor of Dublin's worst tenements.

Again and again, Bono had expressed in interviews that U2 were not about the indulgence of rock 'n' roll as a self-gratifying, ego-boosting and decadent phenomenon but about rock 'n' roll as something which inspires, something which catalyses people to act for their own good. Now in their twenties he, Edge and Mullen had long left the Charismatics behind and through constant travelling had seen and felt a much bigger, more complex world than that of their teenage years. It was time to stop being introspective and start incorporating a social and political awareness in the music itself, where it could be heard by the masses. Starting in August, studio work at Windmill Lane lasted until December. Steve Lillywhite, after doing their first two albums, was loath to do a third one because he felt that things would get formulaic and predictable. Several other producers were tried out but nothing really happened, so Lillywhite again was called in to sit at the controls. It was to be a strenuous job. U2's sound was kneaded and pummelled, reinforced with greater substance and expanded to incorporate acoustic guitars, violin, saxophone and backing vocalists. The Edge got an opportunity to nourish the music with a lap steel guitar, an Epiphone 1940s model, which he had picked up in Nashville. He also started to use his voice, singing solo and accompanying Bono on harmonies. The latter also changed role slightly by playing guitar, something that he hadn't done for a while. The resultant album was clamorously titled *War*.

The record was a crucially important creation for its time. It rallied against the coldness of the eighties, an era which had seen the increasing influence of right-wing governments, the worsening of East-West relations, the threat of nuclear destruction loom larger every day, international terrorist acts become commonplace, and murder, carnage and disorder spread through the world like a contaminating virus. From the Solidarity struggle in Poland to the ceaseless killings in Northern Ireland to the British-Argentinian war in the Falklands to the Christian-Moslem slaughter of the Middle East to American corruption in Central America — it was obvious that no lessons had been learned from the past. What had been learned was that the world was a worse place than was imagined. The youth that grew up to the sound of punk rock also grew up with more knowledge of how close the world was to self-detonation, how manipulative and corrupting the media was, how much power rested in the hands of the few. During the 1960s rock music became socially and politically involved, supporting people who spoke out about Vietnam and civil rights. By the early seventies it had become self-effacing and decadent. The *Rolling Stones'* irresponsible Altamont catastrophe in December 1969 (where beatings and murder were enacted to their music) and their subsequent decline almost reflected the step-by-step erosion of rock music as an instrument of positive change. *U2* had often voiced their dissatisfaction with rock music of the past for not fulfilling that role. *War* was proof that they put their music where their mouths were.

The best track from the album, and *U2's* ninth single, 'New Year's Day' was released in January of 1983. The video which accompanied the single portrayed *U2* as four figures on horseback, galloping across a snow-covered terrain, large billowing white flags projecting upwards from their backs. A shrill, hollow clang describes the rough metallic surface of the music. The ricocheting of spherical sound, so much a part of *October*, has been replaced with a compacted tension — a tension that slowly unwinds itself as the piston-like drums and strafing guitar gather momentum. Bono's voice sounds less hysterical and enters the mix as a disciplined instrument, one which outlines a chaotic world he sees as being 'under a blood red sky'. The organisation of the track allows Edge to really excel himself on the guitar, filling the lengthy non-vocal, middle section with successive riffs and solos that abound with invention. Overall, the *U2* sound has become more aggressive, more controlled, more pointed. The song ends on a note of resignation, unusual for Bono but quite appropriate to the broader view of a more reality-conscious songwriter:

> And so we are told this is
> the golden age,
> And gold is the reason for
> the wars we wage.

Though I want to be with you,
To be with you night and day
Nothing changes on New Year's Day.

Not surprisingly, given a foretaste so strong, given a band with by then such a fanatical following, given the international circumstances and the need for young people to have a rock music they could believe in, the official release of *War* (Island) on 28 February saw it make Irish rock history by dropping into the number one position at the top of the British album charts. A real album of its time, it hasn't dated well and in retrospect could be described as a live album of live music better suited to the concert place than the turntable. This is definitely the case with its opening cut, the controversial 'Sunday Bloody Sunday'. From the musical point of view it is plodding in tempo, loosely arranged and suffers from poor vocal harmonies from The Edge. More than that it is simplistic in structure and after one or two hearings becomes monotonous to the ear. But, and this is the fundamental reason for *U2's* ascendant, it is more than a song, more than music. Any Irish man or woman hearing it can immediately identify the source of its title in the blood-soaked history of their nation. There are two incidents called Bloody Sunday documented in the books. The first occurred during the British-Irish War of Independence, when in 1920 English soldiers gunned down several people indiscriminately at a football match in Dublin's Croke Park. The second was more recent and had been incorporated into songs by both Paul McCartney and John Lennon — the January 1972 massacre of thirteen civilians by British troops in Northern Ireland. 'Sunday Bloody Sunday' stood up to the world and shouted for an end to war. It cites 'the trenches dug within our hearts' as the true culprits for strife at all levels. It subtly denounces the need for rebel songs and brings its message beyond Irish-only connotations into an international context. The words 'when fact is fiction and TV is reality' clearly point to the numbing and corrupting effect of television on the human psyche. Incidentally, this echoes the cutting line, 'the news today will be the movies of tomorrow' by the American rock musician of the sixties Arthur Lee.[7] It would not be the first or the last time that favourable comparisons could be made between the work of Bono and *U2* and that of Lee and his group *Love*.

The subversive nature of *War* continues in 'Seconds', a creeping piece of jangling acoustic guitars and cut-in television sound where Edge distinguishes himself on lead vocals. The lurking frailty of the song and the sinister portents of lines like 'it takes a second to say goodbye' succeed in getting across the precariousness of life in the atomic age. After the superlative 'New Year's Day' comes the noisy 'Like a Song', in which Bono over-stretches his voice to emotionally scream for an end to the tribalism and divisions of man. The instrumentation is superb, Larry Mullen's drums bang, bang, banging through a mesh of Edge guitar breaks. 'And we love to wear a badge, a uniform. And we love to fly a flag,' shouts Bono, as a battlefield of wild music flails around him, Edge's piercing electric guitar spinning icicles of ever-assailing brilliance. Side One ends with the calming 'Drowning Man'. Here, one can easily imagine a mist floating across a far eastern location, like that of say Japan after the holocaust of 1945. Again, biting acoustic guitar rhythms back the lyrics as Bono invokes the power of love — in this context a transcendent force that goes beyond the ugliness of the world. Musically, the arrangement of the song is more colourful than anything else on the album, benefiting much by effective multi-tracked harmonies and Steve Wickham's floating violin. (Wickham was at that point also putting down session takes for the newly formed *In Tua Nua*.)

Side Two begins with 'Refugee' on which a searing electric guitar gives muster to another angry assault on warfare — this time it is the effects of imperialism that are under attack, where innocent people are displaced from their homelands and more often than not offered a dislocating, consumer world as pitiful compensation for their plight. Veering into beat-pop territory, the next track 'Two Hearts Beat as One' rocks forth with a jagged frenzy, lyrically celebrating the joy of human bonding in a music that shunts, slices and dances along. Interestingly, this was *U2's* first excursion into dance music and was released as their tenth single shortly after *War* came out with a special extra re-mix by New York disco producer Francois Kevorkian. The ominous side of *War* resurfaced in 'Surrender', a song about a girl who in forsaking her apartment life ended up on the hostile streets. Here the scrapings of Edge's guitar adequately convey a terrifying experience. The album closes with the poignantly beautiful '40'. The best group effort of the set, its slow tempo is symmetrically balanced between Adam's hanging bass line, Larry's strident drums, Edge's understated electric and acoustic guitars, and Bono's measured vocals. A fitting climax to *U2's* most demonstrative release since they began recording, the song places *War's* out-pourings into a spiritual place. 'I waited patiently for the Lord, He inclined and heard my cry,' sings Bono, who then implores 'How long to sing this song', meaning why do we have to put up with all the evil in the world? The singer then resolves to sing a new song and the piece ends on a joyous note.

War was an unorthodox release for its time, politically provocative and musically out of synch with the general level of post-punk rock. Edge's guitar playing was more sixties/early seventies in fashion and the arrangements of the songs had little in common with the short, sharp, shock music of the times. *U2's* approach to the studio and complexity of song design was more in keeping with the progressive rock attitude than that of a garage band of the punk era. Even if only four of *War's* songs 'New Year's Day', 'Drowning Man', 'Like a Song' and '40' would stand the harsh test of time, the album succeeded in establishing *U2* as a premier-league rock band. Both the spring British tour and the American summer concerts were sold out, long in advance of the group's arrival. Bono would introduce 'Sunday Bloody Sunday' with the line, 'This is not a rebel song, this is "Sunday Bloody Sunday".' Transformed into an anthemic protest live, its impact was heightened by Bono's spectacular use of large white flags on poles — emblems of neutrality, emblems of peace, proferred in the face of partisan symbols. Criss-crossing America the group did up to twenty-five dates a month, Bono getting more and more caught up in the spectacle of the shows. Sometimes he would dive into the audience so uninhibitedly that the whole thing was in danger of going dangerously out of control. At the Los Angeles Sports Arena the crazed lead singer found himself jumping off balconies 20ft from the ground, getting torn to shreds by the crowds that caught him and eventually fighting with the very audience he had come to entertain. One positive side to the

American tour was U2's sympathetic performance at Bill Graham's 'US' festival which attracted three hundred thousand people to see musicians of past and future generations play together in a spirit of peaceful harmony. The ultimate U2 concert of that period was done on 5 June at Red Rocks canyon in Denver, Colorado. The audio/visual recording of this event would later be released partly on record and fully on video, bringing home to European audiences the proportions of U2's messianic American following.

At the end of the tour the group arrived back to Ireland for a rest and then played an unfortunate open-air concert at Dublin's Phoenix Park. U2 were supported by UK groups *Steel Pulse, Big Country, The Eurythmics* and *Simple Minds*. The venue would have been adequate if the stage had been placed in the park itself, allowing plenty of room for all and sundry. Instead, it was set in the grandstand end of the racecourse, the stage facing a small area of tarmac and then the terraced stands. Placed obliquely, only those right in front of the stage could see anything and most of the people present were at the sides. Too many people were allowed in and the area became congested. No refreshment centre was available inside the concert area and if one wanted a drink a push through a dense crowd was necessary. Once one got to the outer fringes a complicated queueing/pass-out system had to be gone through before any refreshment was capable of being consumed. As the heat of the day increased, people got more restless. The other bands were greeted with howls for U2, and their performances suffered accordingly. People were being brought out on stretchers intermittently and on the perimeter I witnessed the horrible sight of bouncers beating would-be gate crashers with clubs. Dogs were also in force and after seeing people being mauled by wild Alsatians I said that was it. I didn't stay for the show and wondered how a group with such a professed care for their audience allowed a situation nearing that of Altamont take place under their very noses.

I didn't know it at the time, but U2 were themselves getting tired of the spectacle of their show, the rock 'n' roll delusion that they had so often railed against was in danger of engulfing them. If they weren't to become another *Rolling Stones* something would have to be done. After Phoenix Park, Bono talked of breaking up the band, starting again from scratch and re-inventing U2 with the same people. He had called *War* a 'slap in the face', but that slap could have dire consequences if not controlled. Anyhow, the end of 1983 was eventful. In November an album of live material taken from various concerts in the US and Europe was released, and called *Under a Blood Red Sky* (Island). It went straight into the British album charts at number two. Divorced from the actuality of their execution, most of the record's eight tracks sound lacklustre and forced. As a lasting artistic contribution only one song 'Party Girl' really stands up to scrutiny. Originally the B side of the 'A Celebration' single, in the live arena 'Party Girl' becomes instantly more dynamic, more interesting and stands as one of U2's best recorded tracks. *Under a Blood Red Sky*, for all its faults, is worth having for that song alone. U2 also travelled to Japan to do their first concerts there. The year closed with the group, to their credit, appearing at a grand charity gala held in London's Apollo Theatre. Called The Big One, the gala was organised to aid the Campaign for Nuclear Disarmament and served as a positive finale to a stormy year's work.

No longer boys (both Bono and Edge were now married men) U2 were at a crossroads. A repetition of 1983 was to be avoided at all costs. Musically, the band had to crack through the mould of their sound, a sound which, the live album had shown, was getting jaded. A new direction was necessary, but how was it to be achieved? During 1983 Edge had taken some time away from U2 to work with avant-garde musicians Holger Czukay and Jaki Liebezeit (of German electronic rock group *Can*) on an album produced by Francois Kevorkian. *Snake Charmer* (Island), an overtly dance-oriented package, shows the guitar player enjoying himself in a new format. 'Hold Onto Your Dreams', partly written by Edge, is an excursion into a popular form that he had only brushed against on 'Two Hearts Beat as One'. Edge had always admired experimental musicians like Robert Fripp and Czukay, so maybe U2 could move towards that area sound-wise? In order to do this they would have to approach the recording of their next album from an entirely new angle and the best way was to enlist the aid of a new producer. Steve Lillywhite, Jimmy Iovine, Martin Hannett, Chas de Whalley, Bill Whelan and Kevorkian had all done sterling work in the past, but now someone really innovative was required. Conny Plank, Czukay's long-time collaborator, was suggested but an Englishman by the name of Brian Eno would eventually be the one to pull U2's music up to the higher ground.

THE UNFORGETTABLE FIRE

At first Eno wasn't that enthusiastic about working with U2. He had listened to their back catalogue but found little to inspire him there. Bono kept phoning him persistently until he gave in and came to Ireland out of simple curiosity. Eno's work with *Roxy Music* and David Bowie had established him as something of a technical wizard in the rock world, while his environmental and tonal music of the seventies and eighties was unusually advanced. A product of the radical British art schools of the 1960s, Eno had always been interested in breaking new ground. Intensely prolific, he had moved restlessly between rock, classical and jazz music as well as taking in such varied disciplines as fine art, producing, theorising, lecturing, writing, video creation and soundtrack recording. He was always looking for a new challenge and U2's intense desire to work with him was intriguing.

When Eno arrived in Dublin he was presented with a spectacular scenario. U2 were going to get away from the stuffiness of doing everything in a studio and instead freely created their new music in the grounds and large rooms of a huge medieval castle. Eno was stunned when he saw Slane Castle in county Meath. A centrepiece of Celtic history, standing on the banks of the river Boyne, surrounded by burial grounds and stone edifices from ancient times — U2's idea was to catch the ethereal nature of the mystical Irish character. Eno was the perfect choice of producer. He immediately grasped the subtleties of what was required and was impressed by U2 as individuals. 'I'd seldom met a group of people so fierce in their belief in their own music. Something about their honesty as people attracted me. They wanted to build from strength and limitations.'[8]

The project took up most of 1984. The title of the album *The Unforgettable Fire* (Island) came from a book of paintings done by survivors of the Japanese

81

82

81 Edge — his ratchety guitar clang is the distinguishing feature of *U2*'s firebrand rock 'n' roll.

82 Daniel Lanois, the French-Canadian engineer/musician, who co-produced both *The Unforgettable Fire* and *The Joshua Tree* albums.

84

83

85

83 Brian Eno — impressed by *U2*'s commitment, he co-produced *The Unforgettable Fire* and *The Joshua Tree* with Lanois.

84 Bono sings about Martin Luther King and the 'Unforgettable Fire', Nantes, France, November 1984.

85 Larry Mullen Jnr deep in the heart of America — *Joshua Tree* session 1987.

86 Adam Clayton 1984 — European tour.

87 Even if the hair got longer and the clothes more hippie, Bono's social and political awareness was never in any doubt.

86

87

holocaust of 1945, the fire being that produced by the nuclear bombing of Nagasaki and Hiroshima. During the course of its recording a short documentary of the proceedings was filmed by former *Horslips* man Barry Devlin. Screened on RTE television that winter, it is a seldom-seen look at *U2* in the genesis of its creativity. One sees instruments scattered throughout the castle. The four members of the group are driving themselves very hard — Bono screeching vocals into a microphone, Edge bending strings and throwing out licks in all directions, Adam crashing out on a couch, exhausted, and Larry pounding his drums with all his might. The acoustics seem to be pretty strange in the large halls and rooms of the castle. One can see Eno sitting pensively in the background, listening and making suggestions as his Canadian engineer, Daniel Lanois, uses a portable studio set-up to catch the various sounds. The film concentrated on the recording of 'Pride (In the Name of Love)', *U2's* eleventh single and first Top Three British chart hit. One sees Bono struggling with a very high vocal while the Edge tries in vain to synchronise his guitar part. Eno, as ever, works hard to tease out the essence of what they are after. Cutting to Windmill Lane, the footage then shows the realisation of the track. After a frustrating period of getting nowhere, Eno takes a chance and slows down the backing track to suit Bono's vocal. In a flash of inspiration, Larry Mullen then comes up with a suitable drum bridge and the whole thing comes together like magic.

Not all of *The Unforgettable Fire* recordings came as quickly as 'Pride'. There were numerous patchy songs, half-baked ideas and distended periods of lyrical and musical vacuity that dogged the sessions. Given the open-endedness of the execution, it could have carried on for much longer than it did, but sense prevailed and the proceedings were wound up in the autumn. It had been an historic experience both for *U2* and the Irish public — the feeling being that rock music was going to get an injection of something extraordinary, something hewn from the very core of Ireland's heritage. The October 1984 release of *The Unforgettable Fire* saw it cruise right into the number one slot in the British album charts. The second successive *U2* album to do this, their achievement in terms of popularity was incomparable to any other Irish rock band in history.

The Unforgettable Fire was no pop album, contrived into a number one position by savvy marketing ploys, but an upfront, modern, progressive rock album whose relationship to anything else at the time was like that of chalk to cheese. What had propelled it so high was that it was wanted by *U2's* loyal and rapidly burgeoning body of fans who saw in the group a meaningful, fresh new voice for rock music, one that tried harder to make its music matter. The album was unlike anything else ever heard. From its very opening song, 'A Sort of Homecoming', the rain, drizzle, driving snow and sunshine of Ireland's changeable north Atlantic climate rise up at you through the music. Waters flow as smooth as silk through the velvet-like production. The drums wash on your ears like waves pounding on a shore. Edge's guitar ratchets back and forth as if being refracted through some prismatic substance. Bono's voice soars like an avenging angel, intent on making its truthful words ring deafeningly clear.

Dotted with references to American history, the record's strongest feature is the second track, 'Pride (In the Name of Love)', a fearsome requiem for Martin

Luther King. Killed on 4 April 1968, the black, non-violent, civil rights campaigner could have no better tribute. Full of the pain and strength of the black leader's struggle, Bono's lyrics adamantly convey the righteousness of King's cause. The strength that comes through the song is amplified by Edge's scorching guitar refrain, a riff that recreates in sound the image of a burning wheel revolving at high speed. The conciseness and precision of 'Pride' is abandoned for a let-all-hell-break-loose style on 'Wire'. Lyrically obscure to the point of nonsense the song seems to relate to the death penalty and its application in the States. Musically, too many things are going on for a listener to readily warm to the track. The album returns to form on the title track 'The Unforgettable Fire'. It is here that Brian Eno's characteristic Ambient washes and textures really come into their own, stretching the music spatially, giving it a depth that it never had before. Lyrically colourful, the track is imbued with an atmosphere of fog and water, an heroic atmosphere that could be interpreted as either that of pre-civilisation or post-modern. Highly impressionistic 'The Unforgettable Fire' works as a song because the breathy voices, spraying drums and a dramatic string section all fuse into an alchemical mixture of real beauty.

From the band's point of view that track was a tough cookie to crack. It had originated as a simple piano piece that Edge thought might work as film music. After the group arrived back from Japan, Edge and Bono were just messing around one day with the basic motif which they put through a synthesiser and drum machine. When Adam and Larry heard it the composition was worked up to a group creation. Still it was very messy and Bono had to keep adding and subtracting melodies to get it right. During the album session Edge found that the guitar wasn't right so he scrapped playing chords or single notes and opted instead to work it with open harmonies. He considered it his best dance (!) music, but it took a long time to get it right.

The last song on Side One, 'Promenade', is a very introspective type of medium-tempo love ballad whose sensitive arrangement and sparkling guitar sound suit its slightly melancholic air. Side Two opens with '4th of July', an instrumental piece of mood music where U2 simply allow their sound to be enveloped by Eno's Ambient textures. An interesting experiment, it turns out to be a very effective diversion into avant-garde territory. Clayton's simple bass and Edge's flying guitar are transformed by Eno into something akin to an aural aquarium, a veritable science fiction soundscape. Following that comes the potent 'Bad', Bono's anti-heroin plea. Lyrically exceptional in that it flows, communicates and graphically illustrates the singer's meaning, the song stands out as Bono's best effort as a writer since he started. Building slowly through a series of harrowing images, Bono emotively gets across the effect of his seeing a heroin-addicted friend die in Dublin. The music keeps its distance as the distraught vocalist implores the victim to leave behind all the 'desperation', 'dislocation', 'separation', 'condemnation', 'temptation', 'isolation' and 'desolation' by throwing the 'lifeless lifeline to the wind'. It was destined to become one of U2's most respected songs and in concert becomes more stirringly emotional than on record. The North American connotations of *The Unforgettable Fire* re-surface on 'Indian Summer Sky', 'Elvis Presley and America' and 'MLK', the last three tracks of the album. 'Indian Summer Sky', a charging, almost tribal rocker, concerns itself with the plight of the Red Indians in a constricting, capitalist society that has forced them to accept its concrete life in return for everything that was their spirit. The song paints a picture of someone attempting to get back to the elemental forces that were America, the natural environment that is the Indians' real home. The abstract quality of the album turns to confusion on 'Elvis Presley and America', the most opaque track of the set. Here words and music wrench at each other, none finding clear definition in a turmoil of nuance, jangling guitar and hearkening emotion. One only knows it is about Elvis Presley from its title, for the lyrics are much too personalised to have any meaning for an outside listener. Even if it fails on that level, 'Elvis Presley and America' fits in quite nicely with the overall atmosphere of the album. The record was brought to a close with the gospel-like 'MLK', where again Martin Luther King is remembered. Lamenting but spiritually uplifting in feeling, this short song evokes sadness and joy. Its emotion is heightened by its simple structure — just Bono's vocal set against Eno's ominous background treatments, which sound full of incipient thunder and rain.

The Unforgettable Fire could be said to be U2's first real album of music, something which exists as an entity in itself away from the phenomenon of the band. By risking the familiarity of their accustomed ways for an unorthodox, letting-go approach they had succeeded in becoming real musicians. Tracks like 'Pride', 'Bad' and 'MLK' are Bono writing real songs and not the usual flimsy attempts at stream-of-consciousness writing. Edge refined his style, peeling down the basic sounds of his guitar, and simultaneously explored new permutations of sound. Adam's bass playing comes out much more in front. Full of funk and black music slaps, his bass makes the album a very rhythmic listening experience. The most striking factor of the work is the sustained and flourishing drum technique of Larry Mullen Jnr. In places where The Unforgettable Fire seems to be in danger of loosening up too much Larry's kit binds the sounds together. By bringing in Eno and Lanois, U2 circumvented the possibility of stalemate in their art. In a lot of ways they gave themselves the opportunity to start all over again. The big test was how would their audience take to the new music.

Starting in Australia, the Unforgettable Fire tour would last for the remainder of 1984 and right through the first six months of 1985. Early shows were problematic affairs as the band struggled to incorporate the complex new material into their usual set. As time wore on though, the concerts would get more polished and effective. To the surprise of the vast crowds which turned up to see them all over the world U2 would sometimes throw in a cover of a Bob Dylan song or boogie with a Led Zeppelin or Neil Young rocker. The days were long gone when the group were obliged to pour cold water on such musicians of the pre-punk generation. In fact Edge had first learned guitar from Rory Gallagher records and Bono had grown up listening to the music of Dylan and Jimi Hendrix. In the white heat of punk such things were considered regressive but by the mid 1980s U2 had grown to appreciate the music of the past as all part of rock's rich tapestry. As a case in point, during The Unforgettable Fire sessions, Bono had made an impromptu guest appearance at Bob Dylan's Slane Castle concert. The July bash was a legendary affair with UB 40, Santana and Van Morrison all contributing to the greatness of the event. Near the end of Dylan's lengthy performance Bono came on-stage and made a go of accompanying the inventor of folk-rock on two songs, 'Leopardskin Pillbox Hat' and 'Blowin' in the Wind'. Bono muffed his lines and was criticised for making an exhibition of himself in front of so prestigious a figure, yet he had displayed a solidarity with the music of the 1960s.

U2 were a changing band and happenings over the next two years would alter their perspectives even further. As the Unforgettable Fire show juggernauted its way across the globe many people became suspicious of their motives. Taunts of 'ivory tower rock stars' and 'embryonic millionaires' were thrown at them as frequently as words of praise. No matter how sincere they tried to be, U2 were viewed from some quarters as another stadium band, isolated from mainstream life by adulation, wealth and fame. The argument had its pros and cons. Bono had professed his concern for the plight of others and was willing to invest time and energy bettering the situation for the people of his home town and elsewhere. The band had stayed in Dublin, helped expand the facilities there for rock music, employed a lot of Irish people and brought large revenues into a country considered Third World by Western European standards. U2 had also set up Mother Records, a label specifically designed to give an opportunity to up-and-coming or obscure acts to issue a record. In Tua Nua, Cactus World News, Tuesday Blue, Operating Theatre, The Subterraneans and The Hot House Flowers would be some of the Irish bands to benefit from this venture. More importantly, the words of the critics were made to sound hollow when during the beginning of the American leg of the tour Bono and Adam downed tools and swiftly made their way to London to involve themselves in Bob Geldof's famine relief Band Aid record. More than just a gesture of benevolence, Geldof's feat would stimulate a complete re-think among rock and popular musicians of how to use their talents to improve the situation of the needy, the oppressed and the discriminated against. U2 would always be on hand to contribute their share.

The early months of 1985 found the band still gigging around the States. In March they became the first Irish rock band to grace the front cover of Rolling Stone magazine. Their Unforgettable Fire album, having dented the American Top Twenty, drew a lot of positive attention and the Stone went so far as to rate them 'our choice band of the '80s'. Back in England, Island Records chose April to release some special U2 singles packages. The ordinary 7 inch disc features the original album version of 'The Unforgettable Fire' track, but the B side is a new live recording of 'A Sort of Homecoming', produced by Tony Visconti. A double-pack 7 inch contains these tracks but also includes three new items. All out-takes from the Slane Castle recordings, they are 'Love Comes Tumbling', 'Sixty Seconds in Kingdom Come' and 'The Three Sunrises'. 'Love Comes Tumbling' looks back to the Boy days in terms of its guitar sound, is pop-sounding and simply structured by a neat bass and drums backbeat. Lyrically, it is quite abstract. 'Sixty Seconds in Kingdom Come' is more of a musical doodle than anything else, and too vaporous in quality to be memorable. 'The Three Sunrises' is a very uplifting song with 1960s style refrain and harmonies. It commences with a familiar touch of Eno Ambience but really tightens up into the most traditional hard rock of the band's career thus far. Edge's guitar playing is particularly exciting as it trembles and saws electric riffs throughout. The

12 inch version includes the contents of the 7 inch plus finished versions of 'Love Comes Tumbling' and 'The Three Sunrises' (although the difference between these and the out-takes is indiscernible!) and another new cut, 'Bass Trap'. The latter has Brian Eno using all his abilities to treat Edge's sound as pure fabric. With hints of voices in the far distant background the shimmering soft guitar passages animate an aural effect of a deep blue ocean rippling under a clear panoramic sky. It is like a form of aesthetic fantasy music and is the most inspired of the releases. The following month Island in America issued a new pressing of that 12 inch single under the title *Wide Awake in America*. Instead of the five tracks contained in the English copy, this Stateside release features only three of these but compensates with an extra new live recording of 'Bad'. This turned out to be the definitive version of the song on vinyl, where Bono was heard to reach new depths of emotional expression. Unfortunately, because of its dramatic new cover artwork and one previously unreleased track, the record was dubiously imported into Europe where in some shops it was sold for triple the price of its European counterpart!

Still playing hard, U2 were set to return to Ireland in June for their biggest homecoming concert ever in Dublin's Croke Park. Perfectly timed to coincide with the Dublin City Carnival, U2 had gone to the trouble to sponsor an exhibition of words and images connected with the themes of the *Unforgettable Fire* album. At the Grapevine Arts Centre the public could see for themselves the naked truth of Hiroshima and Martin Luther King's struggle. Up to sixty thousand people turned up at Croke Park on 29 June to see the band and by all accounts it was an incredible performance. U2's message was never more clear than when, during 'Pride' and 'Sunday Bloody Sunday' the stadium erupted in unison song and the entire city of Dublin was hailed over with a sonic blast of thousands of voices. This was the last official date of the Unforgettable Fire tour, but one more concert had to be played, and it was in Wembley Stadium, London, the following month. Yes, on 13 July 1985 U2 the band became U2 the legend as they stepped onto Bob Geldof's Live Aid stage. A highpoint of their career, millions of people must have shared the ecstasy, the tears and the sheer joy of seeing them play their hearts out for the people of Africa. This was, for me, one of the greatest moments in Irish rock history. (See coda.)

It would be reasonable to think that after seven years of hard slog, the four members of U2 would now take time off to take stock of their situation. In the strict sense the U2 shop was now temporarily closed, that is of course until another album was due to be delivered to Island. But as individuals and as a group there were a lot of things that had to be done behind and in front of the scenes. Later that summer they made a surprise appearance at RTE's 'Lark by the Lee Fields', a free festival of music organised for the benefit of people in Cork. After that Bono and his wife, Alison, in response to what Bob Geldof had done, made an unpublicised trip to Ethiopia to work for seven weeks in the famine relief effort. On the music front Bono recorded some collaborative material in 1985 which was released near the end of the year. The first of these was with Irish folk rock group *Clannad*. U2 had been fans of their soft Celtic music for quite a while and at many concerts had used their 'Theme from Harry's Game' as a suitable post-show epilogue. The Donegal group wanted somebody to contribute an additional vocal to a song they had written called 'In a Lifetime' and Bono was chosen to be the guest singer. The climactic song, where *Clannad's* Máire Ní Bhraonáin and Bono successfully play off each other's abilities, appeared on the album *Macalla* (RCA) released in October. This wasn't the end of that association, for shortly afterwards Bono, Edge and video director Meirt Avis all took a hand in making the promotional film for the single release of the song. Executed in *Clannad's* windswept home town of Gweedore that winter, it was a suitable representation of all the traditional Irishness and mysticism that 'In a Lifetime' conveyed.

Bono also contributed to an album titled *Sun City: Artists United Against Apartheid* released on the Manhattan/EMI label in November. The track was called 'Silver and Gold' and it won worldwide acclaim for its castigation of Botha's South African regime as well as being critically lauded in music circles for its bluesy intensity. Put down in America with *Rolling Stones* Keith Richards and Ron Wood, the song sprang out of a recording session organised by ex-Bruce Springsteen guitarist 'Miami' Steve Van Zandt. Enraged by the South African system and encouraged by the effectiveness of Bob Geldof's Band Aid idea, Van Zandt decided to organise a special recording revolving around the title 'Sun City' (the place in question being one of excessive white wealth situated in the middle of a poor black settlement). Van Zandt ably persuaded some of the best names in the music business to lend a voice, including Springsteen, Jackson Browne, Lou Reed, Gil Scott-Heron and a highly vitriolic Miles Davis. After returning from Ethiopia, Bono flew straight over to the States to add his strength to the proposed all-star 'Sun City' single and video. When the sessions turned from a single into an album he wrote 'Silver and Gold'. All royalties from the project went to aid oppressed black South Africans. This was a formative experience for Bono for it was with Richards and Wood that he learned the value of the blues.

In 1986 U2 seemed to go out of their way to confound both their critics and their fans. Popping up here and there Bono and Co. were looking and sounding quite different from what people expected of Dublin's 'holiest' rock band. Sporting beards, long hair and scruffy clothes more suitable to a late sixties/early seventies hippie group, both Edge and Bono were now showing the influences of having absorbed a different set of cultural references from those which had inspired their earlier work. Early in the year an appearance on RTE's 'TV Ga Ga' was like that of a wild American country rock combo as U2 beat out two new songs called 'Womanfish' and 'I Trip through Your Wires'. Viewers were left wondering what this new U2 were up to and whether their next album would be in this idiom. Unlike the grand occasion that surrounded the recording of *The Unforgettable Fire*, the making of their fifth studio LP was to be something of a well-kept secret, shrouded in vague hints and non-statements. After Brian Eno opened his Works Constructed with Sound and Light exhibition in London that March it was strongly suggested that the next U2 album would be produced by him as well. Though no confirmations were forthcoming, Eno did come to Dublin that spring to check out some rough material the group had demoed. It transpired that they had worked out quite a bit of new stuff on the Unforgettable Fire tour and that it was to be honed down in segments, then recorded in two-week sessions. The location this time would be Adam Clayton's largish south Dublin house, but work would also take place in all the band's Dublin residences as well as Windmill Lane. There was to be a lot of free time in between the fortnightly recordings, to regenerate but also because Edge was working on his first film soundtrack and Bono had committed the band to some special engagements.

The first of these was the great Self Aid extravaganza at Dublin's RDS grounds on 17 May. Here, with almost every notable Irish folk and rock act, and a few English ones besides, U2 played a short set of music for the benefit of Ireland's unemployed. Headliners on the day, U2 did a belter of a set. Along with the usual standards, a tassle-jacketed and hairy Bono blasted out versions of Eddie Cochran's 'C'mon Everybody', Bob Dylan's 'Maggie's Farm' and John Lennon's 'Cold Turkey'. The latter was re-written to include references to the danger of nuclear reactors and was accompanied by a roaring tape collage of political speeches intercut with the sound of American F III fighter planes and broadcasts from the recent US bombing of Libya. It was a shocking performance, in the best sense of the word. Through their music U2 made a clear statement about how they felt about Ireland's emigration and unemployment problem but also drove home the explicit evil of heroin addiction, nuclear power and America's sabre-rattling power displays.

At Self Aid the group had made a necessary contribution to the state of their homeland and revealed a continuing awareness of world problems. As far back as September 1985, U2 had promised Amnesty International, the world organisation for the release of prisoners of conscience, that they would contribute in some way to their twenty-fifth anniversary year. Lots of ideas were thrown around but when other musicians like England's Peter Gabriel and Sting, and America's Lou Reed, Joan Baez and Jackson Browne all said they'd contribute, a special short 'super-star' tour was organised in favour of Amnesty. So in June U2 again broke off work on their album to do some trouping for a just cause. Under the banner of A Conspiracy of Hope, six special shows were staged across America — starting at the Cow Palace, San Francisco, and ending at Giants Stadium, New Jersey. At the Los Angeles concert Bob Geldof, Bob Dylan and Tom Petty made some guest appearances. In Atlanta Sting reformed *The Police* and U2 jammed with Lou Reed. When the entire party of 8 bands, 36 musicians, 200 tour personnel and 250 tons of equipment reached the East Coast, morale was so high that an extra appearance was put in for the Anti-Apartheid movement. Around an estimated sixty thousand people converged on New York's Central Park on 14 June for the climax of a rally against racism. Several musicians performed and Bono was re-united with Steve Van Zandt as U2 backed him on a sweltering version of 'Sun City'. The finale to the Amnesty tour came the following night in New Jersey where, in front of live television cameras, some former prisoners of conscience gratefully joined the musicians on-stage for an upliftingly appropriate version of Bob Dylan's 'I Shall Be Released'.

As a direct reaction to U2's enthusiastic support, Amnesty's membership soon doubled in America. Having been awoken to the importance of the organisation, the band's involvement didn't just stop at Conspiracy of Hope. Through the pages of their new world-service information magazine *Propaganda,* U2 impressed on their fans the role of Amnesty and disseminated copious amounts of information on world injustice and how ordinary people could improve the situation for those falsely imprisoned. On the first date of the Conspiracy tour, Lou Reed had brought Bono to see an area of San Francisco called 'Little El Salvador'. There in Mission Street he was shown how the locals had covered the walls with anti-American slogans and graphic murals of oppression in their homelands. He was also introduced to a Chilean artist, Rene Castro, who had been rescued from the brutality of General Pinochet's right-wing military regime by Amnesty International. A relationship soon developed and more Latin American people got to know about U2's interest in their problems. The end result of this was that Bono took yet more time off recording to go and see for himself what exactly was happening in places like El Salvador and Nicaragua. In Nicaragua, Alison and Bono were greeted by the Sandinista Liberation Front who since the civil war of 1979 had been waging a running battle with American-backed right-wing forces operating from Honduras and Costa Rica. Bono was mesmerised by how much strength the people had after suffering forty thousand deaths, and with three quarters of a million homeless from the war. Not only men, but women and children were carrying arms, and at a public rally led by Sandinista President Daniel Ortega, Bono witnessed how inspiring the revolution had been. Even though the country was literally under siege by the United States, the people were committed to dying for the cause of freedom. If Bono needed further evidence of the hell-bent paranoid side of American imperialism, he got it in El Salvador. An air of death hung over the country like the plague. Fifty thousand-plus lives had been lost since 1980, mostly to the security forces and the death squads. The people's liberation front was fighting a terrible war and individuals were vanishing every day. Bono was devastated when he met the relatives of the disappeared — those that had been spirited away, tortured and killed at the whim of the military. He was bewildered to find the capital, San Salvador, operating like a normal consumer capitalist city while outside the country was being raped by bullets and bombs. One day, while walking towards a village, Bono was caught up in the mêlée of indiscriminate attack. Soldiers began mortaring the area and heavily gunned aircraft appeared overhead. Shots rang out over the young Dublin singer's head and chaos reigned. Locals informed him that it was a regular occurrence and that he was far enough away from the point of the skirmish not to be hurt. His journey to El Salvador had been a deepening experience and out of it Bono wrote two of his best songs, 'Mothers of the Disappeared' and 'Bullet the Blue Sky'.

Another factor that would affect the content of the next album was the sudden death of a member of the band's crew. Greg Carroll was killed in a traffic accident in Dublin on 3 July. He was riding Bono's motorcycle at the time, in fact collecting it for him. Emotionally scarred, U2 went into mourning and blamed themselves for his death. Carroll was a Maori from New Zealand. The group had met him on the Unforgettable Fire tour and struck up an instantaneous rapport. He made such an impression that he joined their personnel and travelled with them all over the world. A week after he was killed Bono and Larry went to Wanganui in Auckland for his funeral. U2 had first met Carroll in a place called One Tree Hill — Auckland is a city built around five volcanic mounds and this is one of them. Out of remorse and anger, bereavement and sorrow, Bono composed an effusive song in response to Carroll's tragedy. It was titled 'One Tree Hill'.

To the general public most of what was happening to U2 was a closed book. Rumours abounded, the worst being that they were on the verge of breaking up. In August, reports in the British gutter press were dispassionately spelling out the end for U2. The story ran that U2 were facing serious problems because Larry Mullen was in a New York hospital, suffering from a grievous hand ailment and undergoing surgery. By the time the story got through the Irish media, panic had set in and U2 were forced to make a statement. As per usual the British popular press, eager for a career-wounding angle, had blown up a simple problem into an almighty calamity. In fact, Larry wasn't in New York at all but in Dublin, contributing his share to the creation of the new album. It was true that he had had a problem with his left hand and as far back as the Unforgettable Fire tour had to seek treatment. But it was a normal drummer's problem — so much working of the hands often leads to swelling and pain. Larry required a long-term solution and after the tour met an Irish doctor who found a way to control the ailment. A special interview in *Hot Press* magazine put the information in perspective and also produced the first official reports that the album was coming together and due for imminent release.

More detailed information about the record was to come from The Edge. September saw the release of *Captive* (Virgin), a soundtrack album of music that Edge had mostly hammered out in the latter months of 1985. He had always had a soft spot for the cinema and held film directors like Orson Welles in high esteem. Doing a film score was a hankering ambition, so after the Unforgettable Fire trek Edge went off to London and wrote some sequences for a possible film. There he met Michael Brook, a Canadian guitarist and inventor who worked closely with Eno on video installations. Having done the basic work, Edge returned to Dublin to demo the stuff with Larry Mullen. The next step was to sell it to one of his favourite film directors, but here the plan nearly collapsed. Nobody was interested. Not to be fazed, Edge kept trying and eventually contacted English producer David Puttnam. Puttnam put him in touch with a producer named Don Boyd who required a soundtrack for a new film to be called *Heroine*. (It was later changed to *Captive* because of supposed drug references in the original title!) It starred Oliver Reed and was set in France, and director Paul Mayersberg wanted it to have a fairly moody soundtrack. Edge gave him his tape of rough sketches and after a while heard that they would be suitable. More work was in order, though. Flown to Paris to see early rushes Edge would have to re-record the music and sequence it to the flow of the film. Michael Brook was invited to Dublin and work began in earnest near Christmas 1985. Also involved were nineteen-year-old Dublin singer Sinéad O'Connor and U2 stalwart Steve Lillywhite.

The film *Captive* was not a great success with the public. Its threadbare plot about a privileged girl who, on being kidnapped and abused, becomes somehow transformed, looked like the work of an artist groping in the dark. Mayersburg's use of Oliver Reed, flashy photography, exotic locations and bizarre images added up to a vacuous cocktail, a substitute for real cinematic flair. It drowned at the box-office. The only thing the film had going for it was the music, and as an album *Captive* is a great artistic achievement for Edge. Most soundtracks sound limp and disjointed when heard outside their visual context, but here Edge manages to create something of musical value in its own right. With the exception of Sinéad O'Connor's vocal on 'Heroine' and some backing voices on 'The Strange Party', the record is instrumental and reflects Brian Eno's strong influence on Edge's thinking. *Captive* is for the most part an excursion into Eno's world of texture, nuance, layers and atmosphere. 'Rowena's Theme' is full of Celtic twilight — a slow enchanting piece of echoed acoustic guitar, watery piano and picturesque synth treatments. 'One Foot in Heaven', with its percussive bass, overlay hypnotic keyboards and trance-like electric guitar arcs has a very African feel. Both Edge and Michael Brook are very interested in ethnic rhythms and that really comes out here. The same rhythmic tendencies are to be found in 'The Strange Party', but here the use of funky riffing and swampy effects does not bring the composition above the mediocre. A minor shortfall in an album of great continuity, this track is its only weak point. Side Two of *Captive* takes the atmospheric character of 'Rowena's Theme' and develops it into a continuous series of musical interludes — episodic but at once cohesive. 'Hiro's Theme' again has that Celtic spirit, something one could imagine while walking in the Wicklow mountains or the Boyne valley. A children's musicbox melody opens the piece, then it is embroidered by sonorous treatments, the best being a thoughtfully sparse application of electric guitar and some presageful, background rumbling. Eno had often likened his work to painting onto canvas, here Edge was taking his lead and painting with sound an image of an Irish sunset or sunrise onto the mental canvas of the listener. 'Drift' is the record's diamond cut, where Edge crystallises his use of the acoustic guitar into a shifting harmony of echo and slow motion. Highly organic, 'Drift' gives the impression that the guitarist is actually present in the listener's living space. 'The Dream Theme' floats upwards, a soft wash of electronic treatments. It re-states the subtler elements of 'Hiro's Theme'. Here the album completely overlaps with Eno's Ambient work and is obviously much affected by Michael Brook's collaborations with him. Brook had in fact recorded a collection of music under the title *Hybrid* (Editions EG) with Eno and Daniel Lanois earlier in 1985. 'Djinn' is Brook's showcase piece on *Captive*, written and produced solely by him. A dirgy composition, it includes Brook's fascination for swamp percussion and sub-textural, ethnic beats. Brook had also pioneered the 'infinite guitar' — an electric guitar with a scalloped fretboard which could produce an infinite sustain on any note the player wished. On 'Island' Edge uses this guitar to great effect, its creamy tone flying through the music like a high-altitude aeroplane shooting across the clear sky. The song 'Heroine' sounds in some ways out of place with the rest of the album's contents. It was written by both Sinéad O'Connor (ex-*Ton Ton Macoute* and *In Tua Nua*) and The Edge in response to the producers wanting a hit single to go with their film. Although Larry Mullen guests, Edge plays some sprightly electric guitar and Steve Lillywhite was brought in to re-mix, it is O'Connor's silken, tough vocal line that makes the track something special.

During the course of being interviewed about *Captive*, Edge was constantly quizzed about the next *U2* album. He intimated that he was really getting into the 'infinite guitar' and that it might well feature on the new record. It was a definite that Brian Eno and Daniel Lanois were on hand, and recording had produced a lot of surprisingly diverse material. It was to be an album of songs, each one having its own characteristic sound and musical arrangement. Edge humorously talked of Arabic, Gaelic, gospel and even 'swamp' songs all intermingled, but not so much that there would be incoherence. Specific details were avoided and as 1986 drew to a close speculation again was rife about *U2's* long-awaited creation. One rumour said that Bono was now heavily into the post-war American sound of Mississippi guitarist John Lee Hooker and that the album was going to be a blues. Another said that Robbie Robertson, the American ethnic rock guitarist, was involved and that it was going to be a country-style album. No one really knew how it was going to turn out but as time passed, and 1986 became 1987, a great sense of anticipation began to surround its release. It was over two years since *The Unforgettable Fire* — a period in which Irish rock music had gone beyond its insularity to affect the world at large. *U2* had played a major role in re-focusing rock's energy to benefit those shackled by adversity. They had expanded the consciousness of both the public and themselves. Now it was time for their recorded music to ring the changes.

THE JOSHUA TREE

Never before had an Irish rock album risen to such an elevated plane. Internationally, rock music had been decimated by the video age, the quick sell, the trend, and had lost all sense of its roots. A look at the charts in America and Britain confirms the feeling that artists were grabbing at straws in an effort to sell novelty for hard cash. Pop was king. It had pushed rock over to the margins — the experimental, ethnic and electronic enclaves. They were healthy areas but very much on the fringes of people's collective vision. Older rock musicians were still coming out with some interesting music, now and again, but what of the children of punk? Few of them had stayed the course, and if they did their music had failed to blow rock as a form beyond its past into the future. There was a real need for a rock music that was epic, a rock band that was idealistic and passionate enough in its concerns to generate greatness. The ennui of eighties rock had still not produced something to rival the splendour of Jimi Hendrix's 1968 *Electric Ladyland* (Track), or something as compelling as *Led Zeppelin's* 1971 *IV* (Atlantic). *U2* were regarded as the band with enough potential to change that situation. The general feeling, in the early months of 1987, was that their new album just might be the one to bring rock back to its pre-eminent position in popular music.

Released worldwide on 9 March, *The Joshua Tree* (Island 1987) did just that. With its gatefold sleeve, complex music, wealth of social and political perspectives and impressive production, the album was *U2's* most forthright rock-'n'-roll opus. A certain sobriety pervades the monochromatic sleeve photographs of a haggard-looking *U2*, taken in Joshua Tree National Monument. This desert location, situated in Death Valley, California, reflects an emptiness — a need to get back to the essence of things, a need to re-evaluate life in terms of a deserted reality. The photograph on the back of the cover highlights the prickly contours of the Joshua tree itself, a giant cactus and one of the oldest types of American flora. The tree also has spiritual connotations — it was named by early Mormon settlers and symbolised for them the struggle of Old Testament prophet Joshua as he led the people of Israel into the Promised Land. For *U2*, America was the Promised Land of the modern era, the New World where thousands of their fellow countrymen and women had gone for better or for worse.

The album's contents number eleven new songs. Given that up to forty had been recorded in the year-long sessions prior to its release, it's surprising that a double album wasn't constituted. Bono had long promised that he would deliver clear-cut songs and here the discipline towards songwriting strengthens the resulting compositions. Musically speaking, Eno and Lanois contribute much more to *The Joshua Tree* than to *Unforgettable Fire*. As well as backing vocals with The Edge, Eno plays a lot of keyboard instruments and Lanois a variety of extra guitars. At the invitation of Eno, Steve Lillywhite was brought in to re-mix several tracks, making the record a best of both production worlds for the band. The harder surface and more precise nature of its music makes *The Joshua Tree* sound as if the attack of *Boy*, the scope of *October* and the grittiness of *War* had all been funnelled into a common pan and then sieved, leaving only the most essential elements. The ethereal, almost psychedelic nature of *The Unforgettable Fire* is whittled down, but not entirely dispensed with. Even if *U2's* music is now more compacted, more compressed, layers of sound still deck up underneath the mixes.

As far as instrumental quality goes, Bono's voice never sounded better. Relying more on the inflection and intonation of his vocal chords, there is less frenzy and more control, which helps elocute the lyrical impact of the songs. Edge is in top form. His guitars are all present — electric Fenders, the Yamaha jazz acoustic, the Gibson, the Les Paul and, as predicted, Michael Brook's 'infinite guitar'. In a lot of ways it is Edge's playing that makes *The Joshua Tree* such a listening feast. Acoustic slide and bottleneck guitar fit cosily beside hard, feedback electric and out-and-out hard rock styles. There are blues elements, psychedelic elements, heavy metal elements, but also a good smattering of The Edge's individual stroking technique. The guitarist had never spread himself so widely or sounded as competent. The rhythm section of Larry's drumming and Adam's bass playing is less adventurous than it had been on *The Unforgettable Fire*. Gone are the florid splays that Larry employed there. Gone too are the reggae-influenced walking plucks that Adam enjoyed in 1984. What replaces them is a more direct approach — Mullen banging his kit for all it's worth, sometimes making it sound more forceful by accentuating its resonance through electronics and amplification, Clayton throbbing a constant beat, tautly underpinning the music with a stringent determination.

Thematically, *The Joshua Tree* re-iterates a fair amount of the subject matter of *The Unforgettable Fire*. The horror of heroin addiction, the monstrousness of the American right, the mysteries of love and death all bound out through its music. But it is an older, greyer statement from a group of individuals coming to terms with the sheer scope of life. Having spent so many years in America it was this sprawling variegated culture that awed them, disturbed them, disgusted them and attracted them, all at the same time. *The Unforgettable Fire* had coddled its themes in a haze of ideals. *The Joshua Tree*, in contrast, pulls no punches. The paradoxes of the modern world were nowhere as spectacularly prevalent, nowhere as bitingly real, nowhere as huge as in the United States of America. The album puts forward these paradoxes and leaves the listener questioning. U2 were now less sure of an easy-out spirituality. America was a place where religion and spiritualism had been used to further bigotry, to hurt people, to dispossess people, to victimise people and to destroy them. America had also produced great art, its best being by those who had suffered at the hands of its paradoxes. *The Joshua Tree* commendably borrows traces of the black blues and the imagery of some of America's more graphic writers. There are also country and gospel influences running through its multifarious structures. The record isn't just a one-dimensional obsession with one country — problems in Ireland and England are also dealt with, as is the punishing situation of those people Bono had met in Central America. A note on the inner lyric sheet invites people to join Amnesty International and the album as a whole is dedicated to the memory of their recently dead friend, Greg Carroll.

On first hearing, the opening track, 'Where the Streets Have no Name', sounds like it is a continuation of *The Unforgettable Fire*. Indeed, its cluttery mix is similar to that of 'Indian Summer Sky' and Edge's guitar mirrors that of 'Bad'. But soon the differences become noticeable. There is more control, especially in Bono's vocal. The song has a symmetry of design and clarity of form that distinguishes it from the previous album's work. Steve Lillywhite's harshness is complemented by Brian Eno's thoughtfulness. The first thing one hears is Eno's mournful keyboard atmosphere which then segues into a strident instrumental, featuring Edge's by now familiar ratchety guitar playing. Then Bono begins to sing in a new voice, a voice full of register, full of tone. The song pleads for an escape, a seemingly desperate wish to get away from modernism — its names, its cities, its alienation, its decay, its spiritlessness, its pollution, and reaches out for a simpler existence 'high on a desert plain'. It is said that after he came back from Ethiopia, Bono was appalled by the moribund state of the West when compared with the liveliness of Africa. He is also reputed to have spoken vehemently about the destruction of Dublin's historic buildings, pulled down in the name of so-called progress. 'Where the Streets Have no Name' is full of his reactive sentiments. The heroic feel of 'Streets' flows into 'I Still Haven't Found What I'm Looking For', a song which could be viewed as one of questioning realisation that existence and faith are insufficient to satisfy a person's being. An uptempo dance-like track, the bass and drums bounce along against Edge's guitars. Here several different types of guitar overdub are used. A simple bit of string-picking, a hint of electric reverb, a familiar rippling effect, a jangling acoustic, all make a tasty sound, seasoned by the lovely use of Brook's 'infinite' boomeranging in and out of the mix. The music helps lift up a song which lyrically sounds somewhat bleak.

'With or without You' is even more despairing. This song describes a situation of not being able to live with or without a person, but whether this person is meant to be Christ as alluded to in 'the thorn twist in your side' or a loved one, we are never quite sure. Ignoring this lyrical shortfall and looking at the words and music as a combined emotional expression, 'With or without You' can really be singled out as one of U2's finest achievements. A tinkling of synthesised bells

88 *Edge in pensive mood — Wembley Arena, London, June 1987.*

89 *U2 in Death Valley, California, 1986.*

introduces a very physical bass line, then Eno's sailing treatments waft around the rhythm. As Bono's vocal comes in the track literally opens out, bursting forth with Edge's sharding guitar breaks and Larry's drum strikes. About two-thirds of the way through, Steve Lillywhite's powerful touch is then perceived as the noise level increases and the floating *U2* of Eno changes to the belting *U2* of *War*. After a blistering crescendo, Bono resolutely sings the closing lines, 'I can't live, with or without you' and the music steadies itself against the backdrop of Eno's phantom whistling. It then fades out instrumentally, sounding very like the opening, but stronger in fibre. Hardcore critics of U2 could be forgiven for thinking that *The Joshua Tree*, three tracks in, had not strayed too far from old waters. One could imagine questions being thrown around like: What happened to the blues and country influences? Where is the traditional rock 'n' roll of the concert appearances of 1986? The answer comes in the form of 'Bullet the Blue Sky', a concrete impression of America, sung to heavy rock music with Jimi Hendrix-style strafing guitars, and which some people likened to *Led Zeppelin's* 1969 'Whole Lotta Love'. It has more in common with Hendrix's 1969 anti-Vietnam 'Machine Gun' really, and was written by Bono in reaction to American self-righteousness and its murderous effect on Central America. Edge goes full-out to build up a screaming tension as various guitars resound in chaos behind Bono's stark images. Lyrically, the singer had never painted a picture so penetrating. The burning crosses of the Ku Klux Klan, the gambling men, New Orleans jazz, the sanctimonious pseudo-morality of moneyed America — all these elements run together as the word-film tackles the death and dread of US foreign policy of the 1980s.

> And he's peeling off those dollar bills
> (Slapping them down), one hundred, two hundred,
> And I can see those fighter planes
> And I can see those fighter planes
> Across the mud huts where the children sleep
> Through the alleys of a quiet city street
> You take the staircase to the first floor
> And turn the key and slowly unlock the door
> A man breathes into his saxophone
> And through the walls you hear the city groan
> Outside it's America
> Outside it's America ....

Near the end Edge plays a blitzkrieg series of solos and some electric slide that would have Elmore James reeling in his grave. As this climaxes in feedback, Bono, recalling his trip to El Salvador, sings the words: 'See the sky ripped open, See the rain through the gaping wound. The howling of women and children who run [and then the music stops dead, and in a good Yankee accent Bono speaks the chilling pun] into the arms of America.'

The bombshelling 'Bullet the Blue Sky' leads directly to the relative quiet of 'Running to Stand Still', an aching ballad about Irish drug addiction. Bono had been incensed by the amount of heroin dependence in his native Ballymun, and the 'towers' in the line 'I see seven towers, But I only see one way out of here' are the blocks of poor council flats of his family locale. 'Running to Stand Still' concerns a girl desperately trying to escape her predicament, but, getting more deeply involved in the opiate world, basically standing still. The running refers to doing a smuggler's run for hard cash so as to escape the poverty that stimulated the addiction in the first place. Though about Ireland, the track is also shot through with shades of America. Edge's whispering slide guitar echoes the acoustic style of Ry Cooder, Bono's harmonica tails the song off into the region of the blues. The pessimism of the song is enhanced by Lanois and Eno's production — melancholic keyboards, ghostly washes and at one point a thunder effect on Larry's drums all add up to a gloomy picture. A similarity could be drawn between this song and a composition by Arthur Lee of American sixties group *Love* titled 'Signed D.C.'. Both songs are about the evils of heroin addiction, both have simple structures which utilise bluesy acoustic guitar and harmonica. If this seems like a spurious comparison remember that Bono had been listening to *Love* as far back as the early American *U2* tours and had already lyrically paralleled Arthur Lee's writing in 'Sunday Bloody Sunday'. Moreover *Love*, like contemporaries *The Doors*, were all part of the sixties underground rock scene who were ideologically opposed to the American establishment and its mores. Bono had gone on record and stated how much this movement inspired him and if there is a *Love* influence in 'Running to Stand Still' it is a very positive one.

The outward-looking social and political aspect of *The Joshua Tree* is again taken up on Side Two in the song 'Red Hill Mining Town', a personal statement about the scarring effects of the British coalminers' strike of 1984-85 on the private lives of the miners. In a number of lucid images the honourable labour of the miners and their grinding existence is traced out in the context of the wearing strike. It would be very effective if it were not for the turgid mix (actually done by Steve Lillywhite but not credited) and awkward musical accompaniment. The song is seriously hampered in its impact by a lumbering rock undertow which serves to distract attention from the fine lyrics. In terms of melody it is too near that of 'The Unforgettable Fire' song and as a complete item 'Red Hill Mining Town' is saved only by the sublime use of the Arklow Silver Brass Band, a feature which should have been amplified. The next track, 'In God's Country', brings the album back to America. A running heroism pervades this song, with Bono singing about dreaming 'new dreams tonight'. Through a number of suitable references to 'crooked crosses', 'sad eyes', drugged sleep, gold and death, Bono outlines a system which has failed to live up to its great promises of liberty, equality and fraternity. Yet the song is a rallying call to people everywhere to 'punch a hole right through the night' of apathy and political inertia. Its optimism is speared by a rousing music — Edge's acoustic and electric strums fleeting away in the background to Larry and Adam's very danceable syncopation. The theme of redemption through love and the healing power of same, so much a part of *The Joshua Tree's* imagery, come up again on 'Trip through Your Wires', a stomping country blues, replete with loud harmonica and shrieks. Supposedly put down live near the end of the recording sessions, it has a great spontaneity about it. This time the protagonist is coming out of the 'heat and dust of the desert', 'broken, bent out of shape' to be 'put back together again' by the power of love.

Metaphorical or literal, whichever way one reads it, it is pretty good writing.

On the elegiac 'One Tree Hill', Bono again digs deep for suitable words, this time to express his overwhelming feelings of loss for his dead mate, Greg Carroll. It is a heart-rending piece of work. On the one hand sinewy guitars and Eno's idiosyncratic synth playing give it a spectral characteristic but on the other the bright pulsations of the rhythm section make for a lightness of tone. The song speaks of Carroll's funeral not as something final but as part of a brave struggle which transits from life into the afterlife, here symbolised by the ocean, the sea. It would have been easy to sentimentalise the subject matter, but Bono demonstrates a profound sense of his belief by allying Carroll's death with that of martyred Chilean freedom singer Victor Jara and others who have tragically died in an unjust world, in that all of their spirits would unite 'when the stars fall from the sky.' In coloration, the song has a very spiritual quality and at the end, after Edge laid down a scalping bit of electric guitar, the backing music fades out and within seconds a little gospel coda comes on, sung in harmony by Edge, Eno, Lanois and Bono. Snipped straight out of the repertoire of black American church music it is a joyous finale to one of rock's great epitaphs in song.

'One Tree Hill' also includes a lyrical reference to 'The Enduring Chill', a short story by American author Flannery O'Connor. Born in Georgia in the 1920s, O'Connor was a Catholic who wrote about the Deep South in a matter-of-fact kind of way, tracing its grotesqueness, its violence, its spiritual deformity through the lives of ordinary folk. Her work was documentary in style and not without its humour. Bono, in talking about *The Joshua Tree*, spoke about the directness of language he found in the work of American writers, particularly O'Connor, as something that had changed his attitude towards writing. O'Connor was an heir to the tradition of William Faulkner, one of the first writers to capture the reality of life in the Southern States. Full of degeneration, decay, cruelty, viciousness, perversity, grimness, callousness and brutality, his novels dealt mainly with the outcasts of society. Instead of the gentility and dynastic torpor so fondly portrayed by Hollywood up to the 1960s, Faulkner wrote of the mutilation, the idiocy, the lust and incest rife in his Mississippi birthplace. There was also pride, individualism and vitality, but punctuated by darkness, disease and the hatred of white for black. The extremes of the American South were like a reflection of the unbridled immorality of the United States, a country so huge and sprawling where literally anything could happen. The twisted shape of the Joshua tree could be interpreted as symbolising the twisted mind of a Faulknerian or O'Connor character hellbent on destruction. The ultra-realism of the fiction of the Deep South was to leave an indelible mark on American prose and in the modern era it had its fullest expression in two books — Truman Capote's *In Cold Blood* (1966) and Norman Mailer's *The Executioner's Song* (1979). Both works depict real events and were hailed as masterpieces of the new journalism. The song 'Exit' on *The Joshua Tree* is heavily influenced by Mailer's book and the tradition it came from. Partly written by The Edge and a real stormer, 'Exit' is a picture of a man possessed by something, who 'cuts across the land' in 'the howling wind', a man who has got to a point where violence is the only way out. As he gets more worked up and frenzied his hand reaches into his pocket for his pistol, 'his finger on the steel'. What is distinctive about this song is the way the lyrics lead up to a furious instrumental solo which is utilised to convey whatever violence this man had perpetrated. As the track quietly builds up from spooky guitar and bass, and brooding keyboards the tension in the music is released through a whiplash of pounding drums and treacherous guitar breaks. When the shuddering impact of this solo is repeated one realises that the U2 of *The Joshua Tree* is one capable of producing full-blown heavy rock as explosive as that of any band in rock history.

Whether preacher, cowboy, gangster or vigilante, the character in 'Exit' is symptomatic of a reactionary strand of the American psyche which at its most paranoid can be seen working in Central and South America. Covertly using its immense economic and military might to bolster conservative regimes and to do away with leftist revolutionary people's movements, the Reagan administration of the eighties was still playing fanatical defender of democracy in the face of communism. That people were fighting for their right to live as human beings was something that seemed to escape the narrow-mindedness of the American establishment. The final cut on *The Joshua Tree* is Bono's hymnal 'Mothers of the Disappeared', an explication of the suffering caused by the American-backed security forces and death squads of El Salvador. For years these women had been demonstrating in front of government buildings in San Salvador for the release of their husbands, sons and daughters falsely arrested by the regime. No one really knew what had happened but certain sources revealed, in time, that a lot were being secretly tortured and killed. Some would even turn up dead in a plastic bag or cardboard box. Underscored by Eno's electronic keyboard stabs and spellbinding synthesised programming, 'Mothers of the Disappeared' sombrely describes the situation of those 'cut down and taken from us'. Add to that the sounds of machine-gun fire and Edge's mortaring electric guitar blasts and you have a vivid picture of a country in the grip of senseless terror. It is an empathic piece of work, full of the angst and despair of the Salvadorian women — a fitting epilogue to an album that stands up to the myths of twentieth-century life and uncovers the pock-marks underneath.

But one never feels, even on 'Mothers', that U2 are floundering in a sea of depression. The surety of execution, the vehemence of the music and a profundity of thought are at the root of *The Joshua Tree*. After 'Mothers of the Disappeared' one is invited to join Amnesty International so that the situation can be improved. U2 were trying to make sure that the 'slap in the face' they had given with *War* would not be forgotten. As a record, *The Joshua Tree* is the oasis of substance that people had waited so long for in eighties rock. Nearly a third of a million copies were sold in Britain within two days of its release. In Ireland, stores were selling out so fast that people were queuing up for hours to ensure that they would get their hands on a fresh consignment. On 17 March, St Patrick's Day, *The Joshua Tree* pitched itself straight to the number one position in the British charts, making it the third U2 album to do so. Over-zealous commentators likened the effect of *The Joshua Tree* to that of *The Beatles'* 1967 meisterwork *Sgt. Pepper's Lonely Hearts Club Band* (Parlophone), so taken aback were they by its detonating impact. Granted in Ireland and the UK, *The Joshua Tree* sold more copies in its early weeks of release than any other rock or pop album in history, including those of *The Beatles*, but statisticians, fans and the media ignored, in their enthusiasm, such simple facts as the differences between the sixties and the eighties. *The Beatles* were instigators and leaders of a social revolution which affected the course of popular music and the society around it worldwide. *U2* could never be seen in that light, regardless of their elevated position. As for the runaway sales of *The Joshua Tree*, they were impressive but to compare them to those of *The Beatles* was false. During the 'swinging sixties' young people had relatively more money, on average, than in the 1950s but in the eighties the youth market of the Western world had ballooned to such a degree both in its numbers and in its net disposable income that record sales figures between the decades were rendered incomparable. The fact that the people who ranked *U2* as the new *Beatles* were mostly English and considered them a British band said a lot for the credibility of their statements!

In the midst of all this fuss, *U2* were calmly gearing themselves up for an eighteen-month world tour that would bring them to their largest audiences ever. Rumours concerning *The Joshua Tree* had been disentangled by its release. Robbie Robertson, the ex-Bob Dylan/*Band* guitarist obviously wasn't on it but he had been over to Dublin from Los Angeles to record some material with *U2* for probable inclusion on a solo album. *The Joshua Tree* certainly had blues influences but was not a complete foray into the twelve-bar form. In the string of interviews the group gave after its release they explained their broadening musical interests and names like B.B. King, Janis Joplin, Willie Dixon, Hank Williams and Muddy Waters rolled off their tongues with a comfortable familiarity. This re-discovery of archetypal American singers was a going back to the roots of rock 'n' roll — an investigation that had also tapped into folk song as a primary form of popular music. *The Joshua Tree* was stamped with this learning and in a song like 'Red Hill Mining Town' Bono was re-creating the functionary role of the traditional folk song: to communicate something of the people to the people. It was no off-the-cuff decision that, in February, *U2* had journeyed to Wales to make the video for 'Red Hill Mining Town' with Irish writer/film-maker Neil Jordan. Neither was it a flight of whimsy that had them, in March, appearing on RTE's 'Late Late Show' with *The Dubliners, The Fureys* and *The Pogues,* performing a version of 'Springhill Mining Disaster', a lamenting American folk standard.

Across the Atlantic in the United States the audience that had been built up over so many years of touring had soared dramatically after the benefit concerts of 1985 and 1986. With *The Joshua Tree* it expanded even more. Thousands of people collected outside agencies, days in advance of ticket sales in order to see *U2* play. Within hours of going on sale, tickets for seats at arenas and auditoriums across the country were sold out. From 1 April to 16 May the first instalment of The Joshua Tree tour took the band through such places as Arizona, Texas, Nevada, California, Massachusetts, Connecticut and New Jersey. This time American youth took to *U2* like manna from heaven. Incidents like the criticising of Arizona Governor Mecham's cancellation of the state's observance of Martin Luther King's birthday, and the police stopping of them making a video atop a liquor store in Los Angeles because it threatened to cause a civil disturbance, became items of national scandal. The giant NBC and CBS television networks fell over each other in their attempts to get the best *U2*

90-91 Two milestones in *U2*'s growth — from the cover of Dublin's *Hot Press* magazine to that of the prestigious *Time* magazine.

90

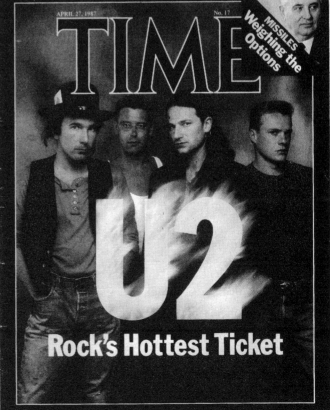

91

coverage. Press conferences and public appearances provoked a reaction near to hysteria amongst the media. On 25 April, after four weeks in the charts, *The Joshua Tree* reached the Billboard ceiling. Never in history had an album by an Irish rock band been to number one in the US charts. That week *U2* were treated to a six-page, front-cover feature in *Time* magazine. Referred to as 'rock's hottest ticket', this alone signified that now *U2* were regarded in America with the same reverence as *The Beatles,* Bob Dylan and Elvis Presley had been in their day. After another appearance on the cover of *Rolling Stone* in May, their first *Joshua Tree* single 'With or without You' rocketed to the number one Billboard chart position.

To most Irish people all of this was an overwhelming occurrence — to some it was the logical certification of the authenticity of a rock culture mostly left untapped by the waves of previous decades. For the Irish music industry it meant a new feeling of confidence in the worth of home product abroad. It also meant that for the first time since the 1960s London had lost its status as the centre of modern rock 'n' roll. As far as the Americans were concerned, Dublin was now the place, the new geographical capital of rock. For *U2* the repercussions of *The Joshua Tree* and the spring/summer American tour went beyond common notions of 'success' and 'celebrity'. What was most important was the new sensibility of the music and its influence on those who heard it. Bono's lyrics were now full of a raw naturalism that fitted easily into the tradition of good songwriting. The moral imperative that in the past had sometimes sounded conceited and cloudy now shone through his songs with a genuine clarity. Musically, *U2* had dispensed with punk's prudishness, especially towards the 1960s and 1970s. Through their own re-awakening they were re-vitalising the work of these and other eras, giving to their audiences a sense of heritage in rock and popular music. On the American tour, during the up to 2½ hour sets, versions of Eddie Cochran's 'C'mon Everybody', *The Rolling Stones* 'Ruby Tuesday' and 'Sympathy for the Devil', *The Doors'* 'Riders on the Storm', *Joy Division's* 'Love Will Tear Us Apart', *The Beatles'* 'Help', Bob Marley's 'Exodus' and Jimi Hendrix's 'The Star Spangled Banner' all cropped up here and there to add flavour to the proceedings. This re-routing of their musical perspective had ultimately saved them from becoming artistically vacant and even with the enormous commercial and critical success of *The Joshua Tree* one felt that in 1987 *U2* still had places to go.

U2 — Discography

Singles

1	U23: Out of Control/Stories for Boys, Boy Girl	(CBS, September 1979)
2	Another Day/Twilight	(CBS, February 1980)
3	11 o'Clock Tick Tock/Touch	(Island, May 1980)
4	A Day without Me/Things to Make and Do	(Island, August 1980)
5	I Will Follow/Boy Girl (live)	(Island, October 1980)
6	Fire/J. Swallow. (Included free live EP with '11 o'Clock Tick Tock', 'The Ocean'/'Cry', 'The Electric Co.')	(Island, July 1981)
7	Gloria/I Will Follow (live)	(Island, October 1981)
8	A Celebration/Trash Trampoline and the Party Girl	(Island, March 1982)

9 New Year's Day/Treasure (Whatever Happened to
   Pete The Chop)   (Island, January 1983)
10 Two Hearts Beat as One/Endless Deep (With free,
   re-mixed versions of 'New Year's Day' and
   'Two Hearts Beat as One')   (Island, March 1983)
11 Pride (In the Name of Love)/Boomerang 2   (Island, September 1984)
12 The Unforgettable Fire/A Sort of Homecoming (live)
   (Gatefold sleeve version included bonus out-take single:
   Love Comes Tumbling, Sixty Seconds in Kingdom Come/
   The Three Sunrises)   (Island, April 1985)
13 With or Without You/Luminous Times (Hold on to Love),
   Walk to the Water   (Island, March 1987)
14 I Still Haven't Found What I'm Looking For/
   Spanish Eyes, Deep in the Heart   (Island, May 1987)
15 Where the Streets Have No Name, Race Against Time/
   Silver and Gold, Sweetest Thing   (Island, September 1987)

12 inch singles (where different from 7 inch)
1 New Year's Day, Fire/I Threw a Brick
  Through a Window, A Day without Me (the last three
  tracks all recorded live)   (Island, January 1983)
2 Two Hearts Beat as One (club version)/New Year's Day,
  Two Hearts Beat as One (album versions)   (Island, March 1983)
3 Sunday Bloody Sunday/New Year's Day, Two Hearts
  Beat as One (the latter two specially re-mixed by
  Francois Kevorkian)   (Island, March 1983)
4 Pride (In the Name of Love)/Boomerang 1,
  Boomerang 2, 4th of July   (Island, September 1984)
5 The Three Sunrises, The Unforgettable Fire/A Sort of
  Homecoming (live), Love Comes Tumbling, Bass Trap   (Island, April 1985)
6 Wide Awake in America: Bad, A Sort of Homecoming
  (both live)/The Three Sunrises, Love Comes Tumbling   (Island, May 1985)
7 Where the Streets Have No Name, Race Against Time/
  Silver and Gold, Sweetest Thing   (Island, September 1987)
Note: 2 (US), 3 (Dutch) and 4 (US) special editions.

Albums
1 Boy   (Island, October 1980)
2 October   (Island, October 1981)
3 War   (Island, February 1983)
4 Under a Blood Red Sky   (Island, November 1983)
5 The Unforgettable Fire   (Island, October 1984)
6 The Joshua Tree   (Island, March 1987)

Miscellaneous
1 They Call That an Accident (film soundtrack)
  U2 contributed two versions of 'October', the LP version
  and one re-mixed by Wally Badarou.   (Island, March 1983)

2 The Edge: *Snake Charmer* (mini six-track album
   with Jah Wobble and Holgar Czukay)   (Island, March 1983)
3 Band Aid: Bono and Adam Clayton contributed to Bob Geldof's
   'Do They Know It's Christmas'.   (Phonogram, December 1984)
4 Artists United Against Apartheid: Bono contributed 'Silver and Gold'
   song as well as vocals to 'Sun City' track.   (EMI, November 1985)
5 'In a Lifetime': song recorded for *Clannad* album *Macalla,* featuring Bono and Máire Ní
   Bhraonáin, later released as a single.   (RCA, February 1986)
6 The Edge: *Captive.* Original movie soundtrack featuring Edge and
   Michael Brook. The song 'Heroine' released as a single, also
   featuring Larry Mullen on drums and Sinéad O'Connor
   on vocals.   (Virgin, September 1986)

Videos

U2 Live, Under a Blood Red Sky
(sixty-one minutes of performance recorded at Red Rocks,
Denver, Colorado in June 1983)   (Virgin, June 1984)

AVANT-GARDE POSSIBILITIES

I The Virgin Prunes

'The Dadaist thought up tricks to rob the bourgeois of his sleep'.[9]
'We are aggressive on-stage, hassling people's heads and kicking people's brains.'
(Gavin Friday, 1980)

Punk had extended many boundaries. For some people it had opened their
eyes to the atrophy that had set into the rock and popular music of the mid-
seventies. For others it had blown the lid off years of frustration. Punk had given
them an adrenalin thrust, a violent yet constructive means to express hostility,
pain and disillusionment — in its way distancing them from the spiritual decay of
Western post-industrial society. In Ireland the levelling process which punk had
brought to the rock scene in turn led to a great leap of faith in the brands of new
music that were to come out of the country. This faith had helped *U2* to erect a
glistening, stately rock palace on the windswept foundations of punk. It also
helped their contemporaries and seminal allies, *The Virgin Prunes*, to construct a
primordial theatre — a torrent of exhibitionist performances and music which
denounced the very meaning of the word civilisation.

The *Prunes* had very close bonds with *U2*. Initially, as friends and accomplices,
the groups evolved together. During their formative years they shared a private
universe known as Lypton Village which would always be mysteriously referred
to in interviews. Band names, Bono Vox and Gavin Friday, sprang directly from
this context. In the early days when *The Prunes* played alongside *U2* they provided
a contrasting bizarre, demonic procession of primalism and transvesticism
accompanied by a spontaneous noise-music, played with a combustible and
dreadful disharmony. Dik Prune, the guitarist, was a masterly axeman, who had
briefly been a member of the embryonic *U2* combo. He was also The Edge's
brother.

The Virgin Prunes first came to public notoriety when they supported *The Clash* in Dublin, in October 1978. It was the English punk outfit's second raid on the capital and it attracted widespread attention. *The Prunes* shocked spectators with their antics on-stage, especially when both lead singers simulated copulation. Pandemonium ensued when vocalist Gavin Friday's blue lurex suit burst at the crotch, revealing all. For a time each successive *Prunes* appearance was a premeditated demystification of values, a mirroring of the animalism of everyday life through a devilish, fantastic, atavistic orgy on-stage. For about four years they took the dark but ever-present elements of life subsumed by the so-called evolution of Western society and unleashed them through an incomparable performance music. The earliest specific line-up was: Gavin Friday (vocals/action), Guggi (vocals/action), Dik Prune (guitar), Haa Lacka Binttii (drums/electronics), Strongman (bass) and Dave Id (solo singer/performer).

The Virgin Prunes stand out in Irish rock history as the only group to attempt and succeed at re-creating the atmosphere of the original European Dadaist movement. During the first quarter of the twentieth century many artists felt cheated by their society, certain individuals taking the view that it was a flimsy, bourgeois compost heap that had rotted into the grimy trenches of war and conflict. In general, art and artists had become the fatted calves who lived off the underbelly of a gluttonous monster. If one wanted to be anarchic, or claim to be part of the avant-garde, how could one acknowledge the legitimacy of such a structure? Surely the function of radical art was to create an alternative by revealing the true nature of man through art's uninhibited gaze? In Switzerland, Germany and France a movement raged to prevent art from resting, besotted, on the mantelpieces of the bourgeois regime. Brilliant figures like Tristan Tzara, André Breton and Marcel Duchamp revolutionised art by instigating a violent intellectual movement known as Dada. Through a series of statements, manifestoes, meetings, groupings, exhibitions and activities, Dada wrought an apocalyptic change in the way people viewed art and artists. The plenitude of the bourgeoisie, which acted as matriarch of good taste and fine-art sensibility, was kicked aside. Good taste had become an habitual curtsy at a gallery opening, run for the well-to-do by the well-to-do. Dada forced the paralytic traditional art world to jump out of its cushioned, leather-bound wheelchair and recognise the naked horror of reality. Marcel Duchamp hung a urinal on a gallery wall. Dada, like punk, was a fundamental rape of old premises. Dada wanted a fresh start and its legacy was the wild and beautiful art known as Surrealism.

Like the Dadaists, *The Virgin Prunes* wanted to slam lazy attitudes and moribund preconceptions. Each public performance and vinyl recording, particularly of the original band, was a slashing of the rock 'n' roll myth, an attempt to do more than cosily entertain. After the chaos of the late seventies, the group abandoned conventional gigging, favouring instead a series of carefully considered 'events'. Their first tactic was to release a record on their own Baby label. 'Twenty Tens, Revenge' appeared at the beginning of 1981 — a puzzling, cryptic, extended-play single, wrapped in a sublime grey sleeve. A romantic drawing of a little Victorian girl and her rabbits on the cover gives no clue to the disturbing nature of the music inside. No cueing speed is given, but it turns out that the four tracks work best at $33\frac{1}{3}$ r.p.m. The first side starts with an ignorant bass, thrashed up with ranting vocals and mad drumming. This moves into a tape loop of random voices, piano and sonic disturbances. The second side is a slow, mournful version of U2's '11 o'Clock Tick Tock'. This song levels out into an atmospheric chant of the Islamic variety. The record asks only questions, questions which the listener has to answer for himself or herself. It caused consternation among the record-buying public attacking the strait-jacket of received tastes and consumer conditioning.

In March 1981 scores of youth — a jigsaw combination of fashion and sub-cultures — assembled in front of an old disused university building called Newman House in Dublin. The tension mounted as there was a long delay before the doors opened. Inside, a scrunching music fell from the walls. It was the first of the *Prunes'* re-emergence experiments. Dave Id recited a stream of garbled words while the rest of the group made ready for the feast. Gavin and Guggi then arrived, wearing dresses and cavorting like two thirsty animals in heat. The musical backdrop used the cut-up aspects of mixed media — tape loops, radio and television extracts pre-recorded and channelled through the speakers as the musicians played. The end result was a grand primalism, with the two singers covered in thick muck, jitteringly intertwined as they flung daffodils into the air. After the show the audience left the concert hall, gulping the night air, dazed by the activity.

The next single, 'In the Greylight' (Rough Trade 1981) was *The Virgin Prunes* in rock mode. Tumbling drums add a new dimension to manic vocals and muffled voices. On the B side 'Moments and Mine', the main bass/drums drive is pre-figured by the ticking of a clock and the rippling of a piano. Here was proof that the *Prunes* could accommodate the standard rock form within their own individual inventions. A small, blond-haired boy popped up on the sleeve, the same kid who played an important part in the early imagery of U2. That summer, Haa Lacka Binttii vacated the group, much to the chagrin of ardent followers who saw his electronic and percussive talents as indispensable to the *Prunes'* drift. It was during this period that the group realigned their activities, pushing their creativity to its limits, producing within a matter of months four pieces of extraordinary work collectively titled *A New Form of Beauty*. Mary D'Nellon (he's not a girl!) joined on drums.

The Dadaists and Surrealists were fascinated by man's conditioning, his apparent ability to accept what he had got used to. They went out on a limb to upset this conditioning, looking on logical order as an unreasonable deception. They thrived on the idea of natural whim and fancy, trouncing the mathematical nature of capitalism with a baton of randomness. The modern world, in their eyes, was too well worked out and anyway it made the few rich, leaving everybody else to live on their senses. Why not rattle the deep subconscious and draw from that the latent animalisms that in truth governed all behaviour? When people looked, thought, spoke or reacted to life in general, it was to the tune of a technological society geared to bourgeois profits. Chief activist André Breton wanted 'beauty' to be convulsive. Rather than put up with silly notions of 'beauty' in art, he likened it to an erotic shiver — quivering on the precipice of sudden realisation.

This was the nature of *The Virgin Prunes'* transmutation of perceptions through

92

93

92 *The Virgin Prunes* in 1982 — they constructed a primordial theatre. *Left:* Guggi; *right:* Gavin Friday.

93 *The Virgin Prunes* were an atrocity exhibition on-stage (Dublin 1982).

94 Gavin Friday *(right)* talks to a Dublin clothes trader sometime in 1983. *The Virgin Prunes'* stage performances belied their genial, everyday normality.

94

A New Form of Beauty. From September 1981 three singles were released by Rough Trade at two-week intervals. They came in 7 inch, 10 inch and 12 inch sizes, each one revealing and reflecting the primitive undercurrents of modern man. in 'Sandpaper Lullaby' and 'Brain Damage', *The Prunes* attack our attitudes towards physical and mental abnormality, the revulsion caused by ugliness, deformation and retardation, in those hooked into the perfectionism of cosmetic Western society. 'The Beast' reaches way back into primeval times, presenting the hellish spirit of a hungry, demented, prehistoric creature. Imagine a tribal gathering around a huge fire — the only source of energy and light — chanting in communal drone, celebrating the kill or enticing the elements, and you'll get an idea of the atmosphere of 'Sweethomeunderwhiteclouds'. The strange but beautiful character of the Australian Aborigine filters through 'Abbágal', an aural recreation of the outback whose humming bush and human inhabitants have changed little since the dawn of time.

A New Form of Beauty was performed in Dublin towards the end of 1981. The Douglas Hyde Gallery and adjoining amphitheatre in Trinity College was the chosen location. For crowds of inquisitive youth it was the event of the year. Anticipation built up as again the doors were kept closed for a long time before the performance. When they were opened, people were first given access to the whitewashed gallery space. Here they were confronted with violent juxta-positions of everyday reality. A large pig's head, dripping blood, rested on top of a mannequin. It faced a mirror on a wall, its festering freshly severed neck pointed outwards. A black box hung suspended from the ceiling. One had to stoop down and stand upright inside it to see what message it conveyed — concrete sounds deafened the ears, the eyes were confronted with ghastly images of decapitation, death and physical torture. In another part of the gallery a table stood on a raised dais, seemingly laid out for dinner — on one side a chair but on the other a urinal, on one plate food, on the other excrement. Guggi had lived in one of the foul, high-rise blocks of flats known as Ballymun Towers, Dublin's asinine sixties solution to housing the city's poor. The claustrophobic and squalid conditions of some of the worst of these flats were reproduced in a corner of the gallery, the tiny space filled with dirt, bits of food, rumpled clothes, a television, a stove, an electric heater and the dank odour of urine. Yet these repulsive conditions had become home for thousands of underprivileged people and, as the *Prunes* pointed out, was in a way a form of 'beauty'. In contrast, another corner presented a leaf-filled grotto draped over with a thin cheesecloth covering, full of oranges and other fruits. Sweet fragrances filled the air as a carnival-type soundtrack played in the background to the twittering of pre-recorded bird sounds. One could crawl into this and experience a curious delight. The crowds were not allowed into the concert area until they had had their fill of the exhibition. Ushered through a corridor, they were then led into the subterranean amphitheatre, by then smoke-filled and throbbing with a visceral taped music. *The Virgin Prunes* then slowly began their ritualistic performance — sacrificing their civilised shells to a lumpen degradation of howling, mud-spattered ridicule. The performance of *A New Form of Beauty* turned out to be the most extreme form of criticism ever of Irish rock's traditional parameters of audience/performer, call and response role-playing. In content it was a vicious sliding tackle on the conservatism of Irish

216

Catholicism, lyrically and visually pissing all over religious conditioning and its effect on sexuality and spontaneous behaviour. What could *The Virgin Prunes* do after this?

The answer was travel. England, Holland and France were subjected to potent doses of subversion. In May 1982 the *Prunes* released their fourth single, 'Pagan Love Song' (Rough Trade), which *Vox* magazine described as a 'sub-psychedelic/psychic piece' with 'amazing brick rhythms'. Guggi appeared all primitive on the sleeve, his face daubed over with thick streaks of warpaint, his hair shaved up into the familiar punk Mohican style. (This haircut became an important visual signal of punk in the eighties. Hard core groups such as *Na — Psalm Sunday* and *The Keltic Klan* wore their hair in exaggerated sculptures after the fashion of the American Indian tribe, the Huron, the subject of American novelist James Fenimore Cooper's book *The Last of the Mohicans*.) Their next Dublin stage performance was more theatrical. The old Television Club ballroom was used, the high stage filled with objects of everyday life — plants, a fur dog, a wheelchair and a parasol all in plain view. The show expressed itself through a mock breakfast, whilst taped music played in the background. It went on for two hours, winding up with a Gothic scenario of death-like mannequins being hauled about the stage. Blackened faces and dead flowers added the final macabre touches to another extraordinary *Virgin Prunes* performance.

The next logical step was a long-playing record. Colin Newman, ex-*Wire* and budding solo musician, was invited over from London to produce the album in Windmill Lane Studios. Released near the end of 1982, *If I Die, I Die* (Rough Trade) was an unusual debut. Each side has a different yet specific texture. The 'brown' side is mystical, abstract, even sensual in tone. Overall it has an Ambient sound — Colin Newman's 'fishy' underwater production featuring throughout. The most interesting tracks are 'Ulakanakulot', with its soft, harmonious tune, and 'Bau-dachöng' which includes the ethnic elements of a bodhrán and jew's-harp. The 'blue' side is more down to earth, four pieces of *Prunes*-style rock and Dave Id's mocking 'Ballad of the Man', where he imitates Bruce Springsteen's sound to a tee. It is a challenging set and most reviewers found it difficult to come to terms with it.

To coincide with the album's release the band appeared on British television, performing on Channel Four's then popular 'Whatever You Want' programme. Public reaction was one of outrage. Tory MPs, the Church and predictably Mrs Mary Whitehouse, voice of moral conservatism, were appalled by scenes of 'simulated intercourse and oral sex'. This signalled a period of upsets for the *Prunes*, who then parted angrily with their manager and left the Rough Trade label because of problems with record distribution. Yet their product was high on demand in Europe, especially in Italy and France, and most of 1983 was taken up with touring. Audiences in America, Canada, Italy, Austria, Yugoslavia, East Germany and France all caught a glimpse of the devilish Dubliners. Returning to their home town in the autumn, a concert at the St Francis Xavier Hall found them more direct in their delivery, abandoning the theatricality of old for a more hard-driving rock 'n' roll performance. A large number of their followers criticised the group for selling out on their original subversive principles but, unbeknown to them, behind the scenes *The Virgin Prunes* had been working hard on an entirely fresh musical direction.

With Dave Ball of English group *Soft Cell* contributing and producing they had been recording material for a new album to be titled *Sons Find Devils* and some singles, notably 'Love Lasts Forever' and 'The Virgin Prunes Present Bob Elvis'. Gavin Friday wanted to expand the band's sound to include influences from the blues and 1940s American and European burlesque music. He was also keen to reflect a new-found interest in the work of dramatist Bertolt Brecht, opera composer Kurt Weill and singer Lotte Lenya who together revolutionised music/performance/theatre in Germany between the world wars. *Sons Find Devils* was to be a collection of songs with cabaret and jazz flavourings, lyrically condemning but also humorous. There were to be songs about God, about the mundaneness of love, about doubt, and two tracks by Dave Id. One piece 'True Life Story', was supposed to be a combination of American fifties twangy rock 'n' roll, thrash psychedelia and experimental music. By all accounts it was going to be a terrific album if *The Prunes* could find a suitable record company to release it — but this seemed to be an impossibility.

At this stage *The Virgin Prunes* were also having personnel difficulties. Guggi, who wasn't that keen on the proposed new approach, left in March 1984 to pursue a different line of work (managing his brother, Peter Rowan, the famous 'boy' of *U2* record cover fame). Dave Id retired from the public eye to work with the band exclusively on studio projects. As time went by no official releases dropped into the record stores but no one seriously contended that the group had split or parted company. Any mentions in the music press always spoke of an ongoing but veiled *Prunes* project. By the summer of 1985 Dik Prune had vacated the guitarist position but a new line-up was in the offing. Mary switched from drums to guitar, Gavin and Strongman remained on vocals and bass while the original drummer, Pod, re-joined. They started afresh by headlining a spectacular Gothic festival at London's Hammersmith Palais. Called The Feast of Flowering Light, this was a veritable celebration of the avant-garde art underground of the eighties, with such names as *Psychic TV* and Kathy Acker also appearing on the bill. It was *The Prunes* who dominated the event with a new cabaret-style show, Gavin Friday playing the 1930s-type music hall impresario to a potent musical accompaniment. Gone were the mind-numbing shocks and the outrageous visual displays. Substituted instead was a polished, streamlined rock music backing a more intellectual stage presentation.

It took until the summer of 1986 for their *Sons Find Devils* project to be realised, this time on their own Baby label through New Rose in Paris. Having recorded new songs and updated other tracks since 1983 the releases were not exactly what had been planned. The rhythmically funky 'Love Lasts Forever' appeared in four different versions: once on a 7 inch, backed by the manic 'True Life Story', twice on an extended 12-inch and again on the album. Now titled *The Moon Looked Down and Laughed* the LP's best feature is the use of acoustic instruments particularly brass and strings. An eclectic collection, its most memorable pieces are the softer version of 'Love Lasts Forever' with its piano and beautiful string section, the rock theatrical 'Heaven' with its bells, synthesisers and military drums, and the title track with its harmonica and rambling vocals. Its slapstick, cod-humour and burlesque songs are indicative of the *Prunes'* persistent

218

individuality and the throwaway rock of some tracks doesn't detract from the album's standing as an unusual and original release. Since then the activities of *The Virgin Prunes* have been sporadic, even though their reputation, music and past achievements have won them a loyal and devoted following throughout the world. Whatever they do, *The Virgin Prunes*, like the Dadaists, can always be looked on as true originals and for a time between 1981 and 1982 they were the most overtly subversive rock group ever to come out of the genre.

Virgin Prunes — Discography

Singles

1 Twenty Tens, Revenge/The Children Are Crying   (Baby, January 1981)
2 In the Greylight, War/Moments and Mine   (Rough Trade, July 1981)
3 A New Form of Beauty 1 (7 inch): 'Sandpaper Lullabye'/'Sleep',
   'Fantasy Dreams'   (Rough Trade, October 1981)
4 A New Form of Beauty 2 (10 inch): 'Come to Daddy'/
   'Sweethomeunderwhiteclouds,' 'Sad World'   (Rough Trade, November 1981)
5 A New Form of Beauty 3 (12 inch): Seven Bastard Suck: 'The Beast'/
   The Slow Children: 'Abbágal', 'Brain Damage',
   'No Birds to Fly'   (Rough Trade, December 1981)
6 Pagan Love Song/Dave Id Is Dead   (Rough Trade, May 1982)
7 Baby Turns Blue/Yeo   (Rough Trade, October 1982)
8 The Faculties of the Broken Heart/Chance of
   a Lifetime   (Rough Trade, November 1982)
9 Love Lasts Forever/True Life Story   (Baby/New Rose, June 1986)
10 Love Lasts Forever (12 inch): 'Lovelornalimbo'/
   'I Like the Way You're Frightened'   (Baby/New Rose, June 1986)
11 Don't Look Back/The White History Book   (Baby/New Rose, September 1986)
12 Don't Look Back (12 inch): 'Let's All Sing of the Tortured Heart'/
   'The White History Book', 'Day of Ages'   (Baby/New Rose, September 1986)

Albums

1 If I Die, I Die   (Rough Trade, December 1982)
2 An Invitation to Suicide (10 inch French import)   (Celluloid, December 1982)
3 Over the Rainbow (a compilation of rarities 1981-1983) (Baby/New Rose, April 1985)
4 The Moon Looked Down and Laughed   (Baby/New Rose, July 1986)
5 The Hidden Lie (live album, Paris 1986)   (Baby/New Rose, June 1987)

Tapes

A New Form of Beauty 4: Din Glorious   (Rough Trade, February 1982)

Videos

Sons Find Devils (live retrospective 1981-1983)   (Ikon/Factory April 1986)

Notes: *A New Form of Beauty* appears complete on a double album released in Italy. The Din Glorious tape contains live recordings from the Douglas Hyde Galley 1981 show and some oddities from that period. *The Invitation to Suicide* record contains the following tracks: 'We Love Deirdre', 'Rhetoric', 'Down Memory Lane', 'Man on the Corner', 'Loved One', 'Go Away Deirdre'. The most extensive analysis of the band's art was carried out by Swiss writer Rolff Vasellari in his 1985 book *Virgin Prunes – The Faculties of a Broken Heart*, published by Black Sheep Press, Zurich.

Avant-Garde Possibilities: the International Background

Before going on to look at the other Irish artists who have worked in the avant-garde rock field, it is necessary to take a brief look at the international background. Most people consider avant-garde rock to be that which uses electronics and relies for the most part on the application of the synthesiser. If one delves deeper into the subject one finds that the use of electronics in itself is not the whole picture. What is just as important is the shake-up in approaches to musical composition and presentation, an input which comes directly from the intellectual avant-garde of the twentieth century. It was really the Dadaists who started the ball rolling when they introduced the concepts of 'random cut-ups' and 'spontaneous noise' which made for unpredictability in their audio-visual presentations. From the classical music end came Arnold Schoenberg, the Austrian composer, who from 1909 re-defined traditional attitudes to tone and melody by using the twelve-note system known as atonality. No longer was music tied to pre-existing structures and safe, easily digestible passages. Although much criticised during his lifetime, Schoenberg's innovation was to have a profound effect on the course of modern music. His exile to America in the 1930s was to bring him into contact with John Cage, a composer whom many consider to be the great guru genius of the avant-garde.

Cage's chief innovation was to combine Schoenberg's ideas with those of the Dadaists and draw in a whole new range of influences to invent a new musical aesthetic. After finishing his studies he started in the 1930s to bring in Oriental and other non-Western scales into his work. Abandoning the strict Schoenbergian serialism, but retaining its implications, Cage then began to devise rhythmic music that was based on spaces of absolute time not on relative note time. In 1937 he maintained that the future of music rested with electronic media and talked of a new music that utilised film, radio and disc technology. Simultaneously he was exploring percussive sound and the effect of the collision of ethnic instruments like Chinese, Turkish, Javanese and Japanese cymbals and gongs with 'non-musical' anvils, car-brake drums and metal cylinders. This led to the invention of the 'prepared piano', an ordinary piano with bits of metal, wood, rubber or leather stuck between the strings to alter its tone. Cage used this as a percussive instrument to produce music which had all the hallmarks of an Eastern ensemble. His interest in Zen and Hindu philosophy was to continually stimulate the indeterminacy and chance elements of his work. In the 1940s he involved himself in design and dance theatre and was one of the great pioneers of mixed-media performance art. By the 1950s he was using magnetic tape collage, radio frequency distortion, pick-up cartridges, contact microphones and feedback circuitry to add an electronic dimension to his creations. Cage's re-invention of music also spread to the use of noise and speech deformation. Even computer-generated permutations were used in the 1960s. With presentations like *Variations V* in 1965, Cage's startling assemblages could be seen at their most pointed — dancers triggered dissonant noise and music as they jumped around sensitive antennae sticking up from a stage, an array of visuals 'cut-up' in quick succession projected from panels behind them, Cage and his associates sat in the foreground monitoring and altering the machinations of a multitude of wires, circuits and electrical voltages. His total rejection of serious nineteenth-century musical values — including its use of written script for which he substituted symbolic patterns and graphs based on the *I Ching*, the Chinese Book of Changes — did and still does shape the character of avant-garde, rock and pop music.

On the European side, Schoenberg's greatest disciple was Karlheinz Stockhausen. Advocating 'total serialism' in 1953, he started working in Cologne on music that would result in the first pure electronic compositions. Each note had to be built up separately, individual sine waves making up timbres, all edited precisely to make an exact tone. In contrast to Cage, Stockhausen was meticulous about preparation and everything was annotated and scored. After this breakthrough he mixed real and artificial sound to examine the interplay between them and to widen the scope of his difficult electronic work. Later he began to investigate the relationship between freedom and determination in a piece of music, seeing chance as a way to bring about 'intuitive music-making'. He also investigated the spatial quality of music, its coloration, its speed, its dynamics. Some of his work was completely devoted to the investigation of one or a small number of notes, chords and sounds. The extension of this aspect came in the form of 'minimalism', a wave of music that emanated from the sixties' and seventies' work of such American composers as Terry Riley, Steve Reich and Philip Glass. Here repetition and slight variation were used to create expansive hypnotic pieces. The idea was to create a mood through subtly shifting nuance rather than outwardly presenting a precise theme.

Of course allied to these great strides in serious music was the refinement of sound technology. Minimalism owed a lot to the potential of the magnetic tape recorder to generate loops. Cage and Stockhausen relied heavily on the tape machine since it was a perfect device for collage, chance and re-creative experiments. Invented in 1935, the tape recorder's first real application in the avant-garde world was in the form of 'musique concrète'. Originated by French radio engineer Pierre Schaeffer in his Paris studio and developed with composer Pierre Henri, musique concrète centred on taping all sorts of sounds from everyday life and manipulating them with pitch, echo and editing effects. This could be used on its own or fed either at random or sequentially into a musical composition. In tandem with changes in the use and style of magnetic tape came those in connection with 'synthetic' sound production. As early as 1915 there existed an oscillation device which could produce an electrical tone whose sound was alterable by the flick of a knob. By 1929 the French had linked together a number of oscillators to make the first primitive sequencer. Also in that year came the mass production of a Russian invention known as the theremin. This hand-sensitive sound machine sprouted antennae and its whistling sound was first used in commercial rock by *The Beach Boys* on 'Good Vibrations' (Capitol 1966). (Jimmy Page also used one during *Led Zeppelin* concerts of the early seventies!) Most of these early discoveries had little more than novelty value and it was not until Laurens Hammond marketed his electric organ in 1935 that the public took note of the significance of electronics in music. Eventually, in 1944, the synthesiser arrived. It went beyond previous hardware by being able to shape and modify oscillation tone, making the sound pliable for the first time. Improvements were made and by the 1950s RCA in America had created a synthesiser that could produce any sound a composer desired. This equipment was large and unwieldy and had to be housed as permanent installations attended on by dozens of white-coated staff. This problem was circumvented by Robert Moog, who in 1965 brought the synth to the people in the shape of his modular unit. Moog and Vox portable models became very popular in the sixties and seventies since they used a polyphonic keyboard system to 'touch' the tones and required little maintenance.

In 1967 the ramifications of what had previously happened in electronics and among the serious musical avant-garde hit rock with full force. Nowhere could it be better seen than in *The Beatles' Sgt. Pepper's Lonely Hearts Club Band* (Parlophone). At the time Paul McCartney was very interested in Stockhausen, John Lennon was working from electronics of all descriptions, George Martin, the producer, was experimenting with tape after the fashion of Pierre Schaeffer, and George Harrison, like Cage, was bringing Eastern philosophy and note structures to bear on the music. Post-*Pepper* rock felt that it could justifiably go in any direction it wanted, but only the few really had the ability to create bona-fide avant-garde material. English group *Pink Floyd* used long, expansive, unfurling aural dreams and staggering visual displays in their output of the sixties and seventies. Structured on a simple pulse, their sound was always embroidered with a complexity of guitar, drums, bass and electronic keyboards. German band *Kraftwerk* used electronics to construct a sound so tense and resilient that one could immediately picture highways, bridges, building and locomotives on hearing their records. Fellow countrymen *Can* produced a thick fusion of jazz, ethnic and rock, coated with an almost industrial layer of electronics. Not surprisingly, chief contributor Holgar Czukay was a student of Stockhausen's. In 1974 British intellectuals Robert Fripp and Brian Eno collaborated on *No Pussyfootin'* (Island), an album which realised aspects of tape delay mechanisms in rock for the first time. Although there are many artists who have used avant-garde ideas and electronics in rock since *Pepper*, none has made an impact quite like that of Eno.

Taking the stance of an artistic 'non-musician' and incorporating the thinking of John Cage into his creative method, Eno left his first rock group *Roxy Music* in 1973. Over a series of solo albums he brought the idea of utilising the studio as an instrument more prominently into rock. Simultaneously, he established a record label called Obscure in order to produce and make available serious avant-garde work by English and American composers — even John Cage was involved. In this context Eno hit on the idea of 'discreet music', a type of sound that was as enjoyable as it was ignorable. From this came his 'Ambient' series of recordings — a set of environmental musics which used tonality coloration and electronics to paint sensitive aural-scapes. 'Ambient' meant an expansion of the innovations of Stockhausen and the Minimalists, intersected with those of John Cage and Pierre Schaeffer. In 1977 Eno's contributions to David Bowie's *Low* and *Heroes* (two RCA albums) established him as the primary avant-garde force in mainstream rock and popular music. Since then, through collaborations too numerous to itemise, Brian Eno had continued to place the work of the radical fringes of music clearly in the public domain. His interest in tape technology, chance progression, studio treatments and an open-endedness in execution have made for an exciting output; and his multi-faceted creativity has built upon the precedents of earlier twentieth-century innovators. Eno's fame tends to overshadow others working along similar lines, and it is to the stimulating work of Irish musician-artists Roger Doyle, Stano and Nigel Rolfe that we must now turn.

2 Roger Doyle

Criminally ignored in his own country, Roger Doyle has been stretching the limits of modern music in several directions since the 1960s. As a serious composer he has taken radical concepts in 'found sounds', musique concrète, pure electronic sound, interlocking instruments and serialism to produce the most difficult and sometimes disquieting music of recent times. His career has veered into rock, where unusual scores and barren soundscapes have greeted drum machines and strong electronic rhythms. As an actor, he has attempted a 'future music' by combining theatre projects and sound installations in a mixed-media whole. An eclectic creator he finds no problem in melting elements of opera, electric/acoustic avant-garde music, computer technology and rock into his work.

Roger Doyle was born in Dublin in 1949. He was classically trained in the piano from an early age. At the age of fourteen he amused himself by banging barrel tops in the grounds of a derelict building in his native Malahide. He quickly graduated to playing drums in local band *The Malabeats*. He became involved with improvisational groups *Jazz Therapy* and *Supply Demand and Curve* who freely mixed folk, classical, rock and jazz, using unusual time signatures. He toured Canada with the latter but after a stint of two years was lured into the realm of serious academia. Since the bulk of his group work was done at night, mostly for fun, Doyle had been devoting his days to studying in the Royal Irish Academy of Music, Dublin. He was fascinated by the oscillator and aspects of computer programming and telecommunications. He was genuinely turned on by electronic music and was exposed to the musique concrète of French composer Pierre Henri during a holiday in Paris. According to Doyle: 'I was in a record shop in Paris and a friend of mine said go and buy that record there. It was totally new, and I had no idea how he got the sounds, but it was wonderfully familiar to my soul.'[10] By 1974 Doyle had won a valuable scholarship to study composition and instrumentation at the Royal University of Music, The Hague.

With money left over from this venture he financed the production of five hundred copies of his first album *Oizzo No* in 1975. A completely avant-garde piece of work, both Brian Dunning (flute) and Jolyon Jackson (cello) assist. Prepared piano, uilleann pipes, Irish harp, tin whistle, drums, clarinet and viola also feature. Random bits of conversation, 'found sounds' and environmental noises cut in here and there. On a track titled 'Why is Kilkenny so Good', the music is interspersed by a harrowing conversation relating to self-doubt, alienation and fatal drug addiction. This record, though extremely rare, is an essential introduction to the world of Roger Doyle.

Coming to grips with concepts and techniques, Doyle then busied himself in the wire-strewn studios of the Institute of Sonology in Utrecht. Working from John Cage's premise that 'silence' and 'sound' were equally important, Doyle built up compositions that emphasised 'quietude' in relation to musical form. It was like taking an empty vessel of 'silence' and filling it very slowly with sound reverberations. 'Solar Eyes' from this period resembles an aural vat of submarine 'quiet' with outside notes plopped into it at regular intervals. After some time spent at the Experimental Radio Music Centre in Helsinki, he got the opportunity to broadcast 'Solar Eyes' — both backwards and forwards — on international radio. It appeared on his second album, the spartan *Thalia*, which was released by CBS in 1978.

The next two and a half years were spent in Holland, Finland and Ireland obsessively working with editing, utilising all the techniques inherent in magnetic taping, multi-tracking and splicing. The influence of the French school of music concretists Schaeffer and Henri, as well as their associates Pierre Boulez and Edgard Varèse, was never as clear in Doyle's work as in the output of this time. 'Finestra' and 'Rapid Eye Movements' are the most intense pieces of musique concrète ever to be put on vinyl, and defy normal listening habits. 'Finestra' sounds like a giant hoover being switched on and off or an enormous tape machine which sucks in and blows out pockets of sound randomly. 'Rapid Eye Movements' is more interesting and contains several thousand taped snippets of everyday life. It begins with a far off piano, played softly as the waves of the sea wash on some distant shore. The piano is sustained as footsteps, radio broadcasts, noisy public address systems and a confetti of 'found sounds' literally encroaches on the listener, increasing in loudness all the time. On hearing it most people would be hard pushed not to switch 'Rapid Eye Movements' off, so dissonant, so discordant was its sound. In effect it places the receptor in the curious position of having to make a decision about what he or she was hearing. Basically, 'Rapid Eye Movements' challenges the listener's preconceptions about the roles of sound and hearing in modern music. Both pieces surfaced on an LP, released by United Dairies in 1981 under Doyle's new working title *Operating Theatre*.

After adapting and directing the music chapter 'Sirens' from James Joyce's *Ulysses* for the stage, Roger Doyle then formed his own music-theatre group also under the banner of *Operating Theatre*. His reasons were simple: 'I formed this with actress Olwen Fouere as a breakaway from wordy theatre where the actors sit around talking.' A grant from the Dutch ministry of culture put the first show on the road in 1982; it consisted of 'seven pages of text and loads of music and gestures.' A more extroverted attitude led to the production of *Miss Mauger*, an accessible album of modern music distributed by the independent Kabuki label in 1983. One side plays at 45 r.p.m. the other at 33⅓. The track 'Rampwalk' sounds like aural liquid, so beautiful and hypnotic is its character. The louder, more percussive pieces, have rock elements but remind one essentially of film soundtracks inspired by ethnic cultures. 'Dragon Path' opens with a reverberating gong and echoes aspects of China or Mongolia through an ocean of sound. 'Confectioners' has a snowy characteristic, almost like music for Eskimos.

From there Doyle's direction was towards an open plain of expression, where simplicity and effectiveness, melody and sonority were the key traits of *Operating Theatre's* art. On the one hand he provided music and sound for a seventy-five-minute theatrical-style event called *The Diamond Body*. Written by poet Aidan Carl

Mathews and performed by Olwen Fouere in Ireland, England and America between 1984 and 1985 *The Diamond Body* was critically praised for sustaining fresh perspectives on mixed-media performance. On the other Doyle pushed his music into the post-punk minimalist rock enclave. Punk had been responsible for a return to minimalism in the exploratory avant-garde area of rock music. Aided and abetted by increasingly sophisticated and compact technology, those who so wished could apply electronics to the 'standard' rock sound any which way they liked. Doyle's latter-day work was very affected by these changes. In 1984 he acquired the use of a Fairlight Computer Music Instrument, a technical piece of equipment whereby the programmable information store of a modern computer is used in conjunction with a synthesiser to sample and reproduce any sound imaginable.

To the untrained the Fairlight is considered a novelty, something which can produce nice synthetic sounds at the touch of a key. To Doyle it was like all the different electronic possibilities that he had been exploring in his career, refined into one easily accessible sound generating system. He began composing on it in earnest and was excited by the outcome of what he termed his first popular song, 'The Queen of No Heart'. About this time Doyle made the acquaintance of Bono from *U2*, who was keen to take piano lessons from him. Doyle's biggest problem had always been the business of releasing his music into the marketplace — it was considered too avant-garde to appeal to the mainstream and too experimental to appeal to anyone else. But now that he was moving towards songwriting and electronic sound the time seemed right to give the public a good strong dose of his music. Bono was quick to realise this and through the *U2* Mother label, Doyle's new music was released in the summer of 1986.

Appearing in 7 inch and 12 inch versions, *Operating Theatre's* 1986 product was some of the best new music of the eighties. The single 'Queen of No Heart' is an epic driving rock song in the *U2* mould. Sean Devitt plays drums, Elena Lopez sings and Doyle does everything else. He finds little difficulty in making convincing guitar breaks and background atmospheres sound from his Fairlight. The B side 'Spring Is Coming ...' is more like rock-opera and is much enhanced by Olwen Fouere's background soprano vocal. The 12 inch is actually called 'Spring Is Coming ...' and works like a mini LP, adding three extra takes to the contents of the 7 inch. 'Part of My Make-up', written by Doyle and Fouere, has an Oriental feel to it. Doyle's treatments sparkle with Eastern promise as Fouere dramatically intones her lyric images as if on the stage of a Noh play. The other two tracks are instrumentals, Doyle showing just how powerful the Fairlight can be in the right hands. 'Atlantean' is an excerpt from a larger piece written for a television documentary. Here one is given enough to taste the lovely Slavik drone of its dashing keyboard arpeggios. 'Satanasa', an out-take from the *Diamond Body* production flows with all the sense of a classical composition. Measured percussion, the ticking of a clock and an ominous wintry string section summon up the ghosts of Shostakovich and Tchaikovsky at their most emotive.

Long overdue for international appraisal, Roger Doyle inhabits that grey area between the fringes of the serious avant-garde and those of new interesting rock. With no public recognition to speak of his dedication to his art is all the more admirable. One thing is certain and that is, whether it be through *Operating*

Theatre or another vehicle, Doyle will continue to stimulate and confound in the years to come.

Roger Doyle — Discography

Singles

1 *Operating Theatre:* Austrian/Positive Disintegration   (CBS 1981)
2 *Operating Theatre:* Blue Light and Alpha Waves/Rampwalk   (CBS 1982)
3 *Operating Theatre:* Queen of No Heart/Spring is Coming With a
  Strawberry in the Mouth   (Mother 1986)

Albums

1 Oizzo No   (Roger Doyle 1975)
2 Thalia   (CBS 1978)
3 *Operating Theatre:* Rapid Eye Movements   (United Dairies 1981)
4 *Operating Theatre:* Miss Mauger   (Kabuki 1983)
5 *Operating Theatre:* Spring is Coming ...   (Mother 1986)

3 Stano

One of the major distinguishing features of avant-garde music was and still is in its approach to creativity. As John Cage had earlier shown, a fresh perspective could result in the making of completely new sounds that would be impossible through strict classical composition. No other Irish rock musician comes as near to Cage's improvisatory dictum as does Stano. A self-confessed 'non-musician', Stano has completely shunned historical achievements in any musical form, opting instead for a naive working method that formulates sound out of an organic framework. Most people if they were to attempt something like this would end up with a selection of indiscriminate noise works of unbearably low quality, but Stano's intuitive grasp of sonic architecture has resulted in possibly the most individual hybrid of rock, experimental and electronic music ever to come out of Ireland.

Born John Denver Stanley, Dublin 1960, Stano grew up in Artane and showed no inclination towards a 'musical' career as a child. Attending the local Christian brothers school and then the technical college, his first choice of lifestyle was that of the army. After five months there he settled down to become a carpenter. But Stano had always been a non-conformist. His early schooldays had been chequered by a rebellious streak and at the tech. he had been noticed for his distinctive writing abilities. Even though an avid fan of Bob Dylan's, it wasn't until punk happened that Stano took an active interest in rock music. During the late seventies/early eighties, Stano hung around the Dublin punk scene, went to gigs, and befriended Johnny 'Rotten' Lydon of *The Sex Pistols*, who then often came to Ireland to get away from the hustle and bustle of London's whirligig music business. Stimulated by the energy of punk, Stano teamed up with Dublin combo *The Threat* and started to play synthesiser. Purveyors of a gritty ultra-realist sound their first single 'Lullaby in C'/'High Cost of Living, (Web 1980) was well received and made British radio airplay. Like a lot of groups of the punk period they didn't stay the course and broke up after a short time.

95 Roger Doyle operates the Fairlight computer instrument.

96 Stano — the true non-conformist.

97 Nigel Rolfe presenting 'Amerikaye' from his *Island Stories* album 1986.

Not to be discouraged, Stano used all his free time away from his carpentry job to experiment with sound. Acquiring two tape machines he began recording from everyday sources, inventing his own version of musique concrète from television transmissions, gurgling tap water, walking footsteps, tinkling bottles and clattering plates. Stano found that by walking around with a tape recorder on him he could chance upon interesting combinations of sounds. Later these would be re-mixed into other things to make suitable collages. He was also writing a lot of poetry — word associations that were not literally translatable. Open to much interpretation, Stano's writing was intended to work on the level of the subconscious like a form of dream stimulus. Exploring many areas, he used his carpentry to design physical sculptures, visual constructions that could accompany the sounds he was hearing in his ears. Through a musician friend, Vinnie Murphy, Stano was encouraged to follow his muse in a studio context and early in 1982 his first solo record was released.

The single 'Room'/'Town' on Vox Enterprises was an interesting debut. Lyrically two icy observations of fragile, broken reality, the arrangements sound quite unusual. In a deadpan voice Stano sings of stagnant isolation in a room, to the accompaniment of Vinnie Murphy's plaintive piano. His own drum machine rhythms and crashing background noises enhance the gloomy mood of the piece. 'Town' is more in the traditional punk mould, Stano angrily evoking the sense of desperation in alcoholic street violence through a funky rhythmic sound. Its quirky drum-machine segments, synth parts and grand piano ending all help to communicate a chaotic scenario. On the strength of this one record Stano made a reputation for himself among the public and press of the rock underground. Saving his money he bought more time in the studio and with a deal from Deke O'Brien's Scoff label completed an album's worth of material. *Content to Write in I Dine Weathercraft* came out in 1983 and demonstrated to those who thought Stano a depressing artist how varied and lively his work could be. Including 'Room', the album has eleven tracks in all. Acting as lyrical contributor, sound arranger and producer, Stano involved the talents of many musicians during the recording sessions. Ex-Van Morrison man Jerome Rimson plays a neat slap rhythm bass on 'White Fields (in Isis)', a real dance cut. 'Seance of a Kondalike' features the acoustic strains of 'Mo Chara' (my friend), a sitar-like instrument played by its inventor Michael O'Shea. Here Stano experiments with his vocals, screaming and screeching behind the Arabesque pattern of O'Shea's beautiful string tapping.

O'Shea's Eastern influence is also felt on the poignant 'A Dead Rose' where he plays both Indian sitar and his Mo Chara to Stano's elegiac vocal. 'Whale' is equally sad; a short song about the cruelty of animal killing, it is unusually scored by a chunky mid-tempo acoustic guitar riff. This is an album of much variety — tape-loop experiments, heavy guitar sounds and Brecht/Weill-type burlesque tracks all snugly fitted together under Stano's direction. 'Out of the Dark into the Dawn' is the record's finest take and relies heavily on the emotively powerful piano playing of Roger Doyle. To this Stano adds an aquamarine-type drum sound, the sweet voice of Suzanne Rattigan, and a hint of other vocals. Almost Ambient in texture, this soothing composition has the effect of enthralling one to reverie.

Content to Write in I Dine Weathercraft is a uniquely accomplished collection of music from an untutored, inexperienced 'non-musician'. Even the early experimental solo work of Brian Eno looks pale in comparison. Wrapped in a simple, 'homemade' grey sleeve, the album made no impression whatsoever on the Irish or English record-buying public. Very few people actually heard it at the time, but those few critics who did raved about it. One English writer went so far as to label it an 'eccentric classic'. Words like introverted, recluse and outsider were thrown around too readily by rock journalists who really couldn't see the enormous ground-breaking nature of Stano's work. Here was somebody with little or no knowledge of avant-garde music and electronics who was in reality applying all the innovations of twentieth-century music to his vision of sound. In the studio, Stano would just let things happen. If an idea entered his head, then it would be tried. Musicians were brought in not for their virtuosity in a particular style but because they made a specific sound. Positioning of microphones, splicing of tape, backward tracking — whatever the studio threw up to him — Stano woud incorporate into his compositions. Vocals were more important for their intonational qualities than their literal meaning. Few could have guessed the spontaneous methods in Stano's designs from the highly polished music of *Content to Write*. In time the album would become globally recognised as exemplary of new directions in contemporary music.

Mixed-media performances, involving slides, film and other artists/musicians, as well as more advanced recordings using computer electronics, made up his 1984 projects. His unorthodox mixture of words and unprepared music became more rock-oriented on his second album, *Seducing Decadence in Morning Treecrash* (a record that did not receive a general release until 1986!). Although more lyrical the eight-track *Seducing Decadence* is a much darker affair than *Content to Write*. Utilising the unusually treated guitar sounds of Gurdi (ex-*Microdisney*) and Donald Teskey, a harder rhythmic drum sound courtesy Seán Devitt and the multi-instrumental talents of Vinnie Murphy, Stano pushes his creations fully into the desolate territory of post-industrial decay. Full of chaos, sliding avalanches of sound, disintegrating images and junkyard/scrapheap elements, Stano's new visions chart a downward spiral of human alienation and confusion in the face of the problematic state of late twentieth-century Western capitalism. 'Destruction' acknowledges the negative side of man's make-up, his uncontrollable tendency to destroy life in the name of 'progress' and is potently delivered through a series of liquid textured guitar passages. 'Cry Across the Sea' relates to the damaging effect of the consumer society on individual integrity through a style of music that stitches familiar dance beats and mesmeric polyrhythms into a documentary-type soundtrack. The thunderous noise of 'Ascendancy' is so subversive that it communicates an aural re-creation of the rioting, chanting hordes of Russia's 1917 Bolshevik revolution. And just to knock a few more noses out of joint, Stano weaves Arabic, Oriental, Arctic and Slavik stylisations into the album's overall music plan.

The sounds of *Seducing Decadence* lent themselves to film and other visual media. For live presentations in Ireland and the UK, Stano collaborated with Dublin artist Donal Ruane. Instead of treating the stage like a normal performer would do, Stano chose to pre-tape his music and relay it back on a reel-to-reel in conjunction with Ruane's projected cut-up slide shows and film sequences. Stano would murmur and shout his 'poetry' into a microphone, sometimes sitting down, sometimes out of sight completely. Audiences were befuddled by it all, particularly the violent nature of Ruane's imagery. A thoroughly self-taught expert on media art, Ruane collaged several thousand excerpts from news-reel, film, advertising, documentary and other sources and re-edited them to synchronise with Stano's stage output. At times these images would become nauseatingly repulsive and the entire show resembled an audio-visual compendium of the reality outlined by such writers as William S. Burroughs and Marshall McLuhan. This was the first time that an Irish rock artist had ventured into such territory and its only real equivalent was in the 'media rock journalism' of Sheffield band *Cabaret Voltaire.*

Residing in London between 1985 and 1986, Stano maintained his association with Ruane. Through an independent outlet called Food Records, two tracks from his first album and two from his second (which was still unavailable) were released on an EP under the title 'The Protagonist 28 Nein'. The cover of *Content to Write* was re-designed and made available in Greece and Scandinavia. But like a lot of composers working in the avant-garde area, Stano found it very difficult to get large commercial record company backing. Disillusioned with the staleness of the English scene he returned to Dublin late in 1986 to find that interest in what he was doing had increased enormously during his absence. Scoff Records had acquired European distribution for *Seducing Decadence* through a Berlin label, Dossier. Playlist statements received by Scoff showed that *Content to Write* had been aired on the radio of twenty-seven countries world-wide, including Russia and America, Central and South America, Scandinavia, Eastern and Central Europe and the Far East. In response, RTE Radio featured a lengthy documentary on Stano's art, presented by serious music academic Dermot Rattigan. In this context Stano was given the incisive analysis that his work required. Here he spoke of his music as an attempt to provoke 'smells' and 'feelings' in the mind of the listener, as a way of painting memories, as a form of sculpting in time.

Similar attitudes to musical composition had been expressed by other figures in modern avant-garde music, most notably Brian Eno. The radio programme also included excerpts from Stano's third album *Daphne Will Be Born Again* (Dossier 1987). An entirely instrumental excursion, this record is a more relaxing and uplifting work than its predecessor. It is difficult to associate the optimistic tone of this selection with the unpredictable Stano's pessimistic 'Protagonist' product of 1984/1985. Most of the album's sound originates from his exploration of the Fairlight computer music instrument, a piece of equipment that seemed tailor-made for Stano's requirements. On 'Dream and the Little Girl Lost' he creates a tastefully romantic violin section to go with the bubbly funk riffing and spoken French dialogue of the track. 'Majestics of Majesty' is a spacey concoction of bells, flute and percussion that has very Japanese connotations. The sound of the Japanese koto can actually be heard on 'Nuit Blanche — Winter in Summertime'. A moody set-piece, which displays Stano's gift for getting the best out of any electronic equipment he touches, its Fairlight fabrication combines the shimmering strings of the koto with the sounds of waves, birds, screams and a fearful backing orchestra that aurally describes a sort of Gothic Little Red Riding Hood scenario.

Again the music had a powerful soundtrack quality. In fact a lot of Stano's music had been licensed out for television, radio and film use. In 1987 a selection of tracks from his first two albums including the momentous 'Out of the Dark into the Dawn' were chosen for the French film *Kaleidoscope*. Addicted to studio work, Stano recorded another album before his third one had had the opportunity to make the record stalls. Titled *Before May I Will Change* (not released to date), he considered it the most 'accessible' vinyl proposition of his career. Not content with that he simultaneously began work on a classical piece with Dermot Rattigan as arranger. A multi-talented operator, Stano's contribution to Irish rock cannot in any way be ignored. He is the first Irish rock artist to play the studio like an instrument, the first to allow intuition with regard to electronics, sound and chance occurrences to govern his output. While professing no prior knowledge of historical movements in modern avant-garde music, his work easily slips into the mould of the world's foremost innovations in that field. For Stano it's his gift for the natural arrangement of sounds, no matter from what source, into a highly original music that is the key to his success as a recording artist.

Stano — Discography

Singles

1 Room/Town		(Vox 1982)
2 The Protagonist 28 Nein: White Fields (in Isis), Cry across the Sea/ Out of the Dark into the Dawn, Ascendancy		(Food 1985)

Albums

1 Content to Write in I Dine Weathercraft		(Scoff 1983)
2 Content to Write in I Dine Weathercraft (re-packaged, re-released)		(Magnet 1986)
3 The Protagonist 28 Nein: Seducing Decadence in Morning Treecrash		(Dossier 1986)
4 Daphne Will Be Born Again		(Dossier 1987)

Nigel Rolfe

If it seems peculiar to conclude this short section with a focus on a fine artist, grounded in Art College training, who lives and works via the visual art form, then think again. Englishman Nigel Rolfe embodies everything which is salient about avant-garde music in that his use of electronic sound and the record medium brings modern rock into another entirely new dimension. Taking on the perspective of a 'nomadic Irishman', Rolfe has, since the early 1980s, augmented his atavistic moving sculpture displays with audio-visual installations in order to create a 'future primitive' setting. This space is much more extreme than the early theatre of *The Virgin Prunes* because Rolfe gives his body over totally as an implement of the spectacle, usually rolling himself naked on wet canvas or other substances to create impressions. Considered to be one of the most advanced artists alive in the twentieth century, Rolfe has recently placed more emphasis on the recorded medium, exploring compositional techniques in 'found sounds' and synthesised music that simultaneously work as performance soundtracks and vinyl end-product.

Nigel Rolfe was born in the Isle of Wight in 1950. After attending Art Colleges in Surrey and Bath, he came to live in Ireland during his mid-twenties. His reaons were simple. He wanted to 'get his hands dirty', to move away from object art and the conservative Neo-Expressionism which was starting to take a hold of English art and break out into new terrain. Rolfe saw Ireland as a place where he could 'leap-frog' the institutions, where radical art was possible because there was no real art-school tradition.[11] Rolfe's view was that very few Irish artists had investigated the primitive side of Irish rural culture. Because Ireland as a whole was still agrarian, slightly industrialised and fairly swamped by British and American media culture, its art was perilously caught between several stools. Rolfe saw that Irish art required a stronger identity and for this it had to hook back into the mystical Celtic heritage that invisibly bonded all Irish people. He immediately perceived a sense of communality, a sense of spirit in Irish culture that was lacking in his native post-industrial Britain.

But Rolfe was not unaware that his background in many ways shaped the methods and approaches of his work. During the 1960s and 1970s English art schools had produced many individuals who became leaders in contemporary rock music. Names like Keith Richards, Bryan Ferry, Brian Eno, John Lennon and Pete Townshend easily come to mind. Most of the composers innovating in serious latter-day avant-garde music originate from these liberal institutions. Given his unorthodox education, which stressed continual self-criticism and re-orientation so as to get beyond conditioning processes, Rolfe's art was bound to be different. Just as relevant was the ideology that art needn't be figurative. The most vital attribute of an English art school education of the sixties and early seventies was the way it turned one's head inside out as far as the meaning of art was concerned. Anything could be art, depending on how it was approached. Art became not so much a physical entity but more a mental set that involved both audience and artist. Thus performance and mixed-media art took on important symbolic roles, radically challenging staid painting and sculptural reference points. It was through these forms of expression that Nigel Rolfe would make his biggest impact on the Irish art and music scene.

His first Celtic phase was through sculpture — painstakingly building structures out of wood, some of them in natural locations, others in galleries, even more in unusual 'spaces'. Sometimes these would be destroyed through violent physical contact. The ritualistic creation and destruction had an instinctiveness to it that looked very primitive but at the same time could be interpreted as being representative of the nuclear arms building 'progress' of the Western world. From here he moved to the 'crawling drawings' of the late seventies. Calling them 'sculptures in motion', Rolfe would lie down on areas of flour covered with soot arranged in basic line, star, disc and cross patterns. Like a Shaman or medicine man from the tribal past he would then 'undraw' the floor designs by forcibly dragging and twisting his body all over them. Soon these performances were done naked and gave way to 'ramp drawings' on raised wooden platforms with waterbuckets, and 'target drawings' where Rolfe would dramatically fling himself onto mounds of flour. Such variations as 'face drawings' brought it home to audiences that Rolfe's body was the artistic tool and never before had the distinction between art and artist seemed finer. The intense nature of these living sculpture experiments became more streamlined when Rolfe started to transfer his body imprint onto damp cotton cloth in the early 1980s.

For his *Dark Star . . . Nine Shrouds* presentation at the Project Arts Centre in 1982 he employed video and sound to complement his imprint method. Guitarist Pat O'Donnell and synthesiser/rhythm player Steve Belton composed music for the performance and thus Rolfe entered the multi-media world. Some would say that his work became less potent because of its growing technological sophistication, but those detractors obviously did not see the artist's intention. At the brilliant opening of the *Dance, Slap for Africa* exhibition/event in Paris 1983 Rolfe displayed an uncanny sense of appropriateness in his use of electronic audio-visual props. Central to this Pompidou 'exhibition' were two stretched cotton silhouettes of Africa on which he made naked 'red man running' impressions. Tall colour slides of various tribes-people alternated on and off to make a flickering backdrop. Two videos, one of a gyrating rock dancer, the other of Rolfe's face being beaten, beamed out from either side of the stage. Dramatic lighting and the electronic music of Pat O'Donnell and Steve Belton completed what for Rolfe was a peak achievement in his career. The work seemed to say that no matter how complex our environment becomes or whatever high notions of 'art' or civilisation man holds, the primitivism is always there and impossible to disown.

Rolfe collaborated with Belton and O'Donnell on four more projects in 1983/1984, the most renowned being *The Rope that Binds Us Makes Them Free*. Like *Dance, Slap for Africa* this new multi-media presentation successfully toured internationally but was even more stunning in its impact. Following through on his personal 'body drawing' technique, this time he gave a map of Ireland the treatment. Images of Irish monuments were projected around him as three video monitors flashed their different visual contents. One showed the torso, arms and legs of an Irish girl dancer. Another had Rolfe in the fascinating situation of self-binding his head with an enormous ball of string. The third showed Rolfe again, this time being struck in the face by water. O'Donnell's and Belton's music, as usual, complemented the proceedings. A short text which included the title sentence was also included in the slides and the television screens radiated three distinct green, white and orange hues which obviously represented the Irish flag. A riveting political and sociological statement, the magical rope-binding reference (to be observed in Celtic mythology) worked with the water splash aspect as a direct flashback on Ancient Ireland. Along with the music, this highly charged visual creation encapsulated the history and present situation of the Irish nation through a criss-crossing array of subconscious trigger symbols.

An extremely busy man, Rolfe was involved in art administration, lectureships in the UK and America, multiple exhibitions and shows all over the world, films and videos, designing theatre sets and acting as visiting Professor to Yale University. Despite all these draws on his attention he still managed to develop the musical input into his art. No longer involved with O'Donnell and Belton,

Rolfe worked briefly with American composer Jeffrey Brooks before knuckling down to creating his own music in 1985 and 1986. The new material was conceptually designed as the soundtrack for a multi-media event titled 'Island Stories', debuted at the ICA Gallery London. It served a dual function because the tracks were 'busy' and 'aurally intricate' enough to be released as an album. Thus Rolfe became a proper recording artist when *Island Stories* came out on the Reekus label in the summer of 1986. Assisted by engineer Pearse Dunne, instrumentalist John Duffy, plus a selection of other musicians, Rolfe had produced the LP himself at Windmill Lane Studios, Dublin. The eight pieces that made up *Island Stories* were individually stimulating but admirably flowed together in a suitably cohesive fashion. Rolfe made full use of electronics, involving sequencers, synthesisers and taped excerpts, but never overriding the melodious musical content of the album. Like all his art *Island Stories* was an Irish statement through an organic/technological framework that made new perceptions possible.

The opening track 'African Flower' is a specific anti-apartheid cut-up of taped voices atmospherically mixed with synth treatments and electronically generated tribal drumming. One can hear an emotionally stirring speech by the Rev. Alan Boesak of the World Methodist Church, rallying the black peoples of South Africa with phrases like, 'there can be no turning back' and 'the price is high but the end is near.' P. W. Botha and the South African police also feature. 'African Flower' closed with an appropriate excerpt from a township funeral march. A longer version was made available on 12 inch and proceeds from its sale were donated to the African National Congress. This version includes extra voices, and those of Winnie Mandela and American politicians arguing about the morality of South African apartheid were most prominent. Its B side is an ethnic sounding electronic instrumental ironically called 'P.W. Botha's Funeral March'. The album's second track 'Going Boeing' is a sound collage of various 'noises', voices and effects, underpinned by a pulsating synthesised keyboard/drum music which re-creates the experience of air travel and flight disaster. Amusingly, Rolfe uses a domestic vacuum cleaner here to get across the whistling of aircraft engines starting up. 'Three Monkeys' involves a collapsing drums/bass funk rhythm over which Rolfe speaks an eccentric commentary which centres on Europe's positioning within the international super-power structure. Side One concludes with the strange 'Made in Japan — 39 Years', which starts with Rolfe describing the attitude of a man who wants to buy a gramophone but because of his World War Two experiences refuses to purchase anything Japanese. A synthesised koto gives the exact Oriental touch as Rolfe reels off twenty-nine brand names of everyday appliances made in Japan.

The first side of *Island Stories* could be described as the 'international viewpoint'. Side Two is very Irish. It commences with 'Heartbeat Drumbeat', a bodhrán-based, ethnic, chugging instrumental which commemorates the death of Seán Downes who died after being struck by an RUC plastic bullet in Northern Ireland in the summer of 1984. Explaining the inspiration behind the track on the sleeve notes, Rolfe wrote the emphatic line: 'One heart is stopped and the heartbeat of a nation is stronger.' Christy Moore had a hand in the making of 'The Ostrich', a moving lament about Ann Lovett, the fifteen-year-old girl who died delivering her own child in a country grotto in January 1984. Sung passionately by Rita Connolly, the song comments on the warping effect that traditional Catholicism has on people's lives — the way it approaches areas of behaviour with a blinkered vision making people treat 'taboo' aspects of their reality with the attitude of an ostrich. Moore's folk influence can clearly be heard in the lilting percussive beat that subtly carries the song. 'Amerikaye' is an odd juxtaposition of Russian choral music, deep tuba, held synth notes and spoken words. Here Alanna O'Kelly recounts an experience she and Rolfe had in Galway. They met a Mrs Coleman, a woman of about ninety years, who in all that time had never left her village locale. She could only speak Irish and lived frugally with no running water or electricity. She lived by the sea and the only other country she knew about was 'Amerikaye'. Rolfe was fascinated by the fact that on one side of the Atlantic there existed this huge urban capitalist society while on the other a rural peasant culture slowly meandered on its simple way. The album climaxed with the beautiful 'Breast Mound Bowl' an Ambient composition, reminiscent of the work of Brian Eno, totally created on Yamaha DX7 and Prophet 5 synthesisers. Rolfe wrote it with Queen Maeve's cairn, county Sligo, in mind and as an aural tribute to the mystical Irish landscape which inspires most of his art.

To some, the world of Nigel Rolfe is one of mysterious eccentricity that is best observed at a safe distance. To others it is endlessly fascinating, providing late twentieth-century life with a necessary form of artistic criticism that is as entertaining as it is subversive. Few however have realised how important he is to contemporary music. When analysed it's obvious how full of avant-garde music principles Rolfe's work is. The multi-media ideas of John Cage, Stockhausen's electronic universe, Eno's Ambient techniques, Schaeffer's musique concrète, Jon Hassell's 'future primitivism' and so forth are readily observable in the *Island Stories* project. But what is more exciting about Rolfe is that in an Irish context he has shown that music can go beyond the isolated aural conventions of the past. For him music is a malleable substance that can be used with any number of other media, something to be involved as a means to express but never as an end in itself. Like multi-media artist Laurie Anderson (with whom Rolfe has exhibited in America) he treads the path of the modern-day iconoclast, utilising information technology, electronic equipment and his mortal self to re-make musical communication in terms of the future.

Postscript

The major narrative of this chapter has concentrated on the way Irish rock has changed since the early 1970s, outlining in depth the prominent music and musicians that have brought about that change. The emphasis has been on pivotal phenomena which have shaped and expanded the form. Of course the structure of such an analysis cannot hope to include every artist that has been involved and in places the conceptual and historical perspective has meant that certain people have not been given as much attention as they deserve. In fact there have been omissions which anybody familiar with the area will no doubt observe. In order to give a wider view and a more fair treatment what follows is an A-Z miscellany of individuals and bands, past and present, both in the mainstream and on the fringes, who have contributed something significant to modern Irish rock music.

Auto Da Fé

After her prestigious career as vocalist with *Steeleye Span* and *The Woodsband*, Gay Woods re-emerged in the eighties with *Auto Da Fé*. A highly versatile chanteuse she managed to retain the subtleties of her folk roots within a new electronic rock format. Keyboardsman Trevor Knight and Gay co-wrote the material and formed the main nucleus while travelling members such as drummer Robbie Brennan were recruited for live and studio work. Philip Lynott produced the group's four best singles: 'November November' (ADF 1982), 'Bad Experience' (ADF 1982), 'Man of Mine' (Rewind 1983) and 'Something's Gotten Hold of My Heart' (Red Hot 1984). They are all beautiful songs, carried perfectly by Woods' pristine vocals. *Auto Da Fé* became a popular concert attraction mainly because of Woods' theatrical and colourful stage performances. In 1985 they released two albums *Five Singles and One Smoked Cod* and *Tatitum* on Red Hot Records. A single, this time without Lynott, also appeared called 'Credo Credo'. In 1986 Gay and Trevor changed the title of their act to *Operaracket*. The flamboyant aspects of *Auto Da Fé* were dispensed with for a more serious presentation which featured Gay's voice against a backdrop of cut-up sounds, African rhythms and minimalist keyboard techniques.

Big Self

One of Irish rock's most tenacious and original bands, *Big Self*, arrived in the slipstream of punk in the early 1980s with a solid live reputation and two memorable singles on Reekus 'Surprise Surprise' and 'Don't Turn Around'. Originally a five-piece from the Falls Road in Belfast, the group were joined by Dublin-born Gordy Blair (ex-*Rudi, The Outcasts*) in 1982. The fascinating thing about *Big Self* was that they were an all-white Northern Irish combo who had no truck with either sectarian prejudice or musical cocoonery. Their music mixed as many different styles as possible and could be described as a punk, jazz/rock, new wave, ethnic formulation. They recorded their debut album *Stateless* for the Reekus label in Windmill Lane in 1984, and it showed how well this variation worked in the studio. A hugely atmospheric production, its sinister guitars, reggae rhythms and Gordy's soulful saxophone marked it out as a unique combination of subtlety, diversity and open-mindedness. Even though Gordy joined *Ruefrex* for their 1985 album *Flowers for All Occasions* (Kasper) he returned to the *Big Self* fold soon after.

Blue in Heaven

Quite easily the dirtiest-sounding Irish rock 'n' roll band of the post-punk era, *Blue in Heaven* formed in the early eighties in Dublin. Soon they became notorious for their angry words, jagged rhythm guitars and trouncing drums. While doing support slots at the likes of the SFX Hall, Dublin, the group had that rare ability to be able to command any size of stage with just youth, speed and a frenzied attack. Comprising Shane O'Neill (vocals, guitar), Eamonn Tynan (keyboards), Declan Jones (bass) and David Clarke (drums) they put together some demo tapes, one of which was produced by *U2's* Edge, and secured a record deal with Island UK in December 1983. Their first single 'Julie Cries' is a hostile and intense barrage of emotion, but some hiccups in the making of *All the Gods' Men* with ex-*Joy Division/U2* producer Martin Hannett in 1985 made for a slightly disappointing debut LP. Not to be deterred, they kept up the gigging and soon Island boss Chris Blackwell realised how committed *Blue in Heaven* were to their music. Whisked off to Compass Point Studios in the Bahamas, the band recorded their second album, *Explicit Material* (1986), with Blackwell as co-producer. A much louder, more direct and grinding effort than its predecessor, *Explicit Material* is a definitive rock statement. The June 1986 single 'I Just Wanna'/'Beating in My Head' (Little Flower) was so full of energy, searing guitars, hammering drums and sneering vocals that one felt on hearing it that the rock idiom had only just been invented.

Cactus World News

Indicative of how chance and belief can bring about an unusual combination, *Cactus World News* got together in 1984 out of sheer fortitude. Founder members Eoin McEvoy (acoustic guitar, vocals) and Frank Kearns (electric guitar) teamed up in that year after several aborted attempts at careers in the music business. While searching for other musicians they wrote a melodic rock song with passion called 'The Bridge'. In December 1984 Feargal MacAindris (bass) and Wayne Sheehy (drums) were recruited and a demo was made and sent to *U2's* Bono. The latter was looking for aspiring talent for his fledgling Mother label and wanted to co-produce 'The Bridge' and some other tracks as an EP. While this was being organised, Cactus World News built up an awesome live reputation. Kearns's guitar style was fluent and piercing, McEvoy strummed a loud guitar but balanced this with poetic lyrics, fraught with feeling. This spirited combination was driven outwards and upwards by MacAindris's and Sheehy's fearsome bass and drums. It was a new type of sound, owing something to *U2*, but very much of their own making. On the whiff of a *U2* connection *Cactus World News* were hounded up and down the country by A & R men from England and eventually they went for a sensible deal with MCA Records. At the beginning of 1986 their second EP 'Years Later' came out and proved that the band had an exceptional sound — acoustic/electric guitar rock combined with heartfelt vocals to produce a sound which is dynamic, tempestuous but never bludgeoning. The follow-up single 'Worlds Apart' is even better and in the summer came *Urban Beaches*, an album produced by former *Rolling Stones* desk-man Chris Kimsey in Holland and Ireland. Sometimes noisy, sometimes cluttered but relentlessly invigorating *Urban Beaches* boasts some outstanding tracks. Most notable are the aforementioned 'Years Later' with its threshing guitar mesh, the atmospheric 'State of Emergency' with its driving acoustic guitar and the fascinating 'Maybe This Time' which opens as a ballad but evolves into a stormy sea of cymbals and tugging Spanish and slivering electric guitars. Despite heavy criticism from some quarters *Cactus World News* are a genuinely inventive rock group whose audience abroad, especially in America, is continually expanding.

98 *Auto Da Fe's* Gay Woods 1983.

99 *Blue in Heaven's* Shane O'Neill, 1983.

100 *Blue in Heaven,* Dublin 1983.

101 Eoin McEvoy and Frank Kearns of *Cactus World News* jump for joy after the release of *Urban Beaches* in 1986.

102 Chris de Burgh.

103 *Fastway* in 1987. Dave King *(third from left)* became the most acclaimed heavy rock singer in the world in 1983. That's 'Fast' Eddie Clarke second from right.

104 *The Fountainhead* — Steve Belton *(left)* and Pat O'Donnell *(right)*.

103

104

Paul Cleary

One of Ireland's great young songwriters, Cleary was best known for his formation *The Blades*, who in the punk and post-punk era produced a version of pop/rock that was distinctly appealing. Even though Cleary went solo for 'Some People Smile' (Reekus 1983), a fine acoustic rock ballad, *The Blades* were still very much in the offing. In early 1984 they secured an international record deal with Elektra America. Following through on the new contract a debut album was put down in London with the nucleus of Cleary (guitars, vocals), Brian Foley (bass) and Jake Reilly (drums) plus a variety of session musicians including respected sax player Mel Collins and some backing vocalists. Shockingly, Elektra refused to release the album and in 1985 *The Blades* were dropped from the label. Then Reekus, the company that had championed the band in the past, came to the rescue and negotiated with Elektra so that the recorded material could be distributed internationally. During that time Reekus released a compilation album of *Blades'* singles and rarities titled *Raytown Revisited (1980-1985)*. Feeling that it was time to make a change, Cleary dissolved *The Blades* in 1986 and formed a new group *The Partisans*. As well as ex-*Blade* Conor Brady on guitar this unit boasted *Clannad* drummer Paul Moran and Australian session bass/didgeridoo player player Steven Cooney (ex-*Stockton's Wing*). Always socially and politically sensitive to working class Irish experience and to the inequalities in Irish society, Cleary saw *The Partisans* as a new exploratory vehicle for his writing. This sensitivity was also shown by his controversial decision not to be involved in that year's Self Aid concert. (He had felt that unemployment required a better solution than one benefit gig!) In autumn 1986 *The Blades'* long-awaited first album *The Last Man in Europe* (Reekus) appeared and displayed Cleary's talent for wrapping his strong viewpoints in accessible pop music compositions. 'Downmarket' is a simple tune about basic living that has all the hallmarks of the old *Blades* style. 'Talk about Listening', a track about hard graft for little reward in a warehouse, and 'Those Were the Days', a clever look at the indoctrinating nature of Irish religious schooling, are both reggae-based. 'Boy One' even has an electric sitar and is very much like something out of the *Byrds'* country period. Due to Cooney and Moran's busy working schedules, Cleary re-grouped *The Partisans* with two new members in 1987 and recorded the mini album *Impossible* (Hotwire). An extension of the *Blades'* album this is a mixture of soul/pop songs, one country rock number and a quartet of tracks relating to contemporary working class Dublin life.

Chris de Burgh

Christopher John Davison was born in Buenos Aires, Argentina, in 1947. His father, a British citizen from the Channel Islands, came from a line of engineers who had settled in Australia and then moved to South America. The Davisons had gone there to farm but the Second World War brought Davison senior into the English army. After specialising in intelligence operations in Burma for a number of years, he returned home, but during a short stay in England fell in love with and married the daughter of General Sir Eric de Burgh, Maeve, who was of Irish birth. Chris was the second son of the union and because of his father's continued involvement with British intelligence moved to Malta in the

1950s. Later the whole family travelled to Africa as a result of Charles Davison leaving the secret service and going into the construction business there. From here Chris was sent to Ireland for some primary school education. In 1960 the entire Davison clan settled in Wexford where they began a hotel business in a castle.

Following a spell at an English boarding school, Chris went to Trinity College, Dublin, to study languages. Most of his childhood spare time had been spent playing the piano and as a youth he enjoyed singing popular songs to the self-accompaniment of acoustic guitar. He'd also started writing his own compositions. Soon after graduating he decided on a musical career and pushed himself into the Dublin scene. Nobody wanted to know, so he left for England where the young troubadour odd-jobbed it for a while before landing a recording contract with A & M, the first record company he approached! In the summer of 1974 Chris de Burgh (obviously his mother's name was more suitable for his chosen profession) recorded the album *Far Beyond These Castle Walls*. It is a highly orchestrated singer/songwriter's affair with added harpsichord, pedal steel guitar, mouth harp, harmonium, acoustic bass and backing vocals. It did nothing on the English or American markets but went to number one in Brazil and shifted cart-loads in Europe and Canada.

With his natural flair for songwriting and wilful determination to succeed, de Burgh spent the next decade raising himself to star status all over the world. Through the albums *Spanish Train and Other Stories* (A & M 1975), *At the End of a Perfect Day* (A & M 1977), *Crusader* (A & M 1979), *Eastern Wind* (A & M 1980), *The Getaway* (A & M 1982) and *Man on the Line* (1984) the small bodied, Anglo-Irish entertainer became a certified commercial success especially in Germany, Scandinavia, Canada and Ireland. Unfortunately, from a pure rock perspective his music has little to offer, being neither innovative in nor authentic to that genre. In terms of Irish rock his sound has none of its rousing Celtic quality and could never be termed mystical. Analysing his LP releases down through the years one finds a music that vacillates between bombastic pseudo rock, dull piano tales, pompous overblown audacity and sickly sweet romanticism. It's precisely because of its mid-Atlantic, middle-of-the-road character that Chris de Burgh's recorded output has had such a broad market penetration, yet he is recognised as an Irish artist and the only Irish-based singer/ songwriter to reap substantial international recognition with that style. Moreover he is bountifully sincere in his art and has always been a huge live attraction. In October 1986 he played six sell-out nights in the fifteen thousand capacity RDS Simmonscourt Arena, Dublin, and because of popular demand had to come back early the following year to do four more. Also his interest in getting local radio established in Ireland and his contributions to such worthy causes as Self Aid and Bands Against Drugs (a 1987 video against addictive drugs which also included items from Bono, Bob Geldof and Brush Shiels) showed that he was not just a canny showbusinessman content to sit comfortably atop a mountain of wealth. In 1986 his ninth studio album *Into the Light* went to number one in the British charts as did the catchy ballad single 'The Lady in Red'. By the summer of 1987 that song had also made the upper reaches of the American Billboard Top Ten.

Johnny Duhan

After sorting out his legal position, which effectively tied up his product all through the seventies, Duhan's first solo album appeared in 1982. Formerly of *Granny's Intentions*, his whinging vocal style marked an unusual and distinctive talent. His penchant for piercing commentary and acid lyricism gave his new music a stark direct quality. While the 1982 *Johnny Duhan* on Phillips was quite emotionally autobiographical his sharp pen flowed with more socio-political imagery on his second solo set *Current Affairs* (Plastic Records 1984), 'Woman' and 'Northern Ireland' being the most outstanding cuts. His best song to date has been 'El Salvador', an acoustic rock jewel about the plight of the oppressed in South America which was suitably covered by Christy Moore on his 1984 *Ride On* (WEA).

Fastway

Within a year of formation *Fastway* became the most successful latter-day heavy rock combination to come out of Britain. In a matter of months their eponymous first album *Fastway* (CBS 1983) had risen high on the international charts and shifted well over half a million units in the States alone. Produced by former *Jimi Hendrix* techno-whiz Eddie Kramer, it featured ex-*Motorhead* guitarist 'Fast' Eddie Clarke, ex-*Humble Pie* drummer Jerry Shirley, renowned session bassman Mickey Feat and a little-known Irish vocalist called Dave King. On hearing him sing, old *Led Zeppelin* shouter Robert Plant testified that King was the best hard rock singer in the world. Twenty-year-old King always wanted to be as good as Plant if not better. He had started singing with Dublin heavy metal outfit *Redeemer* in 1980. He was quickly noticed and invited to play with Belfast three-piece *Mama's Boys*. After a couple of jams he wanted room to move and joined *Stilwood*, another Dublin formation, and fronted a lot of acoustic heavy *Zeppelin*-type rock. They built up quite a following in a small Dublin club called the Ivy Rooms, but King wanted more. Some tracks were laid down on tape and seeing a *Melody Maker* advertisement King sent the demo to Clarke in London. Eddie was so knocked out by King's voice that he immediately got back to him, brought him over to London and within a week was paying for studio time. As well as singing, King wrote songs and contributed acoustic guitar passages.

Charlie McCracken (the legendary *Taste* bassist) joined them for their inaugural American tour of 1983. McCracken also stayed for the second album *All Fired Up* (CBS 1984). It was then that *Fastway* turned their line-up into *Stilwood* plus Eddie Clarke. King felt that the group needed more texture and with Shane Carroll (guitar, keyboards), Alan Connor (drums) and Paul Reid (bass) went into Abbey Road Studios to record *Waiting for the Road* (CBS 1986). This utilised the fifty-eight piece London Symphony Orchestra and the Fairlight CMI in the same mix and was critically praised for being an intelligent and progressive heavy rock album. On such tracks as 'The World Waits for You' and 'Change' King, *Stilwood* and Clarke mingle subtlety, emotion and musicality into a form that so many others had bastardised. In 1987 the band made the soundtrack LP *Trick or Treat* again for CBS.

Na Fíréin

Honourable mention must go to Dublin quartet *Na Fíréin*, the only contemporary rock band to write and perform their material entirely through the Irish language. Their debut selection *Sin mar a Bhíonn* (Gael-Linn 1986) was a wealthy collection of songs that pulled the urgency of punk, the softness of folk, the minimalism of the new wave, and the stylisations of sixties rock into an enervating whole. Their lyrical subject matter covered a wide range of relevant issues such as unemployment, the problems of war, alcoholism, the anguish of young love and Celtic mythology. A lot of people reacted negatively to *Na Fíréin's* choice of Irish as a medium of expression. Realistically, these detractors failed to see that even if the lyrical meaning of *Sin mar a Bhíonn* (That's the Way It Is) is obscure to many the strong feelings in the music always come through to compensate.

The Fountainhead

Sophisticated electronic-oriented duo Pat O'Donnell and Steve Belton first became known for their work with artist/musician Nigel Rolfe between 1982 and 1984. Addicted to exploring the possibilities of the new sound technology of the eighties their early experimental creations were done with the basic materials of a 4-track tape recorder, guitar and simple synthesiser. Belton, with his experience of studio engineering, and the song/guitar focused O'Donnell made for an ideal pairing and their grasp of minimalist principles coupled with an original sound soon drew a respectable audience. Constantly upgrading their equipment to include Fairlight Computer, DX7 Digital Memory synth and so on they released the dancy 12 inch single 'Rhythm Method' on their own label in 1984. Within a year this had become a sizeable American disco and College radio hit and secured them a deal with Chrysalis/China Records. Now going under the name *The Fountainhead*, their initiating album *The Burning Touch* was released in June 1986. Subsequent to this they formed a larger band network for live performance but retained a certain amount of the technological ingredients. This was a beneficial move as can be heard on 'Sometimes', a celebratory concert track taken from the Los Angles-recorded 'Too Good Now' EP of 1987. With a full understanding of funk/rhythm motifs and the simultaneous ability to be able to incorporate interesting electronic possibilities into their sound spectrum, *The Fountainhead* are a good example of the new futuristic side of developing Irish rock.

Haa Lacka Binttii

'Illicit sex and the aftermath of Catholic guilt', 'half-baked drag queen', 'buzzsaw guitars and submarine bleeps thrown together in an aircraft hangar', 'if ugliness is beauty, this is very beautiful', 'like really bad acid', 'arse-backwards production values that succeed in intimating a melody'. These are some lines taken from the reactionary British music press reviews of Haa Lacka Binttii and his group *Princess Tinymeat's* 1985-86 record releases. Bintti (or Danny Figgis) was at one time the drummer/electronics person with *The Virgin Prunes* and definitely rates as the strangest, most far-out artist ever to come out of modern Irish rock. Always androgynous in appearance, his outrageous image and unfathomable thrash version of neo-psychedelic punk has made him a notorious presence on the fringe/underground Irish and UK scenes. His first 'solo' single as *Princess Tinymeat* front person, 'Sloblands' (Rough Trade 1985), garnered much attention, mainly because of its sleeve shots of a naked Binttii revealing all! The simplistic reaction of the British press to that and the releases 'Bun in the Oven' (1986) and 'Devilcock' (1987) (all were 12 inch EPs) didn't attempt to understand Binttii's humour, talented electronic or studio musicianship and innate charm. Respected by serious composer Roger Doyle, the weird Dubliner produced the crazy 'Big Spud' EP for fellow thrash rockists *The Gorehounds* in 1987.

Hotwire

Without a doubt the most vital independent record label to germinate from modern Irish rock has been Hotwire, the brainchild of former *Horslips* drummer and director Eamon Carr. The wily county Meath man had always done something different when approaching the music scene, effectively changing things whenever he was involved. *Horslips* had originated Celtic rock and their importance has been well documented elsewhere in this book. After their disbandment, Carr wanted to set up a label that would give new Irish talent a proper outlet, but it took quite a few years to organise. It was seeing a fourteen-piece punk-adelic band called *The Golden Horde* in 1984 that made him realise there was a more anarchic side to the *U2*-dominated situation that deserved exposure. Fired with conviction and enormous energy, Carr quickly picked up on other groups and Hotwire was baptised with the release of the compilation *Hip City Boogaloo*. Its most immediately striking feature was the substantial sound of *Light a Big Fire* whose playwright lead singer Tom McLoughlin came across as a lyricist of no small means. Carr offered to manage and in 1985 released the mini-album *Gunpowders* which reaped great critical and public acclaim. Not wishing to specialise too much Carr nurtured his other finds. He was particularly fond of *The Golden Horde* and any ideas that frontman Simon Carmody had were entertained. Carmody, a walking encyclopedia of sixties rock and collector of obscure knowledge, wanted to get American Robert Anton Wilson in on an album project. No sooner said than done; with Carr producing, the record was put down and put out in 1985 under the title *The Chocolate Biscuit Conspiracy* — the title being an amalgam of US sixties psychedelic group names *The Peanut Butter Conspiracy* and *The Chocolate Watch Band*! Anton Wilson was an oddball character who wrote books about complex conspiracy theories and spoke in terms of 'natural surrealism', 'extra-terrestrial psychology' and other such hokum. The *Chocolate Biscuit* album turned out to be a wild, zany fusion of Wilson intonating fascinating gibberish about such things as Hiroshima, werewolf dreams and CIA-Lee Harvey Oswald clones and *The Horde's* adrenalised garage band crash rock. Because of its total weirdness it quickly became known as a truly original Irish rock underground classic.

Following the appearance of *The Golden Horde's* 'In Reality' EP, a speedy Ramones-style offering, in early 1986 Carmody could be heard again on the more serious *Last Bandits in the World* LP. This is a genuine blues masterpiece with old *Horslips* guitarist Johnny Fean coaxing some lovely slide twangs from his acoustic. (Later that year Henry McCullough put down some tracks with Carmody and Nikki Sudden in a different *Last Bandits* line-up). A very busy year for Carr, 1986 also saw the release of *Buying Gold in Heaven*, a thirteen-track album of *Radiators from Space* cuts from 1977 to 1980, and the fabulous compilation *The Weird Weird World of Guru Weirdbrain*, which is a gold-mine of 'left-field' tracks ranging from some unknown calling himself The Legendary J. O'Connell doing a perfect Elvis Presley impression into a bedroom tape recorder to various frenzied mutations of sixties and seventies punk with a bit of country, folk and blues thrown in along the way for good measure. Critics in the UK and Ireland were rightly bowled over by Eamon Carr's sense of fun, originality and vision in bringing such unheard-of music out of the nooks and crannies of the subterranean scene.

On the management end, *Light a Big Fire* were signed up by Siren in England and numerous singles were released, the most notable being 'Charlene', a convincing anti-heroin pop song. Their album *Surveillance* (Siren 1987) confirmed Carr's instinct that they were an unusual *mélange* since the record was full of imagistic songs backed by a simple rock music that was constantly slipping into different stylisations. Since its inception Hotwire has enabled Carr to get a lot of music exhibited that would be ignored by the larger record combines. Such groups as *The Real Wild West, The Stars of Heaven* and *Paranoid Visions* were given a necessary early opportunity to get started in the recording business, whilst off-the-beaten-track sessions by older, more well known artists could be given an airing. It's true that Hotwire wasn't the first independent label to get going, but it is the only maverick to achieve status in the field of alternative Irish rock music.

In Tua Nua

A rare product of Irish rock is a group that can mix Celtic instrumentation into their sound without it coming out folky or traditional. Up to the inception of *In Tua Nua* in Howth in 1982, any such fusions had always tilted over to the ethnic lane because it was usually from there that uilleann pipers, tin whistlers and fiddlers came. *In Tua Nua* were therefore not really a *Horslips* of the eighties but a new kind of formulation altogether. Founded by Martin Clancy (guitar, keyboards) and Ivan O'Shea (guitars) in order to 'use real instruments not synthesised sounds' a tape 'Welcome the Freshness' was done with flute, clarinet and the violin of Steve Wickham. The demo was distributed to record shops but Wickham, who had recorded with U2 for *War*, had to go on their 1983 European tour. Vinnie Kilduff (uilleann pipes) also guested and when it was over both he and Wickham returned to *In Tua Nua* (the name was of Irish origins with Hawaiian and Indonesian connotations) to make a seven-piece with Leslie Dowdall (vocals), Paul Byrne (drums) and Jack Dublin (bass).

Their wafting sound, reminiscent of West Coast American group *Jefferson Airplane*, was most definitely rock but with an exciting flavour that sketched out real Irish colours. On a visit to Howth before *U2's* Phoenix Park gig of summer 1983, Bono and Jim Kerr of *Simple Minds* saw *In Tua Nua* perform and were floored. Bono immediately wanted to release their heroic song 'Coming Thru' and in 1984 it was the first Mother label single. That summer *In Tua Nua* supported Bob Dylan at Slane Castle and were signed up by Island in the same week. The haunting 'Coming Thru' was included with some new tracks on a tasteful 12 inch gatefold single (a real Irish rock collector's item) titled 'Take My

105 Haa Lacka Binttii (top) and his 1980s thrash rock unit Princess Tinymeat.

106 Zen Alligators — Eamon Carr's shortlived rock 'n' roll jaunt between Horslips and Hotwire.

107 In Tua Nua, with singer Leslie Dowdall (seated).

109

108 Simon Carmody's *Golden Horde* (1987) — a frantic stomp through a thrash rock psychedelia that snatches from *The Ramones* for its attack and from every acid-trip band of the 1960s for its humour. (Simon Carmody *second from right*.)

109 Early shot of Cork's fine *Microdisney* — Sean O'Hagan *(left)*, Cathal Coughlan *(right)*.

110 Since the progressive rock days, Gary Moore has been a constant leading spirit in Irish rock. His 1987 LP *Wild Frontier* incorporated traditional group *The Chieftains* in a new fusion of technology, folk and hard rock.

111 *The Mama's Boys*, a modern equivalent of seminal Irish three-pieces *Taste* and *Thin Lizzy*.

110

111

Hand' (1985) — a compellingly beautiful and emotional recording which had been originally written while teenager Sinéad O'Connor was in the ranks. Their star was in its full ascendant, for 1985 also saw them support U2 at Croke Park as well as releasing a tour de force version of *Jefferson Airplane's* original 1967 hit 'Somebody to Love'. This was actually better than the summer of love classic with Dowdall's voice vastly improving on Grace Slick's. Australian rasta bass/didgeridoo sessioner Steve Cooney had produced their previous product and his eclectic influence could be heard on the African sounding B side 'Sleeping Tide'. Tragedy struck when Wickham threw in the towel to join British band *The Waterboys*, and Kilduff split also. The projected album *Map of Days* was shelved by Island and *In Tua Nua* suddenly found themselves without a record outlet. As compensation a compilation LP, *Somebody to Love*, was put out by Island America and Europe in the spring of 1986.

Doggedly committed to their work, *In Tua Nua* re-grouped with Aingeala De Burca on violin and Brian O'Brien on pipes, and signed with Virgin UK. Continuously gigging and doing some interesting support slots with *Simple Minds* in Scotland and England their first Virgin product, the tightly construed 'Seven into the Sea' backed by the Jack Dublin composed 'Ballad of Irish Love' appeared in the summer. Still recovering from the Wickham/Kilduff separation, *In Tua Nua* survived the worst of traumas to record *Vaudeville* (Virgin 1987), an album of ambitious rock music that has enough classical, folk and Celtic elements and emotional drive to satisfy any listening party that a new kind of Irish rock sound had evolved.

Jolyon Jackson

The death of Jolyon Jackson in London at the end of 1985 was an unfortunate blow to modern Irish music. A choral singer and composer in his youth, Jackson loved the cello. He studied at Trinity College during the 1960s. There he was involved with Roger Doyle in *Jazz Therapy* and *Supply Demand and Curve*. Following that he took after John Cage and combined synthesiser improvisations with movement in his work with the Dublin Contemporary Dance Theatre of the 1970s. A lot of sound-track material was created and Jackson endlessly experimented with new compositional ideas in all manner of musical idioms. His contribution to the 1978 Dublin Festival of Twentieth-Century music, where he improvised on synth and piano, was substantial and up to his premature death from Hodgkin's disease he continued to investigate the rich area of cross-musical pollination.

The Mama's Boys

Sometimes it happens that a group can be producing albums, touring and gaining recognition at home and abroad but rarely reach the pages of the newspaper or magazine critics. For all that anyone has heard of them, *The Mama's Boys* might never have existed, but with a steady release of albums since 1980 the county Fermanagh three-piece deserve some recognition. Pat, Johnny and Tommy McManus came from a traditional folk background in Derrylin. While still young they were encouraged to play music in their parents' pub and soon Pat and Johnny had won themselves All Ireland championships for fiddle and tin whistle. More in tune with rock they formed a guitar-based band under the name *Pulse* and magnetised quite a following in Belfast. Only teenagers, their music was unlike derivative heavy metal since it showed a pronounced knowledge of the subtler side of sixties and early seventies rock. It was Tony Prince of Radio Luxembourg who dubbed them *The Mama's Boys* because of their youth and through an independent label called Pussy *The Official Album*, a sandpaper mix of acoustic, blues and guitar music was released in 1980. The anti-violence 'Belfast City Blues' and sonorous 'Without You' are good songs and in a way *The Mama's Boys* were a modern equivalent to seminal Irish three-pieces *Taste* and *Thin Lizzy*. Barry Devlin (ex-*Horslips*) produced their next two albums *Plug It In* (Pussy 1982) and *Turn It Up* (Pussy 1983) which both had a strident, thick and intelligent rock sound. The cool addictive 'Needle in the Groove' became their most popular tune of this period. Admired by Phil Lynott for their traditional rock values, *The Mama's Boys* did plenty of gigs with *Thin Lizzy* as well as other internationally famous heavy rock outfits like *Hawkwind* and *Wishbone Ash*. They were signed to a worldwide contract by Jive Records, and the albums *Mama's Boys*, *The Power and the Passion* and *Growing Up the Hard Way* were released in 1984, 1985 and 1987 respectively. Despite the use of clichéd, tough-boy, sexist imagery on their album covers the music of *The Mama's Boys* has always tried to retain melody and song structure within a hard rock format.

Metropolis

What may escape a lot of people's attention is that Ireland has a pool of top quality session musicians and sidemen who spent most of their time helping out on recording projects and bolstering group line-ups in transition. On a rare occasion some of them might get together to form a short-lived aggregation. One good example of this is *Metropolis* whose 1981 *Morning Shadows* (Claddagh) is a very high standard jazz/rock album with some exceptional tracks. Paul Barrett played keyboards, Garvin Gallagher did the bass guitars, Don Harris was on drums and percussion, Greg Boland plugged in his electric guitar, while a panoply of twelve-string guitars, trombone, flutes and zither were also used. Proof of how good these musicians are — Sting of English group *The Police* saw them live once and considered their version of his 'Walking on the Moon' to be superior.

Microdisney

In the winter of 1985 Microdisney went to number one in the British alternative rock charts with *The Clock Comes Down the Stairs* (Rough Trade). Guitarist Sean O'Hagan and lyricist Cathal Coughlan had come a long way since the shambolic craziness of their Cork beginnings in the late seventies. Those were the days when *Five Go Down to the Sea* and *Microdisney* were considered a form of musical lunacy that was best ignored. *Five Go Down to the Sea* were to release several singles (most notably 'The Glee Club 12' in '84) while a perversity and a natural charisma were to serve *Microdisney* well. By reducing the early five-man line-up to the essential O'Hagan/Coughlan axis, and through the release of two singles 'Hello Rascals' and 'Pink Skinned Man' in 1982 and 1983, they built up quite a following on the miniscule Dublin underground scene of the time. They received enough encouragement from

BBC DJ John Peel and their London-based label Kabuki in that period for them to move to London and expand the group to include Jon Fell (bass) and Tom Fenner (drums). Because Kabuki were affiliated to Rough Trade, the famous indie label, *Microdisney* were quickly taken on board and their first album, *Everybody Is Fantastic*, is a lyrically disjointed, quirky and claustrophobic debut. Funnily enough, it was their earlier west Cork sound experiments (the Kabuki singles and some moody instrumentals recorded on an eight-track tape machine) that made their name in England. *Microdisney* became hot controversial stuff when that material was released on a compilation record titled *We Hate You South African Bastards* six months later in 1984. The English rock underground gave a thumbs up to these angry young men who had something worthwhile to say and a novel way of saying it.

February 1985 saw the release of *In the World* (Rough Trade), an EP which startled those accustomed to the old-style Disney punkiness. Instead, tracks like 'Loftholdingswood' sparkle with a fresh, surreal-type of jangling electric pop that is decisively innovative. After that came the album *The Clock Comes down the Stairs*. With its deft touches of viola, sax and backing vocals, complex arrangements, wonderful guitar work and Coughlan's intelligent use of the English language, the LP is leagues ahead of the dull fare of their indie counterparts. Evident from the opening track 'Horse Overboard' is a clarity in the music and lyrical projection that has a high-quality pop sensibility. Coughlan's writing is a magnificent crossover of subconscious dream imagery, acidic, political and social commentary and literary prose. 'Begging Bowl' is arguably the standout track; overtly a song about female submission in a typical male dominated relationship, its music is a perfectionist blend of lilting country rock (both Coughlan and O'Hagan were big Gram Parsons fans) and classical viola that comes out sounding Celtic.

In 1986 *Microdisney* added Jim Compton (keyboards) and recorded their third studio set *Crooked Mile* for Virgin with Lenny Kaye, the respected American writer, compiler of definitive album of sixties American garage bands *Nuggets* (Elektra 1972), ex-Patti Smith guitarist and Suzanne Vega producer. The combination of Disney with Kaye resulted in a magic album. Drifting through the grooves of *Crooked Mile* are vestiges of American desert towns, motel life, Nashville dreams and other ideas that are rooted with strong doses of soul, country rock and bluegrass tones. B.J. Cole plays lap steel and pedal steel guitars, in America the favoured instruments of country musicians. Kaye adds string sections and flugelhorns to give the selections a full, top-class production sound. *Crooked Mile* (Virgin 1987) turned out to be an embarrassment of riches, showing that *Microdisney* were interested in expanding their music into newer, more exciting territories at every given opportunity. Yes, it has a commercial sound, yes it is pop, yes it is easy listening *but* it is also subversive. Lyrically, Coughlan gives a panoramic view of life as a struggle against unforeseeable and invisibly powerful odds. In 'People Just Want to Dream' for example, one is presented with a picture of a world strewn with illusionists, escaping through 'carnage magazines', television and drugs. 'And He Descended into Hell' is about a normal working man getting confused and ending up as a street bum. Musically the work is faultless. The latter track features the finest slide guitar playing that has ever been done by an Irish guitarist. Even the Edge's work on *The Joshua Tree* seems slight compared to Sean O'Hagan's ability. For his economy of style, variety in technique and thorough understanding of form, O'Hagan must be rated as a near virtuoso. There are blistering solos and lamenting refrains, chugging riffs and psychedelic snatches, all of them delivered with an expertise that is uncanny. More than that the music is such a broad canvas of Americana, from the sad Nashville-type ballad 'Our Children' straight through gospel, soul and country to the other extreme of sixties bubblegum in 'Give Me All Your Clothes'.

Microdisney are an important and vital Irish rock group simply because they have kept going forward regardless of problems and criticisms. Funnily enough at roughly the same time as they were moving from underground to overground, some of the original members, namely singer Mick Lynch and drummer Rob McKahey, had formed a new anarchic outfit to take their place on the indie scene. *Stump*, as they were called, yet again brought the infuriating Cork madness of the late seventies to the British alternative charts in the form of *Quirk Out* (Stuf 1986), a tongue-in-cheek, loosely arranged collection of funky minimalism with Lynch playing the part of punk jester on a weird musical bender!

Gary Moore

The name Gary Moore should mean something to any Irishman or woman who is remotely interested in their rock culture. Having contributed much to the music of the sixties and seventies, Moore went international and to this day remains the world's best respected of heavy rock musicians. It may be a surprise to learn that Moore is considered to be the most popular Western musician to play Japan. He has released no less than ten solo albums and has endeavoured over the years to keep that melodious quality so beloved of Phil Lynott within the walls of hard rock.

Gary Moore was born in Belfast in the early 1950s and started playing guitar at the age of eleven. Entranced by the 1960s British blues movement, he modelled his early technique on that of Jeff Beck. Drifting to Dublin at age sixteen he met Brush Shiels and Philip Lynott and joined *Skid Row*. While he bent ears with some colossal guitar innovations, he also did more restrained electric playing with *Granny's Intentions* and *Dr Strangely Strange*. After forming the short-lived *Gary Moore Band* he joined *Thin Lizzy*. That wasn't to last long either and soon he opted for the English heavyweight jazz/rock formation *Colosseum II* where he was to find a relatively stable resting ground for three years. There he developed his musical knowledge, studied whole tone scales and became familiar with written scores. In 1977 he returned to *Thin Lizzy* for live shows and in 1978 released *Back on the Streets* (MCA), an album done with Phil Lynott and Brian Downey which includes the classic 'Parisienne Walkways', a superlative meeting of Moore's crying guitar with Lynott's emotive vocals. The following year that song became Gary Moore's first solo British hit single.

A restless spirit, the Belfast wanderer recorded one album with *Thin Lizzy, Black Rose* (Vertigo 1979), went to Los Angeles and formed the hard rocking *G-Force*, subsequently involved himself with Greg Lake and released the album *Corridors of*

Power (1982) with *Deep Purple* drummer Ian Paice. That was his first Virgin release and the beginning of a more solid professional relationship that would emphasise his solo qualities. Unlike many other heavy rock guitarists, Gary had the ability to write good songs and sing them without resorting to mindless histrionics or meaningless solos. This was obvious from the 1983 LP *Victims of the Future* (10/Virgin), which produced 'Empty Rooms' the electric rock ballad that made him an international star. Extensive touring in Europe, Japan and America had to be undergone to support the success of the record, but Moore took some time off to appear with *Thin Lizzy* for their farewell tour of 1983. In 1984 he went to Ireland to play a string of 'homecoming' concerts and some of the best recorded performances were released later as the video album *Emerald Aisles* (Virgin 1985). During that tour Moore asked Phil Lynott to join him for the Belfast show and because of this the duo went into the studio again and came out with the hit single 'Out in the Fields' (10) — a song which concentrates on the violence of Northern Ireland and points out that killing is a pointless act under any conditions. The single has a B side, 'Military Man', penned by Lynott and the 12 inch has a re-recorded version of 'Still in Love with You', the most heartfelt of Lynott's later period songs. Moore did Lynott the honour of including a version of 'Military Man' (a song written by Lynott while in the aborted post-*Lizzy Grand Slam*) on his highly popular *Run for Cover* album of 1985 (10).

In keeping with the spirit of Lynott, Gary Moore recorded a more Irish-oriented set in 1986, titled *Wild Frontier* (10/1987). Utilising complex electronics, his own hard rocking, three-piece band and some members of *The Chieftains*, Moore was able to achieve an authentic form of Celtic heavy guitar rock music. On the heroic big-sounding 'Over the Hills and Far Away', Moore matches Paddy Maloney's uilleann pipes and the fiddles of Sean Keane and Martin Fay to the Fairlight Computer Music Instrument. A lot of the album is tough, hard-core material that is really for the heavy metal enthusiast, but on some tracks Moore's sensitivity wins the day. 'The Loner', originally written for Moore's idol Jeff Beck, is a bluesy guitar instrumental that has a cool, entrancing effect. But more effective and in keeping with his origins is 'Johnny Boy', a melancholic ballad where the marriage of Moore's voice and Paddy Maloney's pipes is made in heaven. Gary Moore has, since the 1960s, been little regarded in his native land. Even with his enormous international audience his technicality and musical knowledge (he has most of his guitars built to personal specifications) are rarely commended. Down through the annals of Irish rock Moore has consistently given his best to his music, and even if at times it sounds too much like anthemic guitar rock there always has been and hopefully always will be that Gaelic spirit coming through to make it all worthwhile.

Sinéad O'Connor

With a voice as pure as the driven snow, nineteen-year-old Sinéad O'Connor was launched on the world in 1986 when *U2's* The Edge released his soundtrack album *Captive*. Sinéad sang 'Heroine', the only song on the record, and attracted critical praise for her ability to instil her voice with a considerable emotional charge. Possibly the youngest personality to come out of Irish rock, O'Connor started as a professional at the astonishingly tender age of fourteen. This was when she joined *In Tua Nua* for a Dublin studio session and recorded the original version of 'Take My Hand', a profoundly moving piece which became *In Tua Nua's* first Island single. Soon after her stint with the *Nua*, parental pressure brought Sinéad to a Waterford boarding school. But she wasn't to be foiled and after busking around the town with a guitarist friend she fled to Dublin and joined an acoustic/funk outfit *Ton Ton Macoute*. That was in 1983 and within a year her spine-chilling vocal chords had netted her English record company interest. Recognising a star in the making, Ensign London offered her a solo contract and enticed her across the Irish sea. While working up material for her first album, *The Lion and the Cobra* (1987), O'Connor made 'Heroine' with The Edge in Dublin and did a prestigious 'Old Grey Whistle Test' support slot to *U2* in Belfast. With her shaved head and fascinating vocals — that could be softly caressing and howlingly banshee in the space of a single intonation — O'Connor gave a consummately skilled performance. Some may say that a voice and an interesting image are hardly enough to sustain a career in the music business, but Sinéad O'Connor is more than surface and technique. On the self-produced *Lion and the Cobra* album she achieved a rock/roots music for the eighties, which is incredibly diverse in terms of influences. Arabic, Japanese, African, classical, disco and funk sounds are all in evidence. On top of that, O'Connor put a tremendous amount of Irishness into some songs. The arrangement and atmosphere of 'Jackie' gives the impression of being caught out in a slashing storm on a wintry Irish coast. The folky 'Never Get Old' track is made more ethnic by the inclusion of Enya Ní Bhraonáin doing some Irish dialogue. Not to be caught out, Sinéad also included a *Sgt Pepper*-era *Beatles*-type sixties rocker in 'Just Call Me Joe' — a psychedelic piece of shaving *Velvet Underground* guitar, feedback noise and babbled talkover. At twenty years of age, O'Connor was already capable of arranging, producing and recording a brand of rock that few of her contemporaries could even hope to emulate.

Michael O'Shea

Michael O'Shea (born in Newry, Northern Ireland, 1947) dropped out of school at only sixteen and drifted through over thirty-five occupations before he settled down to being a wandering musician. Having sculpted, worked with leather, clothes and pottery, Michael exhibited an eclectic artistic sway. He spent the expansive sixties and early seventies following the hippie freedom trail, travelling the dusty roads of India, North Africa, the Middle East and Turkey. During this seemingly never-ending journey he nurtured his love of instrument-making. In 1978 he spent the summer playing Indian sitar in France. There he met Algerian musician Kris Harpo, who accompanied him on zelochord. Moving from there down to Greece via Germany, O'Shea, in a sudden blast of genius, decided to combine both zelochord and sitar into one instrument. The result was a hollow, wooden box, strung with several layers of steel strings which he called 'Mo Chara' (my friend). This was fitted at a later stage with several electronic phasers, echo units and amplification. The strings would be struck lightly by O'Shea with chopsticks to produce soft resonating patterns which had a traditional Irish folk music rhythm but streamed through with numerous East European and Indian timbres. The application of this radical innovation can be heard on his one LP, *Michael O'Shea* (Dome 1982), on which he waves a misty mystical Celtic fog of sound. The aptly titled 'No Journey's End' is a climactic enunciation of natural forces through an overlying sequence of patterned running tappings. English avant-garde artists/musicians Bruce Gilbert and Graham Lewis (of *Wire*) joined him on Side Two of the album to process the basically acoustic sound of 'Mo Chara' through the technology of the studio. The following year O'Shea could be heard playing both 'Mo Chara' and sitar on Stano's album *Content to Write in I Dine Weathercraft* (Scoff). Michael O'Shea was a familiar figure around Europe at the time; always with his instrument, he could be found sitting in a street or in someone's home launching into another of his ethereal trance-inducing displays. Although very little seen these days, his individuality has given something special to Irish music particularly from the avant-garde point of view.

The Rhythm Kings

After listening to a lot of black rhythm and blues and American rockabillly, Rocky De Valera decided to express his love of fifties music by forming *The Gravediggers* in the late seventies. Despite trends, *Rocky De Valera and The Gravediggers* became one of Ireland's best-loved bands. Their speciality was a no nonsense, down home, boogie-woogie music that was good 'live' dance entertainment. After a short break, De Valera came back with a new group *The Rhythm Kings*, whose effective mixture of urban, teenage imagery, quick-step, foot-tappin' rock and black beat can be heard on the album *Setting Fire to My Heart* (Scoff 1983).

Barry Ronan

Ronan made history by releasing a 'modern rock album' with songs written and performed in the Irish language. *Tráth* (Gael-Linn 1983) tells of young life on the Aran Islands, the Irish-speaking outlands off the west coast of Ireland. For those fluent only in the mother tongue it was a welcome invitation to the world of contemporary rock music. The work utilised Paul Barrett on the Fairlight Computer Music Instrument and Don Harris (ex-*Peggy's Leg/Metropolis*) on percussion and drums.

Ruefrex

Eight years from formation to firm album may seem like an eternity, but for Belfast band *Ruefrex* what was always important was sticking to your principles and getting the message across in your own musical way. Paul Burgess and the rest of his Protestant pals had from the start committed themselves to cutting down the sectarian dividing lines of their birthplace and through the years that resolve had never weakened. It was the punk insurgence of 1977 that brought *Ruefrex* together. Debuting with *Stiff Little Fingers*, they played every conceivable Northern Irish venue — pubs, ghettoes, ballrooms — until they were dutifully given a recording chance by Good Vibrations. Their crackety drums, meshing guitars, slim solos and angry vocals brought them John Peel airplay, but that was as far as they could bring it then. Having always done day jobs, the band went on ice until Kabuki Records persuaded them to put out songs again. Paul Burgess, who did all the writing but took the drum seat, and Allan Clarke (vocals) marshalled their forces and stung the English (but for obvious reasons not the Irish) scene with 'Wild Colonial Boy' (1985), a great barraging melodic punk anthem which hit hard at American supporters of the IRA. Burgess proved that he was a songwriter of inimitable precision when it came to giving a Protestant perspective on Northern Ireland. This crystalline portrait has the ring of nauseating truth that few Southern Irish could admit to. Lines like 'All this time we're trying hard to keep the niggers down . . . It really gives me quite a thrill to kill from far away' are hard to take but impossible to ignore. Stiff records gave *Ruefrex* a deal on the strength of this song and the album *Flowers for All Occasions* came out at the tail-end of 1985. Here Burgess brings the reality of working-class Protestant life into high-resolution exposure through a music that is a resounding punk bash but with a kick of a melody. A first for Irish rock, it is an ultra-realist .picture of death, faint hope, blood-soaked hypocrisy, sacrifice and emotional upheaval which sounds like a cross between the literary scenarios of Joyce and the punk noise of *The Sex Pistols.* 'Paid in Kind' is like a miniature novel, Burgess drawing out a sinuous array of bristling images as he recounts an IRA hitman's clandestine mission of terror. There are references to Bram Stoker and James Plunkett in other songs, but in some cases the incessant grind of the music obliterates the effect of the writing. For this reason two tracks 'Even in the Dark Hours' and 'Flowers for All Occasions' stand well above the rest. The first is an emotional reading of separation through death, where the music is relaxed and spaced enough to give the appropriate tone. The second could be honoured with the distinction of being termed a Northern Irish rock masterpiece. Lyrics melt perfectly together in poetic flow as Burgess effortlessly describes the early marriage of a poor couple which is blown apart by sectarian killing. The sociological sketch is poignantly supported by a sparse, acoustic guitar, electric bass and percussion music. A rap on the head to all those with 'bibles clutched in bloody hands' this song says it all in the verse 'There are flowers for all occasions, floral tributes to the dead. Orange lilies, shamrock green, bloody scarlet, poppy red.'

Feargal Sharkey

When Northern group *The Undertones* disbanded during the summer of 1983, it was a sad day for Irish rock. The Derry band that had given so much to punk/pop were forced by record company problems and the fickle public to throw in a premature towel. Their talented vocalist, Feargal Sharkey, whose shrill, sky-reaching singing style was *The Undertones'* hallmark, emigrated to England soon afterwards and teamed up with electrobop musician Vince Clarke to form *The Assembly.* They had immediate success with a number four British chart entry 'Never Never' on Mute records in November of 1983. Satisfied that he could manage a solo career, but aware that he had been categorised as a rough, Catholic boot-boy type, Sharkey set about learning the rudiments of how to go about presenting yourself in the world of eighties perfectionist pop. He went to classes and workshops and acquired useful skills in video and sound production. When he was ready, he started afresh with Virgin Records, releasing the boppy 'Listen to Your Father' in 1984. His new, polished image and ritzy-sounding

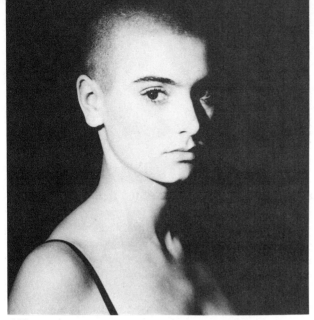

112

115

116

112 Sinéad O'Connor, whose voice is capable of being softly caressing and howlingly banshee-like in the space of a single intonation.

113 Rocky de Valera, who in the 1980s produced boogie-woogie music and quick-step, foot-tapping rock. For years he was one of Ireland's ubiquitous live performers.

114 Feargal Sharkey. A move to England and a stint in a workshop enabled him to top the charts in 1985.

115 *The Stars of Heaven. Left to right:* Stan Erraught, Bernard Walsh, Stephen Ryan, Peter O'Sullivan.

116 *That Petrol Emotion* letting rip — Steve Mack *(left)*, John O'Neill *(right)*.

117 Pierce Turner *(left)* with one of America's most celebrated modern minimalist composers, Philip Glass *(right)*.

118 Andy White — he takes the early 1960s streaming style of Bob Dylan and re-moulds it in terms of Northern Irish reality.

music made him very popular, and in the winter of 1985 he had his first number one hit with the soulful 'A Good Heart'. His follow-up album, *Feargal Sharkey* (1985), demonstrated his talent as an original interpreter of other people's songs. Produced by *Eurythmic* Dave Stewart, the collection is quite a distance away from *The Undertones'* simple style, but it yields some interesting tracks like the elaborate version of Dylan's 'It's All Over Now Baby Blue', a good jive song in 'You Little Thief' and a masterful Motown cover with 'Someone to Somebody'. Because of his new-found direction, Feargal Sharkey became a respected artist in America, so much so that he did a video with Bob Dylan and collaborated with, of all people, actor Jack Nicholson on a songwriting project!

The Stars of Heaven

Dubbed by the BBC's John Peel as 'Dublin's finest' band in 1986, *The Stars of Heaven* descended on the UK airwaves with their first Eamon Carr-produced single 'Clothes of Pride' (Hotwire) in 1985. Their minimal rock sound, with its harmonic emphasis on texture and definite West Coast America/country strains, is a uniquely interesting music and in January 1986 *The Stars* became the first Irish band in six years to debut their material with a John Peel session. In Ireland, young rock bands have for years steered clear of country, since the land has always been riddled with fourth-rate cabaret country and western acts who place more emphasis on the cowboy flick image than the content of their music. For Stan Erraught (guitars, lyrics) and Peter O'Sullivan (bass, vocals), punk was always the starting point of making music. Erraught in particular had been constantly on the Dublin music scene since punk blew in, playing in various outfits like *The Modernaires* and *The Peridots* (whose 'Open Season'/'Calm' in '81 is exceptional by any standards). It took the duo six months to find Stephen Ryan (guitars, lyrics, vocals) and Bernard Walsh (drums) and with a name adopted from the Bible, *The Stars of Heaven* were born. The emphasis was on musicianship and having a healthy attitude to distant influences — *The Byrds* and *The Velvet Underground* being a few of the many. 'Clothes of Pride' gave an inkling and the Peel sessions certainly gave a wider view, but it wasn't until the release of *Sacred Heart Hotel* by Rough Trade in autumn 1986 that one could really grasp the full richness of *The Stars'* sound. Guitars chime and vocal harmonies ring in a spatial music where the tasteful use of drums and bass brings you on a guided tour around the many sights of rock, past and present. The title track is incredibly smooth, its guitar riffs reminiscent of Arthur Lee's sixties group *Love*, but with a clarity and arrangement that brings you accurately into the modern era. Lyrically it is an enthralling observation of hotel-bar life, based on Erraught's own impressions of what he saw in Galway. On 'Moonstruck' the fast punkiness of the instrumentation is coated with that familiar jingle-jangling Roger McGuinn guitar sound which on 'So You Know' becomes a powerful full-out duel between Ryan and Erraught in the psychedelic '8 Miles High' mould. 'You Only Say' is a tough, crash-bang rocker which dips into post-'White Light White Heat' *Velvet Underground* circa 1969 era. And when one thought that the country element was only a shade, they finish the record with a snappy, barnyard stomp in 'Man without a Shadow'. The refreshing nature of *Sacred Heart Hotel* was to win *The Stars* across-the-board British press approval and a high place in the indie charts. On the 1987 EP *Before Holyhead* (Rough Trade), the group got the opportunity to take more time in the studio, thus benefiting Stephen Ryan's vocals and adding more punch to their sound. From the touching acoustic guitar instrumental of its title cut to the wistful feel of Erraught's Dun Laoghaire sketch 'Widow's Walk', *Before Holyhead* is ample proof that the music of *The Stars of Heaven* is some of the brightest around.

That Petrol Emotion

The break-up of Derry band *The Undertones* in 1983 may have seemed like a sad day for pop, but for chief songwriter John O'Neill it was a blessing in disguise. In 1984 he formed *That Petrol Emotion* with Raymond Gorman (guitar) in order to give vent to his political and social viewpoints. Avowing that 'this is not the new *Undertones*', O'Neill, his brother Damian (bass), Ciaran McLaughlin (drums) and Gorman had seen enough of pop commercialism and wanted to tear asunder what they saw as the cosy confines of eighties alternative rock. *That Petrol Emotion* played a music that burned with real anger, passion and a sense of imperative. By March 1985 they were well settled in London and had found a singer, an American called Steve Mack. Soon two singles 'Keen' (Pink) and 'V2' (Noise A Noise) were wailing their way around the English indie charts and John Peel's radio show. They were characterised by piercing electric guitars, ranting vocals and a deafening loudness but also by O'Neill's well-tuned eye for chorus, melody and harmony. On top of that they held out a nationalist Catholic viewpoint on the Northern Irish question with anti-British sleeve notes simply stating the injustices of such practices as the army's use of plastic bullets and the strip-searching of internees in Armagh women's jail.

Their third offering 'It's a Good Thing' is an almighty single; put out on Demon in spring 1986, it is a perfectly constructed piece of anti-system rock, with wall riff guitars splicing Mack's tuneful vocal to the accompaniment of minimal pointed guitar lead. Considered by some to be the best white rock single of its time, 'It's a Good Thing' was followed by *Manic Pop Thrill* (Demon), an album recorded in Rockfield studios in Wales. Elsewhere this book has commented on how rock originating from Ulster is seldom unaffected by its climate of unrest. In the punk era many bands were able to communicate the war-like situation of their environs through the clatter of basic four-four noise music, but since then few had managed to survive and adapt their sound to the changing times. *That Petrol Emotion* on the other hand were seen as something new, another re-formulation of rock sound that drew many strands from the past but still had that 'now' ingredient. *Manic Pop Thrill* was an LP that had no competitors and thus it went to the top of the British independent album chart in June of 1986. Its inner sleeve contains an extract from Michael Davitt's 1904 *The Fall of Feudalism in Ireland*; its strong words give an unequivocal indication of how O'Neill and company feel about the continued British presence in the North. Importantly, *That Petrol Emotion* left the clear political statements to the sleeve notes because the tracks themselves are musical creations based on the harmony or otherwise of sound and not proselytising verses. On its first three tracks *Manic Pop Thrill* is certainly jagged and insidious in its design, but lyrically it focuses its grey lens on the human side of Ulster's problems. Interestingly, the appeal in the songs is that they were instantly appreciable by anyone, for the landscape of emotional problems and turmoil they cut across is universal. 'It's a Good Thing' in particular is applicable to any couple, young or old, in that it emphasises the importance of human contact no matter how untenable the situation seems to be. At times though, *The Petrols* could not help but let their strong distaste for Unionism come through as on 'Circusville' which might be described as an incisive look at the turmoiled mental state of an individual beaten down for so long that he or she has to gain retribution through assassination.

Again it would be foolish to place *That Petrol Emotion* into an agit-pop for the Republican cause slot, for *Manic Pop Thrill* has some genuine surprises. O'Neill's 'A Million Miles Away' is a lovely little pop ditty about lost love, framed in the charming lustre of *The Velvet Underground*'s sound *circa* 1967. 'Lettuce', again by O'Neill, is a full-blown psychedelic creation, a parody of the kind of thing favoured by American sixties garage bands complete with satellite guitar licks. Lyrically it cleverly denigrates the false euphoria of drug imbibing. 'Blindspot', a song of vain hope co-authored by Gorman (who did his fair share of songwriting) is another *Velvet Underground*-sounding track, this time more 1968 styled with its creamy guitar picking echoing that of Sterling Morrison and the Lou Reed-like vocals of Steve Mack. In 1987 *That Petrol Emotion* continued to cause a commotion on the English music scene with the release of 'Big Decision' (Polydor), a high tech piece of durable O'Neill pop/rock which rallies Northern Irish youth to stay put and help improve the unfortunate situation of their province. Its lyrical content and sleeve design, again with anti-British information, this time about the workings of the juryless Diplock courts, was quite controversial and garnered substantial music press attention. Even if their successive LP *Babble* didn't match the sparkling *Manic Pop Thrill, That Petrol Emotion* were still the only Northern Irish rock band with punk roots to make a significant impact on the English alternative music scene of the late eighties.

Pierce Turner

An unusual meeting of Irish lyricism, modern, avant-garde classical music and American rock comes in the form of Pierce Turner whose debut LP *It's Only a Long Way Across* (Beggars Banquet) was put down with Philip Glass in New York sometime in 1986. Turner was born and bred in Wexford and was a soprano singing champion as a boy. Although very fond of his country upbringing and the literary and song traditions of his native land, Turner chose to emigrate to America in the early 1970s. Accompanied by his guitar-playing friend Larry Kirwan, Turner settled in East Greenwich Village and put together a funk-oriented four-piece called *The Major Thinkers*. After quite a bit of local attention on the bar circuit, the group wanted to release a record but major labels weren't interested. Not to be short-circuited Pierce had a mini-album of demo takes released in Ireland. Ironically it became a high-demand import item in the States, the track 'Avenue B Is the Place to Be' attracting good radio and disco exposure. Epic picked up on the band, who found themselves suddenly playing to thousands of people as they supported such groups as *Simple Minds* and *UB 40*. An album was recorded but the company wanted a singles band so *The Thinkers* found themselves adrift. Kirwan became a playwright and Turner got down to crafting more elaborate sounds. Fate brought him into contact one day with Philip Glass, the renowned American minimalist composer whose piano works were archetypes in the field of contemporary avant-garde composition and whose operas, particularly *Einstein on the Beach* had innovated a completely new language for the genre. Glass knew about Turner because his son had a *Major Thinkers* record, and he was impressed by the Wexford man's ideas for an eclectic kind of pop album. They collaborated and what came out was *It's Only a Long Way Across* (Beggars Banquet 1986) produced by Glass and his electronic partner Kurt Munkacsi. Here Turner's penchant for lyrical expansiveness is perfectly matched by Glass's ability to precisely space whatever sounds he's working on. An appropriate song about an emigré's Irish reflections, 'Wicklow Hills' would have come off pretty bland in most producers' hands but with Glass a natural hypnotic quality was readily perceived. Throughout the album, tasteful brass and string arrangements can be heard, courtesy Glass, and one track, 'How It Shone', comes off as the perfect marriage of Irish emotional lyricism with neo-twentieth century avant-garde music. On this Turner conveys an impressionistic account of childhood, drawing on personal experience of a July day in Wexford. The details of the memory and the emotional way in which they are recounted is redolent of Van Morrison's work — for example 'And It Stoned Me' from *Moondance*. But the structuring of the carefully looping string segments which sway to and fro around the vocal place the track firmly out of the jazz oeuvre of Morrison into that of modern-day composition. It was a fascinating new direction for an Irish rock artist, something which revealed to Irish rock in general that there was still quite a bit of unexplored territory out there to investigate.

Andy White

With a talent for collating unusual word images and an invective wit, and with acoustic guitar and tape machine his only props, Andy White became a noticeable presence on the English and Irish music scenes of 1985. Then going under the moniker of *Andy White and the Ghost of Electricity*, it was a trouncing, surrealistic composition, delivered in a vocal style not that dissimilar to Bob Dylan *circa* 1965 called 'Religious Persuasion', that made his name. A thumping rhythm undercut a profuse stream of lyrics all relating to Northern Irish religious prejudice. Lines like 'I was up against persuasion of a religious kind' and 'Being afflicted by religion of the persuasive kind' are those of an outsider to the narrow-minded mentality that has tarnished so much of Ulster's history. In the climaxing couplet 'Someone's gotta stand up or nothing's gonna change 'til religion is re-arranged' White spits out his reason for following in the footsteps of Dylan. 'Religious Persuasion' may be a post-punk version of 'Subterranean Homesick Blues' but it is a phantasmagorical protest song of a kind that had never been realised quite from that point of view. White had left Belfast in 1981 to go to Cambridge University to study English. Of a fairly mixed religious background he considered himself a Protestant, but one that had no respect for the factions of Unionism or the IRA. He was an individual with a healthy respect for good sixties music and the better side of punk, who liked to perform rambling songs about his homeland in his spare time. After a brief stint with the BBC he went fully into the music business and released 'Religious Persuasion' through Stiff. An appearance on 'The Old Grey Whistle Test' was an approval seal that led to a Decca recording deal and the album *Rave on Andy White* (1986). Dylan's pervasive influence is obvious in song titles such as 'Tuesday Apocalypse No 13' and 'Vision of You' and in the occasional use of harmonica and Hammond organ that remind one of the sound of *Bringing It All Back Home* or *Highway 61 Revisited*. Even if the stylisations owe much to somebody else the lyrical content is all White's doing, representing a form of imaginative song films that could only be of Irish origin. Among its contents is a rollicking skit called 'The Soldier's Sash' (a clever word-play on two famous Irish songs, one the Republican national anthem of the South, 'The Soldier's Song', and the Unionist 'The Sash My Father Wore') which points to the hypocrisy of hiding behind an emblem and allowing it to justify any wicked deed. 'Reality Row', 'The Walking Wounded' and 'Things Start to Unwind' are uncompromising communications of a situation that has to be lived through to be understood — the North in White's words is a place 'where the madmen lead the blind', 'where a trigger pulls from the past' and whose population's problems are filed by the Government of England 'in the dead letter zone'. In other places the album veers between the totally zany as on 'Rembrandt Hat', a humorous piece of nonsense writing, and the wistfully poignant as exemplified by the folk-style 'I Will Wait', a track distinguished by the tin whistle and sax playing of Rod McVey. Andy White made such an impression on his musical peers that Van Morrison invited him to open for his *No Guru, No Method, No Teacher* tour of 1986.

CODA

Occasionally when rock musicians involve themselves with mainstream social and political issues they can have an immediate impact because of their access to the mass market. In 1975 Bob Dylan caused a furore when he led a movement to free a black boxer, Hurricane Carter, who had spent nine years in prison for a crime he did not commit. The response was overwhelming, as it had been on 1 August 1971 when George Harrison organised the concert for the starving peoples of Bangladesh at New York's Madison Square Garden. The ex-*Beatle* paid all the $\frac{1}{4}$ million-dollar take into a relief fund.

In the 1980s it was Dublin-born grandfather of punk, Bob Geldof, who did something that altered people's perceptions of the role of a pop or rock musician in society. Late in the winter of 1984 the northern reaches of Ethiopia were ruined by the worst drought in centuries. A rampant famine spread right across into the Sudan and conditions got so bad that only a few hundred out of every ten thousand could be fed by relief workers. The situation was grim and the first TV and newspaper reports hammered home the naked death to the cushy West. Initially most people did little in response except express sympathy to each other — or switch to another channel. At best some sent in a financial donation to fund the relief work. Bob Geldof was not to be one of these. The same spark that fuelled his energies in *The Boomtown Rats* glowed like a red-hot coal when he saw the images of misery emanating from his TV set. In a flash of genius he decided to do something to help — as many pop stars of the day as could be persuaded would be brought together to record a unison single. The proceeds generated from its subsequent sale would be used to pay for food and medical supplies which, in turn, would be ferried to Africa as quickly as possible.

First off, Geldof's idea was to restructure the record industry for this one very special recording. Nobody was going to make a profit, only the sufficient margins necessary to keep the record selling would be retained. Geldof, through his persuasiveness, made all the businessmen waive their profits — a difficult task, since retailers make a large margin on record sales. Out of the £1.35 to be paid for the single, 96.03p would go to Africa, with 17.46p going to the necessary manufacturing and distribution, leaving 3.5p for mandatory discounts. Unfortunately, Margaret Thatcher's Tory regime would not budge on the 18p value added tax being slapped on the record in the UK. Her more sensitive Irish neighbour balanced the situation though and was able to totally waive taxes, thus allowing Geldof to reap as much funds as he could get from his inspired project.

Bob had written a song called 'It's My World' and contacted Midge Ure of *Ultravox* to write a tune around it. They eventually came up with a full arrangement titled 'Do They Know It's Christmas/Feed The World' and booked recording time in Trevor Horn's Sarm West studios. On a wintry Sunday near the end of November 1984, reporters and television crews invaded the area around the studio as the most popular performers in Britain arrived for the historic occasion. English pop idol Boy George flew in from America by Concorde to be present while *Spandau Ballet* broke their Japanese tour to be there. Bono and the rest of *U2* halted a strenuous American trek to be part of the session. High-profile stars Sting, George Michael, Simon Le Bon, Paul Young, Paul Weller and Phil Collins were there, while members of *The Boomtown Rats, Kool and the Gang, Heaven 17, Duran Duran, Culture Club* and *Bananarama* provided the backing choir. Even older artists from the 1960s joined in.

Bob Geldof had managed to overcome the petty rivalries between pop stars and had got them all together to record his song. He had even persuaded *Wham!*, Jim Diamond and Nik Kershaw, all potential number one stars to sacrifice their chances and make his song the Christmas number one — they even wore famine relief publicity 'Feed the World' tee-shirts when performing on 'Top of the Pops'. The recording was done in twelve hours with Bob taking a backstage role as the others sang. Paul Young started off the song, Boy George came in on the refrain, and each singer in turn added his section. Bono's voice was loud and clear and soared high on the chorus. The event was recorded and televised throughout the world. A media blitz occurred. Robert Maxwell gave Geldof the cover of the *Daily Mirror* and all sorts of people started offering trucks, jeeps and even aeroplanes. Geldof had tapped into the most powerful current of rock and popular music and caused a worldwide wave of response. On 7 December 1984 the record, released by Phonogram, was an immediate number one hit in the British charts, selling a keen one million copies during its first week of release, making it the fastest-selling single record of all time. Five factories were kept busy pressing the disc. The 12 inch version had extra contributions from superstars David Bowie and Paul McCartney who could not make it to the recording session. By the summer of 1985 the record had sold a staggering eight million copies.

The fact that Bob did not just stop there but followed up his move was proof that he wasn't doing it for the selfish reasons that a lot of his detractors were suggesting at the time. He made sure that the money was properly spent, flew to Ethiopia and with famed charity figure Mother Teresa really got down to the nitty-gritty of feeding the needy. This had a tremendous media impact and roused several black musician stars in America to make a move. The singer Harry Belafonte, stirred by Geldof's initiative and sensing a lack in his own country, contacted ex-*Commodore* Lionel Ritchie so that a special recording could take place in the Band Aid mould. Stevie Wonder, Michael Jackson and Quincy Jones were the first to give their support and soon after legends Bob Dylan, Bruce Springsteen, Paul Simon, Tina Turner, Ray Charles, Diana Ross, Dionne Warwick and Smokey Robinson pledged their talents.

On Monday 28 January 1985, in Los Angeles, California, the most prominent names in American popular music were all present at the annual music awards. After the ceremony a sizable group filed into one of A&M's prestigious studios to record a sweet song, co-written by Lionel Ritchie and Michael Jackson, titled 'We Are the World'. The occasion turned into an event, its ten-hour duration being video-taped in its entirety. Bob Geldof himself flew in to take part and as Quincy Jones directed the choir he acknowledged that there was a powerful energy in the ensemble, something unique and commendable. On release the single 'We Are the World' (Columbia) topped the American charts and a double album of previously unreleased material by the artists involved, and those who couldn't make it, generated millions of dollars for Geldof's relief fund. Because of the strong black element in the enterprise, some of the money was used for the poor and homeless of America, who are mostly deprived blacks.

Bob Geldof was achieving a global impact, and it was at this time that the thirty-three-year-old Irishman came in for snide comments and criticism from the cynics who make up the worst aspects of the media. At the time, people would lament about Bob's 'last stand', saying that he was only in it for the publicity and media profile it gave him. Others even said that because his band, *The Boomtown Rats*, weren't happening anymore, Geldof was cunningly getting his kicks elsewhere. No matter what anybody said, what he had done was unprecedented, and it was a sincere and brilliant idea. Such feelings were confirmed when Bob Geldof literally changed the world for a day by organising the greatest rock 'n' roll event in the history of the globe!

BOB GELDOF'S LIVE AID FOR AFRICA

At first it was only a rumour. Every now and then, in the newspapers or on the television, a comment or two would be passed on what Bob Geldof was trying to do. There was going to be a special charity concert for Ethiopia and Sudan, with all the proceeds going to the starving peoples. The story was treated with a 'pinch of salt'. Three months into 1985, it was reported that Bob Geldof had been refused permission, by the Wembley Arena authorities, to stage any kind of concert. The haggling went on and on. Then, around the end of June when the festival season was at its height — Glastonbury Fayre and The Longest Day (*U2* Special) on the same day, as well as a plethora of free concerts in London — the first startling news of Live Aid came through. It wasn't going to be just any old concert, but a concert unprecedented in the history of rock. Two stadia were to be used, one in the US and one in the UK. There was to be an around-the-world satellite link, as well as an on-the-spot video link-up. The Sky-Lab space station would zoom over both concerts and pick up the transmission. There were going to be hundreds of thousands of people watching and listening, and last, but not least, the best line-up of rock 'n' roll stars the world was ever likely to see on one stage. Concorde, the supersonic airliner, was to be used for some special purpose, and an entire day would be taken up with the event.

Again, the cynics crawled out of their holes and dug their teeth in. This concert was all talk and no action. How could any one person organise something on this kind of scale, and, if it could be done, why hadn't anyone done it before? That was exactly the point, it had never been attempted and Geldof was going to do it. A lot of twenty-four-hour-days were put in. Negotiations and re-negotiations were entered into again and again behind the scenes in the six months leading up the summer. As rain washed out both Glastonbury and Milton Keynes Bowl,

119

119 Live Aid changed rock music from a self-indulgent capitalist enterprise into the most powerful transfer of resources from rich to poor ever seen.

120 Declan Patrick Aloysius McManus, alias Elvis Costello — his performance at Live Aid echoes *The Beatles'* first global link-up in 1967.

121 Sting— his spartan version of 'Roxanne' brought tears to the eyes of millions.

122 A member of the Wembley Stadium audience reminds us how it all started.

120

121

122

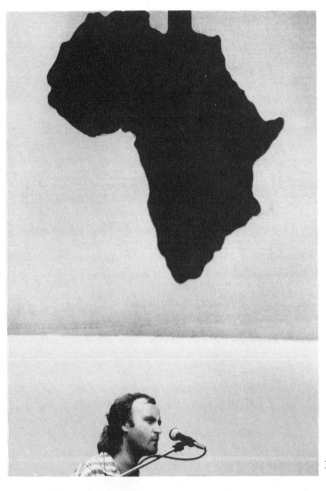

123

123 Phil Collins of *Genesis* fame. Geldof organised Concorde so that Collins could perform in London and Philadelphia on the same day.

124 As Bono drew from the words of 'Sympathy for the Devil' during the performance of 'Bad', one realised that *U2* were cleansing rock's tarnished image, still rusty after the excesses of the sixties and seventies.

125 Grand finale — *left to right:* Pete Townshend, David Bowie, Paul McCartney *(behind)*, Bob Geldof, *Wham!* *(behind)* and Bono.

people were starting to get expectant and excited about the mammoth event that Geldof was trying to pull off. Then like a miracle at the end of June, Wembley Stadium was confirmed, and the situation was a full go-ahead from all parties concerned. It was announced that every performer, from the most popular to the most durable, would be performing one after the other. Each act would be chosen on the grounds of viability and commercial exposure. Each act would play only three songs.

As the days went by, the idea caught the world like an electric current. John F. Kennedy Stadium in Philadelphia was to have a similar event, with the same practical format as Wembley. Bill Graham, notorious as the only organiser of worth in the sixties, was getting all his old friends to donate a live performance free of charge. The whole thing would have a simultaneous video link-up, so that people looking at screens at each concert would be able to see what was going on at the other side of the world. Bill Graham enlisted the help of Hal Uplinger and Howard Mitchell, organisers of the world Olympic games in Los Angeles, to put the giant concert into action, with all the relevant media penetration and ticket advertising. In Britain, Harvey Goldsmith was doing the honours for Bob, while Rogers and Cowan were handling the advertising portfolio. RTE, BBC, MTV and NBC were all coerced to give over an entire day's radio and television free, while governments of other countries were to allow all-day transmission via satellite. Moreover, countries like Russia and Japan were to be involved in a worldwide link-up that aimed to bring the entire extravaganza to the eyes and ears of 1.5 billion people around the planet.

Meanwhile the £8 million raised by the 'Do They Know It's Christmas' record was fast running out. Geldof, along with a core of one hundred relief workers, had chartered three ships to transport food and supplies to Port Sudan. Tons of food, however, were lying at the port because it was impossible to get into western and central Sudan. The rail links had been destroyed by torrential rains and the dirt tracks had been turned into quagmires. The lorries that were available were twenty years out of date, but, as the concert was gearing up, Bob Geldof was informed of a deal with a Middle Eastern oil company that put a hundred more transports at his disposal. Still, in northern Ethiopia, the feeding centres were enormous, the distribution of grain just as problematic, and communication just as impossible. Hundreds of thousands of people were subsisting on a meagre ration, and the shortage of rain, which had caused the famine, had turned into a deluge, bringing with it rock falls, pneumonia, disease and congestion. The situation was worsened by the inability of some starving stomachs to digest the food provided, political and security problems, and the real need to get seed, tools and knowledge to the populations, so that intermediate self-sufficiency could be attained. Without a certain stability, the death toll would increase for another year at least.

To Geldof this was the priority — not the petty whims and fancies of the rock 'n' roll intelligentsia. It was easy for him to convince all the stars to give their services free, for, in the words of David Bowie, 'who could refuse?' The problem was co-ordinating their activities so that they would all be free on the same day. Managers and record companies could be convinced of its importance by pointing out the publicity value of playing such a spectacularly televised event.

The musicians would play to their biggest audience ever, and the fans, in turn, would get more value from a £25 ticket than for any other event in their entire lives. They would also spend money on tee-shirts and souvenirs. Of the 600 million television sets in the world, 500 million would be locked into Live Aid. Viewers would be asked to donate money in return for being privy to the century's most important rock 'n' roll show. The money would all go to Africa, and it was estimated that £50 million would be the figure for the first day, with more coming in thereafter.

Bob Geldof was fast becoming superhuman and extraordinary. Seldom does any one individual do something that affects the entire world for the good of everyone — with no losers, only winners. Geldof was architecting such an enterprise that people everywhere were dumbfounded by his clarity of vision. Live Aid was going to unite the world and pour millions of pounds into a famine-stricken land. *Woodstock* had been the apotheosis of the first rock music generation. It had united people and music in a spirit of peace and understanding. It was good, and millions had felt the positive attitudes of its generation. Yet these attitudes did not transform themselves into anything more. Geldof wanted to utilise the collective spirit of people and music, which had been the essence of Woodstock, and transform it into long-term social and political change. Live Aid was going to be a practical success, and everybody wanted it that way. Sixteen hours of non-stop music would be beamed by fourteen international satellites throughout the world. When tickets went on sale for the twin concerts, they were sold out within a matter of days.

At Wembley, the 72,000 seats were divided into ticket categories of £25 (ordinary), £100 (press) and £250 for the VIP box. Tension spread as starting times for the concerts were announced as 9.30 p.m. in Philadelphia and 12 midday in London, on Saturday 13 July. As Bob Geldof's 'impossible' project exploded on the world that fateful Saturday, a fever of expectation rose as everybody wondered who would be there and what surprises the day would hold. The biggest story was that *The Beatles* would reunite, celebrating their 1967 television link-up of the live recording of 'All You Need Is Love'. But this phenomenon was of a different colour. The co-ordination and negotiations alone would break many men. The strain of the many legal and technical requirements meant a lot of people, and walls, had to be gone through. Whatever the barriers, Geldof's stamina was unyielding and every problem was knocked down with a stubborn Irish optimism. The whole idea was so extravagantly charitable, for the first time promising to harness the global tug of rock music to unprecedented heights. Like tumbling cards, everybody gave way to the unshaven lad from Dublin, who, eight years previously, had been a hard-core punk rocker 'looking after number one'. Something, somewhere along the way, had clicked, and Live Aid was the fulfilment of a rare and special vision.

At twelve o'clock, as promised, flanked by the Prince and Princess of Wales, Bob Geldof rose to the tumultuous cheer of a packed Wembley Stadium. The sun was beaming down in all its summer delight and if anything went wrong then 1½ billion people would be very, very disappointed. But the point was that nothing was going to go wrong; the spirit of the day was that no amount of bad luck could re-direct the positive force of Bob Geldof's conviction. At 12.15 p.m., after all the hours of slog, telephone calls, negotiation, persuasion, heartache, disappointment, victory, stage-building, co-ordination, tenacity, blood and guts, the strength of one man's vision poured out to the world, as the first chord was struck by the first group of the day. *Status Quo's* 'Rockin' all over the World' found its appropriate place, and one felt that nobody could better this collective spirit in a million years.

Live Aid Wembley Stadium London Bill
(12.15 p.m. to 10 p.m. 13 July 1985)

1 *Status Quo*
2 *The Style Council*
3 *The Boomtown Rats*
4 Adam Ant
5 *Ultravox*
6 *Spandau Ballet*
7 Elvis Costello
8 Nik Kershaw
9 Sade
10 Sting, Brandford Marsalis and Phil Collins
11 Howard Jones
12 Bryan Ferry and David Gilmour
13 Paul Young and Alison Moyet
14 *U2*
15 *Dire Straits* and Sting
16 *Queen*
17 David Bowie
18 *The Who*
19 Elton John, Kiki Dee and George Michael
20 Freddie Mercury and Brian May
21 Paul McCartney
22 Bob Geldof and Bono Vox lead the 'Do They Know It's Christmas' ensemble

Each successive performance had its own highlights. Each artist was playing to their largest possible audience and the public in turn were not just isolated groups of fans, but an essential part of a global phenomenon, aiming to co-ordinate a life-saving miracle. To attempt to criticise or analyse the performers or songs would, in this case, be a devaluation of the meaning of the exercise, but there were indeed some very special moments that some people would remember for the rest of their lives. When Bob himself came out with *The Boomtown Rats*, the surge of feeling and emotion was obvious. 'Drag Me Down' and 'Rat Trap' were sung with panache, but it was on 'I Don't Like Mondays' that Geldof reached a level of true communication with the people, when the whole of Wembley erupted and sang the song for him. It was indeed a moving and special moment in his career.

A strange melancholy hung in the air, as performers acquitted themselves with emotional grace, on a stage on which the whole world's eyes were to be transfixed for an entire day. Elvis Costello introduced an 'old Northern English folk song', and strummed a unique version of 'All You Need Is Love' in homage to the first worldwide pop music link-up. Sting, of *The Police*, and his side-man soprano saxophonist Brandford Marsalis gave a brilliant set alongside Phil Collins. Sting was nearly in tears, and attempted to reduce everyone to crying by playing a sad, slow, jazz version of his hit song 'Roxanne'. When the crowd heard that *U2* were on their way, the banners waved and the cheers roared in greeting. The four Irishmen strolled on to greet everybody with 'Sunday Bloody Sunday',

Bono looking completely mesmerised by the event, as the rest of the group went full-out on the instrumentation. Still in a trance, Bono viewed the populace, put his foot on one speaker monitor, and breathed the words of 'Bad' into an atmosphere of complete quiet. Suddenly, Bono dived into the crowd from the high stage, and, against the security guards' wishes, hugged a girl with such force that in an instant he had turned the whole affair into a powerful spiritual communion. He continued to sing 'Bad', but, as a homage to rock 'n' roll, improvised the lyrics to 'Satellite of Love', 'Ruby Tuesday', 'Walk on the Wild Side' and the eerie 'Sympathy for the Devil'. U2 were, in a word, devastating.

English group, Queen, were able to capture the audience in an auto-suggestive mock Third Reich collection of songs, but it was David Bowie, who for so long has profited through rock 'n' roll, who came out the best of the British. His clean-cut, light blue suit, and perfect delivery of 'Rebel Rebel', 'TVC15', 'Modern Love' and the anthemic 'Heroes', made him a genuine star on that day. As the curtain went down and the stage lit up the night, the piano strains of a familiar old Beatles song cut the air. The excitement surged across the world as Paul McCartney sang the sad 'Let It Be', and yet again everybody joined in. Pete Townshend and Paul McCartney held Bob Geldof aloft to tremendous cheers and rapturous applause. Then the entire ensemble congregated for Bob to conduct 'Do They Know It's Christmas', with Bono leading the entire troup, arm-in-arm with Paul McCartney, his voice sailing above the entire arena. Bob Geldof's realism had won through. He had succeeded in turning the spirit of rock 'n' roll into a real transfer of wealth to the under-privileged and starving. All the legends who had made rock 'n' roll over the previous twenty years had followed in his footsteps. Bob Geldof had just become the global figurehead for all the good dreams and hopeful fantasies that rock had promised to deliver, but somehow never did. He had proven that if you can give, you can give more, and for a brief while on that stage on 13 July he truly transcended his own, and everybody else's, limitations.

Over in Philadelphia, the hundred thousand spectators were treated to a less spectacular and in many ways more indulgent concert, where some performers continued to portray the exhibitionism and weaknesses that rock music had been so regularly criticised for. Opened shortly after 9 p.m. by film star Jack Nicholson and folk-musician, protest veteran Joan Baez, the expectancy raged high. It was deflated, however, by indiscriminate performances by Bryan Adams, Madonna, The Cars, Black Sabbath, Reo Speedwagon and the atrocious Power Station. English groups went down with a certain respect, but the first really emotive and touching set came from Canadian songsmith Neil Young, whose grasp of rural American history reminded everybody of what it was like to feel pain. His renditions of 'Sugar Mountain', 'Helpless' and 'The Needle and the Damage Done' were priceless. Bob Geldof had acquired the loan of Concorde for a day, and it was used to ferry Phil Collins from London to Philadelphia. He arrived in time to drum for an immaculate Eric Clapton, and take the drum seat for a group who had promised never to reform. Yes, somehow Bob Geldof had managed to persuade Peter Grant to allow Led Zeppelin to reform for this one auspicious occasion, and the Americans went wild as Robert Plant, John Paul Jones and Jimmy Page once more performed 'Stairway to Heaven'. Mick Jagger and Tina Turner did a hilarious duet on 'It's only Rock and Roll', and the grand old man of protest, Bob Dylan, bitterly finaled with the suitable 'Blowin' in the Wind'.

During both concerts huge video screens were beaming what was happening at either end on site but the time difference meant that the American spectacle went on into the early hours of the next morning, 4 a.m. to be precise. All through, Bob Geldof was available for BBC television to hammer it home to viewers that they were bound to donate money if they were viewing the show. BBC presenters Mark Ellen and David Hepworth could not leave their plastic personalities and annoying habits at home, and Hepworth in particular forced an exasperated Bob to come out with 'fuck the address ...' at one point. Geldof continued to be emphatic and stressed: 'There are people dying out there, so give me the money; take the money out of your pockets and don't go to the pub tonight.' All television networks that ran the concerts were allowed to do so only if they ran a phone-in money collection. Included were videos specially made by countries not involved in the concerts. Russia, Japan, Australia and Germany, to name but a few, contributed video clips of their most famous groups.

Despite the odd hiccup, the broadcasts were full of surprises. Bono Vox was outspoken on the BBC, and commented that: 'For the price of Star Wars or the MX missile defence budgets, the deserts of Africa could be turned into fertile lands. The technology is with us. The technocrats are not.' Udo Lindenburg, on behalf of German rock musicians, read a cruel indictment of the global situation, accusing 'governments in Washington and the Kremlin of being sick in their heads'. He rallied people to 'rise up against world insanities'. David Bowie was so together and direct about his commitment that he said he would 'do it again like a shot'. Bowie had also made a highly entertaining video of 'Dancing in the Streets' with Mick Jagger, especially for those looking at the event on television. Cliff Richard just ambled into the studio off the street and played a couple of old favourites. Moreover, in Dublin, Tony Boland was overwhelmed with donations and offers of help. Philip Lynott auctioned off his beloved reflecting bass guitar, and Taoiseach (Prime Minister) Garret FitzGerald came on and donated a staggering $\frac{1}{4}$ of a million pounds to Bob Geldof's relief fund. As the hours slipped by the money piled in, but still a completely exhausted and white-faced Bob Geldof would not stop his pleas for more help and future commitment.

When Bob announced afterwards that, 'It was the best day in my entire life', he was also talking for a large section of the Irish people. With an enormous sense of national pride, it was the Irish who contributed most to the £50 million that the concert generated. Obviously the mid-nineteenth-century potato famine was still fresh in their memories. It worked out that, on the day, each person had contributed the equivalent of £1 to the fund, while within two weeks Ireland had given a staggering £7 million. This, compared to the UK, was enormous since the latter could only manage £14½ million from its sixty million population.

When Bob and Bono stood on the Live Aid stage and led the finale to an emotional crescendo, they must have been aware of the status that Irish people and Irish musicians had been elevated to. After decades of struggle, Irish rock musicians had reached a pinnacle of achievement that went far beyond the parameters of their chosen profession. Geldof and Bono seemed to have a perfect understanding of what rock 'n' roll' could do in the eighties and that was to utilise its power on the imagination to change reality by transferring real value from the rock arena into the hands of those in rigid, disgusting and inhuman poverty.

Note: Band Aid and Live Aid were to trigger off an entire stream of rock music enterprises directed at improving some of the world's worst poverty and discriminatory situations. In the wake of Live Aid, Geldof himself travelled to Africa and, after helping to administer the practical side of the scheme, set off around the world visiting governmental institutions in Australia, America and Europe on a crusade of fund-raising which equalled that of his previous projects. By May 1986 £120 million had been generated through his efforts but more funds were still necessary to even approach overcoming the complicated problems in Ethiopia, Sudan and Chad. That month Geldof announced Sport Aid — a global sporting event of Olympian dimensions whereby one week was set aside for simultaneous sporting activities in countries East and West, whose energy was directed at famine relief. Inaugurated by an Ethiopian runner carrying the burning torch of life, it finished spectacularly a week later with his arrival in New York, an emotional happening which signalled millions of people in twenty-four different countries to commence the Race Against Time, a series of localised marathons that again raised incredible sums of money for Africa. Of the many commendations that Geldof received internationally following his colossal Aid feats the most interesting was his knighthood by the Queen of England in June 1986. It was a curiously ironic thing for an Irishman to receive a knighthood, but what made it unique was that Geldof was the first musician in the history of contemporary rock to receive such an accolade.

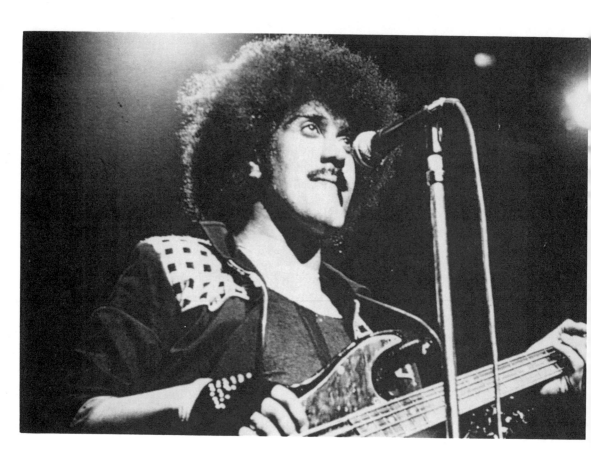

In remembrance of

Philip Lynott

1949 to 1986

On 4 January 1986 the shocking news filtered through the media that Phil Lynott was dead. That evening he had died at Salisbury General Hospital, London, from heart failure and pneumonia following blood poisoning. He had been in intensive care for eleven days following his collapse from kidney and liver failure on Christmas Day of 1985, having celebrated Christmas in his English Surrey home. Phil Lynott's death came at a time when his career had just changed direction and was set to crest another wave. Shrouded in the same mysterious circumstances that clouded the death of his idol Jimi Hendrix, it is certain that continual use of narcotics precipitated Lynott's tragic end. The similarities to Hendrix's death were uncanny. Unspecified narcotics were found in the bodies of both men. On the nights of collapse lengthy troughs of time separated the discovery of each in a semi-conscious state before their subsequent hospitalisation. Phil was aided by his wife Caroline, who drove him seventy miles to the nearest medical centre on the fateful night. For some cruelly insane reason they were turned away. Only after another twenty miles drive was Phil admitted to Salisbury General Hospital. As was the case with Jimi Hendrix an extensive coroner's report and inquest was automatically undertaken after a death under such tragic circumstances. Philip Lynott was only thirty-seven when he died.

During 1984 Phil had disbanded *Thin Lizzy* because he felt the group had run its course. He wanted a fresh challenge and this came in the form of *Grand Slam* 'a hard rock band with the emphasis still very much on the songs'. Writing a lot of new material and rehearsing regularly, Phil had great difficulty in acquiring a recording contract. Disgusted by record-industry apathy, Lynott laid the group to rest and went into incubation. His return to the mainstream was greeted with smiles by an ever-loving audience who knew that Phil could not be kept down for long. During the summer of 1985 he teamed up with old friend Gary Moore and recorded 'Out in the Fields', which reached number five in the British charts. As usual, Lynott's personal vision of Ireland was to the forefront in a song that bitterly criticised the political strife of Northern Irish sectarianism. His appearance on British television performing the song with Gary Moore was marred by a drug-possession charge which he picked up on his return to Ireland via Dublin airport. He was later acquitted in the Dublin courts. Working intensely on a new direction he decided to record a single with Englishman Paul Hardcastle called '19', a song he had written with *Grand Slam*. Acquiring a solid solo recording contract with Polydor, he formed a new backing band and went to Texas to make a video for '19', which eventually charted. Around that time he was also very busy in Ireland. A film about the Irish war of independence was due to be shot in 1986 and Lynott had been approached to write the soundtrack. On top of this Phil was helping *Clann Éadair*, a group of Howth fishermen who played traditional Irish music, to finish their debut album. Their first collaboration had been in 1984 on the beautiful single 'A Tribute to Sandy Denny' (Crashed), an evocative mixture of Lynott's emotional vocals and *Clann Éadair's* whistling acoustic sound. Philip had always helped up-and-coming Irish musicians. He was inundated with offers during the latter half of 1985 to reform *Thin Lizzy*. Childhood friend and lifelong companion, Brian Downey, was all set to join him on his first album of 1986 and Lynott was firmly committed to re-uniting *Lizzy* for a series of summer stadium gigs. The truth of his career then was that Phil Lynott was far more interested in rock music and his future than anything else. The insensitive English gutter press tore his life to shreds just days after his death in an attempt to cash in. Their lies and false testimonies only made the truth more real and Lynott's death more of a tragedy. He may have used drugs, but his belief in the power of rock music and his awesome output was his true epitaph.

Travelling back to those years of struggle when Irish rock was playing second fiddle to the showbands, Philip Lynott was a true visionary. A black youth in a white society, life presented itself to him in a series of unforgettable images that had to be written down. By appearing with a number of interesting bands, the tall, black figure with the swimming romantic drawl became an integral part of the Dublin scene. With a psychedelic dress sense and an ear for progressive sounds, he went all-out to push the showbands and the complacent aside and created a new era of music in Ireland. At the age of twenty he formed *Thin Lizzy*, a magical three-piece which contained the essential ingredients of innovation, charisma and technique. They were the cream of their generation. With Eric Bell's sensitive guitar and Brian Downey's bright drumming, Philip found the perfect cushion for his intensely emotional lyrics that embodied so much of the contemporary Irish culture of their time. As the momentum gathered and his fame spread he became Ireland's first rock hero abroad. *Thin Lizzy* jumped from success to success and were Ireland's leading heavy rock group of the 1970s. Line-up changes were many, but Lynott always led the group in an heroic fashion back and forth across America and Europe. Those halcyon decades of the sixties and seventies saw Irish rock change from a promise to a reality. The most memorable sight from those times was that of Phil Lynott bending the strings of his reflecting bass guitar to the cheers of thousands of youth who realised that this musician was playing for them the sounds of their generation. I personally regret that Philip will not be able to turn the pages of this book and fondly remember the legacy of those few brave musicians who went against the grain of the mediocre and broke all the rules in order to change and grow — musicians like Brush Shiels, whose 1986 acoustic ballad 'Old Pal' (CMR) was suitably reminiscent of Lynott's past. Without Philo, Irish rock music would never have found its pride or its strength. Every person who reads this book or listens to his music should remember him forever as Ireland's first great rock poet.

SELF-AID

A Pictorial Essay

DUBLIN

17 MAY '86

127

127-28 Masterminded by RTE's Tony Boland and Niall Mathews in the wake of Live Aid, Self Aid was to gather together a significant cross-section of musicians, old and young, in the name of a just cause, that of Ireland's ever-worsening unemployment. The slogan 'Make It Work' was the title of a song by Paul Doran written specially to mark the occasion.

129 *The Pogues* — Shane McGowan *(left),* Spider Stacey *(right).*

130 Frank Kearns of *Cactus World News.*

131 *Clannad's* Máire Ní Bhraonáin with that famous symbol of Irish culture, the harp.

132 Freddie White — a real survivor of the 1960s folk and rock era.

133 Martin Fay of *The Chieftains* coaxes a tune from his fiddle. The fact that an avowed traditional Irish folk group could feel comfortable playing to a predominantly rock-oriented crowd proved that a lot of barriers had been broken down over the years.

134 Paul Brady, Irish folk rock's most revered son, delivered a set that was unanimously described as an emotional highpoint.

135 'If Van Morrison was a gunslinger he'd shoot copycats' was how the man introduced his Self Aid set. Although in belligerent humour, he nevertheless presented three new songs which had that same mix of the ethereal and Celtic that has made him the stuff of legend.

129

130

131

128

133

134

132

135

136 For the man who had inspired it, Self Aid was to mark the end of an era. This was the last public concert by *The Boomtown Rats. Left to right:* Pete Briquette, Bob Geldof, Gary Roberts.

137 With a softness of voice, delicate guitar style and powerful stage presence, Christy Moore reminded everyone at Self Aid that even if the message was serious the foremost purpose of Irish music was to communicate and entertain.

138 Rory Gallagher in full flight. Absent from his native land for years, his Self Aid appearance was eagerly awaited and just as eagerly lapped up.

139 Self Aid had started with Brush Shiels doing a fitting tribute to Philip Lynott, the man most conspicuous by his absence. Twelve hours later Gary Moore and the last line-up of *Thin Lizzy* gathered together to pay their respects the only way they knew how. Gary Moore *(foreground)*, Scott Gorham *(behind)*.

140 A shocking performance, in the best sense of the word. *U2* topped all expectations with a ferocious rock 'n' roll set that included versions of Eddie Cochran's 'C'mon Everybody', Dylan's 'Maggie's Farm' and John Lennon's 'Cold Turkey'. Edge *(left)*, Bono *(right)*.

141 Máire Ní Bhraonáin, Bono, Bob Geldof and Chris de Burgh bringing the proceedings to an end with a rendition of the Self Aid song 'Make It Work'.

136

138

137

139

140

141

NOT THE END BUT THE BEGINNING

It would be myopic to believe that what has happened to Irish rock since the early 1960s is a finite story that can be easily parametered within the covers of a book. No writer could hope to account for the hundreds of solo musicians and groups that are constantly bubbling under the surface hoping one day to break into the consciousness of the public. They may not yet have recorded or may have just initiated their recording career, or are maybe known only to a few, but their presence has to be acknowledged. On top of that, rock music does not exist in a vacuum but has always been aided by all the music business people who promote concerts, run studios, manage acts, host radio programmes and work hard to give whatever music is being created the necessary infrastructure for it to develop.

Some of these people have added so much to the convivial climate that has nurtured Irish rock that it would be a crime not to give them their due. Pat Egan is just one of those people. Dublin born, he started his career as a disc jockey and journalist in the sixties before establishing Ireland's first underground record shops. His interest in music led him into promotion and for a time in the 1970s he was the only entrepreneur with the ability to attract interesting foreign rock artists to these shores. He would constantly put on unknown Irish bands so they could benefit from the exposure. His most noteworthy contribution was during the sixties when Irish rock was in its infancy. Through his journalistic activities he championed the new beat and progressive groups who were then constantly struggling against a showband hegemony. *Thin Lizzy*, Rory Gallagher and *Skid Row* were all given their first critical recognition by Egan through his *Hitsville* and *New Spotlight* magazine columns. Another promoter who deserves credit is Jim Aiken from Belfast, who showed that Ireland could mount large scale rock 'n' roll concerts on a par with anything in Europe or America. His first conspicuous success was *The Rolling Stones* at Slane Castle which attracted nearly a hundred thousand people in 1982. Since then he has been responsible for people like Bob Dylan, *Simon and Garfunkel*, *Queen*, Elton John, Bruce Springsteen and David Bowie recognising Ireland as a welcome place to play when for years such huge international stars perennially missed the Emerald Isle in favour of Britain or elsewhere.

One name which constantly crops up when looking back through rock history both in Ireland and abroad is that of B.P. Fallon. A spectral figure, he is known for the vibe he can create between people and has always had a passionate love and deep respect for rock music's potential. Educated in England in the early sixties he was the first authentic hippy media personality on RTE. On shows like 'Sounds like B.P. Fallon' he was the first to do interviews with the likes of Jimi Hendrix and John Lennon. He quickly moved from that to working for *The Beatles* Apple label and then Chris Blackwell's Island organisation. Such names as *Traffic*, *King Crimson* and *T. Rex* were part of Fallon's professional orbit. It was while being involved with Bowie during his Ziggy Stardust phase that B.P. became publicity man for *Led Zeppelin* in the early seventies — then the biggest rock act in the world. After many other colourful experiences and a time with *The Boomtown Rats*, Fallon returned to Ireland where he began a legendary series of radio

142

142 Pat Egan *(right)* with Albert Lee at Eric Clapton's 1981 Dublin concert. Egan was responsible for rock journalism, record retailing and rock promotion gaining respectability in Ireland.

143 BP Fallon (1982) — a veritable walking encyclopedia of rock music history.

144 Dave Fanning in 1981 — Ireland's most progressive and best-loved disc jockey.

145 Phil Lynott *(left)* with Pat Egan *(centre)* and Rory Gallagher *(right)* in 1972. Irish rock was still in its infancy, but men like these would ensure its rightful place in the world at large.

143

144

145

programmes titled 'The B.P. Fallon Orchestra'. Its lengthy two-hour format of interviews interspersed with music, provided continually original material and was a worthy contribution to Irish rock culture. For example in 1986 he devoted no less than three entire shows to Henry McCullough and *Sweeney's Men*. A veritable walking encyclopedia of rock music history, Fallon's sensitive presence and admirable writing and broadcasting skills have added much to the popular understanding of the form.

Staying with radio, Irish rock has benefited considerably from the setting up of RTE Radio 2, the official national music channel. Since the late seventies one man in particular has given young Irish musicians the encouragement and confidence to go forward by featuring their music on his lengthy, four-nights-a-week rock show. His name is Dave Fanning and, along with producer Ian Wilson, he has given airtime to more up-and-coming Irish bands, groups and solo artists than all the pirate stations put together. Listened to avidly in the UK and Europe, Dave Fanning's rock show has been instrumental in giving untried and untested music a chance to be heard. Moreover, through the session system where young groups record some tracks in RTE for airplay purposes, many have found swift record company response and eventual contracts.

No rock scene is really complete without a representative periodical publication. It took quite a few years for Ireland to develop the art of rock journalism. In the sixties and early seventies one had various interesting but shortlived organs devoted to disseminating the facts in and around the contemporary music of the day. *Hitsville* and *High Times* did trojan work in their time and *New Spotlight/Starlight* always devoted a couple of pages to rock, but not until the arrival of *Hot Press* in 1977 could the country say it had a proper representative journal that could compete with English papers such as *New Musical Express* and *Melody Maker*. Steered by editor Niall Stokes, *Hot Press* developed through the vital punk years and in the eighties was to become recognised as the most authoritative music magazine in Ireland and the UK. Its continuous and exhaustive coverage of Irish rock and folk has been a welcome and necessary part of the development of a serious popular music culture.

There are countless other individuals who are working every day towards making Ireland a better place for rock music. The 1980s has seen this country become, in terms of technical facilities and equipment, an enviable place in which to record. There are more record labels and a greater variety of record shops. Most importantly, there is a very high level of awareness concerning the worth of popular music to the nation. In 1987 the Arts Council took a serious interest in rock, and raised it to the status of 'art' by allocating a portion of its administration and funding to look into the area. Also in that year *The Irish Times* published a small but significant item on the first Irish rock archive which had been started in the Linenhall Library, Belfast, by one Robert Bell. Whatever happens in the future it is true to say that the story of Irish rock doesn't just end with *The Joshua Tree* or Self Aid. In a way the evolution of the music which has been detailed in these pages has only just begun. In years to come we will hear many new and different voices; some of them may be aware, some of them may not, that they are following in the footsteps of a long line of predecessors.

During the winter of 1986 an American Indian/Canadian musician flew into Dublin to be met by a hurricane and some serious flooding. He was whisked by car to a house in the outlying mountains and given a bed to rest his weary bones. Culture shock, flight fatigue, and a punishing work schedule in America; scoring a film for Martin Scorsese, working on a solo album, helping Eric Clapton on another LP and so forth had left him in a temporary state of sensory overload. The next morning he went downstairs to where four musicians were banging out some serious rock and roll. The chunky lead singer jumps up and says 'Let's go!' while the worldweary North American thinks 'Oh God! Let's go where?' The band were U2, the musician was Robbie Robertson, ex of Bob Dylan's halcyon mid-'60s touring days and of the premier American roots group of the same period, The Band. This was the man who wrote 'The Weight' familiar from the *Easy Rider* soundtrack of 1969. Anyhow his very first solo LP came out in October 1987 and on this superlative work co-produced with fellow Canadian Daniel Lanois were two cuts featuring U2, the best being 'Sweet Fire of Love', the song instantly created after Bono had laid down the gauntlet above.

'Sweet Fire of Love' contains everything great about what happened to U2 during and after *The Joshua Tree*. The rhythm section of Larry Mullen and Adam Clayton breaks out from the very heart of rock history, literally pulling one into the sound. Bono and Robbie take vocal roulette while he and Edge trade licks. This is jamming inside a big tradition but the finale took my breath away and still does. Edge hikes up his guitar, pulling off piercing slices that are so perfectly economical and one thinks well that's mighty fine but then it happens—the effects pedals are heaped on and Edge heads straight through that black hole left by Jimi Hendrix and into another realm. Whatever happened to U2 in America was all evident on this last Edge guitar break. They wanted to reaffirm the greatness of classic rock 'n' roll and what better place to start than with Hendrix, the undisputed inventor and master of sizzling electric rock guitar.

The full document of this change arrived a year later in the form of the double LP *Rattle & Hum* (Island). In Britain it sold 600,000 copies on release in October 1988, making up 25% of all album sales in the UK and at the time ranked as the fastest selling LP of all time. In America it stayed at number 1 for three weeks. The pre-album release single 'Desire' was to be U2's first number one single in the British Isles. *Rattle & Hum*'s contents were raw, rootsy, and very American. The band had gone to Memphis to ensconce themselves in Sun Studio of Elvis Presley fame and record various tracks. One 'Love Rescue Me' had been written with Bob Dylan who also added backing vocals, another a rousing blues 'When Love Comes to Town' featured a riveting vocal and guitar performance by blues legend B. B. King. Other highlights were 'All Along the Watchtower' performed à la Hendrix in San Francisco using The Greateful Dead's equipment; the rhythm & blues thump of 'Desire', the black Harlem Gospel version of 'I Still Haven't Found

What I'm Looking For', Edge's Irish ballad 'Van Diemen's Land', and a tribute to John Lennon in 'God Part II'. Soulful tracks such as 'Heartland', recorded in Dublin with Brian Eno and Daniel Lanois and 'All I Want Is You' featuring a Los Angeles recording with beautiful strings courtesy of Van Dyke Parks are some of U2's most poignant songs.

Yet for me the most telling moments of this venture are two live performances. The first, 'Silver & Gold' (Denver, Colorado, November '87) where Bono ad-libs his anti-apartheid feelings before saying the classic line 'Am I buggin' you? Don't mean to bug ye! Edge play the blues'—and play them he does, with even more intensity than on 'Sweet Fire of Love' and not the slow twelve-bar either but a newer, grittier, harder form of rock guitar solo. Jimmy Page had certainly been bettered here. The second, 'Bullet the Blue Sky' (Tempe, Arizona, December '87) was introduced by an actual section from Jimi Hendrix's Woodstock show of '69 in 43 seconds of 'The Star Spangled Banner'. Again Edge goes right over with the sliding riffs and Bono reacts with a better version of the song than on *The Joshua Tree*. This is all recorded perfectly in Phil Joanou's *Rattle & Hum* movie made with £5ml worth of the band's money and released around the same time. Although not the box office smash Paramount had expected it did capture U2's love of the music with some of the best onstage footage ever put to celluloid. However, anybody expecting a Dylan type *Don't Look Back* rockumentary was to be disappointed with almost no revelations of volatile artistic personalities. Subsequent U2 activities were Spring '89 involvement in the Russian Greenpeace album with the likes of Sting, Peter Gabriel, REM, David Byrne etc plus the posthumous release of Roy Orbison's 'She's a Mystery to Me', a song written for him by Bono & Edge. While worldwide gossip raged about what the band would do next, June '89 saw the opening of Dublin's City Centre Arts Complex, a docklands centre built with the help of U2 money and the first of its kind in Europe where incipient creativity whether it be in music or other arts could be given top rank facilities to grow. Aside from the development of their Mother record label to include such local musicians as Stano, The Word, The Dixons, The Black Velvet Band, An Emotional Fish, and even The Golden Horde plus an album, *Old Friends*, by revered American country singer Guy Clarke; and Bono's painting, photography, and poetry activities; the most significant fact about U2 was stated by Bono in his last important interview of the period (Hot Press, January '89) when he unflinchingly said "Basically, we're The Grateful Dead of the '90s."

And The Hothouse Flowers were proclaimed the Irish Beatles. Fronted by native Irish speakers Liam Ó Maonlaí and Fiachna Ó Braonáin this busking group had made it to the pages of *Rolling Stone* before their second single release 'Don't Go' in December '87. Mixing bass, piano, bodhrán, Hammond organ, bouzouki, mandolin, saxophone, acoustic/electric guitars and anything else, they came up with a bluesy/soul version of Irish folk-rock that won them fans everywhere. The acoustic version of 'Don't Go' is superb and after pulling off the impossible by appearing to an approximately 500 million people in June '88 via a Eurovision Song Contest. Their debut album *People* (London) went straight to number 1 in the Irish and number 2 in the British charts. A strange collection of pastoral soul, funk, pop, rock and much else that brought memories of James Brown meets Van Morrison meets Tim Buckley to mind, the album nevertheless got much attention and contained one surefire touch of genius in 'If You Go'. A real pop phenomenon, they were going down a treat in Britain and Ireland (selling out in Dublin a 25,000 venue in September '88) and did reasonable club business in America.

The idea that Ireland is in any way overshadowed by U2's success is nullified by the sheer quality of other rock releases during the 1988–1989 period. Aslan, fronted by Christy Dignam and from North Dublin, had achieved considerable airplay with the perfect pop debut single, signed to EMI and released the Irish number 1 LP *Feel No Shame* in March '88. A potent brew of soulful, anthemic, emotional rock, the pressures of fame split the group within months, the charismatic Dignam leaving the others to go it without them and rebuild a solo career. That April The Stars of Heaven received a rare and deserved 12-star review in Hoto Press for their beguiling piece of perfection 'Speak Slowly' (Rough Trade), an album sprinkled with beautiful references to American groups like Big Star, Love, and The Byrds while holding onto a misty Irish feel observed through the prism of a modern musical lexicon. 'Lights of Tetouan' is beautiful refashioned sixties pop, '2 O'Clock Waltz' is as precise a piece of soft Irish rock as one will find in the genre. An out-take, 'Wheels', was used in the Steve Martin comedy film *Planes, Trains & Automobiles* some months later. In May '88 came In Tua Nua's second helping in 'The Long Acre' (Virgin), a spirited mix of rock, folk instrumentation, and good hooks that brought the troupe to North America later that year with new violinist Lovely Previn. Houston, Austin, Dallas, El Paso, Tucson, San Diego, Los Angeles, San Francisco, Boulder, Chicago, Madison, Minneapolis, Cincinnati, Detroit, Toronto, Boston, Providence, and New York all revelled to Howth's finest.

The end of 1987 saw both The Radiators and Stiff Little Fingers, two of Irish punk rock's best bands, reform and play live. This resulted in the re-release of *Ghostown* (Chiswick) in April '89 for the former. An album that is considered a Joycean rock musical vision of late twentieth-century Dublin without peer, it contained the new Philip Chevron composition 'Under Cleary's Clock'. Stiff Little Fingers were greeted by a sell-out Irish/European tour which interspersed such folk standards as 'Love Of The Common People' and 'The Wild Rover'with more fiery material such as 'No Sleep 'Til Belfast'. A double live LP *See You Up There*, came out on Virgin, early '89, to remember the occasion. Fellow Northerners That Petrol Emotion continued on their highly controversial anti-Royalist way with *End of the Millenium Psychosis Blues* (Virgin) in September '88, a record that just teemed with the cutting-edge atmosphere of occupied Ulster. The end of that year saw punkish groups A House and My Bloody Valentine release two important records in *On Our Big Fat Merry-Go-Round* (Blanco Y Negro) and *Isn't Anything* (Creation) respectively. A House looked to the independent sound of early '80s British bands such as The Cure but with definite Irishness while My Bloody Valentine (an original Dublin formation that regrouped in London with two English girls) occupied a universe all to themselves. *Isn't Anything* went on to occupy the number 1 slot in both the Irish and British independent charts in the winter '88/'89 period. Their music was accelerated, polished to a sheen, sprinkled with psychedelia, and tremendously visceral. As good as anything else independent 'punky' music was producing at the time, a trip to America's East Coast, especially New York, won them even more followers in the summer of '89.

Of all the new groups up and running for the sun the one most likely to get close are Dublin's Something Happens! whose debut October '88 album *Been there, Seen that, Done that* (Virgin) was the complete item. Bursting with intricately woven songs, originality, love, beauty, and freshness it won unanimous praise on both sides of the Irish sea. This was emotional Irish rock with dozens of unexpected twists and turns and some gorgeous melodies as on 'Beach' and 'Forget Georgia'. It matched the insistence of punk/new wave with a broader perspective as evinced on the acoustic tracks 'Both Men Crying' and 'Be My Love'. A lovable bunch led by singer Tom Dunne their sense of humour and slightly neo-hippy image attracted much attention. A sign of their zealous commitment was after Virgin America stalled on releasing their debut they self-financed a summer '89 tour of the American East Coast plus some dates in Los Angeles and Hollywood. The reaction was such that the worthy record entered at number 2 in the U.S. import charts.

On the folk side it could be said that the late 1980s period was never a better time for its revitalisation. The merger brought about by Shane Mac-Gowan's Pogues between the more anarchic side of modern rock and straight Irish traditionalism was continued with 'Me Walk Fol De Do Fol, The Diddle Idle' on the January '88 record *If I Should Fall from Grace with God* (Stiff). Though the irreverence and hard-drunken Irishness is still apparent, other influences: jazz, East European, Spanish are here in evidence. Most importantly the contributions of Philip Chevron's 'Thousands Are Sailing' and Terry Woods' 'Streets of Sorrow' raise the proceedings considerably. Woods' moving ballad for Northern Ireland segues into 'Birmingham Six', an attack on dubious British arrests for suspected terrorism which was banned outright on UK radio. Chockfull of ballads, commiserations, re-membrances, melancholia, and plain knees-up-crack music this was an important record. MacGowan's reputation as a sort of Brendan Behan of rock had earned him respect from Dubliners such as Bono as far as Hollywood film stars and even Bob Dylan who in 1989 expressed wishes to play and even write with The Pogues. On the release of *Peace and Love* (WEA) it was difficult to believe that the same bunch who had goofed around in Alex Cox's spaghetti-western pastiche *Straight to Hell* (1986) could produce such great music as 'Down All the Days' (a remarkable tribute to Irish writer and artist Christy Brown), 'USA' and 'Night Train to Lorca'.

If Kevin Burke, Andy Irvine, Jackie Daly, and Arty McGlynn were injecting authenticity back into the Irish/American scene on the albums *Patrick Street 1 & 2* (Green Linnet '88, '89), Davy Spillane was creating marvellous new fusions out of both cultures. His *Atlantic Bridge* (Tara) appeared in Ireland in late '87 and elsewhere in early '88 to laudatory reviews all round. The cream of American country and blue grass pickers, Albert Lee, Jerry Douglas, and Bela Fleck joined seasoned Irishmen Christy Moore and Eoghan O'Neill on a celebration and a half of new acoustic music possibilities. If one wanted to hear how the history of American folk and Irish folk intertwine this is without a doubt its definitive statement. Spillane's uileann pipes on the title track effortlessly glide into Fleck and Douglas's dobro/banjo hootenanny jam. A live session/studio set featuring Spillane's own Irish combo plus guitarist Rory Gallagher was released in 1989 titled *Out of the Air* (1989).

Of all the eclectic musics that were coming out of Ireland the most potent brew of rock and folk was produced by Scots group The Waterboys on their Irish album *Fisherman's Blues* (Chrysalis). Having relocated to Spiddal in Galway, recruited fiddler Steve Wickham full-time, Mike Scott, Anto Thistlewaite, and Trevor Hutchinson finally found their spiritual home. Over recording sessions that lasted throughout 1986, 1987 and 1988 the band threw every conceivable formation of acoustic musics together to come up with marvellous tunes like 'When Ye Go Away' (with a marvellous fiddle reel by Charlie Lennon), the country waltz of 'And a Bang on the Ear' and the W. B. Yeats derived 'Stolen Child' (with the help of Gaelic singer Tomás MacKeown). The Waterboys' instant adoption by the Irish was rooted in singer Mike Scott's sense of community and ability to convey the very essence of rock's evergreen popularity. In concert Scott and Co. could blend songs as diverse as Van Morrison's 'Sweet Thing', Dylan's 'Rainy Day Woman', McCartney's 'Blackbird', and such ditties as 'What a Wonderful World' and 'Je T'Aime' into their set with gay abandon. On successive, sold-out tours, many talked à la U2 of The Waterboys redeeming rock for future generations and given the brilliance of the contents of *Fisherman's Blues* the fact it was an Irish experience makes it all the more historic. Like Dylan and The Band in Woodstock during the late sixties, The Waterboys Irish years of the late eighties are times that have already passed into myth.

While The Waterboys were stirring up emotions as far West as the Aran islands, the summer of '89 also saw one of Ireland's finest modern music exports, Clannad, celebrating in their family pub in Gweedore, Co. Donegal. Ostensibly an occasion to mark the 21st year of their father Leo's pub the band were presented with an award to mark 300,000 copies sold of the superb June '89 compilation LP *Past Present* (RCA), a mixture of their renowned mist of sound music ('Newgrante', 'Theme from Harry's Game'), blissful Irish ballads ('Coinleach Glas An Fhómhair') and more rockier material ('In a Lifetime' with Bono and 'Something to Believe In' with Bruce Hornsby). The last title came from the big production album *Sirius* (October '87) which had been put down in Dublin, Wales, London, and Los Angeles with the help of American producers Greg Ladanyï and Russ Kunkel.

Though railed by the critics for being too FM rockist, such tracks as 'Skellig', 'White Fool', 'Many Roads', and the heavenly 'Something to Believe In' had a filmic quality that just struck a chord somewhere in the subconscious. Always creating, the group also put out the soundtrack *Atlantic Realm* (BBC) in early '89.

Talk of Clannad brings us neatly to family member Enya, without a shadow of a doubt one of Ireland's great success stories. After creating for nearly two years in the Artane house of production/writing team Nick and Roma Ryan, Enya spent months in England working on the digital mix of what was to become the definitive compact disc statement of the technology conscious era, *Watermark* (WEA). A single from the album *Orinoco Flow* went straight in at number one in the UK, in autumn '88, staying there for three weeks. The album shifted 300,000 copies almost immediately and within less than a year had become a multi-million selling phenomenon worldwide with number ones in Japan, New Zealand, Australia, Europe, and, of course, Venezuela where the real Orinoco river flows. Even demands were coming in from Eastern bloc countries for live performances and 100,000 were reckoned to want to see the golden girl live in Estonia. In America it had had an accelerated flight into the Billboard Top 50. This type of global penetration, and from an artist who was hardly known in her own country not alone outside, was like a fairy story come true for the lass from Gweedore. Shy, retiring, and armed with a devotion-like attitude to her art Enya is now ranked up there with U2 as an example of Irish popular music at its very best. Her music is drift through with the airs, feelings, and images of an Irish landscape; her voice is multi-layered for harmonies, again and again her melodies slowly unfurl, the keyboard instrumentation full of classical nuance architects the music in stately splendour. At the time of release *Watermark* perfectly encapsulated the New Age sound of digital synthesis. Her Clannad roots are clearly evident throughout and nowhere are they better expressed than on 'Na Laetha Geal M'Óige', a tribute to her young Irish days that includes a splendid uileann pipe solo by Davy Spillane.

While people like Barry Moore, with the album *Luka Bloom* (Mystery '88) and successive American touring, maintained the ideal of folk protest Van Morrison was rediscovering his Irish roots with The Chieftains. Near the end of '87 Morrison was to be seen at England's Loughborough University espousing in seminar re 'the power of music to change consciousness'. Those expecting Van to carry on in a dour, philosophical way were to be pleasantly surprised at his collaboration with Ireland's most renowned exponents of traditional sounds. The summer '88 *Irish Heartbeat* (Mercury) LP confounded expectations and showed a man enjoying himself immensely. The record contained two Morrison originals, 'Celtic Ray' and the title track, which sparkled in the fresh light of Chieftain fiddles, whistles, flute and bodhrán. The fun element was apparent on uptempo numbers 'Star of the County Down' and 'Marie's Wedding' but it was the famous ballads 'She Moved Through the Fair' and 'My Lagan Love' that were truly a revelation.

Categorically, Morrison added to the genre with breathy emotive vocal performances that come near to his very best. On tour the ensemble of the Van Morrison band and The Chieftains brought much tears and laughter to audiences worldwide and even Van himself couldn't resist the fun atmosphere of Paddy Moloney and friends onstage. Having got that out of his system, Morrison returned to more spiritual concerns on the summer '89 album *Avalon Sunset* (Polydor). Straight to number 1 in the Irish charts, this showed him reassessing a Christian perspective and included guest performances from both Cliff Richard and Georgie Fame. Replete with the familiar orchestral jazz textures and Celtic vibes it was a highly commercial package that contained only two singular additions to the Morrison canon in the form of the wafting 'Contacting My Angel' and the spoken word reminiscence 'Coney Island'.

Other interesting rock, folk, pop, crossover, and whatever artifacts released by Irish artists '87–'89.

The Adventures: The Sea of Love (Elektra 1988)
Altan: House With a Heart (Green Linnet 1988)
Any Old Time: Phoenix (Dara 1987)
The Babysnakes: Sweet Hunger (Revolver 1988)
Bagatelle: Cry Away the Night (Harmac 1987)
Don Baker: Almost Illegal (Gasworks 1989)
The Big Noise: Raise It to the Rooftops (Big Noise 1988)
Mary Black: By the Time It Gets Dark (Dara 1987)
Mary Black: No Frontiers (Dara 1989)
Black Velvet Band: When Justice Came (Elektra 1989)
Cactus World News: No Shelter (MCA 1989)
Courier Soundtrack LP (Virgin 1988)
Cry Before Dawn: Crimes of Conscious (Epic 1987)
Cry Before Dawn: Witness for the World (Epic 1989)
Cypress Mine: Exit Trashtown (Solid 1987)
De Danann: Ballroom (WEA 1987)
De Danaan: A Jacket of Batteries (Harmac 1989)
Chris de Burgh: Flying Colours (A & M 1988)
Philip Donnelly: Town & Country (Dublin 1988)
Roger Doyle: Light Years (Operating Theatre 1988)
Roger Doyle: The Love of Don Perlimplin and Belisa in the Garden (Operating Theatre 1989)
Johnny Duhan: Reefer & the Model Soundtrack (Trax 1988)
Jim Fitzpatrick: Erinsaga (Ringsend Road 1989)
The Fleadh Cowboys: High Ace to Heaven (Sidekick 1989)
The Fountainhead: Voice of Reason (China 1988)
The Four of Us: Songs for the Tempted (CBS 1989)
Gavin Friday & the Man Seezer: Each man kills the thing he loves (Island 1989)
The Fureys & Davy Arthur: Scattering (Harmac 1988)
Ghost of an American Airman: Some Day (Plain Paper 1988)
Rory Gallagher: Tattoo/Blueprint (Castle '89)
Rory Gallagher: Live in Europe/Stagestruck (Castle '89)

Dolores Keane: Dolores Keane (DK records 1988)
Live For Ireland (Self-Aid 1986): (MCA 1987)
Donal Lunny: Direach Eisithe Ag (Gael-Linn 1987)
Philip Lynott: Ode to a Black Man (Tribute) (Hot Press '87/Solid '89)
Taohg Mac Dhonnagan: Solar Gorm (Gael-Linn 1989)
Arty McGlynn & Nollaig Casey: Lead the Knave (Ringsend Road 1989)
Microdisney: 39 Minutes (Virgin 1988)
Christy Moore: Voyage (WEA 1989)
My Bloody Valentine: Ecstasy (Lazy 1987)
Nightnoise: At the End of the Evening (Windham Hill 1988)
Maura O'Connell: Western Highway (Raglan 1987)
Sinéad O'Connor: The Value of Ignorance (Chrysalis Video 1989)
Mícheál Ó Súilleabháin: The Dolphin's Way (Venture 1987)
Mícheál Ó Súilleabháin: Oileán (Venture 1989)
The Prunes: Lite Fantastik (Baby 1988)
The Radiators: Dollar for Your Dreams (Comet 1988)
Relativity: Gathering Pace (Green Linnet 1987)
Scullion: Cooler at the Edge (Grapevine 1988)
Feargal Sharkey: Wish (Virgin 1988)
Sierra Leone: Prologue (Communiqué 1988)
Silent Running: Walk on Fire (Atlantic 1987)
Silent Running: Deep (Atlantic 1989)
Skid Row: Skid (CBS, re-issue 1988)
Skylark: Skylark (Ceirníní Claddagh 1987)
Something Happens!: I Know Ray Harman (Virgin 1988)
Stano: Only (Mother 1989)
Stiff Little Fingers: Live & Loud (Link 1988)
Stiff Little Fingers: See You Up There (PVG Video 1989)
Stiff Little Fingers: Inflammable Material/Nobody's Heroes (EMI re-released 1989)
St. Vitus Dance: Love Me, Love My Dogma (Probe 1987)
Stockton's Wing: Celtic Roots Revival (Raglan 1988)
Mary Stokes: Tough Times (Hot Press 1989)
Stump: A Fierce Pancake (Ensign 1988)
That Petrol Emotion: Seen and Unseen (Virgin Video 1989)
Tuesday Blue: Shibumi (EMI 1989)
Pierce Turner: The Sky & the Ground (Beggars Banquet 1989)
U2: The Unforgettable Fire Collection (Island Video 1989)
Virgin Prunes: Heresie (Baby 1988, dble LP)
Aidan Walsh: A Life Story of My Life (Kaleidoscope 1987)
Barry Warner: What's Happening?—The Story So Far (Solid 1989)
Andy White: Kiss the Big Stone (Decca 1988)

Note: Raw performances and a view into left-field bands could be gleaned from such compilations as *Live at the Underground* (1987 Underground) and three Comet LPs, *1, 2, & 3* (Comet '87–'89).

Promising ensembles up & running '87–'89

Azure Days, Energy Orchard, The Joshua Trio, QED, The Swinging Swine, Swim, The Stunning, Missing Link, Scale The Heights, The Four of Us, The Black Velvet Band, Rex & Dino, The Fat Lady Sings, Hey Paulette, The Word, The Slowest Clock, The Real Wild West, The Candyshop, The Belsonic Sound, The Subterraneans, Hallelujah Freedom, The Harvest Ministers, The Fireflys, The Dubh Chapter, Thee Amazing Colossal Men, Shaine, Venetian Blond, An Emotional Fish, Burning Embers, The Big Noise, Cypress Mine, The Dixons, Into Paradise, The Power of Dreams, A House, Ghost of An American Airman. . . . (and that's just the tip of the iceberg).

Appendixes

1 Historic Irish Singles Chart: July 1967

1 Black Velvet Band
    Johnny Kelly and The Capitol Showband (Pye)
2 A Whiter Shade of Pale
    Procol Harum (Deram)
3 There Goes My Everything
    Englebert Humperdinck (Decca)
4 Carrie Anne
    The Hollies (Parlophone)
5 She'd Rather Be with Me
    The Turtles (London)
6 Alternative Title
    The Monkees (RCA)
7 Okay
    Dave, Dee, Dozy, Beaky, Mick and Tich
    (Fontana)
8 All You Need Is Love
    The Beatles (Parlophone)
9 Boston Burglar
    Johnny McEvoy (Pye)
10 All for Me Grog
    The Dubliners (Major Minor)
11 Then I Kissed Her
    The Beach Boys (Capitol)
12 Silence Is Golden
    The Tremeloes (CBS)
13 Land of Ginger Bread
    Gregory and The Cadets (Pye)
14 Waterloo Sunset
    The Kinks (Pye)
15 Old Maid in the Garret
    Sweeney's Men (Pye)
16 The Happening
    The Supremes (Tamla Motown)
17 The Curragh of Kildare
    The Johnstons (Pye)
18 Enniskillen Dragoons
    The Ludlows (Pye)
19 Seven Drunken Nights
    The Dubliners (Major Minor)
20 Irish Soldier Boy
    Pat Lynch and *The Airchords* (Pye)
21 Talking Love
    Sean Dunphy and *The Hoedowners* (Pye)
22 Here Comes the Nice
    The Small Faces (Immediate)
23 Paper Sun
    Traffic (Island)
24 Funny Familiar Feelings
    Tom Jones (Decca)
25 I'll Come Runnin'
    Cliff Richard (Columbia)
26 Dedicated to the One I Love
    The Mamas and the Papas (RCA)
27 Seven Rooms of Gloom
    The Four Tops (Tamla Motown)
28 Strange Brew
    Cream (Reaction)
29 Don't Sleep in the Subway
    Petula Clark (Pye)
30 I Got Rhythm
    The Happenings (CBS)

Note: Chart is official Radio Caroline compilation culled from *New Spotlight* magazine.

2 Relevant Irish Singles Entering the Irish Charts 1962 to 1979

(In alphabetical order according to artist)

Artist	Song	Position*	Month	Year	Label
The Boomtown Rats	Looking after Number One	2	August	1977	Mulligan
The Boomtown Rats	Mary of the Fourth Form	12	October	1977	Mulligan
The Boomtown Rats	She's So Modern	10	April	1978	Mulligan
The Boomtown Rats	Like Clockwork	5	June	1978	Mulligan
The Boomtown Rats	Rat Trap	2	October	1978	Mulligan
Brendan Bowyer and The Royal Showband	Hucklebuck	1	January	1965	AMV
		4	March	1976	EMI

Artist	Song	Position*	Month	Year	Label
Emmet Spiceland	Mary from Dungloe	1	February	1968	Inset
Emmet Spiceland	Báidín Fheidhlimí	6	April	1968	Gael-Linn
Emmet Spiceland	Bunclody	8	October	1968	Page 1
Granny's Intentions	Never an Everyday Thing	7	November	1968	Deram
Horslips	Johnny's Wedding	10	March	1972	Oats
Horslips	Green Gravel	20	August	1972	Oats
Horslips	Dearg Doom	8	May	1973	Oats
Horslips	King of the Fairies	7	August	1974	Oats
Horslips	Daybreak	2	July	1976	Horslips
Horslips	Exiles	9	November	1977	Horslips
Horslips	Toora Loora Loora	9	September	1978	Horslips
Orange Machine	Three Jolly Little Dwarfs	14	July	1968	Pye
Radiators From Space	Television Screen	17	June	1977	CBS
Reform	I'm Gonna Get You	12	September	1973	Young Blood
Reform	You Gotta Get Up	3	May	1978	CBS
Spud	The Wind in the Willows	5	December	1974	Philips
Spud	Anna Livia	10	September	1977	Release
Sugar Shack	Morning Dew	17	February	1968	Tribune
Sweeney's Men	Old Maid in the Garret	6	May	1967	Pye
Sweeney's Men	Waxies Dargle	5	February	1968	Pye
Thin Lizzy	Whisky in the Jar	1	November	1972	Decca
Thin Lizzy	Randolph's Tango	14	May	1973	Decca

Highest position achieved.

Special thanks to Larry Gogan for permission to cull the above placings from his book of Irish charts. Through the years no consistent Irish charts have been available — in the sixties *New Spotlight* magazine had a Top 30, then when it came into the seventies, it had a Top 20. With a change of name to *Starlight*, it continued to do a Top 20 chart. After 1979 no Irish chart consistent with the above information was available.

3   Relevant Irish Singles Entering the British Charts 1964 to 1989

Month	Year	Artist	Song	Position*	Label
February	1965	Them	Baby Please Don't Go	6	Decca
April	1965	Them	Here Comes The Night	3	Decca
February	1973	Thin Lizzy	Whisky in the Jar	6	Decca
July	1976	Thin Lizzy	The Boys Are Back in Town	8	Vertigo
August	1976	Thin Lizzy	Jailbreak	31	Vertigo
January	1977	Thin Lizzy	Don't Believe a Word	12	Vertigo
August	1977	Thin Lizzy	Dancing in the Moonlight	14	Vertigo
August	1977	The Boomtown Rats	Looking after Number One	11	Ensign
November	1977	The Boomtown Rats	Mary of the Fourth Form	15	Ensign
May	1978	The Boomtown Rats	She's So Modern	12	Ensign
June	1978	Thin Lizzy	Rosalie	20	Vertigo
July	1978	The Boomtown Rats	Like Clockwork	6	Ensign
November	1978	The Undertones	Teenage Kicks	31	Sire
November	1978	The Boomtown Rats	Rat Trap	1	Ensign
February	1979	The Undertones	Get Over You	57	Sire
March	1979	Thin Lizzy	Waiting for an Alibi	9	Vertigo

Month	Year	Artist	Song	Position*	Label
May	1979	Gary Moore	Parisienne Walkways	8	MCA
May	1979	The Undertones	Jimmy Jimmy	16	Sire
July	1979	Thin Lizzy	Do Anything You Want To	14	Vertigo
August	1979	The Boomtown Rats	I Don't Like Mondays	1	Ensign
August	1979	The Undertones	Here Comes the Summer	34	Sire
September	1979	The Starjets	War Stories	51	CBS
October	1979	Stiff Little Fingers	Straw Dogs	44	Chrysalis
October	1979	Van Morrison	Bright Side of the Road	63	Mercury
November	1979	The Undertones	You've Got My Number	32	Sire
December	1979	Thin Lizzy	Sarah	24	Vertigo
February	1980	The Boomtown Rats	Someone's Looking at You	4	Ensign
March	1980	Stiff Little Fingers	At the Edge	15	Chrysalis
April	1980	Philip Lynott	Dear Miss Lonely Hearts	32	Vertigo
May	1980	The Undertones	My Perfect Cousin	10	Sire
June	1980	Stiff Little Fingers	Nobody's Heroes/Tin Soldiers	36	Chrysalis
July	1980	Thin Lizzy	Chinatown	21	Vertigo
July	1980	Philip Lynott	King's Call	35	Vertigo
August	1980	The Undertones	Wednesday Week	11	Sire
August	1980	Stiff Little Fingers	Back to Front	49	Chrysalis
October	1980	Thin Lizzy	Killer on the Loose	10	Vertigo
December	1980	The Boomtown Rats	Banana Republic	3	Ensign
January	1981	The Boomtown Rats	Elephant's Graveyard (Guilty)	26	Ensign
March	1981	Philip Lynott	Yellow Pearl	56	Vertigo
March	1981	Stiff Little Fingers	Just Fade Away	47	Chrysalis
May	1981	The Undertones	It's Going to Happen	18	Ardeck
May	1981	Thin Lizzy	Killers Live (EP)	19	Vertigo
May	1981	Stiff Little Fingers	Silver Lining	68	Chrysalis
July	1981	The Undertones	Julie Ocean	41	Ardeck
August	1981	U2	Fire	35	Island
August	1981	Thin Lizzy	Trouble Boys	53	Vertigo
October	1981	U2	Gloria	55	Island
December	1981	The Boomtown Rats	Never in a Million Years	62	Mercury
December	1981	Philip Lynott	Yellow Pearl (re-entry)	14	Vertigo
February	1982	Stiff Little Fingers	Listen	33	Chrysalis
March	1982	Thin Lizzy	Hollywood (Down on Your Luck)	53	Vertigo
April	1982	U2	A Celebration	47	Island
April	1982	The Boomtown Rats	House on Fire	24	Mercury
November	1982	Clannad	Theme from Harry's Game	5	RCA
November	1982	Chris de Burgh	Don't Pay the Ferryman	48	A & M
February	1983	U2	New Year's Day	10	Island
February	1983	Thin Lizzy	Cold Sweat	27	Vertigo
April	1983	U2	Two Hearts Beat as One	18	Island
May	1983	Thin Lizzy	Thunder and Lightning	39	Vertigo
July	1983	Clannad	Newgrange	65	RCA
July	1983	The Undertones	Teenage Kicks (re-released)	60	Ardeck
August	1983	Thin Lizzy	The Sun Goes Down	52	Vertigo
January	1984	Gary Moore	Hold on to Love	65	10/Virgin
February	1984	The Boomtown Rats	Tonight	73	Mercury
May	1984	Clannad	Robin the Hooded Man	42	RCA
May	1984	Chris de Burgh	High on Emotion	44	A & M

Month	Year	Artist	Song	Position*	Label
May	1984	The Boomtown Rats	Drag Me Down	50	Mercury
August	1984	Gary Moore	Empty Rooms	51	10/Virgin
September	1984	U2	Pride (In the Name of Love)	3	Island
November	1984	Feargal Sharkey	Listen to Your Father	12	Zarjazz/Virgin
December	1984	Band Aid	Do They Know It's Christmas	1	Phonogram
February	1985	Les Enfants	Slipaway	89	Chrysalis
February	1985	The Boomtown Rats	A Hold of Me	78	Mercury
May	1985	U2	The Unforgettable Fire	6	Island
June	1985	Mama's Boys	Needle in the Groove	88	Jive
June	1985	Gary Moore/Philip Lynott	Out in the Fields	5	10/Records
July	1985	The Adventures	Feel the Raindrops	58	Chrysalis
August	1985	Feargal Sharkey	Loving You	26	Virgin
August	1985	Gary Moore	Empty Rooms (re-release)	23	10/Records
November	1985	Feargal Sharkey	A Good Heart	1	Virgin
November	1985	Philip Lynott	Nineteen	76	Polydor
December	1985	Band Aid	Do They Know It's Christmas (re-release)	3	Phonogram
January	1986	Feargal Sharkey	You Little Thief	5	Virgin
February	1986	Clannad/Bono	In a Lifetime	20	RCA
February	1986	Zerra I	Rescue Me	82	Mercury
February	1986	Cactus World News	Years Later	59	MCA
March	1986	The Pogues	Poguetry in Motion (EP)	29	Stiff
April	1986	Feargal Sharkey	Someone to Somebody	64	Virgin
May	1986	Cactus World News	Worlds Apart	58	MCA
May	1986	Chris de Burgh	Fire on the Water	88	A & M
June	1986	Clannad	Robin of Sherwood	80	RCA
August	1986	Chris de Burgh	The Lady in Red	1	A & M
September	1986	The Pogues	Haunted	42	Stiff
September	1986	Cactus World News	The Bridge	74	MCA
September	1986	Chris de Burgh	Fatal Hesitation	44	A & M
October	1986	The Edge/Sinead O'Connor	Heroine	89	Virgin
November	1986	Bob Geldof	This is the World Calling	25	Phonogram
January	1987	Chris de Burgh	A Spaceman Came Travelling	40	A&M
January	1987	Band Aid	Do They Know It's Christmas (re-release)	86	Phonogram
January	1987	Gary Moore	Over the Hills and Far Away	20	IO/Virgin
January	1987	Philip Lynott	King's Call (re-release)	68	Vertigo
February	1987	Jake Burns & The Big Wheel	Breathless	99	Jive
February	1987	Microdisney	Town to Town	55	Virgin
February	1987	Bob Geldof	Love Like a Rocket (re-mix)	61	Phonogram
March	1987	Gary Moore	Wild Frontier	35	IO/Virgin
March	1987	U2	With or Without You	4	Island
April	1987	The Pogues & The Dubliners	The Irish Rover	8	Stiff
May	1987	That Petrol Emotion	Big Decision	43	Polydor
May	1987	Gary Moore	Friday on My Mind	26	IO/Virgin

June	1987	Cry Before Dawn	Gone Forever	80	Epic
June	1987	U2	I Still Haven't Found What I'm Looking For	6	Island
July	1987	That Petrol Emotion	Swamp	81	Polydor
July	1987	That Petrol Emotion	Dance	64	Polydor
September	1987	Gary Moore	The Loner	53	IO/Virgin
September	1987	U2	Where the Streets Have No Name	4	Island
October	1987	Mama's Boys	Waiting for a Miracle	85	Jive
October	1987	That Petrol Emotion	Genius Move	65	Virgin
December	1987	Gary Moore	Take a Little Time	75	IO/Virgin
December	1987	Mama's Boys	Higher Ground	88	Jive
December	1987	U2	In God's Country	48	Island
January	1988	The Pogues & Kirsty MacColl	Fairytale of New York	2	Pogue Mahone/Stiff
January	1988	Chris de Burgh	The Simple Truth (A Child Is Born)	55	A & M
February	1988	Feargal Sharkey	More Love	44	Virgin
February	1988	Sinéad O'Connor	Mandinka	17	Ensign/Chrysalis
March	1988	The Pogues	If I Should Fall from Grace with God	58	Pogue Mahone/Stiff
March	1988	Microdisney	Gale Force Wind	98	Virgin
May	1988	Sinéad O'Connor	I Want Your Hands on Me	77	Ensign/Chrysalis
May	1988	The Adventures	Broken Land	20	Elektra
May	1988	In Tua Nua	All I Wanted	69	Virgin
May	1988	Cry Before Dawn	Gone Forever (re-issue)	84	Epic
May	1988	Hothouse Flowers	Don't Go	11	London
July	1988	The Adventures	Drowning in the Sea of Love	44	Elektra
July	1988	The Pogues	Fiesta	24	Pogue Mahone/Stiff
July	1988	Hothouse Flowers	I'm Sorry	53	London
August	1988	Stump	Charlton Heston	72	Ensign/Chrysalis
September	1988	Hothouse Flowers	Easier in the Morning	77	London
October	1988	U2	Desire	1	Island
October	1988	Adventures	One Step from Heaven	26	Elektra
October	1988	Enya	Orinoco Flow	1	WEA
November	1988	Sinéad O'Connor & Karen Finley	Jump in the River	81	Ensign/Chrysalis
November	1988	In Tua Nua	Wheel of Evil	90	Virgin
November	1988	Chris de Burgh	Missing You	3	A & M
December	1988	The Pogues	Yeah, Yeah, Yeah, Yeah, Yeah	43	Pogue Mahone/Stiff
December	1988	U2	Angel of Harlem	9	Island
December	1988	Enya	Evening Falls	20	WEA
January	1989	Gary Moore	After the War	37	Virgin

January	1989	Chris de Burgh	Tender Hands	43	A & M
February	1989	The Waterboys	Fisherman's Blues	32	Ensign/ Chrysalis
February	1989	That Petrol Emotion	Groove Check EP	95	Virgin
March	1989	Chris de Burgh	Sailing Away	78	A & M
March	1989	Stiff Little Fingers	Wild Rover EP	83	Virgin
March	1989	Clannad	The Hunter	91	RCA
March	1989	Gary Moore	Ready for Love	56	Virgin
April	1989	U2/B.B. King	When Love Comes to Town	6	Island
June	1989	Enya	Storms in Africa (Part 2)	41	WEA
June	1989	Cry Before Dawn	Witness for the World	67	Epic
June	1989	U2	All I Want Is You	5	Island
July	1989	Clannad/Bono	In a Lifetime (re-issue)	17	RCA
July	1989	Van Morrison	Have I Told You Lately That I Love You	74	Polydor
July	1989	The Pogues	Misty Morning, Albert Bridge	41	Pogue Mahone/ WEA
July	1989	The Waterboys	And a Bang on the Ear	51	Ensign/ Chrysalis
August	1989	Clannad	Hourglass/Harry's Game	99	RCA

[*denotes same week of entry*

This list shows highest positions attained by Irish singles in the official British rock and pop music charts as shown in the trade magazine Music Week. As of 1989 © British Phonographic Institute (BPI). Compiled by Gallup for BPI, Music Week and BPC.

The song 'Do They Know It's Christmas' was conceived by Bob Geldof. The original release of the single stayed five weeks at the number one slot making Geldof the first Irish rock artist to achieve three number one hit singles in the British charts in the brief space of six years. The high placing of his Band Aid single the second time round makes his contribution, in the light of achievements in other areas, consummately unique. *Thin Lizzy* are the Irish rock group with most entries in the British singles charts ever. From 1973 onwards Phil Lynott penned no less than seventeen song entries for the band while three more of his solo songs charted. Adding in his success with the two Gary Moore singles 'Parisienne Walkways' and 'Out in the Fields', Lynott must be rated as Ireland's outstanding commercial rock artist of the 1973 to 1985 period.

During the 1987–89 period there were some important re-entries by Chris de Burgh: 'The Lady in Red' (no. 74, February 1987); The Pogues: 'If I Should Fall from Grace with God' (no. 79, April 1988) and U2: 'With or Without You' (no. 94, July 1987), 'I Still Haven't Found . . . (no. 95, September 1987), 'Where the Streets Have No Name' (no. 80, November 1987).

Remember the above list concerns itself only with Irish music and musicians relevant to the text. They were not the only artists to break the British charts. Between 15 February 1964 and 22 July 1967 ballad group *The Bachelors* had eleven singles in the Top Thirty including hits 'Diane' (no. 1, February 1964) and 'I Believe' (no. 2, March 1964). Smooth, easy-listening singer Tony Christie had two hits: 'Yellow River' (no. 1, June 1970) and the catchy 'Is This the Way to Amarillo' (no. 18, January 1972). Our first ever Eurovision Song Contest winner, Dana, reached the number one spot with 'All Kinds of Everything' in April of 1970 and from then until January 1977 had six singles in the Top Thirty-Five. Showband man Joe Dolan put three singles into the Top Thirty between April and August of 1969, the highest being 'Make Me an Island' (Pye) which peaked at number five. Everlasting Irish traditional group *The Dubliners* had three singles in the Top Fifty between May and October of 1967: 'Seven Drunken Nights' being the highest at number eleven in May. Our second Eurovision Song Contest winner Johnny Logan entered the chart at the number one spot in May of 1980 with 'What's Another Year' (Epic). In 1987 he won the contest again with 'Hold Me Now' (Epic) which went to No. 2 in June of that year. His 'I'm Not In Love' (Epic) graced the chart at 51 in September. Still driving the middle of the road lane *The Nolans*, all sisters, placed six singles in the Top Twenty (May 1980 to April 1982) with 'Attention to Me' (Epic), their highest placing at number nine in May of 1981. The most interesting Irish popular artist was the teenybop singer Gilbert O'Sullivan, who slotted no less than fourteen singles into the chart between January 1971 and November 1980. They are worth listing.

Gilbert O'Sullivan (singles)

	Month	Year	Song	Position	Label
1	January	1971:	Nothing Rhymed	8	MAM
2	April	1971:	Underneath the Blankets Go	48	MAM
3	September	1971:	We Will	16	MAM
4	January	1972:	No Matter How I Try	8	MAM
5	March	1972:	Alone Again Naturally	4	MAM
6	July	1972:	Oooh Wakka Do Wakka Day	8	MAM
7	November	1972:	Clair	1	MAM
8	April	1973:	Get Down	1	MAM
9	December	1973:	Why Oh Why Oh Why	6	MAM
10	March	1974:	Happiness Is Me and You	19	MAM
11	August	1974:	A Woman's Place	45	MAM
12	January	1975:	Christmas Song	12	MAM
13	July	1975:	I Don't Love You But I Think I Like You	14	MAM
14	November	1980:	What's in a Kiss	19	Epic

4 Relevant Irish Albums Entering the British Charts 1970 to 1989

Month	Year	Artist	Album	Position	Label
February	1970	Taste	On the Boards	18	Polydor
April	1970	Van Morrison	Moondance	12	Warner Bros.
October	1970	Skid Row	Skid	30	CBS
May	1971	Rory Gallagher	Rory Gallagher	32	Polydor
December	1971	Rory Gallagher	Deuce	39	Polydor
May	1972	Rory Gallagher	Live in Europe	9	Polydor
September	1972	Taste	Live at the Isle of Wight	41	Polydor
February	1973	Rory Gallagher	Blueprint	12	Polydor
August	1973	Van Morrison	Hardnose the Highway	22	Warner Bros.
November	1973	Rory Gallagher	Tattoo	32	Polydor
July	1974	Rory Gallagher	Irish Tour '74	36	Polydor
November	1974	Van Morrison	Veedon Fleece	41	Warner Bros.
September	1975	Thin Lizzy	Fighting	60	Vertigo
April	1976	Thin Lizzy	Jailbreak	10	Vertigo
October	1976	Rory Gallagher	Calling Card	32	Chrysalis

Month	Year	Artist	Album	Position	Label
November	1976	Thin Lizzy	Johnny the Fox	11	Vertigo
April	1977	Horslips	The Book of Invasions	39	Oats
May	1977	Van Morrison	A Period of Transition	23	Warner Bros.
September	1977	The Boomtown Rats	The Boomtown Rats	18	Ensign
October	1977	Thin Lizzy	Bad Reputation	4	Vertigo
June	1978	Thin Lizzy	Live and Dangerous	2	Vertigo
July	1978	The Boomtown Rats	A Tonic for the Troops	8	Ensign
October	1978	Van Morrison	Wavelength	27	Warner Bros.
February	1979	Gary Moore	Back on the Streets	70	MCA
March	1979	Stiff Little Fingers	Inflammable Material	14	Rough Trade
May	1979	Thin Lizzy	Black Rose	2	Vertigo
May	1979	The Undertones	The Undertones	13	Sire
September	1979	Van Morrison	Into the Music	21	Phonogram
September	1979	Rory Gallagher	Top Priority	56	Chrysalis
November	1979	The Boomtown Rats	The Fine Art of Surfacing	7	Ensign
March	1980	Stiff Little Fingers	Nobody's Heroes	8	Chrysalis
April	1980	The Undertones	Hypnotised	13	Sire
April	1980	Philip Lynott	Solo in Soho	28	Vertigo
September	1980	Stiff Little Fingers	Hanx	9	Chrysalis
September	1980	Van Morrison	Common One	53	Mercury
October	1980	Thin Lizzy	Chinatown	7	Vertigo
November	1980	Rory Gallagher	Stage Struck	40	Chrysalis
January	1981	The Boomtown Rats	Mondo Bongo	6	Ensign
April	1981	Thin Lizzy	The Adventures of . . .	6	Vertigo
April	1981	Stiff Little Fingers	Go For It	14	Chrysalis
May	1981	The Undertones	Positive Touch	17	Ardeck
August	1981	U2	Boy	52	Island
September	1981	Chris de Burgh	Best Moves	65	A & M
October	1981	U2	October	11	Island
December	1981	Thin Lizzy	Renegade	38	Vertigo
February	1982	Van Morrison	Beautiful Vision	31	Mercury
April	1982	The Boomtown Rats	V Deep	64	Mercury
May	1982	Rory Gallagher	Jinx	68	Chrysalis
October	1982	Stiff Little Fingers	Now Then	24	Chrysalis
October	1982	Chris de Burgh	The Getaway	30	A & M
October	1982	Gary Moore	Corridors of Power	30	Virgin
February	1983	Stiff Little Fingers	All the Best	19	Chrysalis
March	1983	U2	War	1	Island
March	1983	Thin Lizzy	Thunder and Lightning	4	Vertigo
March	1983	The Undertones	Sin of Pride	46	Ardeck
March	1983	Van Morrison	Inarticulate Speech of the Heart	14	Mercury
April	1983	Fastway	Fastway	43	CBS
May	1983	Clannad	Magical Ring	26	RCA
November	1983	Thin Lizzy	Life	29	Vertigo
December	1983	U2	Under a Blood Red Sky	2	Island
December	1983	The Undertones	All Wrapped Up	67	Ardeck
February	1984	Gary Moore	Victims of the Future	12	10/Virgin

Month	Year	Artist	Album	Position	Label
March	1984	Van Morrison	'Live' at the Grand Opera House Belfast	47	Mercury
May	1984	Chris de Burgh	Man on the Line	11	A & M
May	1984	Clannad	Legend	16	RCA
⌈October	1984	U2	The Unforgettable Fire	1	Island
⌊October	1984	Gary Moore	We Want Moore	32	10/Records
February	1985	Chris de Burgh	The Very Best of Chris de Burgh	6	EMI
February	1985	Van Morrison	A Sense of Wonder	25	Mercury
April	1985	The Mama's Boys	The Power and the Passion	82	Jive
August	1985	Chris de Burgh	Spanish Train and Other Stories	78	A & M
August	1985	U2	Wide Awake in America	11	Island
September	1985	Gary Moore	Run for Cover	12	10/Records
November	1985	Feargal Sharkey	Feargal Sharkey	12	Virgin
February	1986	Clannad	Macalla	33	RCA
May	1986	That Petrol Emotion	Manic Pop Thrill	84	Demon
May	1986	Cactus World News	Urban Beaches	56	MCA
June	1986	The Undertones	Cher O'Bowlies	96	Ardeck
July	1986	Gary Moore	Rockin' Every Night	99	10/Records
August	1986	Van Morrison	No Guru, No Method, No Teacher	27	Mercury
August	1986	Chris de Burgh	Into the Light	2	A & M
October	1986	Chris de Burgh	Crusader	72	A & M
December	1986	Bob Geldof	Deep in the Heart of Nowhere	79	Phonogram

[*denotes same week of entry*

Month	Year	Artist	Album	Position	Label
March	1987	U2	The Joshua Tree	1	Island
March	1987	Gary Moore	Wild Frontier	8	10/Virgin
May	1987	That Petrol Emotion	Babble	30	Polydor
June	1987	Enya	Enya	69	BBC
September	1987	Van Morrison	Poetic Champions Compose	26	Mercury/ Phonogram
November	1987	Clannad	Sirius	34	RCA
November	1987	Phil Lynott & Thin Lizzy	The Best of . . .	55	Telstar
January	1988	The Pogues	If I Should Fall from Grace with God	3	Pogue Mahone/Stiff
February	1988	U2	The Joshua Tree Singles	100	Island
February	1988	Sinéad O'Connor	The Lion and the Cobra	27	Ensign/ Chrysalis
May	1988	The Adventures	The Sea of Love	30	Elektra
June	1988	Hothouse Flowers	People	2	London
July	1988	Van Morrison & The Chieftains	Irish Heartbeat	18	Mercury/ Phonogram
September	1988	That Petrol Emotion	End of the Millenium Psychosis Blues	53	Virgin
October	1988	Chris de Burgh	Flying Colours	1	A & M
October	1988	U2	Rattle and Hum	1	Island
October	1988	The Waterboys	Fisherman's Blues	13	Ensign/ Chrysalis
November	1988	Enya	Watermark	5	WEA

February	1989	Gary Moore	After the War	23	Virgin
May	1989	Clannad	Past Present	5	RCA
June	1989	Van Morrison	Avalon Sunset	13	Polydor
July	1989	The Pogues	Peace and Love	5	Pogue Mahone/ WEA

Note: Album entries sorted from official charts contained in Music Week trade magazine. Charts © British Phonographic Institute (BPI), compiled by Gallup for BPI, Music Week and BBC. Position number shows highest point reached. From the beginning of 1985 Music Week started to incorporate the sales of cassettes and compact discs into the album charts. As of January 1989 BPI considered Top 75 and not Top 100 to be the official British album chart.

Thin Lizzy were the first Irish rock group to have a long stay on the British album charts—sixty-two weeks in fact with *Live and Dangerous*. Of Thin Lizzy's fourteen albums, eleven of them charted over the eight years from 1976 onwards and Phil Lynott even put his first solo LP *Solo in Soho* into the Top Thirty in 1980. Chart analysis becomes difficult when looking at the output of U2. Their *War* album was the first Irish rock LP to drop in at the top. That year, 1983, U2's *Boy* and *October* fluttered in and out of the Top Seventy-five. By January 1984 *Under a Blood Red Sky* had gone Platinum (300,000 copies plus) while *War* went certified Gold (100,000 copies plus). For the first nine months of 1984 *October, War* and *Under a Blood Red Sky* jostled the other albums in the Top Hundred by continually re-entering. After their *Unforgettable Fire* had showed its face at number one it stayed in the Top Thirty for the rest of that year. The pattern of U2 album re-entries continued in 1985 with highest placing being *Boy* (77, July), *October* (76, July), *War* (29, August), *Under a Blood Red Sky* (11, August) and *The Unforgettable Fire* (9, August). Of course with 1987's classic *Joshua Tree* album interest in the group's back catalogue was at fever pitch. By May 10th *Unforgettable Fire* and *Joshua Tree* had sold 600,000 copies apiece in the UK, while *Under a Blood Red Sky* had racked up sales of 900,000. Among the numerous re-entries that year the highest were *Unforgettable Fire* (45, March), *War* (67, July) and *Under a Blood Red Sky* (23, August). During 1988 the pattern continued with February seeing their LPs back up there with *The Joshua Tree* at a very high 13 plus re-entry highs for *Unforgettable Fire* and *Under a Blood Red Sky* at 64 and 73 respectively. In 1989 both *Rattle & Hum* and *Joshua Tree* flew up and down the chart, peak placings *Rattle & Hum* (15, January) and *Joshua Tree* (55, July). By August 1989 *The Joshua Tree* had been 111 weeks on the British album charts. If one includes *Wide Awake in America* on 27 July, U2 achieved, for an Irish rock band, an unprecedented six LPs in the charts at the same time—their entire output up to then. (Note: *Wide Awake in America* was in reality a 4-track single which went over the American industry length standard for an album by a mere fraction. U2's popularity meant that it was a high import demand item during a period when no other product was forthcoming from the group. The fact that the cassette version featured the same four tracks on both sides reflected the dubious nature of this 'album'.) In 1986 their back catalogue was still in evidence on the chart (*Under a Blood Red Sky* staying on for over nine months) and highest placings were *Unforgettable Fire* (36, January), *Under a Blood Red Sky* (33, February), and *War* (67, February).

Chris de Burgh's *The Very Best of Chris de Burgh* re-entered the charts numerous times since its high placing in February 1985, and in August 1986 it got to 44, while in February 1987 it made 77. His *Into the Light* re-entered twice at 83 in August 1987 and 99 in January 1988. In 1989 his *Flying Colours* made it to 63 second time around. *Clannad* also figured greatly with a new peak of 15 in April 1985 for *Legend* which in 1986 bobbed up on six different occasions, the highest being 60 in May. *Macalla* reappeared three times, reaching 80 in April. In August 1985 that radical folk rock band The Pogues went straight in at 13 with their *Rum, Sodomy & the Lash* LP (Stiff). In January 1988 this re-entered at no. 96. Other important re-entries and rising peaks for 1988 were: Sinéad O'Connor's *The Lion & the Cobra* (90, April), The Adventures, *Sea of Love* (72, July), The Pogues, *If I Should Fall . . .* (99, July), *Hothouse Flowers* (22, August), *Van Morrison/Chieftains* (99, August). For 1989 it was Enya, *Watermark* (6, January), The Waterboys, *Fisherman's Blues* (26, February), Enya, *Watermark* (7, June), and Van Morrison, *Avalon Sunset* (49, August).

Again, not only rock musicians penetrated the British album chart over the years. Those green balladeers The Bachelors hit the number two position on 27 June 1964 with their first collection of songs

The Bachelors and 16 Great Songs (Decca) and put six more albums in the Top Twenty-Five between then and August of 1969. A selection of their tunes under the title 25 Golden Greats made number thirty-eight on 22 December 1979. Those roving traditional Dubliners pumped four long-players into the listings within an astonishing ten months of each other. The best placing of all in the Top Thirty-five was their first album A Drop of the Hard Stuff (Major Minor) at number five in May of 1967. Finally, ever-smiling fire-side crooner Val Doonican put ten albums in the Top Forty from 12 December 1964 to 22 May 1977. He made number one with the aptly titled Val Doonican Rocks But Gently (Pye) on 2 December 1967. He had scored a number two with his first offering Lucky 13 Shades of Val Doonican (December 1964) and reached the same notch with The World of Val Doonican (June 1969). Other interesting Irish records to note were James Galway & the Chieftains in Ireland (RCA, no. 32, April 1987), The Dubliners 25 Years Celebration (Stylus, no. 43, May 1987), and The Fureys & Davey Arthur: Furey's Finest (Tristar, 65, December 1987).

Notes

Chapter 1 **From Beat Music to Progressive Rock**

1   Ian Whitcomb took up residence in America between 1965 and 1969. After his hit he did the rounds doing tours with Herman's Hermits, The Rolling Stones, The Dave Clark Five and The Beach Boys. Albums recorded were a mixed bag, running from You Turn Me On (Tower 1965) through rock, to Under the Ragtime Moon (United Artists 1972), a full academic exposition of ragtime music. He also contributed to The Los Angeles Times. His return to Britain saw him start a book on the history of popular music from Tin Pan Alley onwards. After the Ball — A History of Pop (Penguin, London 1973) was an excellent book, highly informative, while being witty and readable. EMI released a double album in tandem with the book. He became the first presenter of the BBC's 'Old Grey Whistle Test' in 1971. He continued to travel, using his talents as a singer and pianist in relation to his vast knowledge of popular music. Other publications include the historical works Tin Pan Alley (Paddington Press 1975) and Whole Lotta Shakin' (Arrow Books 1982) and his complete semi-autobiography Rock Odyssey — A Chronicle Of The Sixties (Hutchinson 1983).

2   The Action were: Peter Adler (sax, vocals), Colm Wilkinson (guitar) and Ian McGarry (drums).

3   Clubs in Dublin during 1960s: The Scene, Sound City, The '5' Club, The Moulin Rouge, Club A Go Go, The Flamingo, The Apartment, Club Arthur and Club Caroline.

4   Paul Charles was involved with more Irish groups than anybody else in Ireland. His Northern Irish perspective and close management association with Van Morrison make him a singular observer.

He was also a keen rock journalist in Belfast and Dublin during the sixties.

5   The Wheels were one of the craziest groups to come from the North. Their lead singer, Brian Rossi, used to sing from inside a coffin or swing from a balcony as part of his opening act. Herbie Armstrong and Rod Demmick were also in the group. Herbie was a very good friend of Van Morrison's and Van toyed with the idea of joining The Wheels, but he got a phone call from Bert Berns in America and went over there instead. Herbie and Rod recorded an acoustic rock album for MAM called Little Willie Ramble in the early seventies. Herbie Armstrong later teamed up with Morrison again during the latter's Wavelength tour as guitarist. He also played guitar on Morrison's Into the Music and Common One albums. Utilising Pee Wee Ellis (sax), Mark Isham (trumpet), John Platania (guitar) and Peter Van Hooke (drums), regulars from Van Morrison's backing group, Armstrong recorded his solo album Back against the Wall for MMC in 1983. Rod Demmick worked with a lot of seminal London pub rock groups and later English star David Essex during the 1970s.

6   Note on Henry McCullough: On return to Ireland in 1968 he joined the folk group Sweeney's Men. After this brief experiment he threw in his lot with Joe Cocker's Grease Band and recorded the classic blues/ rock album With a Little Help from My Friends for A&M in early 1969. Cocker's rising fame brought McCullough to play the legendary Woodstock festival of that year. Another album, Joe Cocker! (A&M 1970), was recorded in the wake of the American success but Cocker defected soon after to work elsewhere. McCullough stuck with The Grease Band and the group recorded sessions for the Jesus Christ Superstar album (MCA) in 1970. Inevitably the group recorded their own album, an excellent set called

simply *The Grease Band* (Harvest 1971). Unfortunately the group soon after fell into disarray and McCullough joined *Spooky Tooth* for one album *The Last Puff* (Island 1970).

In January 1972 he was hired by Paul McCartney for his new band *Wings* and cut his teeth on the controversial 'Give Ireland Back to the Irish' single (Parlophone 1972) which was written by McCartney as a response to the Northern Irish Bloody Sunday massacre of the period. McCullough toured and recorded the LP *Red Rose Speedway* (Parlophone) with Wings but the partnership dissolved in July 1973 when musical and personality clashes became too frequent. McCullough gigged with the *Carol Grimes London Boogie Band* before re-uniting *The Grease Band* to record *Amazing Grease* (Goodear 1975). This group expanded to include Glaswegian rhythm and blues singer Frankie Miller and sessions were cut in London and later brought to San Francisco to be released as Henry McCullough's first solo LP *Mind Your Own Business* on George Harrison's Dark Horse Records in 1975. McCullough stayed in the US for the Frankie Miller album *The Rock* (Chrysalis 1975), but returned to London for *Marianne Faithfull's* 1976 record *Dreamin' My Dreams* (NEMS). In 1977 Henry joined Roy Harper for *Bullinamingvase* (Harvest), but had to leave soon after as a result of tensions. McCullough teamed up yet again with *The Grease Band* for another Marianne Faithfull album titled *Faithless* (NEMS 1978). In 1980 an album, *Darkness Darkness*, came out on Polydor; McCullough did this in Ireland with ex-*Animal* Eric Burdon. McCullough has often been nicknamed the super-sessioner of Irish rock yet his solo output has been slight. He released his second lone venture in 1984, an album appropriately monikered *Hell of a Record* (Line).

7   Ed Deane, Pat Nash and John Ryan were recruited into electric folk band *The Woodsband*. For about a year they toured Europe and cut one album. Differences in temperament between the very serious Terry Woods, a folk purist, and the more extroverted ex-*Granny's* men led to quick dissolution. On one of their excursions to Castletown House to perform, they met English star Donovan, who was looking for a band. (Pete Cummins, John Ryan and Philip Donnelly were caught up in his band, which did a tour of the British Isles in 1972 before that too dissolved.) John Ryan and Pete Cummins then got into meditation. Meantime, Johnny Duhan was doing solo gigs in Dublin and was soon joined by Ed Deane. The pair spent three relaxed years as a rock duo — a reaction by two artists in their early twenties to dicey managers and precarious business scenes. In 1975 Johnny Duhan left Ireland to record an album in London with *St James's Gate*. He had spent three good years with Ed Deane and considered the resultant

album a mistake. In subsequent years Duhan experienced an incredible amount of hardship as one record company after another failed to release his recordings because of company restructuring problems. Eventually it wasn't until the 1980s that one of Ireland's great talents of the 1960s could allow his music to surface on vinyl again.

8   *Andwella's Dream* (one of several line-ups): Dave Lewis (guitar, vocals), Nigel Smith (bass), Wilgar Campbell (drums).

9   Both tracks were A and B sides of *Taste's* first single on Major-Minor.

10   A traditional arrangement.

11   Also surfacing from that period (1969) on the Song label is another single 'Saturday Morning Man'/'Mervyn Aldridge'. Gary Moore sings in a Stevie Winwood mode. Both sides are densely psychedelic, uniquely complex, acoustic sounding and in musical terms radical.

12   Three-piece *Skid Row* performed at an open-air festival in the Phoenix Park, Dublin, autumn 1969, the bill comprising Ireland's most progressive acts: *Taxi, Tara Telephone, Orange Machine, Granny's Intentions, Orphanage* and *Dr Strangely Strange*.

13   A single was released as a taster called 'Mr De Luxe'/'Night of the Warm Witch' (CBS 1971).

14   Gary Moore experienced numerous problems in starting his own band, but *The Gary Moore Band* finally settled after acquiring £20,000 from CBS. *Grinding Stone* (CBS 1973) features Irish musicians Frank Boylan (bass), Pearse Kelly (drums) and Philip Donnelly on rhythm guitar. A Moog synthesizer is also used on some tracks. The music is much different from *Skid Row* — softer and folkier. 'Sail Across the Mountain' is electric music but intimate and subtle. Of the six tracks the seventeen-minute 'Spirit' is a light exercise in synth/guitar music. Obviously Moore had tired quickly in *Skid Row* and now found a musical and spiritual release in a looser format. The following year saw the guitarist temporarily involved with *Thin Lizzy*, managing to play live and cutting a single into the bargain. During the summer of 1975 he teamed up with English jazz rock stalwart Jon Hiseman to form *Colosseum II*, again revving up his guitar work into the techno-flash histrionic gear that has become his trademark. Albums with *Colosseum II* were three: *Strange New Flesh* (Warner Brothers 1976), *Electric Savage* (MCA 1977) and *Wardance* (MCA 1978). After a number of temporary stints with *Thin Lizzy*, Moore eventually settled with a new group *G Force* in Los Angeles. While developing his solo career he worked with ex-*Emerson, Lake and Palmer* frontman Greg Lake on two albums, *Greg Lake* (1981) and *Manoeuvres* (1983), both on Chrysalis.

15   Lynott's bass guitar came from Brush Shiels,

who bought it from Robert Ballagh of *The Chessmen.*

16   *Orphanage* name derived from popular hippie hang-out inhabited by folk group *Dr Strangely Strange.* Band line-up consisted of Joe Stad (lead guitar), Pat Quigley (bass), Terry Woods (five-string banjo), Lynott and Downey.

17   Eric Wricksen had plenty of experience playing in *The Trixons* showband in Europe and Scandinavia.

18   The 'New Day' single (Decca 1971) contained four tracks: 'Dublin', 'Remembering Pt 2', 'Old Moon Madness' and 'Things Ain't Working Out Down at the Farm'. Bar 'Dublin', all tracks are indulgent forays into heavy rock, featuring piercing solos by Eric Bell. The group obviously wanted to see what would happen if they let go on all sides. Bell uses a lot of wah-wah and reverb on his guitar, cutting up the songs with lush breaks. The songs, as usual, are auto-biographical. One can trace the use of the word 'farm' again as a personal space. 'Things Ain't Working Out Down at the Farm' contains the famous refrain — a real soul rap — 'And he said it's you and me and me and you and me and me and you and you and me and me and you and you and me!' One of Lynott's live favourites at the time, the song always caused a stir.

19   At the tail-end of the song, Lynott sings, 'God it's a shame there's no more *Dr Strangely Strange*', a reference to the break-up of the Irish group of that name.

20   Famous Irish artist who established himself during the seventies for his Celtic art work.

21   Title of Philip Lynott's first book of poetry issued in 1974.

22   After a lengthy break Bell joined the *Noel Redding Band* (ex-*Hendrix*), then the reformed *Skid Row*, eventually forming his own *Eric Bell Band.*

23   Between 1972 and 1973 a comprehensive underground rock paper called *High Times* came out under the editorship of Michael Kiley. Modelled on America's *Rolling Stone*, the paper covered the Irish rock scene with more depth than had hitherto been attempted. Excellent photographs, extensive reviews and interviews were its mainstay, while rock and folk were its musical preoccupations. It was definitely a 'progressive hippie' magazine in line with the goings on of a certain percentage of Irish youth at the time.

24   *Mushroom* consisted of: Aonghus McAnally (guitar), Colm Lynch (drums), Mickey Power (organist), Pat Collins (fiddle), Alan Brown (bass).

25   *Fruupp* released four albums before their disbandment in 1976: (R) *Future Legends* (Dawn 1973), *Seven Secrets* (Dawn 1974), (R) *The Prince of Heaven's Eyes* (Dawn 1975), *Modern Masquerades* (Dawn 1976).

(R) = recommended.

26   A fairly progressive thing was executed by *The Freshmen* Showband. Led by keyboardsman Billy Brown, they established their reputation by doing *Beach Boys* covers better than the Wilson brothers

themselves. In 1970 they released an album called *Peace on Earth* (CBS), a concept work with full orchestration, done in collaboration with Micheál MacLiammóir, who quoted texts from the Bible in a lugubrious voice. This was performed live and was fairly risqué for a showband.

27   *Supply, Demand and Curve:* Roger Doyle (drums, piano and composer), Brian Masterson (bass), Jolyon Jackson (flute and cello), Paddy Finney (classical guitar and vocals). With Greg Boland, Fran Breen and Rosemary Taylor, to name but a few, coming in to work on the group's debut album, their music approximated more to jazz by 1976. *Supply Demand and Curve* (Mulligan 1976) utilises ARP synthesisers, Moog synthesisers, cellos, tin whistles, recorder, melodica, bells, fairground organ, acoustic and Fender pianos, electric and acoustic guitars, electric bass and assorted percussion. Definitely a musicians' group, the work sparkles.

28   *East of Eden:* Joe O'Donnell (violins), Martin Fisher (bass) from England, Jeff Allen (drums) from Glasgow, Garth Watt Roy (vocals, guitar) from India.

29   *Pumpkinhead* were chiefly Thom and Cathy Moore, Rick and Sandy Epping, with (on the Mulligan album) Ciarán Brennan (double bass), Robbie Brennan (drums, congas), Kevin Burke (fiddle), Donal Lunny (bouzouki), Jimmy Faulkner (slide guitar).

Chapter 2   **Folk into Rock**

1   Michael Gray, *Song and Dance Man — The Art of Bob Dylan* (Hamlyn, London 1982).

2   Unfortunately this recording has long since been erased by RTE archives due to storage difficulties.

3   *Sweeney's Men* were re-united in the autumn of 1986 for a special studio session orchestrated by Irish radio personality B.P. Fallon. The session was broadcast as part of a three-programme tribute to the career of Henry McCullough, who had spent many years in his native Portstewart recovering from a serious hand injury.

4   *Horslips'* first guitar player was Gus Guest but he was quickly replaced by Declan Sinnott who appears on 'Johnny's Wedding' (Oats 1972). Sinnott did not care for the intensity of the group's music and lifestyle so he quit after some months.

5   After *Horslips* had called it a day, Eamon Carr and Johnny Fean continued to play music in a local rhythm and blues outfit called *The Zen Alligators*, scoring several Irish hit singles and entertaining many with their gusto brand of raunchy material. Barry Devlin, in between his work for advertising, cut a concept album titled *Breaking Star Codes*, based on

the signs of the zodiac. Jim Lockhart became a producer on national radio while Eamon Carr continued to be involved in the music business. Johnny Fean and Charles O'Connor kept up their interest in *The Host* and Fean was much in demand as a session guitarist. With Eamon Carr as producer and new wave vocalists Nikki Sudden and Simon Carmody, Fean recently laid down the most striking acoustic guitar playing of his career on an album called *The Last Bandits in the World* (Hotwire 1986).

6   This beautiful translation was done by native Irish writer and poet Lorcán Ó Treasaigh.

7   The first *Clannad* compilation album appeared near the end of 1986 on K-Tel Records titled *Clannad — The Collection*. Track listing was: Theme from Harry's Game, Closer to Your Heart, Lady Marian, Newgrange, Mhorag's na hÓró Gheallaidh, Níl Sé 'n Lá — Caisleán Óir, In a Lifetime, Now is Here, Na Buachaillí Álainn, Down by the Sally Gardens, Dúlamán, Robin (the hooded man).

8   The bulk of this essay was based on an interview I did during the summer of 1986 for *Hi-Fi Review* magazine.

9   Quotation reproduced from Christy Moore interview, *Vox* magazine, May 1982, by Con Ó Laoghaire.

10   Original copies of *Ordinary Man* on WEA contained a song called 'They Never Came Home', which recalled the terrible plight of forty-eight teenagers burnt to death in a Dublin ballroom disco on St Valentine's Day 1980. Due to court proceedings revolving around compensation for the children's relatives, Moore was judged to be in contempt and the record was banned. The album had to be re-issued in the UK on Demon with a substitute track appropriately titled 'Another Song Born'.

11   Philip Donnelly was a member of *Elmer Fudd* and *The Gary Moore Band* and toured with Donovan in the early 1970s. His love for country music brought him to Nashville where he became a session guitarist of note, appearing on dozens of records. His most prestigious work was with *The Everly Brothers* and *The Byrds* on their respective re-union tours.

12   *Hotfoot* was an acoustic swing band in the Django Reinhardt vein founded by fiddle player Pat Collins and guitarist Jimmy Faulkner in 1982. After a number of years Faulkner left to be replaced by Bill Whelan, and, with the addition of Robbie Brennan (drums), Dave McHale (piano) and Declan McNelis (bass), the band went electric, releasing a highly rated album of swing jazz cum folk-rock, *Hotfoot* (Mystery 1986). The band's career was over-shadowed by the unexpected death of McNelis in April 1987.

Chapter 3   Van Morrison

1   Van Morrison's *Them* were subject to continual personnel problems. In the summer of 1964 the gigging line-up was Billy Harrison (guitar), Alan Henderson (bass), Pat McAuley (organ) and Ronnie Millings (drums). After the first London studio sessions Jackie McAuley replaced Ronnie Millings on drums. During 1965 the McAuley brothers jacked it in completely and returned to Belfast. Millings was re-recruited on drums and Peter Bardens took over on organ. Friction about artistic control reached its height when Billy Harrison, the appealing lead guitarist, walked out never to return. *Them* even returned to Belfast in the latter half of 1965 to try and re-orient themselves. Joe Baldi was taken on as guitarist before being superseded by Jim Armstrong, with Eric Wricksen reclaimed for piano, John Wilson (drums) and Ray Elliott (sax). By the end of the year, Pete Bardens was back on keyboards and by 1966 Terry Noone had taken over the drum stool. Even he was replaced by David Harvey for the US tour. Even though that was the last official *Them* the group members were to have interesting careers without Van Morrison. Ray Elliott, Jim Armstrong, Alan Henderson, David Harvey and a new singer Kenny McDowell continued on as *Them* and through *Flip* magazine in America got a new deal and flew across the Atlantic. Embracing psychedelia they recorded *Now and Them* (Tower 1968) but Elliott found the going too weird and settled in Canada. A slimmed-down *Them* then recorded *Time Out, Time In for Them* (Tower 1968) which even featured the sitar. McDowell and Armstrong also got fed up with the American West Coast and went back to Belfast to form SK'BOO. Henderson moved into country rock and remained in America to record *Them* (Happy Tiger 1970) with session musicians such as Ry Cooder. Another *Them* album, *In Reality*, was released by Happy Tiger in 1971 featuring a similar arrangement, but Henderson had milked the idea dry. Meanwhile Jackie and Pat McCauley had founded *The Belfast Gypsies* who played every type of music in a crazed fashion. They recorded one album, *Belfast Gypsies* (Grand Prix 1967), before dis-integrating. Jackie McAuley came to England and formed the folk oriented *Trader Horne* with ex-*Fairport Convention* singer Judy Dyble and released the gentle *Morning Way* album on Dawn in 1970. McAuley then went solo and recorded an album of excellent material backed by jazz sessioners titled simply *Jackie McAuley* (Dawn 1971).

Around the same time John Wilson, who had become famous with Rory Gallagher's *Taste*, was getting rave reviews in the British music press for his group *Stud*. After three well-received albums he did session work in London, played with Brush Shiels in Ireland and returned to Ulster to become its most famous session drummer. Sessionist Peter Bardens went solo in the early 1970s before joining the much rated jazz/pop group *Camel* to record seven albums throughout the decade. After a disastrous fling with Jesus Christ Superstar-style rock opera on the album *Truth of Truths* (Oak 1971), the American-based Alan Henderson decided to re-unite *Them* once more in the late 1970s because of a growing cult following in West Germany. Teaming up again with Billy Harrison, who had settled in county Down and was working for the post office, and Eric Wrixen plus new drummer Billy Bell and cabaret singer Mel Austin, *Them* recorded *Shut Your Mouth* (Decca 1979). It was described as bluesy rock, with all compositions written by Harrison. Even though *Them* quickly fell apart due to old wounds, Harrison went on to record a solo work *Billy Who* (Vagabond 1980) before returning to the post office in Bangor. Jim Armstrong was not to fall into obscurity for in the late seventies he made a comeback effort by forming *Light* and recording an eponymous debut album for Mint Records in 1978. For the most part the *Them* musicians continued to play music and, excepting the accidental death of Pat McAuley in a drowning accident in Donegal during 1984, all have survived the traumatic incidents of the past.

2   All Van Morrison quotations taken from original Decca press material published in October 1964.

3   The last single to be released by *Them* on Decca Records featuring Van Morrison. Their last single proper was an historic song entitled 'The Story of Them Parts 1 & 2' which took up both sides of the disc. It recounted the history of the group from The Maritime Club days onward and appeared on Major Minor in 1967.

4   Eclectic Music Company Limited 1965, now known as Pattern Music, i.e. Paul Simon. All rights reserved.

5   During this period of homecoming Van Morrison decided not to perform in Belfast, probably because of the growing war situation there. Moreover, his parents had long moved out to Marin County where they were enjoying the success of their record retailing business and since most of his old friends had emigrated, Morrison didn't feel the need to concentrate on the North.

6   Between the beginning of 1975 and the end of 1976 Van Morrison's life became an open book for idle media fantasies. Some thought he was engrossed in Gestalt therapy, Celtic mythology and Jungian psychology, others thought he was recording albums with *The Rolling Stones, The Pretty Things* and *The Crusaders*. Even when he made unexpected appearances at large rock festivals in Britain and the US as an audience member, the media were quick to distort the facts. In reality, Morrison was planning a change of residence to Britain, enlisting the business aid of English promoter Harvey Goldsmith and spending most of his time in the Manor Studios, Oxfordshire, with Dr John recording material for the album *A Period of Transition* (Warner Brothers 1977).

7   The Dr John years saw Van Morrison playing with a strange variety of musicians like George Benson, Carlos Santana, Mick Ronson, Brian Auger and Roger Chapman — all rated talents who saw in the Belfast man a true kindred spirit.

8   W.B. Yeats's lines were written on 4 September 1938 as the last part of his poem 'Under Ben Bulben'. They are inscribed on his gravestone in Drumcliff churchyard, county Sligo.

Chapter 4   Modern Music

1   Jim Miller, *The Rolling Stone History of Rock and Roll* (Picador 1981).

2   Charles Shaar Murray, *The New Musical Express*, (1977).

3   Bob Geldof in conversation with Andy Kershaw on BBC television's 'Old Grey Whistle Test', March 1987.

4   *New Musical Express*, October 1981.

5   U2 interview, *Vox* fanzine, 1980.

6   From James Henke's 'Here comes the next big thing', 19 February 1981. (Reproduced from official U2 booklet.)

7   'A House is Not a Motel' from *Love*'s *Forever Changes* album (Elektra 1967).

8   Brian Eno, RTE, 29 December 1984.

9   Dawn Ades, *Dada and Surrealism* (Thames and Hudson 1974).

10   All Roger Doyle quotes taken from conversation with the author, summer 1984.

11   Both Nigel Rolfe quotes taken from the book *Nigel Rolfe — Sculptures in Motion* (Nigel Rolfe 1986).

Credits

quotation © 1981 *Rolling Stone* magazine; lyrics to Bob Geldof's 'Looking After Number One' © 1977 Sewer Fire Hits (under Copyright Control); Bob Geldof quotation courtesy *The New Musical Express* 1977; lyrics to *The Boomtown Rats'* 'Another Piece of Red' and 'Banana Republic' © 1981 Sewer Fire Hits (under Copyright Control); lyrics to Philip Chevron's 'Television Screen' © 1977 Rockin' Music Ltd. (Complacent Toonz Ltd.); lyrics to *Stiff Little Fingers'* 'Alternative Ulster' © 1978 Rigid Digits Music; lyrics to *U2* songs 'A Day Without Me', 'I Will Follow', 'Into the Heart' and 'The Ocean' © 1980 Blue Mountain Music Ltd.; lyrics to *U2* song 'Tomorrow' © 1981 Blue Mountain Music Ltd.'; lyrics to *U2* songs 'New Year's Day', 'Sunday Bloody Sunday', 'Seconds', 'Like a Song' and '40' © 1983 Blue Mountain Music Ltd.; line taken from Arthur Lee's 'A House is Not a Motel' © 1967 Carlin Music Corporation (reproduced by kind permission); quotation taken from Dawn Ades *Dada and Surrealism* © 1974 Thames and Hudson Ltd.; chart placings © BPI, compiled by Gallup for BPI, *Music Week*, and BBC; lyrics to Paul Brady's 'The Island' © 1986 Rondor Music Ltd.; all lyrics quoted from Van Morrison's 'No Guru, No Method, No Teacher' © 1986 Essential Music; lines and words from *U2's* 'Bad' © Blue Mountain Music Ltd. 1984; all lyrics quoted from *U2's* 'The Joshua Tree' © 1987 Blue Mountain Music for the United Kingdom, Chappell Music for the rest of the world; quotations from Ruefrex's 'Wild Colonial Boy' and 'Flowers For All Occasions' © 1985 Paul Burgess (Copyright Control); lines taken from Andy White's 'Rave on Andy White' © Chappel Music Ltd./Big Rain Music Ltd. 1986; also appreciation to *New Spotlight*, *Vox* magazine and the *U2* press office.

Credits for Photographs

Below we list the photographs that appear in the book. They are listed by photographer, where known, and by source where this is not known. We have tried hard to find all the copyright owners, but in some cases we have drawn a blank and would be grateful to hear from anyone who can help in this area. The page number is followed by the picture number in brackets.

Alicino, Christine, Courtesy Opal Ltd. 188 (82)

ASM Records 239 (102)

BBC 101 (41)

Beggar's Banquet 257 (117)

Brennan, Robbie private collection 16 (3)

Butler, Elvera. Courtesy Reekus 227 (97)

Carr, Eamon private collection 246 (106)

Catlin, Andy 1 (left, right) 2, 3, 27 (11), 90 (34), 110 (45, 46, 47), 140 (57), 149 (63), 157 (64, 65, 66), 188 (83, 86), 189 (88, 89), 203 (90), 238 (99, 100, 101), 247 (109), 256 (116), 266 (119, 120, 121, 122), 267 (123, 124, 125), 278 (127, 128, 129, 130, 131), 279 (132, 133, 134, 135), 280 (136, 137, 138), 281 (139, 140, 141)

CBS Records 239 (103)

China Records 239 (104)

Chrysalis. Courtesy RTE 76 (28)

Clifford, Dave 116 (73, 74), 215 (94)

Cooper, Bill. Courtesy Pat Egan private collection 283 (142)

Corbijn, Anton. Courtesy CBS 174 (76), Courtesy Island 189 (85), 203 (89)

Cummins, Kevin 163 (70), 257 (118)

Dara Records 101 (42)

Decca Records 61 (21), 116 (50, 51), 257 (118)

Doyle, Denis. Courtesy Rough Trade

Selective Index

[(p) = photograph]

The Author: Mark J. Prendergast was born in Ireland of mixed Irish and North African blood. He grew up in the Dublin area. Music has been his lifelong passion and during college days he found himself spending more time at his part-time job in Golden Discs record store than at his studies. From this he moved to writing for *The Irish Times* about the rock music scene. His articles appeared in that newspaper and also in *The Sunday Tribune, The Magazine, Vox* fanzine. He now freelances for music magazines in London. This book is the culmination of years of interest, experience and research.